Eradicating Energy Poverty

"This is a book that breaks new ground on energy poverty. Based on detailed and extensive field work across different geo-climatic zones, the author specifies institutional and policy changes required to decentralize energy systems. This book goes beyond the existing frames of looking at energy, dominated by industrial, corporate and urban needs. By centering his concerns on the needs of the poor, Manashvi brings to the fore the necessity to look at energy in a decentralized and integrated manner to addresses concerns of sustainability."
—Satyajit Singh, *Vice Chair, Global Studies, Professor, Departments of Political Science & Global Studies, University of California Santa Barbara, California*

"This book is one of its kind. Ambitious in scope and methodology, it addresses a difficult area in the Politics of Technology. Using his disciplinary training in both the physical and social sciences, he deftly weaves social, economic and cultural perspectives from the lens of the political. It is a valuable contribution to two areas: as a study of technology from the social scientific standpoint, to Social Studies of Science; and as a deeply grounded and analytical appraisal of policy creation and evaluation, to Public Policy studies."
—Madhulika Banerjee, *Professor, Department of Political Science, University of Delhi, Delhi*

"The book stands out for evidence-based research on policy making. Energy access and policy intervention seeking to ensure access of basic energy to households have been the focus areas of energy policy space for decades. But this book brings a new paradigm by defining the importance of socio-cultural milieu in understanding the nature and demand of energy end use. The incisive case studies lend credence to the message that the book carries–the message that for the policy to move from a mere statement of intent to being an instrument of change, there is a need to delve into the setting of culture, values and practices that the people in rural areas live with, assess the nature and extent of energy poverty and then, design policy encouraging use of locally available resources for a sustainable future. The author holds a promise for change through a deadly combination of his practical experience as a bureaucrat and strong research skills as a hard-core academician."
—Sushanta K. Chatterjee, *Chief (Regulatory Affairs), Central Electricity Regulatory Commission*

"The ambition at the heart of this work is to gain a comprehensive understanding of energy poverty through research based on primary evidence. This impressive work seeks to understand and explain the gap between policy and practice in provision of electricity through a rigorous study of institutions, politics and lived experiences in rural India. It provides a fresh insight by studying how local power relations influence policy implementation. It argues for a radical shift in approach to rural electrification: from conceiving electricity in purely technical terms to one that gives due recognition to socio-cultural and political dynamics at the local level. Without such a shift, the author argues, creation of an effective mechanism for equitable distribution of electricity will continue to remain a challenge. This important message from an outstanding practitioner has relevance well beyond the subject of this work."

—G. D. Badgaiyan (IAS retd.), *Princeton University Alumnus and Former DG: National Centre for Good Governance*

Manashvi Kumar Singh

Eradicating Energy Poverty

Overcoming 'Barriers' to Decentralized Energy Systems in India

Manashvi Kumar Singh
Indian Administrative Service
Chandigarh, Punjab, India

ISBN 978-981-16-7072-5   ISBN 978-981-16-7073-2 (eBook)
https://doi.org/10.1007/978-981-16-7073-2

© The Editor(s) (if applicable) and The Author(s), under exclusive license to Springer Nature Singapore Pte Ltd. 2022
This work is subject to copyright. All rights are solely and exclusively licensed by the Publisher, whether the whole or part of the material is concerned, specifically the rights of translation, reprinting, reuse of illustrations, recitation, broadcasting, reproduction on microfilms or in any other physical way, and transmission or information storage and retrieval, electronic adaptation, computer software, or by similar or dissimilar methodology now known or hereafter developed.
The use of general descriptive names, registered names, trademarks, service marks, etc. in this publication does not imply, even in the absence of a specific statement, that such names are exempt from the relevant protective laws and regulations and therefore free for general use.
The publisher, the authors and the editors are safe to assume that the advice and information in this book are believed to be true and accurate at the date of publication. Neither the publisher nor the authors or the editors give a warranty, expressed or implied, with respect to the material contained herein or for any errors or omissions that may have been made. The publisher remains neutral with regard to jurisdictional claims in published maps and institutional affiliations.

Cover credit: Maram_shutterstock.com

This Palgrave Macmillan imprint is published by the registered company Springer Nature Singapore Pte Ltd.
The registered company address is: 152 Beach Road, #21-01/04 Gateway East, Singapore 189721, Singapore

Dedicated to my teachers and Aanya

Foreword by S. K. Tandon

With the human population racing to almost seven and a half billion, and having added a disproportionately large percentage of that in the last century, it is a matter of no surprise that we are beginning to be increasingly confronted with the issue of stress on our existential resources—water, air, land, food, and energy. It is now common knowledge that we live in a human-dominated age—the Anthropocene. This term, popularized, by the Nobel Laureate Paul Crutzen at the turn of the century has deep roots in human activities of all times, and invokes different threads of thought in the minds of naturalists, scientists, environmentalists, social and political scientists, and those involved in governance and policy frameworks. Notwithstanding the many perceptions of the term Anthropocene originating in different disciplinary domains and settings, the Anthropocene conjures up mental images of the beginning of the Industrial Era almost two centuries ago and the energy systems that became available to humans at that time.

The Industrial Era has been marked by the development of efficient energy systems, more notably those that were based on fossil fuels. The availability of energy systems led to other developments including that of the mechanization of agriculture, which in turn changed the land use patterns of large swathes of land in different continents. The nexus between water-food-energy has become more evident now, than ever before.

In the above context, it was indeed most heartening to learn from one of my former students from the University of Delhi and currently an IAS officer of the Punjab cadre, Dr. Manashvi Kumar, that he has written a Monograph on Energy Poverty, a theme that needs a comprehensive exploration with a multi-disciplinary perspective. His forthcoming Monograph on 'Eradicating Energy Poverty: Overcoming "Barriers" to Decentralized Energy Systems in India', I sincerely hope, will be a step that will lead towards energy becoming more inclusive, and the reduction of inequity both across and within large countries, such as our own. This monograph is timely and relevant, and shall constructively inform policy issues in the future on this important subject.

This work, at its core, is about triggering an energy system change for providing energy access and making it inclusive. For this to happen, both aspects, the production and consumption of energy, require consideration. Like other sustainability issues, the water-food-energy nexus has to be viewed as a coupled social-environmental system; and energy provisioning has to be conceptualized in a socio-economic context. Furthermore, there is the dimension of attendant politics that is associated with the governance of the energy systems.

Dr. Manashvi Kumar has made an intense intellectual journey that, according to him, links 'rural electrification with a social phenomenon that is contextually embedded in cultures and spaces of energy consumption'. He has grappled with the complex issues of availability, access, distribution, affordability, and the acceptability of an energy service. In doing so, Dr. Manashvi Kumar has built on three conceptions, i.e. constitutive, systemic, and action-theoretical.

This monograph is extremely well researched. It has not only laid out the broad contours of the subject of Energy Poverty, but has explored its many dimensions in the context of rural electrification involving an ideological transformation to prosumerism—a process wherein a passive consumer of energy stands transformed to an active and engaged consumer, instead of an idea that takes into account the local energy 'capital' in its entirety.

It is my earnest hope that this important multi-disciplinary monograph will have wide acceptance amongst energy professionals, academics, and policy experts representing different segments of the energy sector.

Professor S. K. Tandon
Formerly Pro-Vice Chancellor
University of Delhi
New Delhi, India

Currently Visiting Professor
Indian Institute of Science
Education and Research
Bhopal, India

Foreword by Satish B. Agnihotri

Energy is an essential ingredient of human development whether at the level of a society or of an individual. Recall Lenin's remark 'Communism is soviet power plus electrification of the whole country'. Soviet power did not last, but electricity for all remained the goal of any developing country, India being no exception. Not surprisingly, household electricity consumption and HDI show such a strong correlation.

But electricity is not the only facet of energy, the quantum and quality of fuel used in a household is an equally important parameter. What fuel you use, how much and how you use it can shape the quality of one's life. In a household context therefore, these twin aspects of energy could be used to define the concept of energy poverty. Development interventions therefore aspire to make electricity available for all and improve the availability of clean fuel. The predominant mode of doing this is by focusing on the supply side of the problem and tackling it in a top down, centralized, and undifferentiated manner.

This is precisely the problem Manashvi Kumar engages with and passionately so. But he does this in a systematic and rigourous manner critically examining the concept of energy poverty and its applicability to the Indian context and our approach to rural electrification. He marshals evidence in support of his arguments systematically, richly contributing to our struggle to bring power for all by a given date. More importantly, he argues persuasively in favour of decentralized production of electricity and within it, giving renewable energy (RE) the attention it deserves.

To do so, Manashvi actually takes us through the length and breadth of Bharat which is not quite India, in terms of its energy usage profile. He covers different geo-climatic zones in Himachal Pradesh, Punjab, Gujarat, Rajasthan, Uttar Pradesh, Bihar, and Andaman and Nicobar Islands. He uses a sound sampling methodology and his work is an excellent guide to field research for young scholars.

A strong case is made out for understanding the context-specific nature of the demand as against the current paradigm of centralized planning, and undifferentiated nature of supply, disrupting in the process the rural social fabric. Of course, any development intervention that questions the power status quo leads to this problem. Rural electrification or supply of LPG have to factor this reality in.

This is in fact the issue at the route of various intervention failures Manashvi has elaborated in his case studies across the country. The supply centric 'one size fits all' approach cannot anticipate these 'icebergs' of political power. The widening definition of rural electrification is itself a testimony to the political accountability process at macro-level. The distribution of electricity within the village is equally so where some hamlets or tola remain deprived. Villages in the vicinity of a power plant remaining in dark is also a question of political power. Even within a household, as our experience at IIT Bombay in a 'million solar lamps' programme has shown, the kitchen may not get the bulb in a hurry if it gets it at all! Technical solutions that wish away politics, a la Ferguson's anti-politics machine, are bound to face with failures and very sub-optimal outcomes. However, Manashvi needs to wonder if the decentralized RE can succeed when the urban does not adopt de-gridding, energy efficiency, or DSM? The assertion that 'The rural energy landscape of India should eventually be dotted with decentralized energy systems promoting micro-level energy governance' begs a question—why just the rural?

The book makes out a convincing case for the adequacy of the RE to cater to the demand of most of the rural settings examined. A combination of solar and biogas appears to be more than adequate for this purpose in most cases. However, the narrative also takes us to rural Himachal Pradesh where the energy consumption patterns start mimicking 'India' lot more closely. This raises twin issues; energy governance and dynamic nature of the evolving demand. The governance issue contrasts a hilly state that is able to supply its citizen both electricity as well as LPG, while a plain state is not. The divergent paths of Uttarakhand and UP are a testimony to this issue.

This dynamic nature of the demand, that would eventually rise to the 'regional average', has a bearing on the question of grid connected and grid independent power supply. Are we fobbing the rural off with second best solution or 'Nakli Bijli' as some respondent observes in Tayyabpur village? This brings back memories of a Doordarshan programme in 80s covering a solar energy pilot in a village in Himachal Pradesh. The villagers being interviewed asked an important question—when will they get the 'Khambhe waali bijli'! We may, therefore, need to use the grid both as a fall back option and to evacuate the surplus local power generated through decentralized RE. The distributed energy generation is likely to succeed then in an entrepreneurial model and not as a community-based effort. The community can legitimately ask as to why and how long should it 'shoulder the responsibility' of what is considered a service that the state is bound to provide and which it does to the urban citizen!

In this backdrop, the rich texture of Manashvi's analysis of Energy Poverty deserves a fulsome praise. In his own words energy poverty is 'episodic, local, contextual, relative and symptomatic'. But I will caution that the issue of poverty need not be mixed with that of efficiency. The power user in Andaman Island is source agnostic—whether supply comes through diesel or solar does not matter as long as it is subsidized. It is the government that has to look at the subsidy burden. The contextual nature of the energy poverty is a rich area of research opened up by the author. As of now, energy poverty lies in the eyes of the beholder. If its measure is difficult in commodity space could we look into the space of capabilities or functionings at least? This is a point to ponder over.

One is left wondering as to what the realm of solutions is going to be. Can we look at decentralized RE generation as a grid augmenter rather than burdening it with distribution; a task that often requires the formal power of enforcement? Should the urban not set the example in de-gridding first? For the fuel part should we not follow Kirk Smith's maxim of making the available clean instead of only making the clean available. This is particularly so as different types of fuels co-exist even in rich rural settings. We also need to wonder as to why has the mobile phone penetrated the rural settings or why is the solar micro-dome gaining its popularity unlike the RE. A wishful dream perhaps is to have a storage technology so cost effective that most households could afford to buy a 'storage can' or a 10 unit or 20 unit (kWh) 'dabba' from the store next door and, in emergent situation the mother could ask çhhotu, or chhoti for that matter, to go and fetch a 2 unit kaa dabba (storage can) to meet the immediate requirement of power. That dabba or storage can will be the ultimate vindication of Manashvi's painstaking analysis.

A big thank you Manashvi for thinking out of box and raising crucial concerns in our journey towards energy for all through your stupendous work!

Mumbai, India

Satish B. Agnihotri
Emeritus Fellow CTARA IIT
Bombay

Acknowledgements

The present piece of work is a formal culmination of events on account of passionate and endless support from people who were colleagues, seniors, friends, and also those who happened to be all eyes and ears during the course of this inquest.

I consider it my first and foremost duty to express my gratefulness towards Dr. Sushanta Chatterjee (Chief, Regulatory Affairs, CERC, New Delhi) who has been a constant critique and a mentor. He played the most difficult part of being patient with me. He was there, 'always' as a friend and guide ever since I made up my mind to venture into the electricity sector. He has been associated with the erection of the skeletal framework of this present work. I would endlessly remain indebted to him ever for his exemplary sense of commitment, passion, and dedication.

I call upon myself now to express my gratitude towards Professor Ignacio Perez-Arriaga, Visiting Professor at MIT Energy Initiative and Centre for Energy and Environmental Policy Research (CEEPR), Sloan School of Management, MIT, Massachussetts Avenue, USA and Director of the BP Chair on Energy and Sustainability at Instituto de Investigacion Technologica (IIT), Universidad Pontificia Comillas, Alberto Aguilera, Madrid, Spain. He has been extremely generous in terms of allocation of his precious time in reviewing the contents of this piece.

It is my duty now to thank my *neural support system* for her constant motivation and support. I *dedicate* this piece to Ms. Gurneet Tej, IAS who has been the sole inspiration behind my academic pursuits. I am indebted to her, not only for her patience with me as an individual, but also for being a regular critic of my writings. She took all the pains to go through the entire content of this draft umpteen times to bring it out in its present form despite her pressing professional engagements.

I shall be doing injustice towards this piece without mentioning Sh.Kumar Rahul, (Assistant Professor, Political Science, at Ramjas college, University of Delhi) who has been a friend, philosopher, and guide to me for almost two decades. He has been an extremely hard taskmaster. I am grateful to him for helping me improve my writing with his impressionist remarks.

I shall be miserably failing in my duties for not being grateful to my parents for their constant support, motivation, and endless blessings. I express my heartfelt gratitude towards them for being with me and standing by my side during immensely adverse and trying circumstances.

Lastly, I express my sincere thanks towards Sh. Darshan kumar, Sh.Iqbal Singh, and Sh. Aman (District Collectorate, Roopnagar, Punjab), Sh.Surjit Singh (Surjit Photo-studio, Roopnagar, Punjab) and Sh.Gagandeep Singh (RS farms, Roopnagar, Punjab) for their relentless support in assisting me with data-entry, preparation of photomosaics and drawings.

Prologue

General

The context in which this present piece nests, is best described in terms of cultures and spaces of energy consumption that forms the bedrock of societal functioning. The study is situated in the overarching domain of lived experiences of rural India, in terms of access and end-use of energy. This text lays emphasis upon creation of base line data, for a realistic understanding of demand for energy end use, and the locally available resource potential to meet the same. The local energy resource potential has been evaluated for two sources of renewable energy—(a) solar and (b) biogas. Spread across different geo-climatic zones and physiographic divisions, the piece banks upon mixed-method investigative paradigm for assessing the design-reality gap in the action arena of energy policy that drives access to energy end-use. The evidence from the field shows that energy demand is highly individualistic at the granular level of a civil structure (a dwelling unit), and the consumption is invariably guided by other important factors as the social, economic, and political which are together embedded in the *cultural*, which normally escapes the policy framing lens.

Mega-scale energy production systems (based on either conventional or non-conventional resources of energy) promote passive consumerism of energy as a service. This approach distances the remote consumer, further, from the policy process governing access to primary energy. The larger policy design framework prevents the local end-user of energy from becoming a necessary party while recognizing his responsible role towards: (a) climate change mitigation, or (b) the need for energy conservation, or (c) the need for efficient use of energy, and (d) the overall objective of need-based usage of energy. The rural, small consumer needs to be educated and guided for being conscientiously aware of the nation's obligations towards adoption of an energy systems change, being a responsible geo-political entity.

Currently, for a rural end-user of energy, there remains no differentiation between power derived from two different sources—a) green power (renewable energy-based power generation from clean and non-polluting fuels) and, b) brown power (oil and gas-based power generation from polluting fuels). He is operationally and functionally too remotely situated to understand the costs and benefits (relative—both economic and social) of different sources of power generation. Therefore, there is a need for a course correction of policies governing energy access. This approach calls for creation of a guild of *prosumers* who can actively engage with the process of an energy systems change. Prosumer would understand the costs and benefits affecting his individual and collective choices as well, for he becomes an active part of a socio-technical transition triggered by an energy system change.

Therefore, unpacking of spaces and cultures of energy consumption would require active engagement with the prosumer. There remains a huge gap to be filled in terms of optimizing potential realization of renewable resources that are available locally. There is a pressing need to assess the differential resource potential within different options of renewable energy sources (RES). The renewable energy sources still are strongly looked upon as an alien element (intruder) by the conventional energy sector, which dictates and dominates policy formulation. This text tries to understand the energy demand dynamics in respect of the local element of energy consumption. There is need for a balanced policy approach for deciding amongst all the sources of alternate power generation which should be guided by local resource availability and, local demand based on contextual empirical evidence.

An energy community approach in policy hinges upon—the philosophy of demand side management (DSM) of energy that calls for an emphasis on the humanist element of energy consumption. We require a community-centric, anthropomorphic approach. Therefore, there is a requirement for alternate policy approaches directed towards providing energy access to rural India. There is a need to assess the local in terms of available, cleaner resources of energy and in terms of differential usage and responses, to energy access initiatives. The foremost need is—to duly and adequately address the issue, being able to create robust, responsive, and resilient communities.

Target-Based Policy Approach (TBP): What Could Be an Alternative?

With ambitious plans to use renewable—particularly solar PV—to satisfy rapidly increasing electricity demand, India shall lead the Asian economies with the greatest need for additional power system flexibility in the coming decades. As our lives became more digital and interconnected, our dependence on electricity shall increase manifolds. And while electricity offers multiple advantages, consumers often do not realize the carbon footprint of their own electricity use. Thus, an energy system change calls for an adequate exposure to different technologies for seamless acculturation. The customer needs to understand the myths associated with a technology type before being directly exposed to it.

There is a general consensus that access to energy supplies is extremely essential. For, it is the driver for mechanistic sectors that in turn drive the economy and contribute to improvements in services delivery. However, this framework (approach) largely captures the macro-perspective of energy access at the level of a nation as a geo-political entity. Therefore, in the absence of any policy framework for data capture at the minutest level of rural India, the essence of evaluation of energy access loses its significance. Another important element that still longs for its long due recognition is linked to the end use to which an energy service is put. This aspect largely depends upon the typology of micro-consumer base. It is strongly subjective in character, given the plurality, and the cultural heterogeneity of the Indian subcontinent, of rural India, in particular.

Moreover, it is extremely important to understand the centrist human element for a real time, effective management of rural, domestic small loads (actual energy demand) that represent the real flavour of the 'local' consumption needs—as highlighted earlier. These requirements are phrased in terms of questions which have been asked throughout the text: (a) Who are the actors and networks telling the narratives? (b) What are, according to them, the goals, scales, and framings of the programmes and their dynamics? (c) Do the narratives focus on shocks or on stresses, and on control, or on responses, and lastly, (d) What appraisal approaches close down upon any given narrative, and open up towards other alternatives? All these questions have been treated, and answers attempted in the chapters that follow. The piece lays out in the repository of case studies (Chapter 2), and in the subsequent chapter showcasing—local empiricism—highlighting the household energy budgets, the local load demand, the local renewable resource potential, and the extent to which the local resource potential meets the local energy demand (Chapter 3). These narratives express the social construction of reality in terms of responses of the policy recipients to the policy doses, they have been exposed to. The evidence-based policy (EBP) approach exposes the design-reality gap in the extant approaches, aimed to ameliorate the present living conditions vis-à-vis access to electricity (energy).

Detailing of Chapters

This piece of work marks an important contribution to the subject of energy poverty based upon prolific use of context-specific immersive study techniques. The study approach lays further emphasis upon local renewable resource modelling for a comprehensive mapping of energy resource, in niche areas of consumption. This text highlights a strong imperative in terms of need to build upon this work further, for a better-informed policy process while broaching the subject of energy access and energy service provisioning.

The innovative feature of the present work is that, it makes a case at the outset that energy poverty is a consequence of a complex set of—socio-spatial relations and therefore, it is imperative that all research on energy access should consider the structures and institutional arrangements within which energy services are provided and consumed. This particular theoretical stance encourages a plural approach that places central value on understanding the heterogeneity of energy demand within a country like India, with extensively marked variations in social and ecological structures.

There are three committed purposes that form an essential part of the lesson-sharing process in the present work. First, the case studies elaborate upon the definitive and determinate roles played by technology in challenging social-ecological resilience. Second, it is important to bear in mind the differences between two essential aspects of this study in terms of— (1) problem framings in the context of demand aggregation in the rural spaces of energy consumption, historicity of rural electrification policies, and (2) the similarities and dis-similarities in the different approaches to improve energy access. This aspect attains primacy for the third purpose, which is, to identify the pace and direction of energy systems transition, that present critical energy governance challenges, at the lowest level of energy consumption. Managing such transitions becomes a key task for the existing instrumentalities that guide policies and programmes.

Chapter 1 in a Nutshell

It is against this fitting theoretical framing that the first chapter presents its contents in three different sections. The first section introduces the readers to the world view on energy poverty. The second section depicts the spatial disposition of this phenomena in the context of rural India. While trying to identify issues circumscribing the phenomena, the section presents in brief, the chronicles of schemes and policies directed towards emancipating rural India from the drudgery of access to primary energy and energy services. This section lays emphasis upon deciphering signs and symptoms of energy poverty in rural India while trying to understand the gap between (a) the talk on energy access, (b) the policy texts entrusted with the task of ensuring access to energy, and (c) the bigger and larger arena of implementation that is defined by context which remains strongly susceptible to local realities. This section further brings to its readers the reasons for choosing an elaborate mixed methods approach for unravelling and sorting four interlacing issues that deserve attention: (1) the flavour of energy poverty in rural India, (2) the flaws in the definition of an electrified village as detailed in the policy texts, (3) the need for a paradigm shift from a TBP approach to a context-based EBP approach for ensuring energy access to rural India, and (4) servicing local energy demand through a realistic mapping of local renewable energy source potential (RESP).

The third section provides a comprehensive and detailed exposition of the research methodology that has been adopted to pursue the themes of understanding and measuring energy poverty in India. The careful attention devoted to setting out of rigorous sampling universe, the sampling frame and the sampling unit presents a comprehensive backdrop to the readers to appreciate the complexity of energy poverty phenomena. The effort entailed a well-balanced use of quantitative and qualitative research methods to develop an effective tool kit for extrication of a social phenomenon from its camouflaged presence. The research design presented in the chapter bears a testimony to the fact that it took almost two years for collection of scattered pieces of evidence from across the subcontinent (details in Chapter 1).

The Arsenal of Case Studies in Chapter 2

The array of case studies is placed in Chapter 2 of the text. The gamut of cases is spread across different geo-climatic zones and physiographic divisions of the Indian subcontinent. The cases cover such politico-administrative locales as: Andaman and Nicobar Islands, Dhundi in Gujarat, Tayyabpur in Bihar, Bahadurpur in Punjab, and Lohati Pasai in Uttar Pradesh. A descriptive, exploratory, and explanatory approach has been followed in respect of each of the cases while trying to highlight the associations and dissociations with their respective contexts in terms of acceptance by the community, followed by a proposed model of prescription as to what could have been done differently for a graded engagement leading to acceptance of the initiative. The demonstrative pilots such as the IMWI—Tata (SPICE) and the Mera Gao Power (Lohati Pasai) are richly illustrated with photomosaics, composite and schematic maps, and further complemented by an overlay of empirical data on energy availability for a variety of sources. The sifting of the slew of ethnographic material, the mapping of energy availability, and the tracking of political economy mechanisms undertaken by the author expose the huge range of heterogeneity emerging from differences in local conditions.

There is also clear and substantial evidence that the schemes do not regard the local communities as being repositories of knowledge regarding energy use of sources. Rather, they are often driven by the logic of their programmes, and impose a set of rules and conditions that are incongruous with the context of communities. This particular dimension rings alarm bells throughout, rather sharply and repeatedly, in this large and very packed chapter. It iterates the urgent need to reintegrate the theoretical concepts of collective action through interweaving the impact of local, cluster and district, and state level institutional arrangements. The importance of case studies as a research tool to facilitate the accessing of rich narratives and to improve the author's ability to identify the less readily voiced features of social life such as tacit knowledge is brought out effectively in this chapter. The depiction of energy availability as graphical representations provided in the text serve as an effective visualization of this method, that are reader friendly and readily comprehensible.

The case studies are driven by: *within a single unit analysis* approach, which provides a deep, vertically integrated framework to broach the subject through an immersion procedure. The plethora of cases spread across various regions helped to raise and answer the following questions while trying to identify flaws (weaknesses) in the extant energy access programmes and policies.

(a) Is there a case for low modernism (as against high modernism) for the rural energy sector as the demand is largely driven by local consumption contexts? Would that necessarily entail a process re-engineering (largely being socio-technical)—opposite of high modernism in a lower form in terms of scale and scope?
(b) Is there a need to build capacity to enable cohesive and smooth adaptation of subtle forms of 'modernism' in its lower (less complex) form? Would these capacities be within the local institutional framework (local institutions of self-government) or outside (within the existing regulatory frameworks)? What kind of complexities (in terms of process conception and design) need to be erased while attempting to create the necessary social and institutional infrastructure at the micro-level, before one builds on the physical super structure?
(c) How do we build the 'rationality' for collective action for decentralized energy systems (DES)? What would be the elements of such rationality? What kind of specific design elements would be required to be put in an institutional framework to achieve pareto-optimal efficiency for renewal energy sources?

The EBP Approach Placing of Scattered Pieces of Evidence from Across Rural Spaces of Energy Consumption and the Collective Learnings from Case Studies on Modes of Energizing Communities

Chapter 3 examines evidence from the villages of Profullynagar, Amargarh, Motivarnoli, Kakira, Bhikuchack, Anher to provide deeper insights into the lessons that can be learned from the installations of solar and other innovative energy source schemes to improve the conditions in the rural electrification sphere across states in India. The author concludes that there is structural blindness with regard to comprehending that the provisioning of energy access is neither a simple nor straight forward proposition. The most severe shortfall of the energy initiatives of both the state and non-state actors has been that they have only addressed, at best, the technical requirements for energy provision. The attempt has been cursory.

They are at sixes and sevens when it comes to a considered opinion of how to work with the wide-ranging heterogeneity in conditions in rural India. The challenge is to breakdown the resistance to facing up to the multifarious nature of energy poverty and to bring the rural community to the centre of policymaking. *This consideration, the author shows is an anathema to policy makers and the private sector—as they appear to have 'lost' the contours of the social and ecological aspects of energy provision.* This very important finding that emerges from the very detailed analysis of a large data collection exercise, and from a veritable library of case studies underlines the importance of evidence-based policy approach towards addressing socio-technical issues, and adopting a policy and programmatic course correction thereafter.

Energy Demand Collectivism Expressed Through Coalescence of the Patterns of Differential Consumption in Differing Contexts

The penultimate Chapter 4 of the text highlights the fact that energy policy estate in India follows a centralized trajectory of extension of policy infusion without assessing the local nature of passive consumerism in terms of energy needs assessment. The unilateral policy design in respect of providing energy access is bereft of an essentialist dogma based on collectivism through coalescence of needs of the local. In the absence of any framework for *demand capture* for requirements of energy services, the executional aspiration in terms of access to electricity coupled with the daily consumption of 1 unit (kWh) of electricity appears to be presumptuous. The argument refers to an inherent flaw in the contemporary policy regulating provision for energy access.

Standardization of Requirements of a Rural Consumer

Propelled by a standardization vacuum for assessing quality, reliability, and reasonability of rates in relation to electricity supply for a rural, domestic customer, the policy remains functionally distant from its desired objectives. Thus, there appears to be a huge gap between the constitutional aspirations, the policy texts and the context defined by the action arenas. This piece of work makes an attempt towards a clinical analysis of the *impolitic policy* conception and execution of schemes providing access to energy services by using interdisciplinarity and a mixed method approach to identify gaps in programme design and execution.

The Human Element in Energy Consumption
Understanding the human dimension in a rural energy eco-system entails local energy demand profiling, understanding choices and preferences, and behaviour of a passive consumer of electricity. The text lists the sequencing of various centralized rural electrification policies and programmes aimed towards bringing an energy system change while improving access to energy services. However, the experience from the field is indicative of incoherence between policy conception, design and execution on account of the singular fact—non-recognition of needs (energy demand) of the local. The programmes appear to follow a target-based trajectory driven by supply side management (SSM) principles rather than being based on demands realism (realistic idea of local nature of energy demand).

The Chinks in the Policy Armour
Thus, the policy process appears to be bereft of two principal essentialities—(a) the anthropological focus (the missing human element in energy action) and (b) recognition of energy poverty as the central theme of rural electrification policies and the related thematic programmes directed towards improving energy access. The chapter highlights the contextual complexities of labelling a passive consumer and a rural area as 'energy poor' within the contemporary rubric of 'energy poverty'. The exclusive focus of this work has been on empirical evidence collection for an incisive understanding of energy poverty nested in socio-cultural spaces. The central focus of this text is to understand 'demands realism' in diverse spaces and cultures of energy consumption which describe the local energy landscape of rural India.

Conclusion—Context-Based Policy Requires Assessment of Local Realities
Local energy action in the form of community driven, small scale energy generation and consumption systems has the locale-specific potential to recast the 'centralized policy framework' governing energy generation, transmission, and distribution. Decentralized energy systems paradigm calls for—(a) evidence-based policy for local resource assessment, and (b) context-specific energy needs assessment for overcoming barriers to decentralized energy systems in India.

The text underlines need for: migration from target-based approach towards evidence-based approach for designing context-based policies in respect of energy demand, and secondly a parallel shift from a techno-economic regime towards a socio-technical regime embedded in 'appropriate' contexts. While proposing the said prescription, the conclusive section proposes a model that tries to assimilate all the issues pertaining to design issues of the centrist energy access policy and presents a strong case for decentralized energy systems in India through recognition of signs and symptoms of endemic energy poverty in rural India. The textual policy prescription also tries to address related issues that lie at the heart of the policy formulation process—that is: non-adherence to the constitutional mandate which emphatically lays down the policy prescription—'rural electrification, energy access, energy distribution whether by conventional or non-conventional means is the subject matter of the institutions of local self-government., the gram panchayats'.

What Has This Piece of a Work Tried to Answer?

This text has made an attempt to highlight the importance of contextual understanding of design and reality gap in policies trying to ensure energy access across rural India. It makes an arduous attempt in linking contextual evidence to the current policy frameworks highlighting the need for course correction. The following thematic queries force one to ponder over the extant *target-based approach* towards driving energy access to rural India based upon—a) extension of central grid and b) massive, mega-scale roll out of 'only' one source of renewable energy, thus creating an exception within the homogeneity of RES.

While trying to understand the energy poverty phenomenon in the associated spaces and cultures of energy consumption, the institutional framework was found wanting in terms of engaging with the problem of asymptomatic as well as symptomatic existence of this phenomenon. The book attempts to answer one single question: Is rural India energy poor? And, more importantly an inscribed observation- If my life style is not energy intensive, do I qualify to be energy poor.

Scope, Limitations, and Key Takeaways (Learnings)

The present work is a means to engage constructively with existing bodies of knowledge on energy supply, technology, energy access, and energy services that affect an individual end-user and the society. What needs to be understood is the fact that this study is nested in the domain of social sciences where issues have been raised and discussed in terms of narratives around institutions, structures, frameworks, processes, and people. Recent years have seen a multiplication in the use of multiple methodological approaches in most areas of public policy.

Differential Approaches to Plural Policies

While the attention of researchers and practitioners has thus far primarily focused on the technical details of study design, the role of methodological pluralism in policymaking has been a relatively under-researched topic. Likewise, the bulk of 'knowledge use' literature has focused on the role of evaluations, assessments, and scientific research in policymaking, paying little attention to the influence of methods, especially mixed methods. However, the early findings from research on the role of methods in policymaking have pointed in a direction similar to that which has been identified in more general knowledge use research, namely that the direct, instrumental use of methods by policymakers seems to be an exception, rather than a rule. One could therefore hypothesize that scientific assessments, evaluations, scenarios, and indicators tend to influence policies indirectly and through largely unforeseen pathways, for example by gradually shaping frameworks of thought, or by providing stakeholders with 'ammunition' that is useful in their daily political and policy communication battles.

Lack of Uniform Approach in Framing Narratives

Pivotal to the present work is the idea that a situation of unsustainability will be described by different stakeholders in different ways. They will tell their 'narratives' in various ways, thus 'framing' the situation differently, for example, *varying the scale* (from local to regional and to national and thereafter global) or *the action perspective* (from control to adapt, or respond as the current text describes it). Usually there is a dominant narrative, in many cases highly focused on control, large scale, and technology and economy driven. However, the author feels that one should find the time to listen to other 'narratives' as well, in order to be able to discover alternative 'pathways' to sustainability, as the present text argues.

Approaches are employed, on the one hand, to monitor policy performance and foster accountability within frameworks and on the other hand, to promote policy learning. This piece puts forth an argument in favour of evidence-based policy approach for an informed policy conception, design, and its eventual execution.

Agenda for Governance, Research, and Policies to Be Laced with Humanism

Technology-focused literature should be receptive towards sharing of lessons between different areas of study in particular socio-technical and anthropomorphic as the present case. It must attend particularly to the common governance challenges that confront either of the approaches. Therefore, throughout this text I have argued that the focus should be on critical experiences arising from immersion, that should ultimately lead to a transition management approach, for governing sustainable socio-technical transformations. Questions over who governs, whose system framings count, and whose sustainability gets prioritized are all pertinent to social-ecological systems research. This piece of work calls attention towards the fact that future research in both areas (techno-economic and socio-technical) should deal more centrally, and explicitly with these inherently political dimensions of sustainability.

This piece of work is cross-sectional and comparative, primarily aimed at gathering empirical evidence. It is also essentially synchronous on account of constraints of time and finances. The phenomenon under study (energy poverty) is both scalar and vector, and therefore, must be studied comprehensively to make a deeper and better diachronic sense. A time series analysis shall yield better and far-reaching results. Despite the constraints, this study is an attempt to create an empirical framework for an informed demand side management of local energy systems, especially with regard to the rural energy consumption landscape in India.

The author is under all intent to use the productive library of case studies nested in different spaces and cultures of energy consumption and feed it into new theoretical framings—the proto-idea of energy Swaraj. The idea has been tentatively suggested that might be the first stepping stone to a more direct engagement with the energy justice strand of analysis in the field of energy and development in the conclusive sections. I look forward to an active engagement with the readers of this text that shall help the perspectives to broaden further.

Contents

1 **Energy and Society: Unravelling Governmentality of Energy Access**   1
   1.1   General Outline   1
   1.2   Section A: The World View on Energy Poverty and Its Linkages to Overall Human Well-Being   2
       1.2.1   Conceptualization of Energy Poverty   2
       1.2.2   Review of Extant Literature on Energy Poverty   3
       1.2.3   Understanding Definitions and Dimensions of Energy Poverty   5
       1.2.4   Quantification of Energy Poverty by IEA   6
       1.2.5   The Concept of Energy Ladder-Illustrating Energy Poverty   7
       1.2.6   Visualization of Energy Access in Terms of Incremental Categories (Table 1.2)   10
   1.3   Section B: The Indian Case of Energy Poverty, Energy Access Initiatives, and the Policy Design and Reality Gap   12
       1.3.1   The Phenomenon of Energy Poverty in Rural India   13
       1.3.2   The Rural Nature of Energy Poverty (EP)   14
       1.3.3   The Concept of Energy Poverty as Understood in and Around the Indian Subcontinent   15

		1.3.4	Energy Services in Rural Indian Context	17
		1.3.5	The Energy Planning and Governance Framework-Genesis of Rural Electrification	18
		1.3.6	FOUR POINT AGENDA Highlighting the Gap Between Policy and Praxis—The Backbone of the Envisaged Research Design	19
	1.4	Section C: The Research Plan, Design and Methods Deployed to Meet the Objectives of the Text as Detailed in the Introductory Section		25
		1.4.1	Immersion in the Action Arena (Field Study)	25
		1.4.2	Household Energy Budget	26
		1.4.3	General Description of Choice of Interdisciplinary (Multiple) Methods: The Mixed Methods Research Paradigm	27
		1.4.4	Description of Fieldwork	28
		1.4.5	Sampling Design: Sampling Universe, Sampling Frame, and Sampling Unit	29
		1.4.6	Sampling Method and Sample Size	31
		1.4.7	Sequential Description of Methodology	32
		1.4.8	Renewable Resource Potential Assessment Method and Instrumentation	33
			1.4.8.1 Solar Resource Assessment (Instrumentation and Data Modelling)	33
			1.4.8.2 Biogas Resource Assessment	34
		1.4.9	The Tool Box Metaphor	36
			1.4.9.1 Concept of Visual Ethnography	36
			1.4.9.2 Case Study Approach	37
	Annexure A			39
	Annexure B			41
	References			59
2	Case Studies as an Immersive Approach for Unravelling Energy–Society Relations			65
	2.1	Introduction		65
	2.2	Evidence-Based Policy (EBP) Paradigm for Fragile Ecosystems Calls for a Realistic Demand Side Management (DSM) of Energy Loads—Case Study from Andamans		67

	2.2.1	General Ground Scenario: Demography, Socio-economic Structure, Power Generation, and Consumption Scenario in the Islands	67
		2.2.1.1 Climate and Vegetation	68
		2.2.1.2 Current Energy Access Scenario	69
	2.2.2	Familiarization with the Area of Study	71
	2.2.3	Introduction to the Dataset	72
	2.2.4	Discussion, Analysis, and Interpretation of Datasets	77
		2.2.4.1 DSM Through Understanding Load Demand and Consumption Pattern Across a Dwelling Unit (Creation of Load Demand Curves)	89
		2.2.4.2 Assessment of Renewable Energy Resource Potential	90
		2.2.4.3 Solar Resource Assessment Potential	90
		2.2.4.4 Biogas Resource Potential Assessed	91
	2.2.5	Conclusion and Policy Implications	92
2.3	Annexure A: Case Study 2.1 (Andaman and Nicobar Islands)		93
References			107
2.4	The Story of Solar Pump Irrigators' Cooperative Enterprise (SPICE), from a Village: Dhundi, Gujarat		108
	2.4.1	Introduction	108
		2.4.1.1 Claims of the Project Proponent	108
		2.4.1.2 Envisaged Outcome	108
	2.4.2	Dhundi Village—The Action Arena	109
		2.4.2.1 The SPICE Narrative Through Its Curator	109
		2.4.2.2 DSUUSM Becomes a Reality	111
		2.4.2.3 Snapshot of Dhundi Project: The Role of the Local, the Panchayat of Dhundi Village (as Recorded During Discussions)	112

		2.4.2.4	Policy Support from the State-Tripartite Agreement for Installation of Solar Agriculture Pumping System	112
	2.4.3	De-construction of Events and the Outcomes		113
	2.4.4	Commercial Interest of the Member Farmer		114
	2.4.5	Technical Issues Related to Discharge		114
	2.4.6	Analysis and Discussion		115
		2.4.6.1	The Operative Solar-Based Irrigation Policy Dose	115
	2.4.7	Interpreting the Policy Content, Relational Dynamics Between the Involved Institutions and Actors		115
		2.4.7.1	The Demonstration Project Remains at a Secluded Distance	116
		2.4.7.2	Socio-political Structure	116
		2.4.7.3	Socio-economic Structure Prior to the Initiative	116
		2.4.7.4	Evidence of Disruption of the Social, Economic, and the Political	116
		2.4.7.5	Legal and Technical Deviations	118
	2.4.8	Conclusion and Policy Implications		120
2.5	Annexure B: Case Study 2.2 Dhundi (Gujarat)			122
References				130
2.6	Unleashing Dystopia Through Technology Implant: Technological Lock-In Leads to Disruption of Social Order. A Case Study from Tayyabpur: Bihar, India			131
	2.6.1	Introduction		131
		2.6.1.1	The Relational Dynamics Between the Protagonist and the Local Institutions	132
	2.6.2	Why Tayyabpur?		132
		2.6.2.1	Plight of Tayyabpur and Ward No.9 in Particular	133
	2.6.3	Background of the Tayyabpur Solar Micro-Grid Project		134
		2.6.3.1	The Utopian Conception	134

		2.6.3.2	*The Ulterior Design Led to Entrapment: Sharwan Gets Trapped!*	135
		2.6.3.3	*Sharwan Executes the Lease Deed: The Rules of the Utopian Design*	136
		2.6.3.4	*Sharwan Reduced to the Status of an Executant*	136
	2.6.4	\multicolumn{2}{l}{*Conclusive Thoughts—Tayyabpur Solar Micro-Grid: Oblivious of Socio-cultural Moorings?*}	138
		2.6.4.1	*The Role of PRAYAS in the Entire Scheme of Things: Escalating Expectations? Over Hyped Technology Capacity? Politics of Inflation and Exaggeration*	139
		2.6.4.2	*Reference Electrification Model Falls Short of Expectations*	139
		2.6.4.3	*Loopholes in the Rules of the Game—Institutional Oversights and Pitfalls*	140
		2.6.4.4	*The Associated Dysfunctionalities*	141
		2.6.4.5	*A Year Later: The Situation in Tayyabpur*	143
		2.6.4.6	*Policy Prescription: Take Home Message*	144

2.7 Annexure C: Case Study 2.3 Tayyabpur (Bihar) 145
References 155
2.8 *Regulating Access to Energy Through Webs of—Weak Decentralized Institutions, Meek Regulator, and Distanced Local Development and Administrative Set-Up, Case Study from Lohati Pasai, Uttar Pradesh* 156
    2.8.1 *Introduction: The Constitutional Mandate for Governance of Energy Access—Pathways to Energy Service Delivery* 156

	2.8.1.1	The Core Argument: Should Distributed Application of Energy Access Be Nested in Structures Outside the Purview of Formal Institutions?	157
	2.8.1.2	Decentralized Energy Access Grounded in the Theoretical Import of Improved Service Delivery	157
	2.8.1.3	Pre-requisite for Localized Control of Energy Access Through Active Involvement of Institutions of Local Self-Government	158
2.8.2	The Race to Light Up a Dwelling Unit: Transforming Power and Relationships Through Lighting Up Lives in Motipur—A Purwa/Majara (Hamlet) of the Revenue Village, Lohati Pasai		159
	2.8.2.1	The Local Power Relations in Motipur—Socio-political Demographic Structure at Play	160
	2.8.2.2	The Class-Caste-Wise Load Consumption Pattern in the Village	162
	2.8.2.3	The Operative Functionality of Non-state Actor: MGP	167
	2.8.2.4	The Local Agents of MGP in the Energy Action Arena	167
	2.8.2.5	The Operational Dynamics of the Micro: The Actors, the Agents, and the Action Arena—In Terms of Resource Allocation, Access to Resource, and Its Capture	168
	2.8.2.6	Trust Deficit Between the RESCO and the Beneficiaries	170

	2.8.3	The Non-state Actor Challenges the Formal Decentralized Institutional Mechanisms of the State that Govern Energy Access	171
		2.8.3.1 Energy Service Adequacy: A Far-Fetched Assessment of Demand Capture!	172
	2.8.4	Conclusion and Policy Implications	176
	2.8.5	Weak Regulation Fuels Voluntarism and Monopoly by Non-state Actors Providing Energy Access	178
2.9	Annexure D: Case study 2.4 Mera Gao Power (Uttar Pradesh)		179
References			188
2.10	RS Farms: The Biogas Cum Dairy Farm (A Social Enterprise) That Was Not to Be: A Failed Saga of Perceived 'Collectivism, Social Innovation, and Social Enterprise'?		190
	2.10.1	About Bahadurpur: Geography, Demography, and Socio-economic Profile	190
	2.10.2	The Family Genealogical Tree and the Prenatal History of RS Farms	191
		2.10.2.1 The Early days of Conception of the Biogas Plant	192
		2.10.2.2 Creation of Trust—Investing in Human Capital, Accumulating Social Capital: The Beginning	192
		2.10.2.3 Issues, Fears, and Anxieties Eroded Trust	193
		2.10.2.4 The Humble Beginning as an Individual Enterprise	194
		2.10.2.5 The Biogas Unit Becomes a Reality	195
		2.10.2.6 The Recurring (Operation and Maintenance Costs)	195

             2.10.2.7   Expansion
                        and Diversification—From
                        a Biogas Unit Providing Free
                        Cooking Fuel Supply, into a Dairy
                        Farm and a Sweet Meat
                        and Confectionary Unit   195
             2.10.2.8   The Physical and the Technical
                        Details of the Unit   196
             2.10.2.9   Interaction with the Mason
                        (the Chief Architect)
                        and the Principal operator—The
                        Real Heroes   198
   2.10.3   Theoretical Imports Applied to Deconstruct
            RS Farms as a Social, Economic, Cultural,
            and Political Entity   199
             2.10.3.1   Social Enterprise   199
             2.10.3.2   Summing Up the Theoretical
                        Framework for SEs   202
             2.10.3.3   The CPR Framework
                        and the Related Institutional
                        Dynamics   203
             2.10.3.4   The Three Influential Models   203
             2.10.3.5   Summing Up CPR
                        and Institutional Issues   204
   2.10.4   Theoretical Imports Applied to Ram Singh
            (RS) Farms   205
             2.10.4.1   Governing and Managing
                        Animal Waste—Does
                        a Refuse/Reject (End Product
                        of Biological Metabolism) Qualify
                        to Be Treated as a Common
                        Property Resource?   205
             2.10.4.2   Social Enterprises, Institutions,
                        Structures: Processes and Outcomes
                        in Bahadurpur   206
   2.10.5   Role of State and Its Policy Instruments
            and Instrumentalities   208
             2.10.5.1   Mandate of NBMMP   208

	2.10.5.2	Incongruent, Self-Contradicting Policy Designs for Creating Delirium	208
	2.10.5.3	Biogas Takes a Hit Despite Its Potential as a Resource	209
	2.10.5.4	The After Effects of the Macro-policy Design on a Micro-Entity	211
	2.10.5.5	Seeing Like a State, Scott Re-visited—Understanding Events and Fallouts	211
2.10.6	Conclusion, Policy Implications, and Prescription—Does the Case Exemplify a Paradigm of Negotiated Compromise for Pursuing an Economic Interest Sans Creation of any Social Value?		214
	2.10.6.1	Policy Prescription	216
	2.10.6.2	Proposed Role of Social Capital in Developing Consensus for Acceptance of Progressive, Local Energy Systems as an Alternate Source of Clean Cooking Fuel from the Biogas Unit in Bahadurpur (Table 2.9)	218
	2.10.6.3	Concluding Thoughts	218
2.11	Annexure E: Case Study 2.5 Bahadurpur (Punjab)		221
References			237

3 **Collectivization of Local Demand Through Localized Energy Needs and Resource Assessment—Understanding Demands Realism** 239

 3.1 The Local Energy Inaction: The Missing Anthropogenic Dimension 239

  3.1.1 Polysemy Around Rural Flavour of Energy Poverty 240

  3.1.2 What Does the Evidence Bring on the Table? 241

	3.1.2.1	The Island Ecosystem (Village: Profullyanagar, Tehsil and Community Development (CD) Block: Mayabunder, District: North and Middle Andaman, Union Territory (UT))	242
	3.1.2.2	The Mainland Black Cotton Soil Rich Ecosystem (Village: Moti Varnoli, Taluka: Desar and District: Vadodara, State: Gujarat)	245
	3.1.2.3	The Nature of Evidence from the Great Plains (Village: Bhikuchack, CD Block: Belchi, Tehsil: Barh, District: Patna, State: Bihar)	248
	3.1.2.4	The Evidence From (Village: Ghanghaol, Tehsil: Fatehpur Sadar, CD Block: Haswa, District: Fatehpur, State: Uttar Pradesh)	250
	3.1.2.5	Evidence From (Village: Amargarh, CD Block and Tehsil: Sadulshahar, District: Ganganagar, State: Rajasthan)	253
	3.1.2.6	Evidence from Himalayan Foothills (Village: Kakira, CD Block: Bhattiyat, Tehsil: Chowari Khas, District: Chamba, State: Himachal Pradesh)	255
	3.1.2.7	Evidence from the Piedmont Zone of the Lesser Himalayas (Village: Anher, CD Block: Pathankot, Tehsil: Pathankot, District: Pathankot, State: Punjab)	259
3.1.3	Evidence from Case Studies Put Together		261
	3.1.3.1	Learnings from Tayyabpur Solar Micro-grid (Fig. 3.31, Annexure)	261

3.1.3.2	Learnings from Dhundi (Solar Pump Irrigators' Cooperative Enterprise) (Fig. 3.32, Annexure)	264
3.1.3.3	Learnings from North and Middle Andaman District (Demand for Local Renewable Energy Systems: Evidence from North and Middle Andaman District) (Fig. 3.33, Annexure)	267
3.1.3.4	Learnings from the Functional Experience of Mera Gao Power (MGP) (Fig. 3.34, Annexure)	270
3.1.3.5	Learnings from Bahadurpur Biogas Plant—Ram Singh (RS) Farms: The Biogas Cum Dairy Farm (A Social Enterprise) That Was Not to Be (Fig. 3.35, Annexure)	272
3.1.4	Summing Up: The Empirical Evidence from the Fieldwork in Different Geo-Climatic Zones and Physiographic Divisions Establish That at the Micro-level	275
3.1.5	The Case Studies That Have Been Discussed in the Preceding Section Suggest That the Policy Conception and Construct in Terms of Structural Design Require an Immediate Course Correction	276

Annexure	278
Profullyanagar	282
Moti Varnoli	288
Bhikhuchak	294
Ghanghaol	300
Amargarh	307
Kakira	314
Anher	320
References	331

4 Decentralized Energy Systems Entails: Evidence-Based Policy Approach   333
    4.1   *The Pristine Bedrock: The Fountainhead of Aspirational Welfareism*   333
    4.2   *The Aspirational Core—The Constitutional Mandate for Governance of Energy Systems: A Critique of Pathways to Energy Service Delivery*   334
    4.3   *The Burden of Aspirations—As Spelt Out in the Rural Electrification Policy, 2006*   335
        4.3.1   *The Rural Load Demand Variability*   336
        4.3.2   *Act Utilitarianism by Self-Interested Actors*   338
        4.3.3   *The Static Interventions of the Non-state Actors in Providing Energy Services*   339
        4.3.4   *Passive Consumerism and the Extent Policies of Rural Electrification*   339
    4.4   *The Missing 'Local' in Energy Action and the Associated* Polysemy *with* Endemic, Episodic *Texture of Rural Energy Poverty (EP)*   340
    4.5   *Evidence-based Policy Approach to Address Energy Poverty*   341
    4.6   *The Missing Dimension of Energy Systems Decentralization in the Policy Estate as Well as the Action Arena*   342
    4.7   *The Missing Contextual* (Scale, Scope, Time, and Place) *Dimension in Local Energy Access action*   343
        4.7.1   *Localized Action for Active Engagement with Energy Access Framework*   343
        4.7.2   *Positivist Approach for Building Capacities*   344
        4.7.3   *Argument in Favour of a Socio-technical Approach*   345
    4.8   *The New Decentralized Energy Systems Paradigm Based on EBP—Evidence Exposes Latent Tension All Along Vertically Integrated Institutions, Structures, and Processes*   346
        4.8.1   *Conventional, Institutional Frameworks Are Not Good Enough*   348

	4.8.2	Conventional Structures Addressing a Symptomatic Issue Appear to be Lacking in Cohesive Action—Sector Characteristics Need to be Appreciated and Tackled	349
	4.8.3	Shaking Up the Archaic Energy Governance and Planning Structural Frame	350
	4.8.4	The Need for New Policy Based on Cohesive Integration of Conventional and Non-conventional Energy Production Systems	351
4.9		Complex, Multi-stage Policy Formulation in the Renewable Energy Sector	352
Annexure			354
References			357

5 Conclusion: Overcoming Barriers to Decentralized Energy Systems in India — 361

5.1		The World View on Energy Access and End Use of Energy	361
5.2		Re-collecting Experiences of the Microculture of Energy Demand and the Rural Dimension of EP	362
5.3		India Needs to Recognize the Importance of Local Nodes of Energy Consumption for an Effective Engagement with SDGs	363
5.4		Challenges Before India—Balancing Growth and Sustainable Development	363
5.5		Energizing Rural India—Rural Electrification: Context, Relevance, Issues, and Concerns	365
	5.5.1	Governance and Planning-Related Concerns	366
	5.5.2	Policy and Design-Related Concerns	367
	5.5.3	Institutional Concerns	370
5.6		Summing Up Challenges to Implementation of Rural Electrification Projects	371
5.7		Addressing Issues and Concerns: Re-aligning the Lost Policy Focus	372
5.8		The Dilemmas of Energy System Transition	373
5.9		Summing Up—Transcending Barriers and Closure of Design-Reality Gap	375
5.10		Scope for Further Research	378

5.11 *Renewable Energy Technologies (RETs)—Alternate Pathways to Power Generation, Holding a Promise to Service Culture-Specific Demands, Exhibited Through Distributed Loads* — 380
5.12 *Tweaking with the Principle and the Institutional Framework* — 382
5.13 *Tweaking with the Conception and Policy Design in the Rural Electricity Sector* — 383
5.14 *Translating Policy Aspirations into Praxis* — 385
Annexure — 387
References — 389

Bibliography — 395

Index — 405

About the Author

Dr. Manashvi Kumar Singh is an officer of the Indian Administrative Service (IAS), allocated to Punjab cadre. He has an exceptional bachelor's and master's degree in earth sciences, and an award-winning Ph.D. in political science from Delhi University. His repertoire of experience includes regulatory and development administration, and trysts with urban development, indirect taxation, public finance, audit, energy, environment, and power. Prior to joining the premier civil service, Dr. Kumar was a trained geologist and an earth scientist.

His professional and academic interest spans across subjects pertaining to land, water, energy and power, climate change, regulatory capture, government failure, comparative public policy, empiricism, inter-disciplinary and mixed methods research, renewable energy resource modelling, demand side management of electricity, evidence-based policy and policy analysis. He writes on issues pertaining to electricity and energy sector; in particular, the rural electricity sector.

Abbreviations

ABT	Availability Based Tariff
AC	Alternating Current
ADB	Asian Development Bank
APL	Above Poverty Line
APPC	Average Power Purchase Cost
AREP	Accelerated Rural Electrification Programme
ASCI	Administrative Staff College of India
ASLA	American Society of Landscape Architects
BAU	Business as Usual
BCs	Backward Castes
BDO	Block Development Officer
BDPO	Block Development and Panchayat Officer
BIS	Bureau of Indian Standard
BKOs	Brick Kiln Owners
BPL	Below Poverty Line
BU	Billion Units
CAD	Constituent Assembly Debates
CAG	Comptroller and Auditor General of India
CCAFS	Climate Change, Agriculture and Food Security
CCE	Comfort, Communication, Entertainment
CCEA	Cabinet Committee on Economic Affairs
CD	Community Development
CDO	Chief Development Officer
CEA	Central Electricity Authority
CEEW	Council on Energy Environment and Water
CEI	Chief Electrical Inspector

CEO	Chief Executive Officer
CERC	Central Electricity Regulatory Commission
CFL	Compact Fluorescent Lamp
CGIAR	Consultative Group on International Agricultural Research
CHP	Combined Heat and Power
CNG	Compressed Natural Gas
CO	Carbon mono-oxide
COP	Conference of Parties
CP	Conventional Power
CPR	Common Property Resource
CSH	Compulsory Supply Hours
DC	Direct Current
DCHB	District Census Hand Book
DDG	Decentralized Distributed Generation
DDUGJY	Deen Dayal Upadhyay Gram Jyoti Yojana
DER	Distributed Energy Resources
DES	Decentralized Energy Systems
DFID	Department for International Development
DISCOMS	Distribution Companies
DSM	Demand Side Management
DSUUSM	Dhundi Saur Urja Utpadak Sahakri Mandali
DU	Dwelling Unit
EBP	Evidence-Based Policy
ED	Executive Director
EDU	Electrified Dwelling Unit
EP	Energy Poverty
ESCO	Energy Service Company
FB	Filament Bulb
FES	Foundation for Ecological Security
FIT	Feeding Tariff
FOIR	Forum of Indian Regulators
GE	General Electric
GEDA	Gujarat Energy Development Agency
GERC	Gujarat Electricity Regulatory Commission
GERMI	Gujarat Energy Research and Management Institute
GETCO	Gujarat Energy Transmission Corporation
GNESD	Global Network on Energy for Sustainable Development
GoB	Government of Bihar
GOG	Government of Gujarat
GOI	Government of India
GUVNL	Gujarat Urja Vikas Nigam Limited
GW	Giga Watt
HP	Horse Power

HPP	Hired Power Plants
HRT	Hydraulic Retention Temperature
HSD	High Sulphur Diesel
IAY	Indira Awas Yojana
IBRD	International Bank for Reconstruction and Development
ICS	Improved Cook Stoves
IEA	International Energy Agency
IEC	International Electrotechnical Commission
IEG	Independent Evaluation Group
IFC	International Finance Corporation
INR	Indian National Rupee
IPCC	International Panel on Climate Change
IREDA	Indian Renewable Energy Development Agency
IWMI	International Water Management Institute
JERC	Joint Electricity Regulatory Commission
KV	Kilo Volt
KVARH	Kilo Volt Ampere Reactive Hours
KVIC	Khadi and Village Industry Commission
KW	Kilo-Watt
KWH	Kilo Watt Hour
KWP	Kilo-Watt Peak (Power)
LAY	Lohia Awas Yojana
LED	Light Emitting Diode
LNG	Liquefied Natural Gas
LPG	Liquefied Petroleum Gas
LT	Low Tension
MCBs	Miniature Circuit Breakers
MDG	Millennium Development Goals
MEPI	Multidimensional Energy Poverty Index
MFI	Micro-Finance Institution
MGNREGA	Mahatma Gandhi National Rural Employment Guarantee Act
MGNREGS	Mahatma Gandhi National Rural Employment Guarantee Scheme
MGO	Mini Grid Operator
MGP	Mera Gao Power
MGVCL	Madhya Gujarat Vij Company Limited
MIT	Massachusetts Institute of Technology
MM^2	Millimetre square
MMGSY	Mukhya Mantri Gram Sampark Yojana
MNCES	Ministry of Non-conventional Energy Sources
MNP	Minimum Needs Programme
MNRE	Ministry of New and Renewable Energy
MOP	Ministry of Power

MORD	Ministry of Rural Development
MOSPI	Ministry of Statistics and Programme Implementation
MPPT	Maximum Power Point Tracking
MSL	Mean Sea Level
MW	Mega Watt
NAPCC	National Action Plan on Climate Change
NBMMP	National Biogas and Manure Management Programme
NBPDCL	North Bihar Power Distribution Company Limited
NCP	Non-Conventional Power
NDC	National Development Council
NEDU	Non-Electrified Dwelling Unit
NEP	National Electricity Policy
NFP	Not for Profit
NGOs	Non-Governmental Organizations
NH	National Highway
NITI	National Institution for Transforming India
NPOs	Non-Profit Organizations
NSSO	National Sample Survey Organization
NTP	National Tariff Policy
NTPC	National Thermal Power Corporation
OM	Office Memorandum
OMC	Omni Power Micro-grid Company
PDN	Power Distribution Network
PEDA	Punjab Energy Development Agency
PFA	Power for All
PIB	Press Information Bureau
PLF	Plant Load Factor
PMAY (G)	Pradhan Mantri Awas Yojana (Grameen)
PMGSY	Pradhan Mantri Gram Sadak Yojana
PMGY	Pradhan Mantri Gramodaya Yojana
PPA	Power Purchase Agreement
PPTC	Polymeric Positive Temperature Coefficient
PRIs	Panchayati Raj Institutions
PSCC	Pre-Stressed Cement Concrete
PTs	Power Transformers
PV	Photo Voltaic
RE	Renewable Energy (electricity)
REDB	Rural Electricity Distribution Backbone
REM	Reference Electrification Model
REP	Rural Electrification Policy
RES	Renewable Energy Sources
RESCO	Rural Energy Service Company
REST	Rural Electricity Supply Technology Mission

RETs	Renewable Energy Technologies
RGGVY	Rajiv Gandhi Grameen Vidyutikaran Yojana
RPO	Renewable Purchase Obligations
RS Farms	Ram Singh Farms
SAS	Stand Alone System
SAUBHAGYA	Pradhan Mantri Sahaj Bijli Har Ghar Yojana
SBI	State Bank of India
SBM	Swachh Bharat Mission
SC	Scheduled Caste
SDD	State Driven Development
SDG	Sustainable Development Goals
SE	Social Enterprise
SEAP	Sustainable Energy Access Planning
SGTB	Solar Grid, Tayyabpur
SH	State Highway
SHLS	Solar Home Lighting System
SNAs	State Nodal Agencies
SNDs	State Nodal Departments
SPI	Smart Power India
SPICE	Solar Pump Irrigators Cooperative Enterprise
SPP	Solar Power Pack
SPV	Solar Photo-Voltaic
SRTT	Sir Ratan Tata Trust
SSM	Supply Side Management
TBP	Target-Based Policy
TL	Tube Light
TPDDL	Tata Power Delhi Distribution Limited
UG	Under Ground
UNDP	United Nations Development Programme
UNFCC	United Nations Framework for Climate Change
UPERC	Uttar Pradesh Electricity Regulatory Commission
UPNEDA	Uttar Pradesh New and Renewable Energy Development Agency
USAID	United States Agency for International Development
USD	US Dollars
USDA	United States Department of Agriculture
VEI	Village Electrification Infrastructure
W/M^2	Watt Per Meter Square
WB	World Bank
WEF	World Economic Forum
WEO	World Energy Outlook
WHO	World Health Organization
WLE	Water Land and Ecosystems
WTP	Willingness to Pay

List of Figures

Fig. 1.1	Energy planning, governance and execution framework of India	40
Fig. 1.2	Mixed methods research framework adopted for the study	41
Fig. 1.3	Sampling framework deployed for the study	42
Fig. 1.4	Layered sampling framework that was the sub-strata framework for choosing the state/UT, district, sub-division, CD block and village	43
Fig. 1.5	Grid access map showing the expanse of field work across various politico-administrative units	44
Fig. 1.6	Map showing different areas covered across various physiographic divisions	45
Fig. 1.7	Map showing solar energy potential assessment (as a resource) on a real-time basis across various geo-climatic zones of India	46
Fig. 1.8	Map showing the quality and quantity of solar irradiance measured on a real-time basis across various geo-climatic zones of India	47
Fig. 1.9	Comprehensive assessment of biogas as a resource for green energy across different villages undertaken for the study	48
Fig. 1.10	Instrumentation deployed for measuring solar irradiance—CMP3 PYRANOMETER	49
Fig. 2.1	Duration of power supply during a day (*Source* Author, 2016)	74

Fig. 2.2	Duration of power supply from sunset to sunrise (*Source* Author, 2016)	74
Fig. 2.3	Peak demand for power for energy scheduling (*Source* Author, 2016)	75
Fig. 2.4	Least demand for power for energy scheduling (*Source* Author, 2016)	75
Fig. 2.5	Voltage fluctuation (*Source* Author, 2016)	76
Fig. 2.6	Harmonious working of appliances (*Source* Author, 2016)	76
Fig. 2.7	Satisfaction levels with respect to power supply (*Source* Author, 2016)	77
Fig. 2.8	Load profile for a day (*Source* Author, 2016)	78
Fig. 2.9	Load distribution pattern of electrical appliances in kWh (average) (*Source* Author, 2016)	79
Fig. 2.10	Load distribuiton pattern of electrical appliances in kWh (average) (*Source* Author, 2016)	80
Fig. 2.11	Load distribution pattern of electrical appliances (average) (*Source* Author, 2016)	81
Fig. 2.12	Lighting load (*Source* Author, 2016)	82
Fig. 2.13	Electrification status (*Source* Author, 2016)	82
Fig. 2.14	Intensity of solar radiation and its duration (*Source* Author, 2016)	83
Fig. 2.15	Current demand for power vs. potential of solar energy and energy output from biogas (*Source* Author, 2016)	84
Fig. 2.16	Current demand for power vs. potential of solar energy and energy output from biogas (*Source* Author, 2016)	85
Fig. 2.17	Current demand for power vs. potential of solar energy and energy output from biogas (*Source* Author, 2016)	86
Fig. 2.18	Comprehensive snapshot of the villages: Lataw, Swadeshnagar and Profullyanagar through the administrative cone of the Meso-(UT)	94
Fig. 2.19	Schematic map of Lataw, Swadeshnagar and Profullyanagar	97
Fig. 2.20	Ultimate recipients of the power supplied. The photo mosaics reflect the general life style of the residents in the three villages of Lataw, Swadeshnagar and Profullyanagar (*Source* Author, 2016)	100
Fig. 2.21	Schematic snapshot of the contemporary HSD based conventional power supply system in Andaman and Nicobar Islands	101
Fig. 2.22	Oldest power sub-station at Phoenix Bay, in Port Blair (*Source* Author, 2016)	102

Fig. 2.23	Storage, purification and power generation process (*Source* Author, 2016)	103
Fig. 2.24	5 MW capacity SPP of NTPC in Port Blair (*Source* Author, 2016)	104
Fig. 2.25	Transmission set-up of solar power generated (*Source* Author, 2016)	105
Fig. 2.26	Power sub-station with feeders transmitting power from conventional and non-conventional sources of generation	106
Fig. 2.27	Comprehensive snapshot of the village Dhundi, through the administrative cone of the Meso-(State)	123
Fig. 2.28	Schematic map of village Dhundi	124
Fig. 2.29	Energy accounting system. The borewell can also be seen	125
Fig. 2.30	Injection point of the solar energy into the MGVCL feeder	126
Fig. 2.31	Equipment layout plan for the solar irrigation pumps	127
Fig. 2.32	Single line diagram (SLD) for the earthing layout plan of the installed solar pumps	128
Fig. 2.33	'Ideal' well-ise of a solar based irrigation pump functional set-up. The necessary element of water conservation	129
Fig. 2.34	Comprehensive snapshot of village Tayyabpur through the administrative cone of the Meso-(State)	146
Fig. 2.35	Schematic map of Tayyabpur	147
Fig. 2.36	General overview of Tayyabpur village	148
Fig. 2.37	General set-up of the solar micro-grid at Tayyabpur (*Source* Author, 2017)	149
Fig. 2.38	Electrical network of solar power generation plant	150
Fig. 2.39	Set-up for energy accounting (*Source* Author, 2017)	151
Fig. 2.40	Distribution infrastructure of the solar micro-grid along with the nature of energy service	152
Fig. 2.41	Load profile of the village depicting actual load demand	153
Fig. 2.42	Schematic array diagram of the solar micro-grid at Tayyabpur	154
Fig. 2.43	200 kV power substation supplying electricity to Lohati Pasai	160
Fig. 2.44	Photomosaic of Motipur hamlet depicting lifestyle of the local dwellers (*Source* Author, 2016)	161
Fig. 2.45	Average daily load demand in Lohati Pasai village	163
Fig. 2.46	Contribution to total electrical load by individual appliances in kWh, based on actual usage of electrical appliances	164

liv   LIST OF FIGURES

Fig. 2.47	Lighting load of different lighting appliances expressed as a fraction of total load on a daily basis across the revenue village	165
Fig. 2.48	Average diurnal (daily) load distribution pattern across the sampled dwelling units	166
Fig. 2.49	Comprehensive snapshot of the village Lohati Pasai through the administrative cone of the Meso-(State)	180
Fig. 2.50	Schematic map of the village Lohati Pasai	181
Fig. 2.51	Schematic single line diagram for the MGP energy service system. Future level 'escalation' in terms of better services has also been shown	182
Fig. 2.52	Energy access typology in Lohati Pasai	183
Fig. 2.53	System of revenue collection by MGP	184
Fig. 2.54	General life style in the village, Lohati Pasai (*Source* Author, 2017)	185
Fig. 2.55	Generation, distribution and the nature of energy service of the MGP setup in the village (*Source* Author, 2017)	186
Fig. 2.56	Village heads interviewed to assess the functioning of MGP	187
Fig. 2.57	Comprehensive snapshot of the revenue village, Bahadurpur, through the Meso-(State)	222
Fig. 2.58	Schematic map of the village	223
Fig. 2.59	Synoptic view of R S farms	224
Fig. 2.60	Complete cattle assembly zone card the feed area	225
Fig. 2.61	Slurry churning unit and the exterior controls of the sub-surface digester	226
Fig. 2.62	Bio-slurry (a by-product) being filled into a tanker	227
Fig. 2.63	Complete aerial distribution system of biogas supply within the village	228
Fig. 2.64	Un-utilized (idle) biogas-based power generation system	229
Fig. 2.65	'Public attention' and accolades earned over a period of time post commercialization	230
Fig. 2.66	Schematic layout of R S Farms	231
Fig. 2.67	Schematic disposition of the cattle shed and feed area	232
Fig. 2.68	Actual layout of the biogas plant at Bahadurpur (sub-surface)	233
Fig. 2.69	Office memorandum showing the details of LPG connections in Bahadurpur	234
Fig. 2.70	Actual potential of a biogas-based power generation system	235
Fig. 3.1	Duration of power supply in the states and one union territory studied	279

Fig. 3.2	Composite map of Profullyanagar	282
Fig. 3.3	(a) Schematic map of the village Profullyanagar; (b) General pattern of energy consumption and lifestyle in the village	283
Fig. 3.4	(a), (b), and (c) Renewable energy resource potential vis-à-vis the load demand, energy budget, and the load demand on account of appliance usage	285
Fig. 3.5	Fraction of lighting load demand as a percentage of the total load demand contributed by use of different lighting devices	286
Fig. 3.6	Composite map of Moti Varnoli	288
Fig. 3.7	(a) Schematic map of the village Moti Varnoli; (b) General pattern of energy consumption and lifestyle in the village	289
Fig. 3.8	(a), (b) and (c) Renewable energy resource potential vis-à-vis the load demand, energy budget, and the load demand on account of appliance usage	291
Fig. 3.9	Fraction of lighting load demand as a percentage of the total load demand contributed by use of different lighting devices	292
Fig. 3.10	Composite map of Bhikhuchak	294
Fig. 3.11	(a) Schematic map of the village Bhikhuchak; (b) General pattern of energy consumption and lifestyle in the village	295
Fig. 3.12	(a), (b), and (c) Renewable energy resource potential vis-à-vis the load demand, energy budget, and the load demand on account of appliance usage	297
Fig. 3.13	Fraction of lighting load demand as a percentage of the total load demand contributed by use of different lighting devices	298
Fig. 3.14	Composite map of Ghanghaol	300
Fig. 3.15	(a) Schematic map of the village Ghanghaol; (b) General pattern of energy consumption and lifestyle in the village	301
Fig. 3.16	(a), (b), and (c) Renewable energy resource potential vis-à-vis the load demand, energy budget, and the load demand on account of appliance usage	303
Fig. 3.17	Fraction of lighting load demand as a percentage of the total load demand contributed by use of different lighting devices	304
Fig. 3.18	Ghanghaol LOHIA AWAS YOJNA SHLS	305
Fig. 3.19	Composite map of Amargarh	307
Fig. 3.20	(a) Schematic map of the village Amargarh; (b) General pattern of energy consumption and lifestyle in the village	308

Fig. 3.21	(a), (b), and (c) Renewable energy resource potential vis-à-vis the load demand, energy budget, and the load demand on account of appliance usage	310
Fig. 3.22	Fraction of lighting load demand as a percentage of the total load demand contributed by use of different lighting devices	311
Fig. 3.23	Composite map of Kakira	314
Fig. 3.24	(a) Schematic map of the village Kakira; (b) General pattern of energy consumption and lifestyle in the village	315
Fig. 3.25	(a), (b), and (c) Renewable energy resource potential vis-à-vis the load demand, energy budget, and the load demand on account of appliance usage	317
Fig. 3.26	Fraction of lighting load demand as a percentage of the total load demand contributed by use of different lighting devices	318
Fig. 3.27	Composite map of Anher	320
Fig. 3.28	(a) Schematic map of the village Anher; (b) General pattern of energy consumption and lifestyle in the village	321
Fig. 3.29	(a), (b), and (c) Renewable energy resource potential vis-à-vis the load demand, energy budget, and the load demand on account of appliance usage	323
Fig. 3.30	Fraction of lighting load demand as a percentage of the total load demand contributed by use of different lighting devices	324
Fig. 3.31	Policy prescription for Tayyabpur	326
Fig. 3.32	Policy prescription for Dhundhi	327
Fig. 3.33	Policy prescription for Andamans	328
Fig. 3.34	Policy prescription for Lohati Pasai	329
Fig. 3.35	Policy prescription for Bahadurpur	330
Fig. 4.1	Variations in base load demands from different sources in different parts of the country from different sources and formal/informal arrangements. What should be a base line minimum electrical load to take a call for addressing demand realism?	355
Fig. 4.2	Individual contribution by each of the functional electronic appliance (AC or DC) to the aggregate load demand	356
Fig. 5.1	Overcoming 'barriers' to decentralized energy systems in India	388

List of Tables

Table 1.1	Energy ladder	8
Table 1.2	Energy services and access levels	11
Table 1.3	Programmes for providing energy access to rural India	20
Table 1.4	Policies/programmes in respect of renewable energy sources (the lesser twin)	21
Table 1.5	Policy initiatives towards governance of energy sector in India	22
Table 1.6	Stages of universe selection	30
Table 1.7	Depicting the sampling strategy for selecting a village	30
Table 1.8	Average waste yield from different sources (Cattle standard 13.00 kgs)	35
Table 1.9	Real-time configuration of solar irradiance	50
Table 1.10	Potential of biogas as a source of electricity (power) and as a cooking medium (fuel)	58
Table 2.1	Soil and vegetation	69
Table 2.2	Category wise power consumption in the Islands	70
Table 2.3	The trajectory of growth of electricity generation in the Islands	71
Table 2.4	The projected growth of peak demand on an yearly basis	71
Table 2.5	Details of the capacity of the solar plant and the owner cum consumer	111
Table 2.6	Showing the caste-class-wise energy access and consumption	162
Table 2.7	Critique on the service offered	174

Table 2.8	Showing selected definitions of social enterprise/entrepreneurship	200
Table 2.9	Developing consensus by enhancing social capital for local energy entrepreneurship	219
Table 2.10	Equipment/instrumentation details of the generation and distribution system of biogas from RS farms along with unit costing and/or expenditure incurred	236
Table 3.1	For BPL families (per month)	257
Table 3.2	Basic details of village Profullyanagar	287
Table 3.3	Basic details of village Moti Varnoli	293
Table 3.4	Basic details of village Bhikhuchak	299
Table 3.5	Basic details of village Ghanghaol	306
Table 3.6	Basic details of village Amargarh	312
Table 3.7	Basic details of village Kakira	319
Table 3.8	Basic details of village Anher	324

CHAPTER 1

Energy and Society: Unravelling Governmentality of Energy Access

1.1 General Outline

The chapter is segregated into 3 broad sections. The first section (A) deals with the world view on energy poverty (EP). It deals with the following subjects—(a) conceptualization of energy poverty, (b) review of extant literature on energy poverty, (c) understanding definitions and dimensions of energy poverty, (d) approaches towards quantification of energy poverty including energy development index, (e) the concept of energy ladder, (e) visualization of energy access in terms of incremental categories.

The second section (B) follows a two-pronged approach to engage its readers. Firstly, it presents the issues that flow from the preceding section vis-à-vis the phenomenon describing complexities associated with it. The section in the beginning briefly presents the efforts made by researchers in and around India while exploring the prevalence of the phenomenon. In the later part, it exposes the readers to the reasons for choosing an elaborate mixed methods approach for unravelling and sorting four interlacing issues that deserve attention: (1) the flavour of energy poverty in rural India, (2) the inherent conceptual vulnerability in the definition of an electrified village as detailed in the policy texts while trying to ensure energy access, (3) the need for a paradigm shift from a TBP approach to a context-based EBP approach for ensuring energy access to rural India, and (4) servicing local energy demand through a realistic mapping of local renewable energy source potential (RESP).

The third section (C) discusses in detail the schemata of the mixed method approach that forms the core of the specific research design. The research tools were specifically chosen for creating an empirical, baseline dataset to understand the endemic flavour of energy poverty in rural India while exploring the various dimensions of energy access and end-use through lived experiences of the policy recipients.

1.2 Section A: The World View on Energy Poverty and Its Linkages to Overall Human Well-Being

1.2.1 Conceptualization of Energy Poverty

The relationship between energy and society is procreative. Energy availability and consumption establishes the normative parameters explicating the types of lifestyles that are possible, while cultural and political-economic value systems guide the resources from which, and end-uses towards which, energy is expended (Shove & Walker, 2010). Energy usage is integral to socio-spatial relations, and therefore, access to primary energy flows and demand for energy by social spaces of consumption lay emphasis on socio-spatial aspects of energy consumption (Calvert, 2016). Social systems tend to increase in size and complexity in proportion depending upon the quality and quantity of overall energy consumption pattern (Haberl & Krausmann, 2002). The patterns of energy production, supply and use have been consistently changing, as these basic principles of the energy-society-environment hold on to each other (Bazilian et al., 2011). This co-productive and procreative relationship between energy generation, access, and end use warrants a granular understanding of EP at the micro-level at an extremely reduced scale. Thus, we come to a stage where EP can be broadly construed as—the inability to secure a socially and materially necessitated level of energy services in a dwelling unit, located in a socio-cultural space in any geographical realm.

The discussion around the phenomena would remain incomplete without bringing in the role of end use of energy in terms of access to various services driven by varied usage of energy. Energy services embody social practices that are—configured by 'hanging together' of—(a) institutional arrangements, (b) shared cultural meanings and norms,

(c) knowledge and skills of socio-cultural groups, and (d) varied material technologies and infrastructures (Geels, 2002; Walker, 2014). Thus, the fulfilment of energy needs is a crucial component of the functioning that enables individuals to perform their everyday activities and achieve well-being (Nussbaumer et al., 2011; Saith, 2001; Sen, 2009). Energy needs are closely conditioned by social practices, as these reflect the social expectations and settings in which energy use takes place. Thus, an energy service operates across a multitude of scales and sites (Anderson & McFarlane, 2011; Bennett, 2005).

EP thus represents hybrid 'assemblages' of differential and relative explanation as well as understanding across geographies. There is profound terminological messiness around defining vulnerabilities and operationalizing definitions related to the phenomena. Identification of symptoms of energy poverty is an arduous task given the different indicators and metrics for measuring its scale and magnitude. The issue gets exacerbated on account of the varied approaches adopted by scholars and organizations while studying this phenomenon (Birol, 2007). Since there appears to be a problem in terms of defining vulnerability (prone to becoming energy poor), it becomes even more difficult to operationalize the existent definition of energy poverty.

1.2.2 Review of Extant Literature on Energy Poverty

There exists an ocean of literature that consists of different approaches to explain and assess the complex rubric of energy poverty. *Energy poverty can take different forms, including a lack of access to modern energy services, a lack of reliability when services do not exist and concerns about affordability of access.* Affordability can be an issue even in developed countries with universal and reliable access to modern energy. The United Kingdom has been the leader in investigating energy poverty, which it refers to as fuel poverty, with research going back to the 1970s. It initially established a UK fuel poverty strategy in 2001 and a subsequent review in 2012, and concluded that a household could be suffering from energy poverty for three main reasons, namely—(a) low incomes, (b) high energy costs, and (c) energy inefficient dwellings.

The global agenda council reports of the world economic forum (WEF) defines energy poverty as—*the lack of access to modern energy services and products* (WEF, 2010). It is defined as a situation where the absence of sufficient choice of accessing adequate, reliable, affordable, safe, and environmentally suitable energy services is found (Awan et al., 2013). It begins from the premise that all forms of energy and fuel poverty—in developed and developing countries alike—are underpinned by a common condition: the inability to attain a socially and materially necessitated level of domestic energy services (Bouzarovski, 2014).

Problems of energy deprivation in the home are also commonly described via the term energy poverty. This concept has traditionally been used to capture problems of inadequate access to energy in developing countries, involving a host of economic, infrastructural, social equity, education, and health concerns (Pachauri & Spreng, 2004).

Energy poverty has received significant academic and policy attention (Gunningham, 2013; Pachauri & Spreng, 2004; Sagar, 2005), often as a result of its extensive impact on well-being and health. Every year, fumes and smoke from open cooking fires are estimated to contribute to the deaths of 1.5 million people, mostly women and children (World Development Report, 2014). It is a highly gendered problem, with women bearing the brunt of the consequences of inadequate energy access while suffering from systematic discrimination as well as decreased access to resources and decision making (Clancy et al., 2007; Pachauri & Rao, 2013).

Traditionally, energy poverty research in the developing world has mainly been focused on supply side issues, emphasizing the need for extending electricity grids based on the experience of developed world countries (Munasinghe, 1990). Work undertaken by organizations such as the World Bank in particular has highlighted the benefits of extending the coverage of power grids into rural areas (Barnes, 2011; Cook, 2011; Foley, 1992; Pereira et al., 2010), as well as the economic, social, and technical barriers to modern energy access (Watson et al., 2012) including the lack of adequate institutional infrastructures and financial capital (Bhattacharyya, 2006; Brew-Hammond, 2010; Green & Erskine, 1999; Haanyika, 2008; Ilskog, 2008).

A number of authors are using energy poverty frameworks to encapsulate developed-world issues at the nexus of energy efficiency and affordability (Chester, 2010; Harrison & Popke, 2011; Katsoulakos, 2011; Petrova et al., 2013). Moreover, a number of international development organizations and scholars have been focusing on the persistent deficiency of energy infrastructure across large parts of Africa, Asia, and South America.

Thus, it becomes obvious that most of the discourse on energy poverty has focused on measurement and policy, but has not yet developed formal tools to generate numerical estimates of the impacts of energy poverty alleviation, with only few recent exceptions (Bazilian et al., 2012; Catherine et al., 2007).

On the question of whether energy poverty is simply a side effect of income poverty, the study found that the overwhelming opinion was that income poverty is a key driver though, but not the sole cause or even a necessary condition for energy poverty (World Energy Outlook, Special Report, 2017). Currently, there is no internationally accepted measure of energy poverty in developed economies, although there is a growing body of analyses that points to a basket of commonly used measures (Rademaekers et al., 2016), mainly looking at household energy expenditures or subjective assessments of the affordability of energy use.

The most commonly used measure—the spending measure (proportion of households spending more than 10% of their income on energy). In the context of developed economies, based on the spending measure, it was inferred that an estimated 200 million people, over 15% of the total population in developed economies, suffer from energy poverty. The report further says—'*these are broad-brush calculations, reflecting the diversity of approaches, and the lack of commonly agreed definitions and data on the affordability of energy*' (World Energy Outlook, Special Report, 2017, p. 24).

1.2.3 Understanding Definitions and Dimensions of Energy Poverty

There have been regular efforts to study causal links of energy poverty to other dimensions of human life. Efforts have also been made to numerically assess the intensity of the energy poverty phenomenon.

There is a strong relationship between measures of human well-being and energy consumption including electricity. A roughly constant ratio of primary energy consumption has been observed for countries with high levels of electricity use. This ratio was then used to determine global primary energy consumption in the human development scenario. The study established a positive correlation between the human development index (HDI) and annual per-capita electricity consumption (Pasternak, 2000).

A related study further depicts the fact that energy security can assume different proportions in relation to a given community, especially in the context of fuel poverty. This study of fuel poverty assessment in the UK found that fuel poverty in the UK is not going to be of the same order or intensity as that of sub-Sahel Africa. NGOs and practitioners also point at complex processes of energy exclusion, and self-exclusion at the community, household and family level, leading to distinct micro-cultures of energy use (Clancy and Roehr, 2003).

Another study in the UK studied government intervention to eradicate fuel poverty amongst vulnerable families and in the common people. The study explained the relations between measures of fuel poverty and the government's objective definition of the problem. The effort was to investigate the characteristics in different household groups and correlate the same with the issues pertaining to fuel poverty in each household (Catherine et al., 2007).

1.2.4 Quantification of Energy Poverty by IEA

The International Energy Agency's (IEA), energy development index is composed of four indicators, each capturing a specific aspect of potential energy poverty:

- per capita commercial energy consumption, which serves as an indicator of the overall economic development of a country;
- per capita electricity consumption in the residential sector, which serves as an indicator of the reliability of and consumer's ability to pay for, electricity services;
- Share of modern fuels in total residential sector energy use serves as an indicator of the level of access to clean cooking facilities; and
- Share of population with access to electricity (IEA, Energy Development Index, 2011a and 2011b).

Thus, having discussed the various approaches to encapsulate the variegated facets of energy poverty, it is inferred that the phenomena is context specific and therefore, shall respond differently to various testimonials in different cultural settings.

However, there is one comprehensive work that deserves a noteworthy mention. It talks about sufficiency and applicability of existing methods for measurement of energy poverty. This study was performed in the context of several African countries. The study proposed a novel composite index—the Multidimensional Energy Poverty Index (MEPI). It captures the incidence and intensity of energy poverty and focuses on the deprivation of access to modern energy services (Nussbaumer et al., 2011). Based on MEPI for Africa, the countries were categorized according to the level of energy poverty, ranging from sensitive poverty (MEPI > 0.9; e.g. Ethiopia) to modest energy poverty (MEPI < 0.6; Angola, Egypt, Morocco, Namibia, Senegal).

This study concluded that the MEPI could be one tool to monitor, improve, design, and execute good quality policy in the area of energy poverty. From the aforesaid discussion it becomes clear that EP is not a singular feature, nor does it have a universal character. Every single space of energy consumption is its own given context and needs to be evaluated differently. However, this feature of EP makes its extremely vulnerable to diverse, subjective interpretations.

1.2.5 The Concept of Energy Ladder-Illustrating Energy Poverty

The most common concept illustrating energy poverty involves the energy ladder. One study defines the energy ladder as the percentage of population amongst the spectrum running from simple biomass fuels (dung, crop residues, wood, charcoal) to fossil fuels (kerosene, natural gas, and coal direct use) to electricity (Holdren et al., 2000). The idea implies that the primary types of energy used in rural areas or developing countries can be arranged on a ladder with the simplest or most traditional fuels and sources, such as animal power, candles, and wood, at the bottom with the more advanced or modern fuels such as electricity or refined gasoline at the top (Table 1.1).

The ladder is often described in terms of efficiency, with the more efficient fuels or sources occupying higher rungs (Sovacool & Drupady, 2016, p. 6). For example, kerosene is three to five times more efficient than wood for cooking, and liquefied petroleum gas is five to ten times more efficient than crop residues and dung (Barnes & Floor, 1996). Table 1.1 depicts the energy ladder as discussed in a variety of academic studies (Barnes & Floor, 1996; Cook, 2005; Legros et al., 2009; Jones, 2010).

However, the fuel access related dimension of EP discourse frequently distinguishes between traditional and modern fuels assuming that there is a linkage between income levels of households and their fuel choice, generally referred to as the *'energy ladder hypotheses'*. Petroleum products

Table 1.1 Energy ladder

Sector	Energy service	Developing countries				Developed countries	The villages under study as mentioned in Chapter 3
		Low-income households	Middle-income households	High-income households			Placement of the villages based upon the sector, and access plus usage of a given energy service (reference-developing countries)
Household	Cooking	Wood (including wood chips, straw, shrubs, grasses, and bark), charcoal, agricultural residues, and dung	Wood residues, dung kerosene, and biogas	Wood, kerosene, biogas, liquefied petroleum gas (LPG), natural gas, electricity, and coal		Electricity and natural gas	Bhikuchack (low and middle income households)* Ghanghaol (low and middle income households)*
	Lighting	Candles and kerosene (sometimes none)	Candles, kerosene, paraffin, and gasoline	Kerosene electricity, and gasoline		Electricity	Profullyanagar (low and middle income households)** Moti Varnoli (low and middle income households)**
	Space heating	Wood, residues, and dung (often none)	Wood residues, and dung	Wood residues, dung, coal and electricity		Oil, natural gas, or electricity	
	Other appliances	None	Electricity, batteries and storage cells	Electricity		Electricity	

Sector	Developing countries			Developed countries	The villages under study as mentioned in Chapter 3
Energy service	Low-income households	Middle-income households	High-income households		Placement of the villages based upon the sector, and access plus usage of a given energy service (reference-developing countries)
Primary technologies	Cook stoves, three-stone fires, and lanterns	Improved cook stoves, biogas systems, solar lanterns, incandescent and compact fluorescent light bulbs (CFLs)	Improved cook stoves, biogas systems, liquefied petroleum gas, gas and electric stoves, compact fluorescent light bulbs (CFLs), and light emitting diodes (LEDs)		Kakira (high income households)*** Amargarh (high income households)*** Anher (high income households)***

*The households have access to electricity however, they rely on mixed cooking fuels comprising dung cakes, kerosene, and LPG (subsidized). There is heavy reliance on filament bulbs though subsidized LEDs are also used for lighting
**The households have access to electricity however, they rely on mixed cooking fuels comprising dung cakes, kerosene, forest produce (biomass), and LPG (subsidized). There is heavy reliance on filament bulbs though subsidized LEDs are also used for lighting. Further, alternate sources of lighting based upon batteries are also used
***The households have access to electricity and the lifestyle is highly energy intensive. The energy consumption is driven by a mix of electrical appliances. However, there is an interesting mix of cooking fuels and cooking medium despite the fact that they have access to all types of appliances for clean, efficient, and comfortable living. Akin to any developed economy
Source Author (2017–2018), adopted from and based upon Sovacool and Drupady (2016)

such as kerosene and LPG along with electricity are considered to be modern fuels at the top of the energy ladder, whereas traditional fuels such as wood, dung cakes, agricultural wastes are at the bottom.

Fuel choices and the diffusion of particular energy resources or technologies is not a pre-ordained progression along some 'energy ladder' towards more 'advanced' energy systems, but represents a complex diffusion of 'multiple, multi-sited' social practices which are constitutive of normative geographical imaginaries and spatial identities (Nicholls & Strengers, 2014). And therefore, the 'energy ladder hypotheses' does not explain the contextual reality of rural energy poverty.

Regardless of the way it is depicted, the energy ladder suggests a rising gap between how the rich and poor consume energy with implications on equity and affordability (Bazilian et al., 2012). The so-called richest tend to consume much more energy—as much as 21 times more—than the lowest quintiles, the so-called poor which means access to energy, or lack of it, can both reflect and worsen social inequality (Legros et al., 2009).

A significant study looking at Asia highlights that the poor typically pay more for energy needs, yet receive poorer quality energy services on account of *inefficient* and more *polluting* technologies with *higher upfront costs* (Masud et al., 2007). Rural households tend to be poorer and consume much less energy than urban households. And in rural areas, fuel wood, the most common source of energy, is usually harvested in unsustainable ways with severe impacts on forest health and the health of those using it (Sovacool & Drupady, 2016, p. 9). What is needed is a spatially explicit contextual analysis that conceives of energy as one of many basic ingredients across differentially active geographies and their practices of everyday life (Birol, 2007).

1.2.6 Visualization of Energy Access in Terms of Incremental Categories (Table 1.2)

The Advisory Group on Energy and Climate Change, an intergovernmental body composed of representatives from businesses, the United Nations, and research institutes, divides energy access into incremental categories (Sovacool & Drupady, 2016, p. 8).

At the first level, basic human needs are met with both electricity consumption of 50–100 kWh per person per year and 50–100 kg of oil equivalent or modern fuel per person per year (or the ownership of an improved cook stove). At the second level lies productive uses such

Table 1.2 Energy services and access levels

Level	Electricity use	kWh per person per year	Solid fuel use	Transport	Kilograms of oil equivalent per person per year	The placement of the villages under study as mentioned in Chapter 3 based upon Level
Basic human needs	Lighting, health, education, and communication	50–100	Cooking and heating	Walking or bicycling	50–100	Bhikuchack Ghanghaol
Productive uses	Agriculture, water pumping for irrigation, fertilizer, mechanized tilling, and processing	500–1000	Minimal	Mass transit, motorcycle, or scooter	150	Profullyanagar Moti Varnoli
Modern society needs	Domestic appliances, cooling, and heating	2000	Minimal	Private transport	250–450	Kakira Amargarh Anher

Source Author (2017) adopted from and based upon Sovacool and Drupady (2016) as access to mechanical energy for agriculture or irrigation, commercial energy, or liquid transport fuels. Consumption of electricity here rises to 500–1000 kWh per year plus 150 kg of oil equivalent.

At the third level lies modern needs which include the use of domestic appliances, cooling and space heating, hot and cold water, and private transportation which in aggregate result in the consumption of about 2000 kWh of electricity per year and 250–450 kg of oil equivalent. Table 1.2 illustrates this sequential ordering quite clearly (UNDP, 2010).

1.3 Section B: The Indian Case of Energy Poverty, Energy Access Initiatives, and the Policy Design and Reality Gap

While trying to set the tone for understanding energy poverty in an expanded, macro-, socio-economic context, it becomes important to revisit the polysemy around EP in terms of the following vulnerabilities, and inherent labile and vulnerable constructs, in and around the phenomena in a localized, micro-, socio-cultural context.

- Energy poverty is susceptible to attenuation depending on the context.
- Definitions appear to be too weak in respect of operationalization of the phenomena
- Defining vulnerability in terms of contextual grounding meaning who becomes prone towards being labelled as energy poor?
- Different metrics, varied approaches to problem identification?
- Energy poverty appears to be a complex function of preferences, habits, and lifestyles across communities with similar or dis-similar socio-economic functionalities (social, economic, and political).
- EP is marked by variations in intensity across spaces and cultures of energy consumption?
- EP also highlights the variations between met and unmet needs of energy consumption in terms of access to electric power and efficient, clean cooking fuels.
- Effective targeting of policy measures to address the problem of energy poverty?
- A new area of policymaking?

- And therefore, it presents itself as a complex rubric of sociocultural behaviourism reflected in tastes, preferences and energy consumption lifestyles of a passive consumer of energy.

The text tends to raise a larger question, whether rural ecosystems can be universally labelled as energy poor?

1.3.1 The Phenomenon of Energy Poverty in Rural India

Energy poverty appears to be a confounded concept that is understood differently and is described in different ways in literature as seen earlier. It is a difficult concept to comprehend in terms of its physical signs and symptoms. It exhibits a strongly polychromatic nature and manifests itself through mixed symptoms. It appears to be strongly endemic and contextual. This fact renders it even more difficult to summarize as a singular, one-dimensional phenomenon. It has a mixed, symptomatic existence which questions its complex 'fabric and texture' in any given geo-spatial terrain in terms of its magnitude and directionality. Therefore, the phenomena and the concept both are vulnerable in terms of operationalization by means of a single universal definition.

The problem gets aggravated further when examined in rural geographies. It exhibits contrarian hues in terms of availability, access, distribution, affordability, and acceptability of an energy service. Rather, it presents itself as a mixed bag in terms of the laid down standards of its relative temporal and spatial evaluation. It has substantive grounding in the physical terrain (geo-spatial features, both natural and man-made), and the local preferences in terms of prevalent consumer culture and the overall socio-economic context. The local weather conditions have a very important bearing on tastes and preferences as well, especially in terms of usage of any given energy service. The problem of recognition of signs and symptoms of energy poverty gets aggrandized particularly when there is a range of options available to choose from for an end-user in terms of an energy basket carrying varieties of services.

Moreover, the concept presents an enormous dichotomy, where more or less regular and reliable supply of power is encountered as evidence. Driven by this reliability of supply, a dwelling unit, therefore, may have the best of the modern electronic multipurpose gadgets, along with the most primitive forms of solid and liquid fuels for cooking and occasional lighting as well. This is a common feature witnessed across a majority of cases (units of study), showing simultaneous usage of a primitive fuel type for cooking, along with modern electrical appliances for other need-based usages. Energy poverty could therefore be episodic, local, contextual, relative, and symptomatic. Hence, there is an imperative to probe this phenomenon differently for an alternate understanding, and conceptualization from a rural context. Is it paradoxical as a conceptual construct? The present study highlights the contextual complexities of labelling a dwelling unit and a rural area as 'energy poor' within the contemporary rubric of 'energy poverty'. The section lays down the background which underlines the need for evaluation of its symbolic, symptomatic presence in the context of the contemporary discourse around the world and more so, in the Indian subcontinent.

1.3.2 *The Rural Nature of Energy Poverty (EP)*

The rural dimension of energy poverty broadly exhibits the following attributes—(a) it is local in scale, micro in socio-economic, politico-cultural context, strongly multi-dimensional, and depicts asymmetric symptoms (the pieces of evidence are scattered, reinforcing at times and also being inhibitory at certain instances highlighting self-contradiction), (b) it bears strong adherence and exhibits deep-rooted contextual grounding in any given socio-cultural space, (c) the demand for an energy service is strongly dis-similar for different rural ecosystems, (d) there are strong and mixed signals in terms of access to different types of energy service(s) in different geo-spatial settings, (e) it is marked by mixed attributes of active and passive consumerism depending on the means and the ends to be met in the context of an energy service.

It offers an invigorated perspective of the non-universal nature of energy poverty. The energy poverty discourse needs to be cautious of the relationship between energy services and the needs of a rural ecosystem that supports a passive consumer of energy services.

This section lays emphasis upon the importance of—(a) socio-cultural space, and (b) the local politico-economic environment where institutions, agents, and actors (policy recipients) interact for collective welfare. Energy access is one such subject that percolates into societal space to make a difference in the lives of people. The present work engages with the central theme of *energy action* and *energy inaction* operating at different levels in formal institutions, within the functional space of non-state actors, and the socio-cultural realm of policy recipients, while attempting to provide access to energy service. There is a need for granular conceptualization of energy provisioning in the socio-cultural spaces of energy consumption where choices are either non-existent or limited. This entails an embedded approach for a context specific study to dissect the notion of energy service as it is understood by different entities—(1) the state actors comprising regulators, (2) the state nodal agency (*enablers*) entrusted with the task of promoting alternate sources of distributed energy generation, and (3) the non-state actors (private entities)—the rural energy service companies (Chapter 2).

This section tries to link energy service provisioning with location based micro-realities that are contextually embedded in pockets drenched in different hues of social, economic, and political interactions. It builds upon three essential conceptions of energy governance framework and energy service provisioning in rural geographic realms: (1) efficacy of decentralized institutions (analysis of success and failure of local delivery systems), (2) systemic conception of the established regulation framework (analysing the taxonomy of regulatory design in terms of its functionality), and (3) action-theoretical conception (policy implications of translating energy access into constructive engagement for quality energy supply based on locale-specific demand; praxis).

1.3.3 The Concept of Energy Poverty as Understood in and Around the Indian Subcontinent

There have been numerous efforts made by scholars to study the phenomenon in India and in similar geographies proximal to India. In one such study an effort was made to measure energy poverty for Indian households. The study adopted two-dimensional measures of energy poverty and energy distribution that combined (a) the element of access to different energy types, and (b) quantity of energy consumed. The conclusion pointed towards significant reduction in the level of energy poverty due to rapid development in India, further saying that there exists a relation between access and use of energy and poverty, thus conceptualizing presence of EP as an impediment to development (Barnes et al., 2012b; Pachauri & Spreng, 2004).

Another study undertaken in India has presented different approaches for measurement of energy poverty by using Indian household level data. The study found a positive relation between (a) well-being and (b) the use of clean and efficient energy resources. The study further concluded that use of access and consumption of clean and efficient energy increases general well-being (Pachauri et al., 2004).

In yet another work, there was an attempt made to examine the nature of energy poverty in urban and rural areas of India. The percentage of energy poor households in rural parts was 57% and in urban areas the percentage of energy poor households was 28%, whereas the percentage of income poor was 22 and 20%, respectively. The study concluded that the persons in energy poverty were also facing income poverty (Khandker, Barnes, & Samad, 2012; Khandker, Rubaba et al., 2012).

Another attempt of a similar nature was undertaken, which explored the problems related to energy consumption faced by the Indian rural and urban households. The results showed that the extent of energy poverty in rural areas of India was about 89 and 24% in urban areas of India. The study further concluded that poor people spend almost 12% of their earnings on procuring different energy sources. The proportion of population labelled as energy poor did not have access to other basic amenities for sustainable living as well. The study concluded that the consumption pattern of the poor in respect of energy leads to income poverty (Jain, 2010).

An analysis of energy poverty status of Sri Lanka was undertaken based on twin approaches dwelling upon—(a) the quantity of energy consumed in any form and (b) the pricing approach for an energy service. The findings on account of pricing approach established that the country had a very high percentage of energy poor (83%), whereas the quantitative approach revealed that EP is high in respect of cooking due to inefficiencies of cooking stoves (Tennakoon, 2009). Thus, a new complexity gets added to the discourse in terms of efficiency of appliances converting primary energy to secondary end usage.

A similar study in Bangladesh explored the welfare impacts of household and energy use in rural Bangladesh using cross-sectional data. The result showed that although the modern and traditional sources of energy improved the energy consumption of rural Bangladesh households, and further that the impacts of modern energy sources were high as compared to the traditional energy services (Barnes et al., 2010).

Another study of a similar nature from Punjab province of Pakistan discusses the consequences and characteristics of the use of different energy services using a single year energy poverty survey (EPS) data. The study outlined that the rural population of Pakistan makes use of many varieties of energy fuels like firewood, plant waste, kerosene oil, and animal waste. Despite access to these sources of energy, the population of Pakistan faces an energy crisis or energy poverty (Mirza & Szirmai, 2010).

Therefore, in the context of a regional geography of the dimensions of the Indian subcontinent, a committed effort is required to have a nuanced understanding of the complex and composite nature of energy poverty. The phenomena laced with further concentricity in terms of its conceptual vulnerability, and difficult to explore in terms of a micro-granular, rural focus of this text. The text brings in an alternative approach to broach the conceptual understanding of this phenomenon, as the situation in the rural Indian energy consumption spaces presents mixed signals.

1.3.4 Energy Services in Rural Indian Context

The diverse geo-spatial and socio-cultural spaces of rural India present a commonality in terms of consumption of energy in a dwelling unit defined by the pivotal role of energy services. The consumption transition from one space to the other appears to be graded. However, the said commonality fades in terms of its significance on account of the following observations—(a) The problem of recognition of signs and symptoms of energy poverty gets aggrandized particularly when there is a range of options available to choose from, for an end-user, in terms of an energy basket carrying varieties of services, (b) the concept presents enormous ambiguity when regular/reliable power supply for good number of hours is encountered as evidence. Driven by this reliability of supply a dwelling unit, therefore, may have the best of the modern electronic multipurpose gadgets. This however does not guarantee usage on a regular sustained basis, (c) The same civil structure may also have the most primitive forms of solid and liquid fuels for cooking and occasional lighting as well. This is a common feature witnessed across a majority of majority of regional terrains (units of study), showing simultaneous usage of a primitive fuel type for cooking, along with modern electrical appliances for other need-based usages, and (d) the local weather conditions have a very important bearing on tastes and preferences as well, especially in terms of usage of any given energy service (Chakravarty & Tavoni, 2013).

Energy poverty could therefore be episodic, local, contextual, relative, and symptomatic. Hence, there is an imperative to probe this phenomenon differently for an alternate understanding, and conceptualization in an exclusively rural context of contemporary India. Is it paradoxical as a conceptual construct? The text highlights the contextual complexities of labelling a dwelling unit and a rural area as energy poor within the contemporary rubric of energy poverty.

The complexity and heterogeneity of the socio-political and cultural context is normally not taken into account during policy conception (problem definition stage) or during implementation stage, which often results in unanticipated challenges during stages of implementation. There is an imperative for understanding the human dimension in a rural energy ecosystem. There is a pressing need for local energy demand assessment, through a context-based understanding of choices and preferences, and behaviour of a passive consumer of electricity residing in a rural ecosystem.

1.3.5 The Energy Planning and Governance Framework-Genesis of Rural Electrification

The electricity governance architecture at the MACRO level derives its institutional hierarchy and the functional structure of its institutions from the Constitution of India. Electricity, as a subject, is enlisted in the seventh schedule (Article 246), under the concurrent list at serial No. 38 (List III). Hence, it is one of the subjects under the shared purview of the Union and the state governments. However, the functional domain of local energy governance in terms of generation and distribution falls under the exclusive jurisdiction of the local institutions (Fig. 1.1, Annexure A).

Rural electrification (RE) has been the focus of policymaking for several decades now. RE is viewed as a prime mover for rural development. RE started as a plan programme from the first plan. The aims were food security and enhancing the socio-economic resilience of the rural population. The twin components of RE were—(1) pump-set energization for increase of food-grain production, and (2) village electrification. Village electrification, however, presented a dismal picture on account of divested electricity supplies at extremely low rates or for free towards pump-sets. Thus, village electrification has mostly been considered as the lesser twin component of RE. It continued to be very poor on account of the unreliable nature of supply and the lack of poor affordability of the rural people (NDC Report, 1994, pp. 33–42). The noble thought that the use of electricity could bring about an improvement in the standard of living and quality of life in the villages led to the roll out of different flagship schemes for rural electrification in the country have been briefly touched upon below.

Chronological sequence of government schemes for providing improved access to electricity, better lighting, clean and efficient cooking is shown in Table 1.3: period (1974–present): (Annual Report of the Planning Commission, 2013–2014, p. 5) and 2005 onwards: (CERC and CEA, ministry of power). Similarly, Table 1.4 shows the major programmes that aim to harness the renewable energy resource potential. The tables show the programme and the implementing agency. Table 1.5 depicts the policy initiatives taken for the effective governance of the energy sector in India.

1.3.6 FOUR POINT AGENDA *Highlighting the Gap Between Policy and Praxis—The Backbone of the Envisaged Research Design*

A. *Issues related to energy access policies and programmes*

Despite recognition of the need for energy access through rural electrification, the policy outputs have been slow, uncertain, and geographically heterogeneous. Rural electrification as a process (policy prescription) for providing access to improve access to energy is nested within a larger thematic construct of supply side management (SSM). This approach normally does not take into account the needs of a small consumer with a non-energy intensive lifestyle. Though, the extant policy is trying to promote or achieve in the longer run, an energy system change, this transition may not happen at a desired pace. There is a lack of dedicated effort to calibrate energy demand via an in-depth study of societal functioning in terms of its daily energy consumption. Therefore, an effective policy prescription necessitates the integration of social theory and cultural practices to move beyond simplistic assumptions of how individuals make choices related to energy access across rural spaces in different parts of the subcontinent.

There is a pressing need for local energy demand assessment, through a context-based understanding of choices and preferences, and behaviour of a passive consumer of electricity residing in a rural ecosystem (Author, 2017–2018). And therefore, this underlines the imperative for understanding the human dimension in a rural energy consumption ecosystem.

At this juncture, it has become expedient to highlight another systemic issue that ails the programmes aimed to energize every household in rural India. This ailment happens to be a definitional flaw as to how a village can be construed to be completely energized. The earlier definition said

Table 1.3 Programmes for providing energy access to rural India

S.No.	Programme and year of roll out	The agencies responsible for execution
1	Minimum Needs Programme (MNP)—(1974–1979)	State Electricity Boards (SEBs)
2	Kutir Jyoti Scheme—(1988–1989)	State Electricity Boards (SEBs)
3	Pradhan Mantri Gramodaya Yojana (PMGY)—(2000–2001)	State Electricity Boards and Electricity Departments of the state governments
4	Rural Electricity Supply Technology Mission (REST)—(2002)	Ministry of New and Renewable Energy (MNRE)
5	Accelerated Rural Electrification Programme (AREP)—(2003–2004)	State Electricity Boards and Electricity Departments of the state governments along with financial support from: Rural Electrification Corporation (REC), Power Finance Corporation (PFC), Rural Infrastructure Development Fund (RIDF), National Bank for Agriculture and Rural Development (NABARD)
6	Accelerated electrification of one lakh villages and one crore households—(2004–2005)	REC as lead agency for the scheme
7	Rajiv Gandhi Grameen Vidyutikaran Yojana (RGGVY)-2005, (O.M. No. 44/19/2004-D [RE], dated 18 March 2005)	All the previous schemes were subsumed under RGGVY. Rural Electrification Corporation (REC) was the nodal agency for implementation
8	Deendayal Upadhayay Gram Jyoti Yojana (DDUGJY)-2015 (O.M. No.-F. No. 44/44/2014-RE dated 03.12.2014)	Rural Electrification Corporation (REC) is the nodal agency for implementation

(continued)

Table 1.3 (continued)

S.No.	Programme and year of roll out	The agencies responsible for execution
9	UJALA (Unnat Jyoti by Affordable LEDs for All)—2015	It is a joint initiative of Public Sector Undertaking of the Government of India, Energy Efficiency Services Limited (EESL) under the Union Ministry of Power and the Electricity Distribution Company
10	Pradhan Mantri Ujjwala Yojana (PMUY)—2016	The Ministry of Petroleum, Oil and Natural Gas is the nodal agency, based on socio-economic caste census
11	Pradhan Mantri Sahaj Bijli Har Ghar Yojana (Saubhagya) 2017, (O.M. No. F. No 44/2/2016/-RE)	Rural Electrification Corporation (REC) is the nodal agency for implementation

Source NDC Report (1994) and Planning Commission Report (2014), CEA Reports: 2018 and 2019

Table 1.4 Policies/programmes in respect of renewable energy sources (the lesser twin)

S.No.	Programme and the year of roll out	Agencies responsible for execution
1	National Biogas and Manure Management Programme (1979–1981)	Ministry of New and Renewable Energy and State Nodal Agencies
2	Remote Village Electrification Programme (2004–2012)	Ministry of New and Renewable Energy and State Nodal Agencies along with state power departments
3	JawaharLal Nehru National Solar Mission (2009–2010)	Ministry of New and Renewable Energy and State Nodal Agencies
4	Village Energy Security Programme (2012)	Ministry of New and Renewable Energy and Village Energy Committees
5	International Solar Alliance (2015)	Ministry of New and Renewable Energy (nodal ministry), Solar Energy Corporation of India (SECI), and other international agencies
6	PM-Kisan Urja Suraksha evam Uthaan Mahabhiyaan (2019)	Ministry of New and Renewable Energy and State Nodal Agencies

Source Annual report Ministry of New and Renewable Energy—2018 and 2019

Table 1.5 Policy initiatives towards governance of energy sector in India

S.No.	Policy and year of roll out	Gazette notifications and agencies responsible for execution
1	The genesis of the Central Electricity Act of 2003	A paradigm shift (the gazette of India, part-II, registered No. DL-33004/2003, 26/5/2003)
2	National Electricity Policy 2005	(*Source* The gazette of India, resolution No. 23/40/2004-R&R, Vol. II, 2005)
3	National Rural Electrification Policy, 2006	(*Source* The gazette of India, ministry of power, resolution No. 23/2/2005-R&R Vol. III, 2006)
4	National Tariff Policy (2006)	The gazette of India, extraordinary, ministry of power, resolution No. 23/2/2005-R&R, Vol. 3, dated 6/1/2006, pp. 1–21
5	Draft Renewable Energy Act (2015)	Still waiting? (unfulfilled objective of *REST*)
6	National Tariff Policy (2016)	The gazette of India, extraordinary, ministry of power, resolution No. 23/2/2005-R&R, Vol. 9, dated 28/02/2016, pp. 1–38

Source Annual reports of Ministry of Power: 2017 and 2018

that—'A village should be classified as electrified if electricity is being used within its revenue area for any purpose whatsoever (pre-1997)'. This definition was further re-casted as—'A village will be deemed to be electrified if the electricity is used *in the inhabited locality*, within the revenue boundary of the village for any purpose whatsoever'. This was the operational definition of an electrified village prior to the commencement of the electricity act, 2003.

The prelude to the rural electrification policy pursuant to the central electricity act, 2003 provides for a definition (statutory) of rural electrification. The nodal ministry thus decided to classify a village as electrified based on a certificate issued by the gram panchayat and as collated/compiled by the state nodal agency using the machinery of the district committee, certifying that—

(a) Basic infrastructure such as distribution transformer and distribution lines are provided in the inhabited locality as well as minimum of one *dalit basti* (hamlet) where it exists (for electrification through non-conventional energy sources a distribution transformer may not be necessary); and

(b) Electricity is provided to public places like schools, panchayat office, health centres, dispensaries, community centres, etc.; and
(c) The number of households electrified are at least 10% of the total number of households in the village; and
(d) The electricity supply per day is at optimum voltage for lighting during the evening peak hours (*para 2.1 of the un-published draft rural electrification policy*).

When should a village be referred to as an electrified village? There were two definitions in operation earlier: (source—Ministry of Power (MOP), vide their letter No. 42/1/2001-D(RE), dated 5 February 2004, and its corrigendum vide letter No. 42/1/2001-D(RE)-dated 17 February 2004). Therefore, the existent definition, issued and notified by the Ministry of Power (MOP), vide their letter No. 42/1/2001-D(RE), dated 5 February 2004, and its corrigendum vide letter No. 42/1/2001-D(RE) dated 17 February 2004 is reproduced here:

A village would be declared as electrified, if:

(a) Basic infrastructure such as distribution transformer and distribution lines are provided in the inhabited locality as well as the *dalit basti* (hamlet), where it exists.
(b) Electricity is provided to public places like schools, panchayat offices, health centres, dispensaries, community centres, etc.
(c) The number of households electrified should be at least 10% of the total number of households in the village. This is the operational definition currently in vogue.

Thus, it appears that the rural electrification policies and programmes are bereft of two principal essentialities—(a) the central anthropogenic dimension that is central to creation of a comprehensive design of a rural electrification programme primarily for ensuring access to energy, and (b) energy poverty still does not find its much desirable place in any of the policy constructs and the instrumentalities that lay the framework for planning energy access to rural parts of the country. Therefore, it is felt that an alternative approach to understanding rural energy demand is necessary towards attaining the desired aspiration of power for all (PFA) after an empirical understanding of energy poverty and the local energy demand as well.

B. *The nature of rural energy consumption landscape of India*

This comprises a plural and complex heterogeneous mix of energy demand. Therefore, the backbone of the future policies in terms of need and requirements should rest upon twin dogmatic paradigms of: (1) comprehensive demand aggregation and profiling of a rural, domestic consumer situated in a geo-cultural, climatic zone/space and a distinct physiographic terrain, and (2) assessment of local renewable energy resource potential. As, energy consumption patterns vary across the vivid rural energy landscape of India. The characteristic patterns of consumption give rise to heterogeneous and distinct cultural spaces of energy-related functional existence of rural communities (Anderson & McFarlane, 2012). An important feature that needs to be re-emphasized is that the policy design needs to look at an energy consumption landscape as a co-construction of physical, socio-cultural space and societal aspirations, that comes into existence through a series of material and social relations (Dimitriadi, 2000).

C. *End use of energy access in the context of Indian rural setting: Energy service—Evidence based policy (EBP) approach to planning for energy access*

The rural energy consumption pattern has a common thread running across different socio-cultural systems. It showcases a distinctive manner of energy consumption within a dwelling unit comprising single or multiple households. This aspect is fundamentally linked to the local culture that decides the end use of energy (energy services). The local ecosystem needs and preferences define the usefulness of an energy service. It is therefore essential to understand the individual and the community-based determinants of energy use dynamics—in particular for domestic needs to begin within a local set-up. This entails immersion to take place in a broader context of geographical location, and the local socio-economic, cultural, and political environment (Aune, 2007; Chester, 2010; Lutzenhiser, 1992; Stephenson et al., 2010).

D. *Human centric approach and RESP assessment*

Energy has an innate anthropogenic (human) dimension. Human beings are central to the theme of energy generation and its final consumption (Gupta, 2015). Energy generation and its distribution as a resource influences and shapes every aspect of human life on a daily basis. This element necessitates critical understanding of demand aggregation and profiling across socio-cultural systems. The requirement of energy in terms of quantity and quality has a deep grounding in the socio-cultural ethos of an end-user, the socio-cultural setting of which he is a part. Understanding this aspect is critical for scheduling the supply of energy.

A policy can produce long lasting impact in terms of alternative options, designs, models, and approaches to solve a symptomatic problem. Therefore, this section calls for an exclusive focus on evidence collection, documentation, and analysis for an informed policy formulation approach for the rural energy sector based on natural renewable sources.

An EBP approach recognizes the fact that rural energy ecosystems are plural and heterogeneous, based upon differential renewable energy resource endowment, local resource base, as well as consumption patterns. An appreciation of this ground reality should form the basis for the design and governance of energy systems. The section highlights the need for an empirical approach for rural energy demand aggregation. The samples were required to be drawn from different socio-cultural systems from across rural India. The rural energy ecosystems were studied in relation to its socio-cultural context to assess the daily requirements of energy in a civil structure (dwelling unit).

1.4 Section C: The Research Plan, Design and Methods Deployed to Meet the Objectives of the Text as Detailed in the Introductory Section

1.4.1 Immersion in the Action Arena (Field Study)

The work has an innate feature of placing the quantitative analysis in the rightful context of societies, cultures, preferences, policies, and local power relations in terms of politics of access and use of energy. This piece of work has an exclusive focus on rural India. Within the rural setting the focus is on residential, domestic consumers who had access to single-phase formal connection as well as those who did not have a formal access to energy services. The population sample is a fairly representative mix from across different socio-cultural spaces of energy consumption in the Indian subcontinent. The quantitative data collection focus is a civil structure (a dwelling unit), and thereafter, its occupants (respondents) who define the household. A detailed physical investigation was done for a comprehensive assessment of actual ownership of all electrical appliances in a civil structure, and its declared usage by the occupants.

The prime focus of this work was to evaluate and establish empirical load demand of an individual dwelling unit on any given day on a daily basis. This elaborate exercise was followed by creation of load demand profiles for each of the randomly sampled dwelling units. It took into account the need for lighting as an essential energy service. For the assessment of cooking needs of households within a dwelling unit, demand for different types of fuels used for cooking and also for lighting (in case of power supply disruption) was physically studied. *Space heating has been consciously left out for the reason that the sub-continent broadly has a tropical climate in contrast to the climatic conditions of the developed world.*

A concept of energy basket has been conceived in terms of actual usage of appliances and use of fuel mix types as a cooking medium for meeting cooking needs. Based on the products in the energy basket of a dwelling unit, an energy budget has been worked out for individual dwelling units. The study creates daily demand for consumption of energy through the study of end usage for an effective demand side management (DSM) in the rural setting to the level of actual site of usage—a dwelling unit. Further, it captures the local potential for alternative energy resources to service the actual demand for energy. Thus, the text has an unequivocal focus on the human dimension of a rural energy system, the larger context being the physiographic division and the geo-climatic zone, where the sites of consumption are situated.

1.4.2 Household Energy Budget

A special mention needs to be made in respect of *energy budgeting* that was done for a household on a monthly basis. For these purposes, the following expenditures were booked: (1) expenditure incurred for meeting cooking fuel needs (based on quantity of cooking fuel mix types), (2) lighting needs (based on expenditure on alternate source of lighting in case of power supply disruption, or any other informal means), and (3) expenditure towards payment of electricity bills (consumption of formal power). Quantitative assessment of loads, type of appliance loads, lighting loads, etc., has been discussed at length in the subsequent sections.

The preceding context brings in the element of desk research discussed earlier. The literature survey has been carefully chosen to place the context and relevance of this empirical work in line with the policy texts and academic studies pertaining to: (a) rural electrification, (b) energy poverty, (c) access to and end use of energy, and (d) deployment of renewable energy technologies (RETs) as alternate energy production systems for meeting community energy requirements. The central theme of the text is to raise an argument around such issues as—a whether rural India is energy poor? The ancillary queries that are linked to the central theme are—(a) Is there a need to recognize 'rural' nature of energy poverty separately? (b) Can rural energy poverty be alleviated by totally alienating the 'human element' that drives demand for energy in rural areas? (c) Does grid extension appear to be the only solution for eradication of rural energy poverty and whether (d) the solution could lie in following an alternate approach to demand side management to trigger an energy system change! These elements warrant policy instruments to follow an EBP approach for a seamless socio-technical transition.

1.4.3 General Description of Choice of Interdisciplinary (Multiple) Methods: The Mixed Methods Research Paradigm

This text lays emphasis on an interdisciplinary approach for data capture in respect of consumption patterns of energy, aggregation of demand for energy, and understanding passive consumer behaviour. The phenomenon under investigation is energy poverty. The research explores the rural energy consumption landscape of the Indian subcontinent contextually situated in different geo-climatic zones and physiographic divisions (Figs. 1.5 and 1.6, Annexure B). Case studies, structured survey approach, focused personal interviews with experts, analysis of institutional and regulatory frameworks, and its associated structures along with policy documents relating to different approaches to rural electrification form the backbone of the presented work (Fig. 1.2, Annexure B). The details of the methods and their significance have been discussed in detail hereafter.

A fundamental feature of this work has been the resource assessment of alternative energy supply sources, solar and biogas. Real-time data pertaining to different geo-climatic zones and physiographic divisions in respect of solar irradiance was assessed in order to ascertain the resource potential of a given region for an alternate energy solution based on solar energy.

A comparative assessment of locked potential (untapped) of renewable energy generation systems, based on two renewable sources of energy solar (sans human involvement in terms of fuel sourcing) and biogas (involves natural and human element in terms of fuel sourcing) has been attempted. Although there was a strong thrust on creation of empirical database creation, primary census data in respect of livestock and human population also form an integral component of this study.

1.4.4 Description of Fieldwork

The fieldwork was undertaken in different parts of the country with exclusive focus on rural areas. In terms of administrative functionality, the context was a revenue village (Figs. 1.5 and 1.6, Annexure B). Every single studied village has been exclusively mapped through administrative layering and individual 'nazari naqshas' (schematic revenue boundary maps depicting natural and artificial features) for each revenue village has been prepared to lock-in and highlight the context of the study. For a comprehensive understanding of energy poverty, a total of six states and one union territory were chosen at random to give fairness and robustness to the sampling universe (Figs. 1.3 and 1.4, Annexure B).

The existence of energy poverty phenomena was investigated following different approaches. Energy poverty appears to be nested in local spaces and cultures of energy consumption. Therefore, it was necessary for the study to be sufficiently vast in terms of coverage of physical spaces to understand different dimensions of energy consumption. In order to establish its prevalence across the length and breadth of the Indian subcontinent extensive fieldwork was undertaken, along with the use of multiple approaches spread across multiple disciplines (Fig. 1.2, Annexure B). The text highlights the exclusive emphasis that was laid on evidence collection, documentation, and analysis for deciphering signs and symptoms of energy poverty in the context of rural India.

1.4.5 Sampling Design: Sampling Universe, Sampling Frame, and Sampling Unit

The sampling universe was chosen through a multi-stage non-probability sampling method, wherein a state was chosen through a systematic random process (Fig. 1.3, Annexure B). A three layered planimetric (two-dimensional on xy-plane) base map served as the foundation for choice of the sampling universe (Fig. 1.4, Annexure B). Choosing a sampling universe was the first stage of the sampling procedure. The three layer ordering of maps were as follows: the first layer was a map of India depicting energy poverty or off-grid regions (International Energy Agency, 2015, p. 154), superimposed on it was a map of India depicting different geo-climatic zones (based on Koppen system of classification; Oxford atlas and www.mapsofindia.com), followed by a map of India with distinct physiographic divisions placed on the top; Oxford atlas and www.mapsofindia.com.

The second stage of sampling procedure was via random sampling through a superimposed grid on the three-layer map to have a representative and distributed depiction of—(a) spaces and cultures of energy consumption, (b) the situatedness in the geo-climatic zone of energy consumption, and (c) the physical location in terms of topography and geography. The politico-administrative entities (regional and local), viz. the states and the districts therein were chosen at random through this method. The details of the procedure have been shown in Tables 1.6 and 1.7.

As mentioned in Sect. 4.1 above, the fundamental unit of data capture was a civil structure—a dwelling unit. The dwelling unit along with its occupants lie at the core of this work. Both electrified and non-electrified units were chosen at random from within the revenue villages. The present work was restricted to the study of electrified dwelling units (EDUs) with a single-phase power connection connected to the grid. Non-electrified dwelling units (NEDUs) functioning through alternative, informal mechanisms for energy sourcing were also picked up at random. A random mix of communities was studied across the revenue villages. The residents/occupants interviewed had a comprehensive spread in terms of age, gender, class-caste structure and socio-political and economic engagement. Each of the respondents was mapped through his/her unique AADHAR identity in terms of his/her representation.

Table 1.6 Stages of universe selection

Layers	Base maps	Purpose
Layer 1	Map of India depicting off-grid regions	For identifying, scoping, and laying down the purposive significance of sampling design
Layer 2	Map of India depicting geo-climatic zones	For studying insolation and biogas resource assessment potential and its subsequent quantification
Layer 3	Map of India depicting physiographic divisions	For placing the context (EP) in the politico-administrative setting along with socio-cultural spaces of energy consumption, viz. state, district, tehsil, block, village and the dwelling unit

Source Author (2017)

Table 1.7 Depicting the sampling strategy for selecting a village

Sampling methods	Stages	Purpose
Probability sampling (PS1)	Four step procedure: multi-stage systematic random	Selection of macro area; (1) state, (2) district, (3) tehsil/community development block, and lastly, (4) a revenue village
Probability sampling (PS2)	Systematic random	Selection of individual dwelling unit through a randomly chosen natural number

Source Author (2017)

Another aspect for the purpose of quantification and statistical analysis was the kitchen of the household within the dwelling unit. It was extremely important to study the consumption pattern of energy—(a) through conventional sources of power, (b) through traditional sources of energy such as dung cakes, fuel wood, charcoal, kerosene, mustard oil, (c) through alternate sources of lighting. The pattern of LPG consumption in terms of its first use followed by subsequent re-filling cycle was restricted to understanding of cooking needs of a dwelling unit. Thus, there was an exclusive focus on demand profiling of individual dwelling units in terms of: (a) source of primary energy, (b) its end use in terms of ownership and actual usage of electrical appliances (for grid connected dwelling units), and (c) cooking and lighting needs of (off-grid) dwelling units (non-electrified).

1.4.6 Sampling Method and Sample Size

The first stage of sampling for the choice of sampling universe was non-probabilistic purposive sampling. The second stage of sampling for selecting the sampling frame was by means of probabilistic random method. The unit of analysis: the sampling unit (dwelling units, both electrified and non-electrified) were picked up at random. These units had a random mix of above poverty line (APL) and below poverty line (BPL) households (HHs). For each of the revenue villages, 25 numbers of dwelling units were picked up at random.

An exception was created in the case of the union territory of Andaman and Nicobar Islands as the settlement was scattered and dispersed. Therefore, 10% of the dwelling units were chosen at random for the purpose of quantitative analysis from the three villages of Lataw, Profullyanagar, and Swadeshnagar. Moreover, all the three villages from the union territory of Andaman and Nicobar Islands have been chosen for a comprehensive coverage as a complete unit of study (as a case study on DSM), being a distinct politico-administrative unit.

Further, in Tayyabpur village of Vaishali district of Bihar, another 25 numbers of dwelling units were randomly picked up from the village. A part of the village is connected to the grid whereas another portion runs on solar micro-grid (this village has been taken for analysis through case study method; Fig. 1.6, Annexure B). The civil district of Roopnagar in Punjab was chosen for the purpose of an exclusive case study on biogas; 50 numbers of dwelling units were picked up at random from the village, Bahadurpur.

A total of 1025 numbers of dwelling units were used for demand profiling, energy budgeting, and resource assessment in terms of two sources of renewable energy, viz. solar and biogas (waste based). For qualitative analysis through personal interviews and focused group discussions, 50 numbers of individuals were picked up at random from each of the 41 villages. Therefore, 2050 individuals were studied for understanding passive consumerism in respect of grid connected power supply from conventional sources (Figs. 1.2 and 1.3, Annexure B). The results of quantitative analysis for resource assessment potential (solar and biogas) have been shown in Tables 1.9 and 1.10 (Annexure B), respectively. For the purpose of discussions in Chapter 3, seven villages have been picked up at random from six states and the union territory.

The details for qualitative and quantitative assessment in respect of energy demand, usage and energy expenditure have been discussed in detail below.

1.4.7 Sequential Description of Methodology

A. Qualitative data capture through structured (questionnaire survey) and evoking participant response for collection of nominal and ordinal data in respect of: (1) diurnal supply of power, (2) supply of power from sunrise to sunset, (3) scheduling of power supply (peak demand on a daily basis), (4) scheduling of power supply (least demand on a daily basis), (5) quality of power supply (voltage fluctuations) and also in terms of harmonious working of appliances, (6) assessment of formal and informal connections of power (whether metered or otherwise), and (7) satisfaction levels with regard to the quality and quantity of power including reliability of supply (Annexure B, Author, 2016–2017).

B. Quantitative data capture involved transect walk through the villages and into randomly chosen civil structures for physical inspection of every sampled civil structure in respect of (1) assessment of physical ownership of appliances, (2) recording of power rating of an appliance as indicated upon it, (3) actual declared (as participant response) usage pattern of an electrical appliance during a day, (4) assessment of contribution to the total declared load by each electrical appliance, (5) creation of load demand profiles for a village on a daily basis, (6) assessment of lighting load as a fraction of the total load of a civil structure along with usage capture of the different kinds of lighting devices within a dwelling unit, viz. filament bulb, tube light, compact fluorescent lamp (CFL), and light emitting diode (LED).

The purpose of this exercise was to ascertain appliance-based usage and consumption of power for a real-time load estimation in respect of an electrified dwelling unit and also for those units drawing power from other formal and informal sources of power supply (Author, 2016–2017). 100% conversion efficiency assumed while creating load demand (energy conversion losses and efficiency of devices have not been taken into account).

C. Data capture for solar insolation potential (irradiation captured on a daily basis by means of a CMP 3 pyranometer (Kipp and Zonen), radiometer cum data logger (meteon software) on a real-time basis), period: December 2016–October 2017: assessment of quality and quantity of solar insolation during the day from sunrise till sunset for a real-time estimation of solar resource potential (Fig. 1.10, Annexure B).

D. Waste quantification for biogas resource from three different sources of waste: (a) human waste (census 2011 data and physical interaction), (b) animal waste (self, animal husbandry and veterinary department, revenue administration), and (c) kitchen waste plus other biodegradable waste from the dwelling unit (physical assessment through inspection and participant response). This exercise aided in the evaluation of quantity and quality of fuel assessment for biogas generation on a real-time basis (Banks, 2009; Dimpl, 2010; Buswell & Mueller, 1952; and Author, 2016–2017).

1.4.8 Renewable Resource Potential Assessment Method and Instrumentation

1.4.8.1 Solar Resource Assessment (Instrumentation and Data Modelling)

Empirical assessment and evaluation of incoming solar radiation was measured on a daily basis for two to three weeks by means of a CMP 3, class one pyranometer and meteon data logger (Fig. 1.10, Annexure B). The placement and geographic setting of the instrument was done while taking into consideration two factors—the terrain characteristics, and the actual distances between the chosen revenue villages. Local weather conditions had an important bearing on data collection. Another prime concern was to ensure the safety of the instrumentation set-up from any natural or man-made disturbance(s). The placement and instrumentation for solar data capture have been depicted in detail at (Fig. 1.7, Annexure B).

The least count in terms of time interval for recording intensity of the solar radiation was 10 minutes on a daily basis for all the geographic settings. This time logging produced 70–72 datasets for insolation per day, for a daily solar cycle lasting on an average for 12–14 hours duration (Fig. 1.8, Annexure B). The area under the curve was calculated on a daily basis. The total quantum of solar energy on any given day was defined by the value of a particular strength of insolation in W/m^2 (measured on y-axis) and multiplied by the time duration (hours) for which it lasts (measured on the x-axis). The sum of each of such values gives the potential of solar radiance on any given day from sunrise to sunset. The nature of the solar curves is reflective of the actual weather conditions throughout the given day and at any instant of time. This data has been generated across the sampling universe for winter, summer, and the rainy seasons in the context of the Indian subcontinent (standard classification by Indian meteorological department).

1.4.8.2   Biogas Resource Assessment

In order to make a real assessment of biogas potential, the following methods were adopted during the field study. Within a dwelling unit an assessment was made of three kinds of wastes: (a) kitchen and household waste (primarily raw waste and left-over organic matter), (b) human waste, and (c) animal waste generated by domesticated bovine animals, pigs, poultry, etc. (ISAT-GTZ—Biogas Digest, 1998, 1999; Dimpl, 2010; Lemvig Biogas Handbook, 2008). Outside the dwelling unit, a survey was initiated with the help of staff from the animal husbandry department, block office, and revenue department. The team comprised village level workers, daily rated mazdoors (labourers), patwaris (village administrative officer), and panchayat sachivs (secretaries).

The empirical data gathered did not take into account the element of migration. The data was cross-checked with the figures of the animal husbandry department at the tehsil/block level and was certified by the veterinary officer. For quantification of human waste, population data of 2011 census has been taken into account, and for kitchen and household waste responses were gathered from the participants through an open-ended, semi-structured questionnaire.

The waste quantification has been therefore done by taking animal, human, and household waste (preferably food waste from the kitchen). Thereafter, the theoretical model that was taken as the benchmark to calculate the resource potential was based on the work of Buswell and Mueller (1952, pp. 550–552). From this seminal work referred to, the quantitative import has been drawn to assess and optimize anaerobic digestion, for production of biogas (methane) and power in different geo-climatic zones and physiographic divisions chosen for the purpose of this study (Fig. 1.9, Annexure B).

The evaluation parameters that have been considered for evaluation of biogas potential are as follows: (a) up to 75% of a substrate gets converted into biogas, (b) the ratio of methane to carbon dioxide in any given substrate is 55:45 (Buswell equation as an standard, theoretical import), (c) digester efficiency is taken as the same as the conversion percentage of the substrate, (d) for the purpose of methane enrichment the digester type has been taken to be single stage prototype, wet, mesophilic digesters (Banks, 2009: https://www.forestry.gov.uk/.../rrps_AD250309_optimising_anaerobic_digestion.pdf). Table 1.8 shows the standardized quantum of refuse generated by human beings and different categories of animals undertaken for assessment of biogas potential.

Table 1.8 Average waste yield from different sources (Cattle standard 13.00 kgs)

S.No.	Standard Living beings	Quantity of dung/night soil produced (kg/day)	Unit	No	Standard
1	Poultry	0.4	kg	10 Hens	32.50
2	Buffaloes	15.0	kg		0.87
3	Bullocks	14.0	kg		0.93
4	Cows	10.0	kg		1.30
5	Dogs	0.3	kg		38.24
6	Donkeys	14.0	kg		0.93
7	Mules/Horses	6.0	kg		2.17
8	Adult Human	0.4	kg		32.50
9	Sheep	0.5	kg		26.00
10	Pig	2.5	kg	Under 8 score	5.20
11	Goat	0.5	kg		26.00

Source Vikaspedia.in/energy, India Development Gateway (InDG), developed and maintained by Centre for Development of Advanced Computing (C-DAC), Ministry of Electronics and Information Technology, Government of India (GoI) (2016), and Author (2017)

1.4.9 The Tool Box Metaphor

Qualitative research methods comprised long transect walks, visual ethnography, structured questionnaire surveys, and group discussions. Apart from these methods, individual interactions across sections of beneficiaries, experts, political representatives, and administrative staff form an integral part of the qualitative framework tool deployed for this study. There were frequent interactions with the technical staff and officials of the state-run utilities for conventional power supply and state nodal agencies responsible for renewable resources promotion and deployment in the states of Gujarat, Bihar, Uttar Pradesh, and Punjab.

1.4.9.1 Concept of Visual Ethnography

A special tool for this work has been extensive use of visual ethnography. Still photography of general to specific features of a household with regard to energy access and its end use in different rural settings of the Indian subcontinent has been depicted. This method was exclusively adopted to capture the social, the economic, the political along with technology at the level of the micro and the local. The tool effectively helped to understand the necessary elements of energy demand, energy access, and end use of primary and secondary energy (energy service).

Energy poverty as a concept and as a phenomenon is multi-dimensional, composite, and extremely complex. It becomes a mind-boggling task in a country like India, to study its nature (prevalence), given the extent of socio-cultural diversity, which is interlaced with the economic and the political. The subjectivity of the concept increases manifold, even when an arduous attempt has been made to pinpoint the context (rural and local) to make it objective and restricted in terms of scope and resolution.

This study has laid an exclusive emphasis on creation of photomosaics from still photographs. Ethnography per se treats people as knowledgeable, situated agents from whom researchers can learn a great deal by seeing a living and working world. Further, it is an extended, detailed, immersive, and inductive methodology to study a phenomenon being studied locally (Cloke et al., 2004; Whitehead, 2005). The photomosaic strongly reflects patterns of engagements of the subjects in terms of their general lifestyles, shaped by social context, cultural conventions and norms of a particular strata or group. In this study, where the phenomenon (EP) had to be studied in complete relatedness to its context (the observed spaces of energy consumption), a layered analysis became the key to diagnose a problem that presented itself camouflaged in the context.

Visual ethnography helped the author to study the patterns of energy end use across age, gender, occupation, social structure (in terms of class stratification), and cultures across different rural settings (Besio & Butz, 2004; Schwartz, 1989; Tracy et al., 2013; Whitehead, 2005), which are otherwise, physically situated in different geo-climatic zones (climatic condition based) and physiographic divisions (physical terrain characteristics).

Therefore, for an objective, qualitative assessment of energy poverty, the context had to be viewed as holistically as possible. The focus was on deep engagement with the context driven by three primary activities: (a) asking, (b) observing, and (c) sharing. This method for the purpose of this study strongly depicts the ground truths and presents objective evidence for interpretation of associations between energy and society (Schwartz, 1989). The current policy paradigm of grid extension for providing energy access is too distant from the context, whereas on the contrary, it deserves to be as close as possible to the action arena. The action arena should ideally be the sole guiding factor for dictating the policy process. However, this seldom happens in other sectors as well and the energy sector is no exception.

This tool has been effectively used in this study with an exclusive focus of strengthening the evidence-based policy paradigm. Quantitative analysis, as an isolated entity, is not robust enough to study energy poverty, and thereafter suggest policy alternatives to address it. Two kinds of software graphic tools were used to create the photomosaics (*adobe photoshop 7.0, acdsee 10 photo-manager, photo management software*) and schematic maps (*autocad software-version 2012 and 2017*) to work on layers and structures of the 'local'.

1.4.9.2 Case Study Approach

Another special feature of this study is the use of case studies as an effective tool, since the requirements of this study were special. And therefore, a total number of five case studies have been presented in this study. The case studies bear commonality on account of being factual, retrospective, being real-time (and therefore empirical), strongly contemporary and contextual and being descriptive and exploratory in nature. The case studies are as follows:

1. The Andaman story: evidence-based policy (EBP) paradigm for an effective demand side management (DSM) of conventional power supply systems.
2. The story of solar pumping irrigation system cooperative enterprise (SPICE), from a village: Dhundi, Gujarat.
3. The story of the Nonia community and the reference electrification model (REM) for planning and designing micro- and mini-grids (small scale power production units, village: Tayyabpur, Bihar).
4. The story of voluntary governance and monopoly of a RESCO case study of solar energy driven pico-power grid being run by an energy service company, Mera Gao Power (MGP), in the village Lohati Pasai, Barabanki, Uttar Pradesh and lastly,
5. The story of R. S. Farms., village: Bahadurpur, in Punjab: narrative of social entrepreneurship in respect of supply of clean cooking fuel (biogas).

Each of these stories is placed in a culturally alien context. The technology lacks acceptance. There is distrust in the 'local', and therefore, the local power structures control resource allocation. Information asymmetry in respect of any new technology, indigenous or alien (not hitherto commonly deployed for harnessing non-conventional forms of energy), entails sustained and strong efforts towards trust building through active engagement (in terms of gaining familiarity for usage) as every new energy production system shall have its own gestation period in terms of immersing itself completely in different spaces and cultures of energy consumption.

The issues that come up during documentation of these cases provide insights into the functioning of—(a) local policy communities and policy recipients driven by their individual, self, and private interests that should not be ignored either by the MESO (state as a regional entity) or by the MACRO (the union as a national entity), both being the drivers of policies governing energy access. These case studies highlight the gap between policy and praxis. Twin approaches have been followed while writing these case studies: (a) problem-oriented approach, and (b) the analytical approach (case study approach has been discussed in detail as a prelude to Chapter 2 comprising the case studies).

All of these thoughts engage with the plight of the policy recipients who want to create, own, and manage local resources for their larger and collective benefits based on local resource availability including the human and technical skill at their disposal. The need for energy and its demand needs to be socially constructed. The case studies highlight the policy oversights and the myths associated within a specific sectoral element—labelled as 'renewable source of energy' or a cleaner, greener source of energy. The shared experience exposes the chinks in the overall policy design while trying to address issues of energy access across rural India that is home to diverse rural communities with their own demand and consumption specifics. This calls for a micro-analysis of the problem through an evidence-based policy approach to correct the policy trajectory of the electricity sector, in particular the rural dimension of energy access provisioning through extension of the grid and/or deployment of standalone systems that run on a particular renewable energy source.

At the end it can be satisfactorily said that the tools and the interdisciplinary approach adopted for the purpose of this study helped: (a) to link the text (policy) to the context (action arena), (b) to appreciate and understand qualitatively and quantitatively the flavour of 'energy poverty' in terms of the rural Indian context, (c) to analyse and ascertain whether the world view of energy poverty is applicable to the local, rural Indian context, (d) in evaluation and realistic assessment of existing policies oblivious to the local nature of rural demand for energy, and lastly (e) in real-time resource potential modelling for promoting active consumerism at the level of local, thus providing an alternate way of governing and regulating energy access and its end use through DSM.

Annexure A

See Fig. 1.1.

40   M. K. SINGH

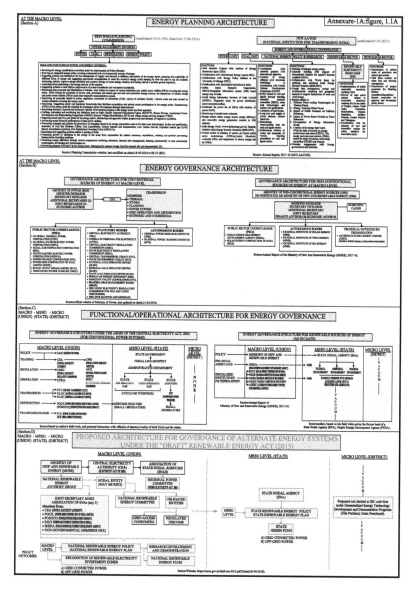

Fig. 1.1 Energy planning, governance and execution framework of India

Annexure B

See Figs. 1.2, 1.3, 1.4, 1.5, 1.6, 1.7, 1.8, 1.9, 1.10 and Tables 1.9 and 1.10.

Fig. 1.2 Mixed methods research framework adopted for the study

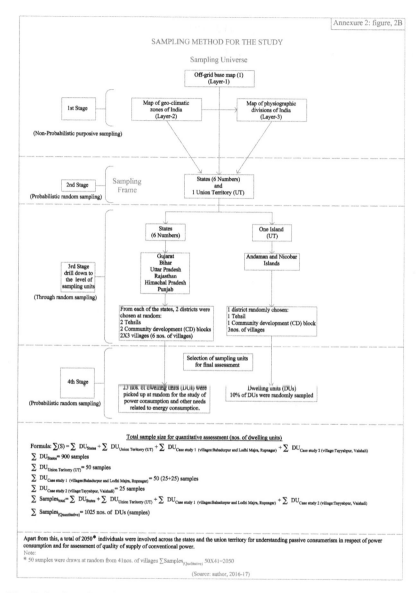

Fig. 1.3 Sampling framework deployed for the study

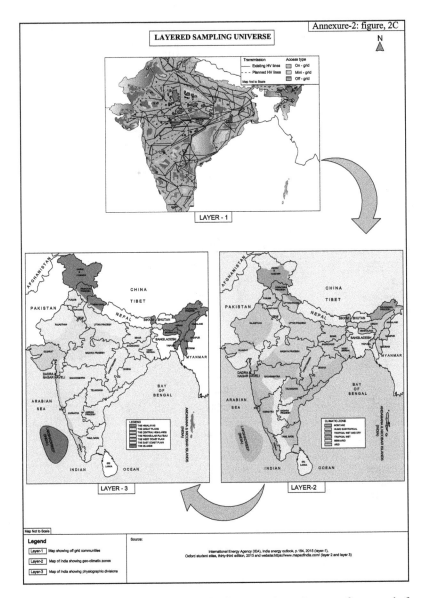

Fig. 1.4 Layered sampling framework that was the sub-strata framework for choosing the state/UT, district, sub-division, CD block and village

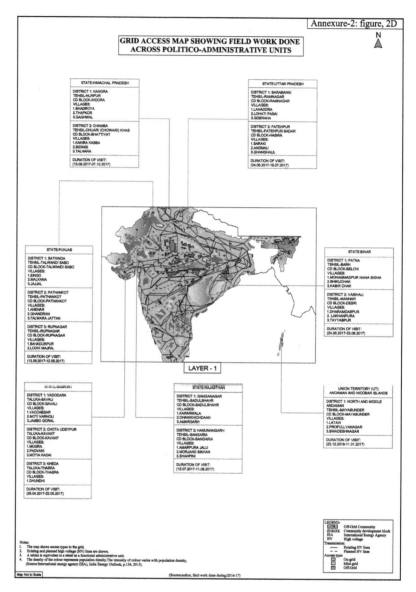

Fig. 1.5 Grid access map showing the expanse of field work across various politico-administrative units

1 ENERGY AND SOCIETY: UNRAVELLING GOVERNMENTALITY … 45

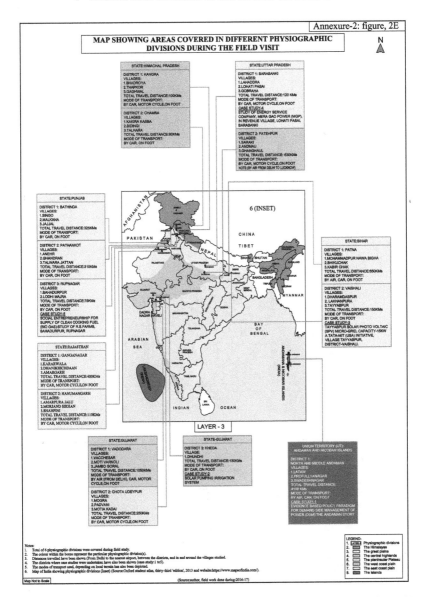

Fig. 1.6 Map showing different areas covered across various physiographic divisions

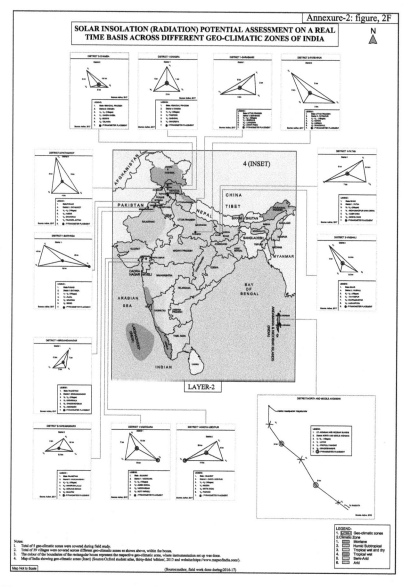

Fig. 1.7 Map showing solar energy potential assessment (as a resource) on a real-time basis across various geo-climatic zones of India

1 ENERGY AND SOCIETY: UNRAVELLING GOVERNMENTALITY ...   47

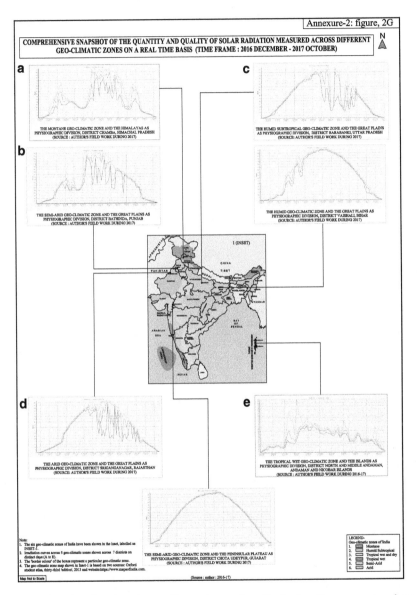

Fig. 1.8 Map showing the quality and quantity of solar irradiance measured on a real-time basis across various geo-climatic zones of India

48　M. K. SINGH

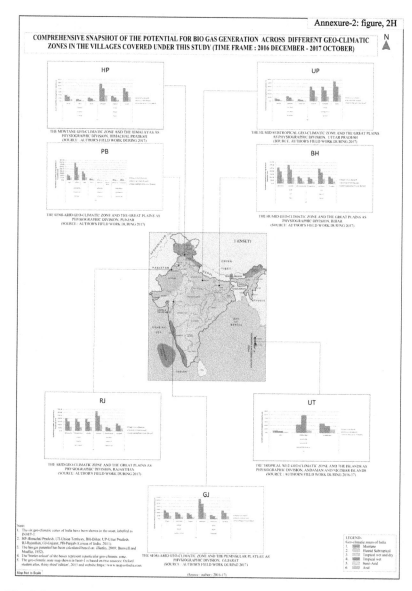

Fig. 1.9 Comprehensive assessment of biogas as a resource for green energy across different villages undertaken for the study

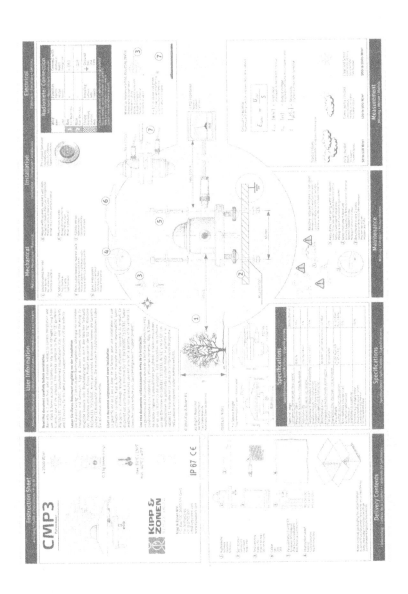

Fig. 1.10 Instrumentation deployed for measuring solar irradiance—CMP3 PYRANOMETER

Table 1.9 Real-time configuration of solar irradiance

S.No.	State	District	Tehsil	Block	Village	Solar irradiance (Watt/m²) Intensity (in Watt/m²)	Duration (in hours/day)	Quality of irradiance (constant/intermittent/erratic)	Energy generated per day (in kWh)
1	UT	North & Middle Andamans	Maya Bundar	Maya Bundar	Profullya Nagar	80	1	Erratic	0.08
2	UT	North & Middle Andamans	Maya Bundar	Maya Bundar	Profullya Nagar	100	1	Erratic	0.1
3	UT	North & Middle Andamans	Maya Bundar	Maya Bundar	Profullya Nagar	250	1.5	Erratic	0.375
4	UT	North & Middle Andamans	Maya Bundar	Maya Bundar	Profullya Nagar	300	4.5	Constant	1.35
5	UT	North & Middle Andamans	Maya Bundar	Maya Bundar	Profullya Nagar	180	2	Erratic	0.36
6	UT	North & Middle Andamans	Maya Bundar	Maya Bundar	Profullya Nagar	40	1.5	Erratic	0.06

1 ENERGY AND SOCIETY: UNRAVELLING GOVERNMENTALITY ... 51

S.No.	State	District	Tehsil	Block	Village	Solar irradiance (Watt/m^2) Intensity (in Watt/m^2)	Duration (in hours/day)	Quality of irradiance (constant/intermittent erratic)	Energy generated per day (in kWh)
7	UT	North & Middle Andamans	Maya Bundar	Maya Bundar	Swadeshnagar	60	2	Intermittent	0.12
8	UT	North & Middle Andamans	Maya Bundar	Maya Bundar	Swadeshnagar	200	2	Erratic	0.4
9	UT	North & Middle Andamans	Maya Bundar	Maya Bundar	Swadeshnagar	250	4	Intermittent	1
10	UT	North & Middle Andamans	Maya Bundar	Maya Bundar	Swadeshnagar	140	2	Erratic	0.28
11	UT	North & Middle Andamans	Maya Bundar	Maya Bundar	Lataw	80	4.5	Intermittent	0.36

(continued)

Table 1.9 (continued)

S.No.	State	District	Tehsil	Block	Village	Solar irradiance ($Watt/m^2$) Intensity (in $Watt/m^2$)	Duration (in hours/day)	Quality of irradiance (constant/intermittent/erratic)	Energy generated per day (in kWh)
12	UT	North & Middle Andamans	Maya Bundar	Maya Bundar	Lataw	450	3.5	Erratic	1.575
13	UT	North & Middle Andamans	Maya Bundar	Maya Bundar	Lataw	200	3	Constant	0.6
14	GJ	Vadodara	Desar	Desar	Moti Varnoli	250	3	Constant	0.75
15	GJ	Vadodara	Desar	Desar	Moti Varnoli	500	2	Constant	1
16	GJ	Vadodara	Desar	Desar	Moti Varnoli	750	5	Constant	3.75
17	GJ	Vadodara	Desar	Desar	Moti Varnoli	500	2	Constant	1
18	GJ	Vadodara	Desar	Desar	Moti Varnoli	350	1	Constant	0.35
19	GJ	Vadodara	Desar	Desar	Moti Varnoli	100	1	Constant	0.1
20	BH	Patna	Barh	Belchi	Bhikhuchak	350	3	Intermittent	1.05
21	BH	Patna	Barh	Belchi	Bhikhuchak	550	2	Intermittent	1.1
22	BH	Patna	Barh	Belchi	Bhikhuchak	700	4	Intermittent	2.8

1 ENERGY AND SOCIETY: UNRAVELLING GOVERNMENTALITY ... 53

S.No.	State	District	Tehsil	Block	Village	Solar irradiance (Watt/m^2) Intensity (in Watt/m^2)	Duration (in hours/day)	Quality of irradiance (constant/intermittent erratic)	Energy generated per day (in kWh)
23	BH	Patna	Barh	Belchi	Bhikhuchak	550	1	Intermittent	0.55
24	BH	Patna	Barh	Belchi	Bhikhuchak	450	1	Intermittent	0.45
25	BH	Patna	Barh	Belchi	Bhikhuchak	300	2	Intermittent	0.6
26	BH	Vaishali	Mahnar	Desri	Tayyabpur	300	3	Constant	0.9
27	BH	Vaishali	Mahnar	Desri	Tayyabpur	500	2	Constant	1
28	BH	Vaishali	Mahnar	Desri	Tayyabpur	650	5	Intermittent	3.25
29	BH	Vaishali	Mahnar	Desri	Tayyabpur	500	1	Intermittent	0.5
30	BH	Vaishali	Mahnar	Desri	Tayyabpur	350	1	Intermittent	0.35
31	BH	Vaishali	Mahnar	Desri	Tayyabpur	150	2	Intermittent	0.3
32	UP	Fatehpur	Fatehpur Sadar	Haswa	Ghanghaul	150	2	Constant	0.3
33	UP	Fatehpur	Fatehpur Sadar	Haswa	Ghanghaul	300	1	Constant	0.3
34	UP	Fatehpur	Fatehpur Sadar	Haswa	Ghanghaul	450	1	Constant	0.45

(continued)

Table 1.9 (continued)

S.No.	State	District	Tehsil	Block	Village	Solar irradiance (Watt/m^2) Intensity (in Watt/m^2)	Duration (in hours/day)	Quality of irradiance (constant/intermittent/erratic)	Energy generated per day (in kWh)
35	UP	Fatehpur	Fatehpur Sadar	Haswa	Ghanghaul	650	1	Erratic	0.65
36	UP	Fatehpur	Fatehpur Sadar	Haswa	Ghanghaul	650	2	Erratic	1.3
37	UP	Fatehpur	Fatehpur Sadar	Haswa	Ghanghaul	600	1	Erratic	0.6
38	UP	Fatehpur	Fatehpur Sadar	Haswa	Ghanghaul	200	1	Intermittent	0.2
39	UP	Fatehpur	Fatehpur Sadar	Haswa	Ghanghaul	700	0.5	Intermittent	0.35
40	UP	Fatehpur	Fatehpur Sadar	Haswa	Ghanghaul	300	2.5	Constant	0.75
41	UP	Fatehpur	Fatehpur Sadar	Haswa	Ghanghaul	200	1	Constant	0.2

1 ENERGY AND SOCIETY: UNRAVELLING GOVERNMENTALITY ...   55

S.No.	State	District	Tehsil	Block	Village	Solar irradiance (Watt/m^2) Intensity (in Watt/m^2)	Duration (in hours/day)	Quality of irradiance (constant/intermittent/erratic)	Energy generated per day (in kWh)
42	UP	Fatehpur	Fatehpur Sadar	Haswa	Ghanghaul	40	1	Constant	0.04
43	UP	Barabanki	Ram Nagar	Ram Nagar	Lohati Pasai	250	2	Intermittent	0.5
44	UP	Barabanki	Ram Nagar	Ram Nagar	Lohati Pasai	400	1	Intermittent	0.4
45	UP	Barabanki	Ram Nagar	Ram Nagar	Lohati Pasai	550	1	Intermittent	0.55
46	UP	Barabanki	Ram Nagar	Ram Nagar	Lohati Pasai	700	2.5	Constant	1.75
47	UP	Barabanki	Ram Nagar	Ram Nagar	Lohati Pasai	850	1.5	Erratic	1.275
48	UP	Barabanki	Ram Nagar	Ram Nagar	Lohati Pasai	750	1	Erratic	0.75
49	UP	Barabanki	Ram Nagar	Ram Nagar	Lohati Pasai	600	1	Intermittent	0.6
50	UP	Barabanki	Ram Nagar	Ram Nagar	Lohati Pasai	400	1	Intermittent	0.4
51	UP	Barabanki	Ram Nagar	Ram Nagar	Lohati Pasai	200	0.5	Intermittent	0.1
52	UP	Barabanki	Ram Nagar	Ram Nagar	Lohati Pasai	50	1.5	Intermittent	0.075
53	RJ	Sriganganagar	Sadulshahr	Sadulshar	Amargarh	200	3	Intermittent	0.6
54	RJ	Sriganganagar	Sadulshahr	Sadulshar	Amargarh	450	2	Erratic	0.9
55	RJ	Sriganganagar	Sadulshahr	Sadulshar	Amargarh	750	3	Erratic	2.25

(continued)

Table 1.9 (continued)

S.No.	State	District	Tehsil	Block	Village	Solar irradiance (Watt/m²) Intensity (in Watt/m²)	Duration (in hours/day)	Quality of irradiance (constant/intermittent/erratic)	Energy generated per day (in kWh)
56	RJ	Sriganganagar	Sadulshahr	Sadulsnar	Amargarh	650	1	Erratic	0.65
57	RJ	Sriganganagar	Sadulshahr	Sadulsnar	Amargarh	500	1	Erratic	0.5
58	RJ	Sriganganagar	Sadulshahr	Sadulsnar	Amargarh	300	1	Erratic	0.3
59	RJ	Sriganganagar	Sadulshahr	Sadulsnar	Amargarh	200	1	Erratic	0.2
60	RJ	Sriganganagar	Sadulshahr	Sadulsnar	Amargarh	50	1.5	Intermittent	0.075
61	PB	Pathankot	Pathankot	Pathankot	Anher	150	2	Intermittent	0.3
62	PB	Pathankot	Pathankot	Pathankot	Anher	300	3	Intermittent	0.9
63	PB	Pathankot	Pathankot	Pathankot	Anher	750	4	Intermittent	3
64	PB	Pathankot	Pathankot	Pathankot	Anher	450	2	Erratic	0.9
65	PB	Pathankot	Pathankot	Pathankot	Anher	300	0.75	Erratic	0.225
66	HP	Chamba	Chowari	Bhattijat	Kakira	25	3	Intermittent	0.075
67	HP	Chamba	Chowari	Bhattijat	Kakira	400	3	Intermittent	1.2
68	HP	Chamba	Chowari	Bhattijat	Kakira	850	3	Erratic	2.55
69	HP	Chamba	Chowari	Bhattijat	Kakira	400	2	Intermittent	0.8

1 ENERGY AND SOCIETY: UNRAVELLING GOVERNMENTALITY ... 57

S.No.	State	District	Tehsil	Block	Village	Solar irradiance (Watt/m^2) Intensity (in Watt/m^2)	Duration (in hours/day)	Quality of irradiance (constant /intermittent erratic)	Energy generated per day (in kWh)
70	HP	Chamba	Chowari	Bhattiyat	Kakira	200	0.5	Intermittent	0.1
71	HP	Chamba	Chowari	Bhattiyat	Kakira	100	1.5	Intermittent	0.15
72	PB	Roopnagar	Roopnagar	Roopnagar	Bahadurpur	200	2	Constant	0.4
73	PB	Roopnagar	Roopnagar	Roopnagar	Bahadurpur	550	2	Constant	1.1
74	PB	Roopnagar	Roopnagar	Roopnagar	Bahadurpur	600	4.5	Constant	2.7
75	PB	Roopnagar	Roopnagar	Roopnagar	Bahadurpur	300	2.5	Constant	0.75
76	PB	Roopnagar	Roopnagar	Roopnagar	Bahadurpur	200	1	Intermittent	0.2
77	PB	Roopnagar	Roopnagar	Roopnagar	Bahadurpur	75	1	Intermittent	0.075

Table 1.10 Potential of biogas as a source of electricity (power) and as a cooking medium (fuel)

Village	Animal waste (in kg)	Human waste (in kg)	Kitchen waste (in kg)	Total waste	Biogas (cu.m)	Electricity (in kWh)	Cooking Fuel (CH_4) (cu.m)	Average energy consumed per day (in kWh)
Amargarh	20,754.18	858.00	633.00	22,245.18	326.73	244.72	106.19	9.58
Anher	4056.90	489.20	315.00	4861.10	71.40	53.48	23.20	7.36
Bahadurpur	3357.38	170.00	83.00	3610.38	53.03	39.72	17.23	11.60
Bhikhuchak	17,413.00	285.60	189.00	17,887.60	262.73	196.78	85.39	0.65
Ghanghaul	26,736.30	880.40	567.00	28,183.70	413.95	310.05	134.53	0.48
Kakira	298.68	307.60	310.50	916.78	13.47	10.09	4.38	10.22
Lataw	488.32	182.40	181.50	852.22	12.52	9.38	4.07	2.95
Lohati Pasai	3292.92	204.80	166.50	3664.22	53.82	40.31	17.49	0.65
Moti Varnoli	3592.00	555.20	301.00	4448.20	65.33	48.94	21.23	1.20
Profullya Nagar	2721.28	183.20	210.00	3114.48	45.74	97.89	14.87	0.81
Swadeshnagar	2847.80	381.20	342.00	3571.00	52.45	39.28	17.05	4.32
Tayyalpur	6042.50	1236.00	790.50	8069.00	118.52	88.77	38.52	0.77

REFERENCES

Anderson, B., Keanes, M., McFarlane, C., & Swanton, D. (2012). In assemblages and geography. *Dialogues in Human Geography, 2*(2), 171–189. https://doi.org/10.1177/2043820612449261

Anderson, B., & McFarlane, C. (2011). Assemblage and geography, royal geographical society, advancing geography and geographical learning. *(AREA), 43*(2), 124–127. https://doi.org/10.1111/j.1475-4762.2011.01004.x

Aune, M. (2007). Energy comes home. *Energy Policy, 35*(11), 5457–5465.

Awan, R. U., Sher, F., & Abbas, A. (2013). An investigation of multidimensional energy poverty in Pakistan: A province level analysis. *International Journal of Energy Economics and Policy, 4*(1), 65–75.

Banks, C. (2009). *Optimizing anaerobic digestion: Evaluating the potential for anaerobic digestion to provide energy and soil amendment* (pp. 1–39). University of Reading. https://www.forestry.gov.uk/.../rrps_AD250309_optimizing_anaerobic_digestion.pdf

Barnes, D. F., & Floor, W. M. (1996). Rural energy in developing countries: A challenge for economic development. *Annual Review of Energy and the Environment, 21*, 497–530.

Barnes, D. F., Singh, B., & Shi, X. (2010). *Modernizing energy service for the poor: A World Bank investment review-fiscal 2000–08* (pp. 1–98). World Bank, Energy Sector Management Assistance Program (ESMAP), 63224.

Barnes, D. F. (2011). Effective solutions for rural electrification in developing countries: Lessons from successful programs. *Current Opinion in Environmental Sustainability, 3*, 260–264. https://doi.org/10.1016/j.cosust.2011.06.001

Bazilian, M., Blyth, W., Hobbs, B. F., Howells, M., & MacGill, I. (2011). Interactions between energy security and climate change: A focus on developing countries. *Energy Policy, 39*(6), 3750–3756.

Bazilian, M., Brew-Hammond, A., Eibs-Singer, C., Modi, V., Nussbaumer, P., Ramana, V. Sovacool, B., & Aqrawi, P. K. (2012). Improving access to modern energy services: Insights from case studies. *The Electricity Journal, 25*(1), 93–114. https://doi.org/10.1016/j.tej.2012.01.007

Bennett, J. (2005). The agency of assemblages and the North American blackout. *Public Culture, 17*(3), 445–465.

Besio, K., & Butz, D. (2004). The value of auto ethnography for field research in transcultural settings. *The Professional Geographer, 56*(3), 350–360.

Bhattacharyya, S. C. (2006). Energy access problem of the poor in India: Is rural electrification a remedy? *Energy Policy, 34*(18), 3387–3397.

Biogas Digest. (1998). Biogas basics (Vol. 1, pp. 1–46). http://biogas.ifas.ufl.edu/ad_development/documents/biogasdigestvol1.pdf. Email: gate-isat@gtz.de

Biogas Digest. (1999a). *Biogas—Application and product development* (Vol. 2, pp. 1–81). https://www.sswm.info/.../ISAT. Email: gate-isat@gtz.de

Biogas Digest. (1999b). *Biogas—Costs and benefits and biogas programme implementation* (Vol. 3, pp. 1–61). https://www.pseau.org/giz_biogas_digest_volume-iii_costs_and_benefits_a.... Email: gate-isat@gtz.de

Biogas Handbook. (2008). *Big>East project, biogas for Eastern Europe* (pp. 1–124). ISBN 978-87-992962-0-0. http://lemvigbiogas.com

Birol, F. (2007). Energy economics: A place for energy poverty in the agenda? *The Energy Journal, 28*(3), 1–6.

Bouzarovski, S. (2014). Energy poverty in the European Union: Landscapes of vulnerability. *Wiley Interdisciplinary Reviews: Energy and Environment, 3*(3), 276–289. https://doi.org/10.1002/wene.897

Brew-Hammond, A. (2010). Energy access in Africa: Challenges ahead. *Energy Policy, 38*(5), 2291–2301.

Buswell, A. M., & Mueller, H. F. (1952). Mechanism of methane fermentation. *Industrial & Engineering Chemistry Research, 44*(3), 550–552. https://doi.org/10.1021/ie50507a033. ACS Legacy Archives.

Calvert, K. (2016). From 'energy geography' to 'energy geographies', perspectives on a fertile academic borderland. *Progress in Human Geography, 40*(1), 105–125. https://doi.org/10.1177/0309132514566343

Catherine, W. P., Brazier, K., Pham, K., Mathieu, L. K., & Wang, W. (2007). *Identifying fuel poverty using objective and subjective measures, centre for competition policy (CCP)* (pp. 1–28) (Working Paper 07-11). Economic and Social Research Council (ESRC). ISSN 1745-9648.

Chakravarty, S., & Tavoni, M. (2013). Energy poverty alleviation and climate change mitigation: Is there a trade off? *Energy Economics, 40*, S67–S73.

Chester, L. (2010). Conceptualizing energy security and making explicit its polysemic nature. *Energy Policy, 38*(2), 887–895.

Clancy, J., & Roehr, U. (2003). Gender and energy: Is there a Northern perspective? *Energy for Sustainable Development, 7*(3), 44–49.

Clancy, J., Kelkar, G., Shakya, I., & Ummar, F. (2007). Appropriate gender-analysis tools for unpacking the gender-energy-poverty nexus. *Gender and Development, 15*(2), 241–257.

Cloke, P., Cook, I., Crang, P., Goodwin, M., Painter, J., & Philo, C. (2004). *Practising human geography*. Sage. ISBN 07619-7325-7.

Cook, P. (2005). *Rural electrification through decentralized off-grid systems in developing countries, green energy and technology*, (ed. S. Bhattacharya), https://doi.org/10.1007/978-1-4471_4673-5_2, Springer-Verlag, London.

Cook, P. (2011). Infrastructure, rural electrification and development. *Energy for Sustainable Development, 15*, 304–313.

Dimpl, E. (2010). *Small-scale electricity generation from biomass, biogas: Part II, experience with small-scale technologies for basic energy supply* (1st ed., pp. 1–17). GTZ-HERA, Poverty Oriented Basic Energy Service, Commissioned by Federal Ministry for Economic Cooperation and Development, Germany.

Dimitriadi, L. (2000). *The spirit of rural landscapes: Culture, memory and messages*. Cult-rural, promotion of a cultural area common to European rural communities, framework programme in support of culture (pp. 1–23).

Energy Access Outlook. (2017). *From poverty to prosperity* (pp. 1–140) (World Energy Outlook Special Report, OECD/IEA). International Energy Agency (IEA). www.iea.org

Foley, G. (1992). Rural electrification in the developing world. *Energy Policy, 20*(2), 145–152.

Geels, W. F. (2002). Technological transitions as evolutionary reconfiguration processes: A multi-level perspective and a case-study. *Research Policy, 31*, 1257–1274.

Green, J. M., & Erskine, S.-H. (1999). Solar (photovoltaic) systems, energy use and business activities in Maphephethe, KwaZulu-Natal. *Development Southern Africa, 16*(2), 221–237. https://doi.org/10.1080/03768359908440074

Gunningham, N. (2013). Managing the energy trilemma: The case of Indonesia. *Energy Policy, 54*, 184–193.

Gupta, A. (2015). An anthropology of electricity from the global south. *Cultural Anthropology, 30*(4), 555–568. https://doi.org/10.14506/ca30.4.04

Haanyika, C. M. (2008). Rural electrification in Zambia: A policy and institutional analysis. *Energy Policy, 36*(3), 1044–1058.

Haberl, H., & Krausmann, F. (2002). The process of industrialization from the perspective of energetic metabolism: Socioeconomic energy flows in Austria 1830–1995. *Ecological Economics, 41*(2), 177–201.

Harrison, C., & Popke, J. (2011). Because you got to have heat: The networked assemblage of energy poverty in Eastern North Carolina. *Annals of the Association of American Geographers, 101*(4), 949–961.

Holdren, J. P., Smith, K. R., Kjellstrom, T., Streets, D., Wang, X., & Fischer, S. (2000). *Energy, the environment and health*. United Nations Development Programme.

Ilskog, E. (2008). Indicators for assessment of rural electrification—An approach for the comparison of apples and pears. *Energy Policy, 36*(7), 2665–2673.

India energy outlook. (2015). *International Energy Agency, world energy outlook special report, OECD/IEA* (pp. 1–187). www.iea.org

International Energy Agency. (2011a). *The Energy Development Index*. IEA. http://www.iea.org/weo/development_index.asp

International Energy Agency. (2011b). *Energy and development methodology* (pp. 1–6). www.worldenergyoutlook.org. © OECD/IEA 2011.

Jain, G. (2010). Energy security issues at household level in India. *Energy Policy, 38*(6), 2835–2845.

Jones, R. H. (2010). *Energy poverty: How to make modern energy access universal?* Special Early Excerpt of the World Energy Outlook.

Katsoulakos, N. (2011). Combating energy poverty in mountainous areas through energy-saving interventions: Insights from Metsovo, Greece. *Mountain Research and Development, 31*(4), 284–292.

Khandker, R. S., Barnes, D. F., & Samad, A. H. (2012). Are the energy poor also income poor? Evidence from India. *Energy Policy, 57*, 1–12.

Khandker, R. S., Rubaba, A., Samad, A. H., & Barnes, D. F. (2012). *Who benefits most from rural electrification? Evidence in India* (pp. 1–39) (Policy Research Working Paper 6095 [WPS6095]). The World Bank Group, Development Research Group, Agriculture and Rural Development Team.

Legros, G., Havet, I., Bruce, N., & Bonjour, S. (2009). *The energy access situation in developing countries: A review focusing on the least developed countries and Sub-Saharan Africa* (pp. 1–142). Environment and Energy Group, World Health Organization and United Nations Development Program. http://www.undp.org/energyandenvironment

Lutzenhiser, L. (1992). A cultural model of household energy consumption. *Energy, 17*(1), 47–60.

Masud, J., & Sharan, D., Lohani, B. N. (2007). *Energy for all: Addressing the energy, environment, and poverty nexus in Asia* (pp. 1–123). Asian Development Bank (ADB). http://hdl.handle.net//11540/225

Mirza, B., & Szirmai, A. (2010). *Towards a new measurement of energy poverty: A cross-community analysis of rural Pakistan* (pp. 1–41). United Nations University (UNU-MERIT), #2010-024. http://www.merit.unu.edu

Munasinghe, M. (1990). Rural electrification in the Third World. *Power Engineering Journal, 4*(4), 189–202.

Nicholls, L., & Strengers, Y. (2014). Air-conditioning and antibiotics: Demand management insights from problematic health and household cooling practices. *Energy Policy, 67*, 673–681.

Nussbaumer, P., Bazilian, M., Modi, V., & Yumkella, K. K. (2011). *Measuring energy poverty: Focusing on what matters* (pp. 1–27) (Working Paper No. 42). Oxford Department of International Development, University of Oxford, Oxford Poverty and Human Development Initiative (OPHI).

Pachauri, S., Mueller, A., Kemmler, A., & Spreng, D. (2004). On measuring energy poverty in Indian households. *World Development, 32*(12), 2083–2104. https://doi.org/10.1016/j.worlddev.2004.08.005

Pachauri, S., & Rao, N. D. (2013). Energy access and living standards: Some observations on recent trends. *Environment Research Letters, 12*(2), 025011. https://doi.org/10.1088/1748-9326/aa5b0d

Pachauri, S., & Spreng, D. (2004). Energy use and energy access in relation to poverty. *Economic and Political Weekly, 39*(3), 271–278.
Pasternak, A. D. (2000). *Global energy futures and human development: A framework for analysis* (pp. 1–27) (United States Department of Energy Report, UCRL-ID-140773). Lawrence Livermore National Laboratory, Livermore.
Pereira, G. M., Freitas, M. A. V., & da Silva, F. N. (2010). Rural electrification and energy poverty: Empirical evidences from Brazil. *Renewable and Sustainable Energy Reviews, 14*(4), 1229–1240.
Petrova, S., Gentile, M., Mäkinen, I. H., & Bouzarovski, S. (2013). Perceptions of thermal comfort and housing quality: Exploring the micro-geographies of energy poverty in Stakhanov, Ukraine. *Environment and Planning A, 45*(5), 1240–1257.
Planning Commission. (2014). *Annual report 2013–14 on the working of state power utilities and electricity departments.*
Rademaekers, K., Yearwood, J., Ferreira, A., Pye, S., Hamilton, I., Agnolucci, P., Grover, D., Karasek, J., & Anisimova, N. (2016). *Selecting indicators to measure energy poverty* (pp. 1–130). Rotterdam: Trinomics, Framework Contract ENER/A4/516-2014.
Report of the National Development Council (NDC) Committee on Power. (1994). *Planning Commission* (pp. 1–173). New Delhi.
Sagar, A. D. (2005). Alleviating energy poverty for the world's poor. *Energy Policy, 33*(11), 1367–1372.
Saith, R. (2001). *Capabilities: The concept and its operationalization.* Queen Elizabeth House.
Schwartz, D. (1989). Visual ethnography: Using photography in qualitative research. *Qualitative Sociology, 12*(2), 119–154.
Sen, A. K. (2009). *The idea of justice* (pp. 1–34). Harvard University Press.
Shove, E., & Walker, G. (2010). Governing transitions in the sustainability of everyday life. *Research Policy, 39*(4), 471–476.
Sovacool, B. K., & Drupady, M. I. (2016). *Energy access, poverty, and development: The governance of small-scale renewable energy in developing Asia.* Ashgate Studies in Environmental Policy and Practice. Routledge, Taylor and Francis Group.
Stephenson, J., Barton, B., Carrington, G., Gnoth, D., Lawson, R., & Thorsnes, P. (2010). Energy cultures: A framework for understanding energy behaviours. *Energy Policy, 38*(10), 6120–6129.
Tennakoon, D. (2009). *Energy poverty: Estimating the level of energy poverty in Sri Lanka.* Report Prepared by Practical Action South Asia. http://www.practicalaction.org.uk/energy/south-asia/docs/region_south_asia/energy-poverty-in-sri-lanka-2008.pdf
Tracy, S. J., Geist-Martin, P., Putnam, L. L., & Mumby, D. K. (2013). Organizing ethnography and qualitative approaches. In *The SAGE handbook of*

organizational communication: Advances in theory, research, and methods (pp. 245–270). Sage.

United Nations Development Programme (UNDP). (2010). *Energy for a sustainable future: The secretary general's advisory group on energy and climate change* (Summary Report and Recommendations). UNDP, New York. www.un.org/chinese/millenniumgoals/pdf/AGECCsummaryreport%5B1%5D.pdf

Vikaspedia, India Development Gateway (InDG). Ministry of Electronics and Information Technology (MeitY). Government of India (GoI). Vikaspedia.in/InDG; home/energy/energy production/bioenergy/biogas. Accessed on 6 August 2016, 7.38 am IST.

Walker, G. (2014). The dynamics of energy demand: Change, rhythm and synchronicity. *Energy Research and Social Science, 1,* 49–55.

Watson, J., Byrne, R., Morgan Jones, M., Tsang, F., Opazo, J., Fry, C., & Castle-Clarke, C. (2012). What are the major barriers to increased use of modern energy services among the world's poorest people and are interventions to overcome these effective? *Collaboration for Environmental Evidence (CEE) Review, 11*(004), 1–91. www.environmentalevidence.org/SR11004.html

World Economic Forum. (2010). *Global agenda council reports.* Summaries of global agenda council discussions from the summit on the global agenda 2009. World Economic Forum. https://members.weforum.org/pdf/globalagenda2010.pdf

World Development Report. (2014). *Risk and opportunity: Managing risk for development* (pp. 1–362). World Bank. www.worldbank.org

Whitehead, L. T. (2005). *Basic classical ethnographic research methods—Secondary data analysis, fieldwork, observation/participant observation, and informal and semi-structured interviewing* (pp. 1–27) (Working Paper Series). Ethnographically Informed Community and Cultural Assessment Research Systems (EICCARS), Cultural Ecology of Health and Change (CEHC).

CHAPTER 2

Case Studies as an Immersive Approach for Unravelling Energy–Society Relations

2.1 Introduction

The section that unfolds hereafter is based upon one of the many critical foundations discussed in this text—*study of human affairs vis a vis energy consumption* (in terms of access to different nature of supplies and varied end uses). Varying typology of cases has been comprehensively presented along the lines of different subject areas. Different orientations, along with different research traditions, have been incorporated to sequentially produce an ensemble of completeness through illustration of facts, examination of phenomenon, drawl of inference, and gradually leading to triangulation through deduction of a hypothesis for each of the cases nested in a different socio-cultural domain. The cases have been extensively chosen for a comprehensive understanding of attributes of: a) variation in energy end use, b) co-variation of end use with access (causality), c) homogeneity and heterogeneity (in terms of access to energy, control over resources, distribution and re-distribution of resources, gains and losses in terms of social capital and other tangible benefits, and supply side versus demand side issues of energy), and d) for gainful insights into relationships.

A noteworthy feature of these case studies is their being exploratory, explanatory and descriptive. Each of these case studies is an empirical inquiry, in which focus is on a contemporary phenomenon within its real-life context and boundaries between phenomenon and its context are not

© The Author(s), under exclusive license to Springer Nature Singapore Pte Ltd. 2022
M. K. Singh, *Eradicating Energy Poverty*,
https://doi.org/10.1007/978-981-16-7073-2_2

clearly evident. The method was found suitable for studying energy poverty- a complex socio-economic and political phenomena. The distinguishing characteristics of the case study approach are hinged upon two contextual realities: (a) a contemporary phenomenon is to be examined in its existential context, and b) the epistemic boundaries between phenomenon (energy poverty) and context (spaces and cultures of consumption) are blurred as the context-specific foundations are yet to be built.

Each of these stories is placed in culturally alien context. The technology lacks acceptance. There is distrust in the 'local', and therefore, the local power structures control resource allocation. Information asymmetry in respect of any new technology, indigenous or alien, entails sustained and strong efforts towards trust building through active engagement as every new energy production system shall have its own gestation period in terms of immersing itself completely in different spaces and cultures of energy consumption. Therefore, the case studies span across: a) explanatory (seeking to answer questions that could explain the presumed causal links in real-life situations/interventions that are too complex) domain, b) exploratory (exploring situations where the policy or pilot intervention does not have a clear, single set of outcomes) domain, and c) descriptive (describing an intervention or a phenomenon and the real-life context in which it is happening, a contemporary event) domain (Yin, 2003).

There was an imperative to probe the phenomena with sufficient amount of vertical, penetrative insight for a 'grounded in'—understanding and conceptualization from a regional context and a mix of alternate perspectives. The case studies present glimpses of purposive sampling, iterative study design, and different approaches to a mixed system of analysis—ranging from caste energy nexus (Tayyabpur village, Bihar) to resource assessment potential for a comprehensive demand side management of rural energy demand (Mayabunder, Andaman and Nicobar Islands) through a story of social innovation at Bahadurpur biogas unit (Ropar, Punjab), energy croppers of the solar pump irrigators cooperative (Dhundhi village, Gujarat), and lastly, the story of experiential learning at the hands of a rural energy service company, Mera Gao Power (Lohati Pasai village, Uttar Pradesh).

An iterative approach was adopted to analyse field notes and interview transcripts on an ongoing basis for a singular (in situ understanding) as well as plural (cross-case understanding) of the phenomenon of energy poverty. Therefore, multiple cases were chosen in order to experience, explore, and explain: 1) a phenomenon and 2) different approaches to provide energy access in diverse regional settings as an ensemble of collective and creative engagements within different socio-cultural orders. There is a conscious attempt made to stay away from generalization that is primarily driven by the need for epistemological harmony (Stake, 1978).

2.2 Evidence-Based Policy (EBP) Paradigm for Fragile Ecosystems Calls for a Realistic Demand Side Management (DSM) of Energy Loads—Case Study from Andamans

2.2.1 General Ground Scenario: Demography, Socio-economic Structure, Power Generation, and Consumption Scenario in the Islands

Andaman and Nicobar Islands occupy a special place in the Indian union. These islands are home to rare species of flora and fauna apart from being strategically sensitive. These islands fall under a specific geo-climatic zone and physiographic division, apart from being a distinct politico-administrative unit (Fig. 2.18, Annexure A). Being ecologically fragile and sensitive, these islands are not similarly placed as other regions in terms of national priorities—a fact which makes these islands a less sought-after subject of study.

There are thirty-six inhabited islands in the long chain of islands: twenty-four in the Andaman group and twelve in the Nicobars. More than 90% of the land in the islands is under forest management (92% under forest cover). The decadal growth rate of population for the islands is 6.86%. The density of population is 46 persons per sq.km. as compared to the all-India density of 382. The different groups inhabiting the islands of Andamans can be classified into two distinct groups, viz. the aboriginals and the later settlers.

The aboriginals belong to the negrito racial stock with pigmy stature, dark complexion, wooly hair, and flat nose. They can be classified into three groups: (a) the Great Andamanese (or Coastal Andamanese), (b) the Jarawas, and (c) the Ongese. These aboriginals permeated the entire group of islands when the British had just arrived. They maintain their self-sufficient economy with the utterly ineffective productive technique-only because they utilized to the utmost all the available materials in the forest and in the coastal sea. The different communities that classify as later settlers are the Burmans, Karens, Bhantus, Mapillas, and the Madrasi refugees from Rangoon and East Pakistan (Sinha, 1952).

These communities earlier had a wide range of occupational possibilities, such as working as agricultural labourer in rich main fields, cultivating others land on half share of yield basis, working as a paid labourer for miscellaneous jobs, making boats, trading with paddy and rice on boats in off-seasons, sawing logs cultivating betel trees, and basketry works. The settler community is currently engaged in such activities as agriculture, vegetable growing, maintenance of orchards, fishing, livestock rearing, and poultry keeping. Apart from such engagements, the different categories are engaged at various levels with the government functioning as well.

Slowly, almost all settlement farmers took on secondary or subsidiary occupations. Household surveys have revealed that only 4% of the cultivating household rely solely on agriculture; the rest supplement their income by various means, chiefly plantations or kitchen gardens, casual labour, household trade, employment in other enterprises, generally government, household industry, and rearing of livestock. A sizable number also derives part of their income from the forest, as forest labour, or from forest fuel, raw materials for household crafts or sundry produce for household consumption (Ghosh, 1994).

2.2.1.1 Climate and Vegetation

For a place so close to the equator, temperatures in the Andaman and Nicobar Islands are moderate. With equable climatic conditions throughout the year, no altitude difference worth the mention and no significant change in the zones of latitude either, the Islands reflect with textbook precision the effect of geological composition on the pattern of native vegetation. The soil characteristics of the island are divided into five broad types, and it may be seen the types of vegetation approximate closely to them, falling also into a similar set of categories as shown in Table 2.1.

The mangrove forests, running along the coastline between high spring tide and mean sea level, around creeks, backwaters, and flat rocky shorts, form a distinct barrier of vegetation that is the first peculiarity of the Andaman forests to hit the eye (Dhingra, 2005).

Table 2.1 Soil and vegetation

Types of soil and terrain	Vegetation found	Village(s) displaying the soil and terrain features alongside vegetation typology
1. Damp marine alluvium, washed by the tides and saline, found at the coast and in creeks affected by tidal action, and the mouth of rivers and nallahs	Mangrove forest, the proximity to the sea and the salinity of the soil, decides the kind of species to be found Generally classified into three-proximal, middle, and distal zones	Profullyanagar
2. Alluvial land out of reach of salinity, along valleys and flat land at the base of hilly tracts, with deeply fertile sandy or clayey loam	Littoral forests and coconut palms where the soil is sandy textured; Giant evergreen canopy forests and cane breaks where it is clayey and deeply alluvial	
3. Low hilly slopes of a poor and hard sandstone or rubble formation and conglomerates, generally with immature soil	Moist deciduous forests with trees that shed their leaves periodically and occupy the well-drained lower slopes	Lataw
4. Hills consisting of yellow–brown clayey soil, of a micaceous sandstone formation, usually the hill caps of no great height	Evergreen tropical forests with three-storeyed canopies	Swadeshnagar

Source Author, 2016–2017; adopted from and based upon Dhingra (2005)

2.2.1.2 Current Energy Access Scenario

Due to the geographical and topographical peculiarities of these islands, including separation by sea over great distances, there is no single power grid for all the electrified islands. Instead, one power house caters independently to the power requirements of a given geographic area/island. The electricity department of the Andaman and Nicobar administration operates and maintains power generation, transmission, and distribution systems along with networks in these islands for providing electric power supply to the general public (Figs. 2.21–2.23, Annexure A). The present total installed capacity of generation of power is around 83.83 MW, with a peak demand of 44.7 MW.

Table 2.2 Category wise power consumption in the Islands

S.No.	Category	Energy in (MUs)	Consumer (%)	Consumption (%)
(a)	Domestic	150.56	82.50	54
(b)	Commercial	39.11	15.22	14.02
(c)	Industrial	18.93	0.46	6.78
(d)	Govt. and Bulk Supply	60.57	1.31	21.71
	Street Lights	9.70	0.51	3.47
	Grand Total	**278.87**	**100.00**	**100**

Source Author, cross-reference, JERC Tariff Order (2018)

The main sources of power are (a) own generation, (b) private purchase from Suryachakra Power Corporation Limited on PPA (power purchase agreement) basis, (c) hired power plants (HPP), and (d) solar plant (Figs. 2.24 and 2.25, Annexure A) of NTPC (National Thermal Power Corporation). The total cost of power purchase comes to about 216.72 crores INR. Over 95% of the power is generated from diesel-based generating stations as there is no other source of energy (Fig. 2.26, Annexure A).

The major component of the cost of supply is the cost of high sulphur diesel (HSD) and lubricants (142.87 crores INR). The major share of the total energy consumption is by the domestic consumers (Electricity Department, JERC, 2018). The category-wise details of consumption and the number of consumers in Andaman and Nicobar Islands are tabulated as below in Table 2.2.

The trajectory of growth of electric power supply in the islands during last 60 years is tabulated below (Electricity Department, 2012) in Table 2.3.

It is interesting to note that the per capita consumption of power is only 492 kWh as against the national average of 1075 kWh (provisional, end of 2015–2016, CEA, 2017). Based on the past trends for demand growth, the electricity department assumes a 5% growth in peak demand per annum. Projections have been made till the year 2021–2022 (CEA and Electricity Department, 2016f). An aggressive demand growth case has been considered in view of the increase in demand due to *envisaged capacity addition plan and availability of surplus power situation*. Demand growth over next 5 years is tabulated in Table 2.4.

The regulator's observation on the current energy supply scenario:

Table 2.3 The trajectory of growth of electricity generation in the Islands

Year	Power houses (nos.)	Total capacity (MW)	Generation (MU)	Per capita consumption (kWh)
1951	1	1.1	0.5	16
1961	1	1.1	1.6	20
1971	10	3.0	4.3	27
1981	16	7.5	10.8	41
1991	32	15.7	51.9	113
2001	34	44.0	118.6	250
2006	34	66.90	183.70	309
2008	41	68.50	200.60	385
2011	43	83.71	241.38	492

Source Electricity Department, Port Blair (2012)

Table 2.4 The projected growth of peak demand on an yearly basis

Time frame	Peak demand (MW)
2016–2017	38
2018–2019	43
2019–2020	45
2020–2021	47
2021–2022	50
2021–2022 (aggressive case)	62

Source Electricity Department, Andaman and Nicobar administration (2016)

In view of the socio-economic constraints of the people residing in the licensee area, the regulator feels that aligning the tariff with the average cost of supply would be unjust to the consumers. The electricity department by all means relies on localized generation and distribution as there is an absence of interconnecting grid. (JERC Tariff Order, 2018)

2.2.2 Familiarization with the Area of Study

The study was undertaken in the revenue villages of Lataw, Profullyanagar, and Swadeshnagar. The villages are situated along the Andaman trunk road that runs across these islands. The villages are located at 7 kms., 26 kms., 35 kms. from the district, and tehsil headquarters of Mayabunder, respectively (Fig. 2.19, Annexure A).

Lataw comprises primarily the Karens and the Ranchis (a mix of pre- and post-1942 group of settlers). These communities are engaged in such economic activities as fishing and casual labour. A large number of them are self-employed, local entrepreneurs running small businesses (retail). About 1–2% of the total population serve the local administration (engaged with the government). The nature of settlement is linear and dispersed.

Profullyanagar is an interior remote village. The community mix mostly comprises Bengalis and Ranchis, majority of them are post-1942 settlers (Dhingra, 2005). The village is scattered in the form of dense clusters radially on either side of the Andaman trunk road. Each cluster has a collection of five to six numbers of dwelling units. Major economic activity in this village is agriculture, the dominant food crop being Burmese rice, followed by cash crop of arecanut (betelnut). Banana plantation is common. Vegetables are grown in small, scattered patches as well.

Swadeshnagar is a large settlement comprising six wards. It has a linear but scattered settlement pattern. Individual dwelling units are located in isolation. Dense foliage is the hallmark of this revenue village. This is true for Profullyanagar as well. The community mix comprises predominantly of Benalis, Ranchis, and some Malyalis. Unlike Lataw, the nature of dwelling units is mostly mixed (kutcha and pucca, hollow brick and mortar) structure. Agriculture remains the main avocation of the residents. Paddy is the dominant food crop. Coconut, arecanut (betelnut), and banana are the major plantations. Some proportion of the population is also engaged in fishing. The lifestyle details of the villages are shown in Fig. 2.20, Annexure A.

2.2.3 Introduction to the Dataset

The captured dataset underlines the importance of anthropogenic dimension of any given energy system framework that ensures smooth societal functioning. *The anthropogenic (human) dimension refers to the rich mixture of cultural practices, social interactions, and choices that influence behaviour of individuals, social groups, functioning of formal and informal institutions while engaging with such critical technical inputs.* There are three broad sets of data.

Dataset A captures the business as usual scenario in these villages vis-à-vis the supply of power. It also reflects the expectations of the consumers with regard to scheduling of energy supply during any given time of day. It is broadly indicative of the time of usage of the energy supply. It reflects the realistic expectations of the consumers of energy.

Dataset B is reflective of the overall lifestyle of the communities. It indicates the general levels of socio-economic affluence in terms of ownership of electrical gadgets and their usage. The data reflects the actual power consumption on an average, on a daily basis by the communities (load profiles have been created based on actual usage of appliances during the day as declared by the respondents from the community mix). The pattern of ownership of lighting appliances and their respective use during the day is indicative of the general levels of awareness of the community towards measures of energy conservation and efficiency.

Dataset C highlights the *latent potential* for power generation in these rural energy ecosystems through tapping of the local natural resource base, primarily from biogas and solar. The actual qualitative and quantitative mapping of local demand for energy has been mapped through creation of baseline data in datasets A and B, respectively. This subsection essentially tries to assess whether the current demand for energy can be met through tapping of the local natural resource (biogas and solar), going even further to service futuristic demands in case the natural lifestyle undergoes a change indicating increased demand for energy.

A. Qualitative analysis: based on dataset A

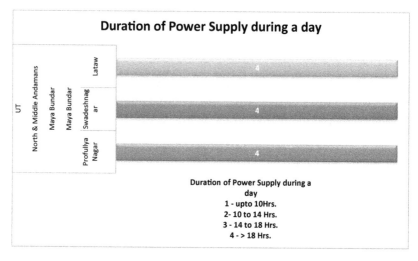

Fig. 2.1 Duration of power supply during a day (*Source* Author, 2016)

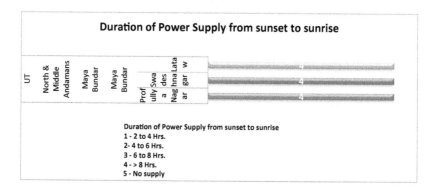

Fig. 2.2 Duration of power supply from sunset to sunrise (*Source* Author, 2016)

2 CASE STUDIES AS AN IMMERSIVE APPROACH ... 75

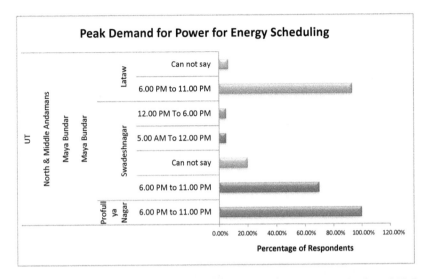

Fig. 2.3 Peak demand for power for energy scheduling (*Source* Author, 2016)

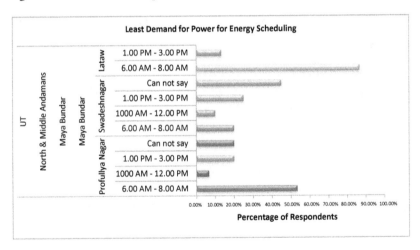

Fig. 2.4 Least demand for power for energy scheduling (*Source* Author, 2016)

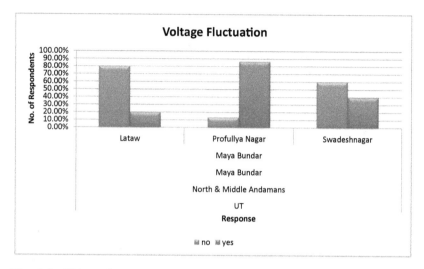

Fig. 2.5 Voltage fluctuation (*Source* Author, 2016)

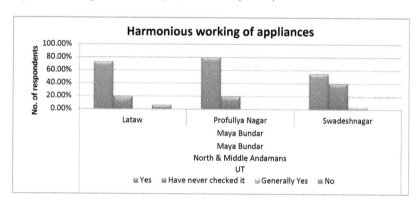

Fig. 2.6 Harmonious working of appliances (*Source* Author, 2016)

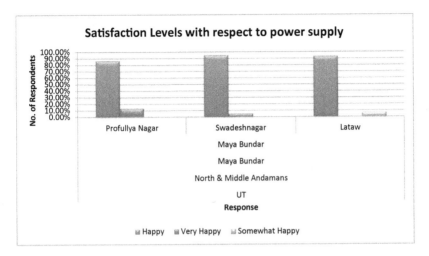

Fig. 2.7 Satisfaction levels with respect to power supply (*Source* Author, 2016)

2.2.4 Discussion, Analysis, and Interpretation of Datasets

The evidence collected is categorized in terms of qualitative (restricted to nominal and ordinal levels of measurement) and quantitative. The public utility (electricity department) is located too far and distant not being contiguous geographically to centres of consumption.

Understanding customer behaviour: as to (a) what they want, (b) how much they want, and (c) when do they want? of energy would be uneasy to comprehend, and practically not feasible in the current energy deployment and consumption scenario. The duration of power supply to these villages is more than 18 hours a day for a 24-hour cycle (Fig. 2.1). Various aspects of consumer response have been shown in the qualitative dataset in respect of the current HSD (high sulphur diesel)-based power generation system.

The quantity of power supplied during the time frame extending from sunrise (6.00 am) to sunset (6.00 pm) is depicted in Fig. 2.2. The supply on a daily basis, in this timeframe, on an average exceeds 8 hours. The response captured in favour of uninterrupted power supply during a 24-hour cycle is depicted in Fig. 2.3. In all the three villages, the response is absolute in terms of the evening time slot of 6.00 pm to 11.00 pm.

The response from Profullyanagar is an absolute 100% in favour of this time slot (Author, 2016). Such clarity in consumer demand can be of immense help in addressing peak demand needs. However, the responses assume a different form and proportion for the villages of Lataw and Swadeshnagar. The responses highlight two important facts: (a) there are three slots for peak demand in Swadeshnagar, and (b) there is one slot in favour of the 6.00 pm to 11.00 pm in Lataw.

B. **Quantitative analysis based on dataset B:**

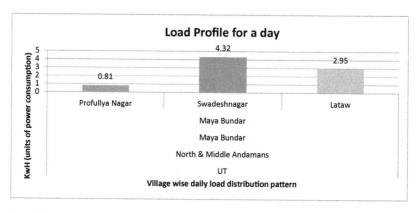

Fig. 2.8 Load profile for a day (*Source* Author, 2016)

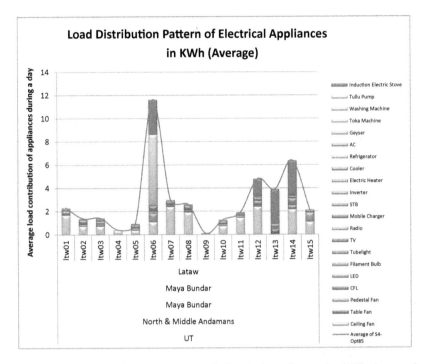

Fig. 2.9 Load distribution pattern of electrical appliances in kWh (average) (*Source* Author, 2016)

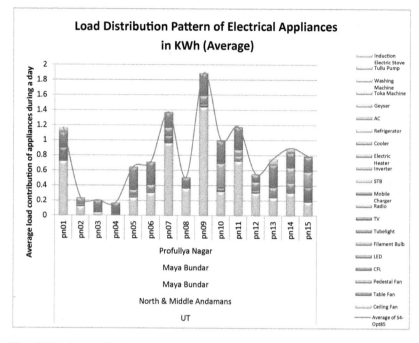

Fig. 2.10 Load distribuiton pattern of electrical appliances in kWh (average) (*Source* Author, 2016)

2 CASE STUDIES AS AN IMMERSIVE APPROACH ...   81

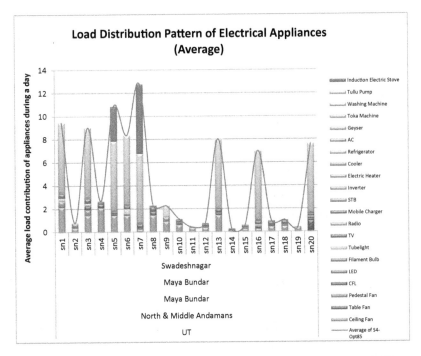

Fig. 2.11 Load distribution pattern of electrical appliances (average) (*Source* Author, 2016)

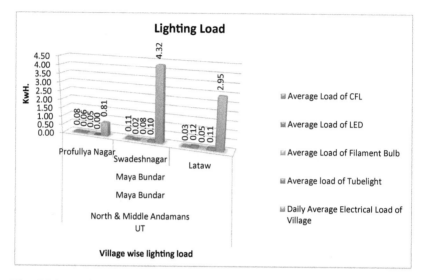

Fig. 2.12 Lighting load (*Source* Author, 2016)

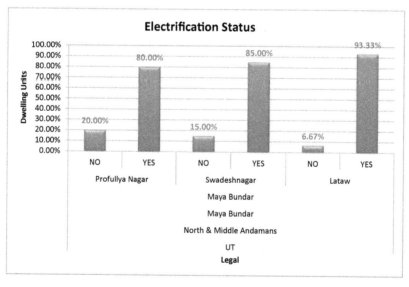

Fig. 2.13 Electrification status (*Source* Author, 2016)

C. **Assessment of renewable resource potential (solar and biogas) based on dataset C:**

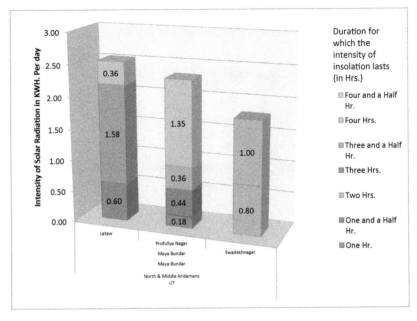

Fig. 2.14 Intensity of solar radiation and its duration (*Source* Author, 2016)

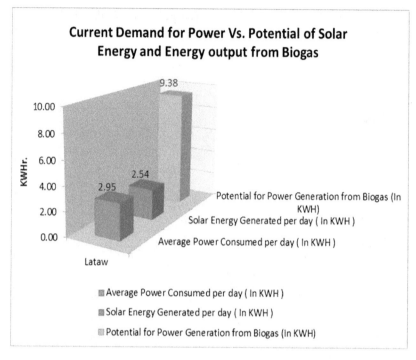

Fig. 2.15 Current demand for power vs. potential of solar energy and energy output from biogas (*Source* Author, 2016)

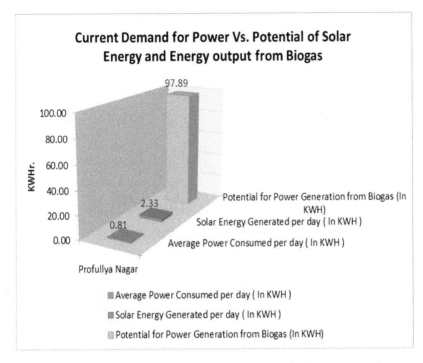

Fig. 2.16 Current demand for power vs. potential of solar energy and energy output from biogas (*Source* Author, 2016)

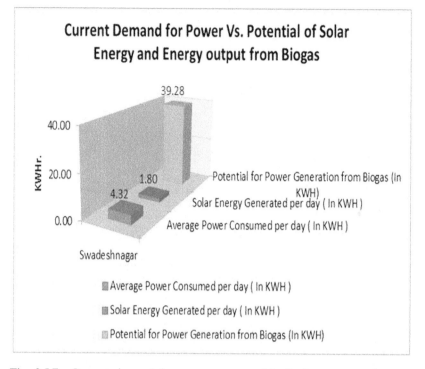

Fig. 2.17 Current demand for power vs. potential of solar energy and energy output from biogas (*Source* Author, 2016)

These timings are different. The responses have a connect with the gender/age/occupational structure of the respondents. Overall, there is a general tilt in favour of the 6.00 pm to 11.00 pm time slot. Another noteworthy feature is the degree of unawareness (information asymmetry) in terms of understanding of a technical subject of peak demand in terms of need for energy. The relative proportion of such customers (respondents) is about 20% Swadeshnagar and only 5% in Lataw.

The situation assumes complex proportions when the respondents were asked about scheduling power cuts (outages). The base load requirements vary considerably and are reflected in variable time slots during the day as shown in Fig. 2.4. There are 4 different time slots reported in the case of Profullyanagar and Swadeshnagar, and two distinct slots for Lataw. The following TOD (time of day) schedule for scheduling least demand for power in Profullyanagar is as follows: (a) a little more than 50% of the respondents are comfortable with the early morning (6.00 am–8.00 am) base load energy scheduling (base load), and (b) almost 20% are in favour of a time slot from 1.00 pm to 3.00 pm.

Coming to Swadeshnagar, the following facts are observed: (a) around 42–43% of the respondents expressed their general inability to respond, (b) around 26–27% opted for the time slot from 1.00 pm to 3.00 pm, whereas roughly 10–12% have opted for the 10.00 am to 12.00 pm slot, and (c) 20% of the respondents have expressed their willingness for the early morning slot from 6.00 am to 8.00 am. Overall, there is general agreement in both the villages towards scheduled power outages, though at different times of the day. The remaining respondents express their subtle resentment mixed with uneasiness towards the idea of power outage, even if scheduled as a 'choice-option'.

In Lataw, the responses are extremely pointed. Around 90% of the population is in favour of the two-hour early morning slot (6.00 am–8.00 am), whereas around 10% are in favour of the afternoon schedule from 1.00 pm to 3.00 pm. The aforesaid responses were in response to such queries as to the requirements of (1) diurnal power supply, (2) supply between sunrise and sunset, (3) energy scheduling for meeting peak, and (4) base load requirements.

The next set of queries pertain to (a) general quality of power supply (voltage fluctuations), (b) working of electrical appliances vis-à-vis quality of power supply, (c) general levels of satisfaction with regard to the duration (reliability), and (d) quality of power supply. Around 85% respondents from Profullyanagar claim that the voltage fluctuates during the day as depicted in Fig. 2.5. The response in favour of voltage fluctuations from Swadeshnagar and Lataw is 40 and 20%, respectively.

These responses were tested against the fact of harmonious working of all electrical appliances owned and operated within a dwelling unit as depicted in Fig. 2.6. In Lataw, more than 70% of the responses are in favour of efficient working of appliances which stands corroborated with the responses in favour of voltage fluctuation. Around 20% say that they never checked out on this issue (Author, 2016–2017). The situation is quite alarming and worrisome in the villages of Profullyanagar and Swadeshnagar. In Profullyanagar, 80% of the responses are in favour of efficient working of appliances, and 20% say that they have never verified this fact. Interestingly, there is a reporting of voltage fluctuation in this village (85% claim, Fig. 2.5), which is self-contradictory.

In Swadeshnagar, 55% of the respondents claim that the appliances work fine. 40% say that they never examined this fact, and 5% generally agree to the fact that the appliances work fine. However, the same respondents report voltage fluctuations (40% claim, Fig. 2.5). This response can be empirically tested against the average quantum of electrical load contributed by (1) the mixed use of electrical appliances, (b) percentages of formal connections to energy source, and (c) general levels of overall satisfaction with regard to the present power supply position.

There is a general consensus towards the fact of harmonious working of all electrical appliances with the current power supply scenario in all the villages. An attempt was made to assess happiness levels with regard to the power supply position on a scale ranging from (0-unhappy) to (4-extremely happy), through interspersed variations of (1-somewhat happy), (2-happy), and (3-very happy). There was no response in favour of the category labelled as (4) or (0). More than 85% of the respondents across the three villages were happy with the quality as well as duration of power supply being provided to them by the electricity department (Fig. 2.7).

The aforesaid qualitative data capture is extremely essential for an informed DSM (demand side management) for scheduling access to energy and managing local load demands on a daily basis. This qualitative assessment creates an avenue for constructive and active engagement, with an otherwise passive consumer of power. These response signals are strong in terms of the fact that they may or may not be in sync with the most modern designs of power systems in terms of power relays and energy management or could be dangerously disruptive to demand assessment and load forecasting. A mega, centralized, remotely situated power generation system is not designed to pick up these small, low priority signals, and therefore, the local utility is seen wanting for a robust DSM.

Another signal that the study picks up is primarily linked to the quality of response, especially with regard to (a) voltage fluctuations, (b) harmonious working of appliances, and (c) general levels of satisfaction. As the distance from the tehsil headquarter increases, the responses gradually became erratic and began to eventually decrepit. The reason can be attributed to such factors as (a) the loads being too remote and interior, (b) diffuse community engagements, (c) fractured political affiliations, and (c) feigned ignorance about energy access and use.

Nevertheless, the aforesaid descriptive data sheds light on several issues related to consumer demand profiling in such geographically alienated ecosystems (Author, 2016–2017). This study points to the significance of such data towards managing (a) real-time dynamic pricing of retail supply of power, (b) rationalization of tariff depending on the type and duration of usage of any electric appliance, (c) effective regulation of loads, and (d) at the same time bringing electricity closer to its consumers in social, cultural, and economic terms.

2.2.4.1 DSM Through Understanding Load Demand and Consumption Pattern Across a Dwelling Unit (Creation of Load Demand Curves)

The second part of the analysis is purely quantitative for an accurate assessment of daily consumption of electricity in a civil structure (dwelling unit). The diurnal average load demand across the villages of Profullyanagar, Swadeshnagar, and Lataw are 0.81, 4.32, and 2.95 kWh, respectively (Fig. 2.8). The load demand curve across individual dwelling units has been depicted in Figs. 2.9, 2.10, and 2.11. The curve running across the individual stack diagram (also known as sub-divided bar diagram) represents the average load consumption of an individual dwelling unit on a given day.

The stack diagram reflects the actual load contribution by an individual electrical appliance to the total load of the dwelling unit, based on its actual usage by the owner. In Swadeshnagar, the major contributors to the aggregate load are such appliances as ceiling fans, induction stoves, and refrigerators (Fig. 2.11).

On the other hand, in the case of Profullyanagar, the major contributors are such devices as ceiling fans and television sets. In the case of village Lataw, the observations are slightly different (Fig. 2.9). Induction stoves are a regular feature in every dwelling unit. Ceiling fans are the next prominent contributor. Almost every dwelling unit has a television set. LEDs, tube lights, and filament bulbs are the common source for lighting. Pedestal fan is also an occasional contributor to the aggregate load though used sparingly. The presence of refrigerators is limited.

An exclusive attempt was made to analyse the lighting load and its contribution to the aggregate load in all the three villages. The respective total electrical load contributed by individual lighting appliances has been depicted in Fig. 2.12. The lighting load for Profullyanagar is the highest (23.4%, CFL > LED > FB > TL), followed by Lataw (10.5%, LED > TL > FB > CFL), and lastly, Swadeshnagar (7.2%, CFL > TL > FB > LED). Compact fluorescent lamps and light emitting diodes dominate the lighting load. However, usage of tube lights and filament bulbs are equally common. This observation is linked to the traditional usage culture and faith in a product.

In spite of the fact the CFLs and LEDs are more energy efficient and are highly subsidized in terms of actual prices and in some cases actually provide free of cost, not many users could be found in these remote terrains, as the local market is still flooded by extremely cheap, locally available, traditional sources of electric lighting. Submersibles are normally not visible (Author, 2016–2017). What is even more conspicuous is the complete absence of water-based coolers. Almost all electricity connections are secured in terms of revenue being metered.

Of the three villages studied, Profullyanagar has 80% formal connections, Swadeshnagar has 85% formal connections, and Lataw bearing 93% formal connections (Fig. 2.13). The average monthly bill of a rural domestic customer in the studied villages ranges from 200 to 500 INR, being heavily subsidized. The actual cost of generation of one unit of power is around 26–27 INR against which, on an average, a consumer is billed 4.50–6.00 INR. The gap is the subsidy component (Author, 2016–2017: electricity department).

2.2.4.2 Assessment of Renewable Energy Resource Potential

The third phase of quantitative analysis pertains to the resource endowment potential for twin renewable sources of energy, viz. solar radiation and power generation potential from biogas generated principally from three forms of biodegradable waste: (a) human, (b) animal, and (c) waste from the kitchen of households.

2.2.4.3 Solar Resource Assessment Potential

The solar insolation potential was measured consistently for the 12/14-hour solar cycle for all the three villages (Fig. 2.14). The three-dimensional (3D) stack bar diagram shows the intensity of solar radiation in terms of units of electricity generated on the left side. On the extreme right side of the plot, the colour codes shown reflect the duration for which a given value of the solar radiation lasts. On the base of the 3D stack diagram, the villages have been shown. The respective solar insolation potential aggregated and averaged out for the entire duration of the field study comes to about 2.54, 2.33, and 1.80 kWh for Lataw, Profullyanagar, and Swadeshnagar, respectively (Fig. 2.14).

2.2.4.4 Biogas Resource Potential Assessed
The assessment of power generation from bio-methane-based generator sets has been calculated by making a detailed quantitative analysis of the waste typology from the different sources discussed above. The potential for power generation has been calculated on the basis of (*Buswell equation, 1952 and Banks, 2009*). Accordingly, the twin potential for generation of power has been assessed in respect of solar and biogas in respect of the three villages. The potential is placed against their actual aggregate loads. In the case of Lataw, on an average the actual daily aggregate load in terms of power consumption generated from HSD (conventional source) is 2.95 kWh (Fig. 2.15).

This load cannot be serviced by a solar-based grid alone (insolation capacity for power generation is 2.54 kWh). However, the current load can be serviced by a biogas-based power generation system (potential assessed to be 9.38 kWh).

Similarly, for Profullyanagar, on an average, the daily aggregate load in terms of power consumption works out to be 0.81 kWh (Fig. 2.16). This load can be serviced by a solar-based grid (insolation capacity for power generation is 2.33 kWh). However, the largest potential is held captive by a biogas-based power generation system (potential assessed to be 97.89 kWh).

Coming to the case of Swadeshnagar, the aggregate demand on an average for power based on actual consumption is 4.32 kWh. The current power demand cannot be met by tapping solar insolation potential alone, which has been assessed to be around 1.80 kWh. However, the power requirements of Swadeshnagar can be met through harnessing its biogas-based power generation potential which has been assessed to be around 39.28 kWh (Fig. 2.17). Further, in this geographic terrain, the quality of insolation is strongly intermittent in terms of intensity. The quality is erratic on account of local wind currents and frequent cloud cover. Therefore, in the absence of a battery-based energy storage system, solar energy-based power generation systems may not be a viable proposition at all, for these islands (Author, 2016–2017). ***Alternatively, biogas-based generation appears to hold great promise.***

2.2.5 Conclusion and Policy Implications

A careful examination, evaluation, and analysis of the data help us to understand the nature of demand that is strongly localized, hazily segregated, and extremely variable in terms of consumer behaviour. The data helps in evaluation of the local resource base and consequently assesses the potential of any renewable 'reserve' to unequivocally qualify as a 'potential resource' holding a promise to match current demand and also can cater to futuristic requirements. This evidence sheds light on the consumer tastes, preferences, and habits which must be studied at regular intervals, in order to ascertain demand fluctuation in terms of usage of electrical appliances.

However, one needs to carefully match the qualitative preferences against quantitative usage (in terms of load burden) for effectively scheduling an energy service as per exact TOD (time of day) requirements of any given consumer base. It may be extremely difficult to predict the duration of usage of an appliance, or a combination of types of appliances being run. Therefore, it becomes even more important to physically investigate the actual load and assess behavioural patterns of power consumption of an otherwise passive consumer. This shall help in better DSM and could also address some of the issues on the supply side as well.

Unless DSM is completely taken care of at the micro-level, a localized, on-site, decentralized, distributed power generation system shall remain an elusive dream. For any utility, irrespective of the generation system (based on any fuel type), this evidence could be of prime importance in order to take care of the power supply system in terms of effective energy management. Since the evidence strongly advocates the promotion of pico-scale, distributed, singular, and/or cluster-based renewable energy applications, it becomes imperative to take into account the ground truth in terms of the physical terrain characteristics and the local weather conditions which are as important as understanding the customer base.

The overall current scenario (evidence) presents a very strong case in favour of decentralized, biogas-based power generation systems coupled with pico-scale solar home lighting systems for catering to direct current (DC) loads in order to have a first-hand demonstration of technology that is primarily alien to the context. The otherwise established, HSD-based conventional power system shall stay as a permanent back-up plan. It cannot be permanently done away with; however, as the new energy system gets established, there can be an ideal thought of gradual roll-back of the conventional HSD-based power supply system. Therefore, the author presents a strong case in favour of a hybrid energy alloy model running on multiple fuels for re-energizing the rural, inhabited energy landscape of the Andaman archipelago on the basis of the gathered evidence (Chapter 3).

2.3 Annexure A: Case Study 2.1 (Andaman and Nicobar Islands)

See Figs. 2.18, 2.19, 2.20, 2.21, 2.22, 2.23, 2.24, 2.25, and 2.26.

94 M. K. SINGH

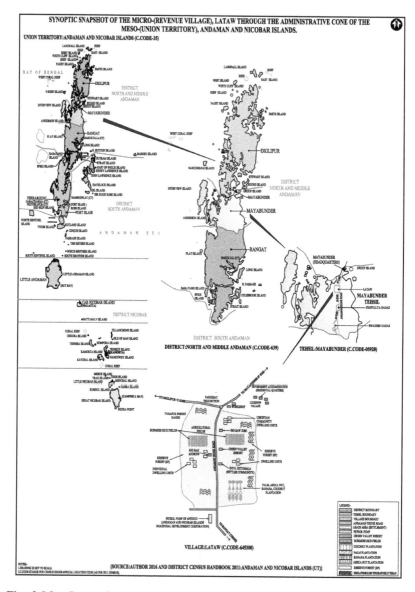

Fig. 2.18 Comprehensive snapshot of the villages: Lataw, Swadeshnagar and Profullyanagar through the administrative cone of the Meso-(UT)

2 CASE STUDIES AS AN IMMERSIVE APPROACH ... 95

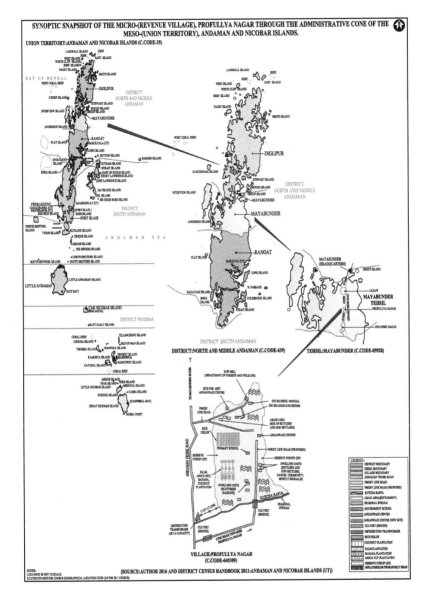

Fig. 2.18 (continued)

96 M. K. SINGH

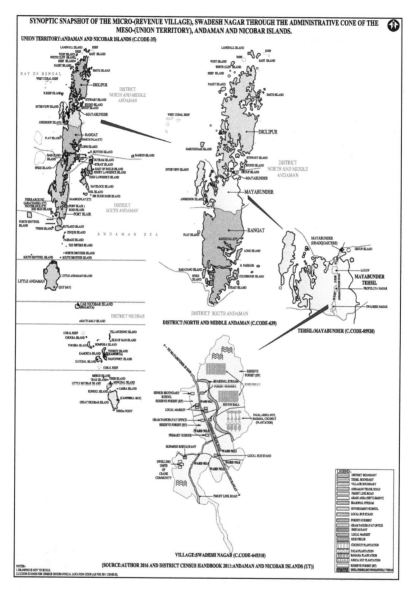

Fig. 2.18 (continued)

2 CASE STUDIES AS AN IMMERSIVE APPROACH ... 97

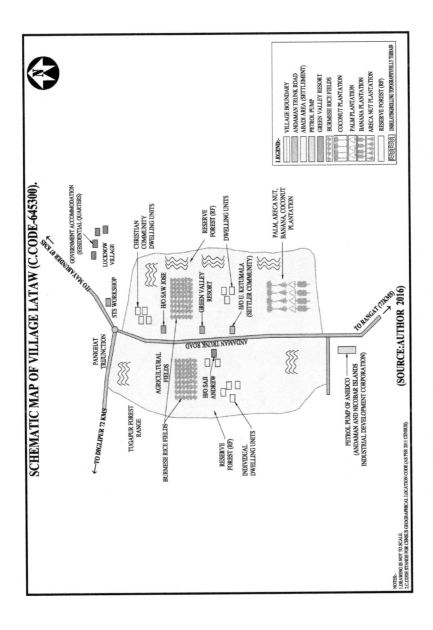

Fig. 2.19 Schematic map of Lataw, Swadeshnagar and Profullyanagar

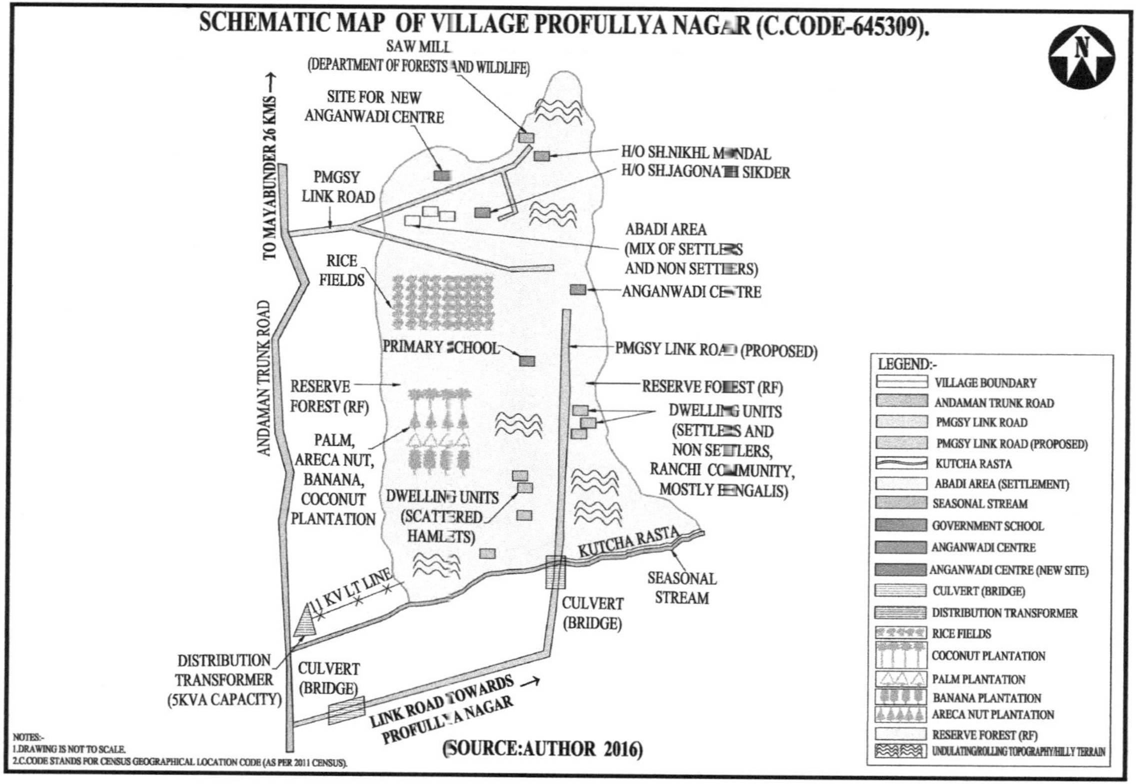

98 M. K. SINGH

Fig. 2.19 (continued)

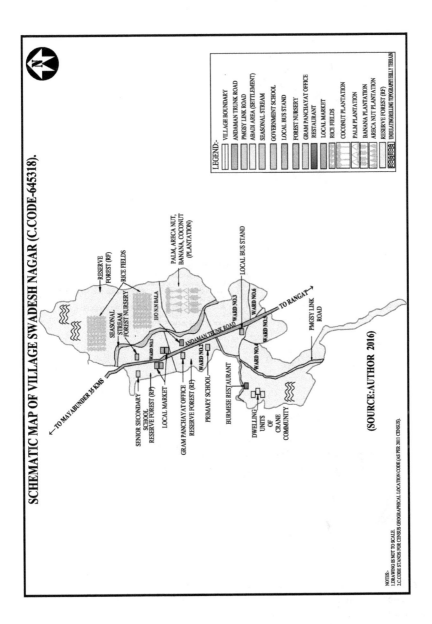

Fig. 2.19 (continued)

PHOTO MOSAICS OF GENERAL LIFE STYLE AND SOCIO-CULTURAL FEATURES

LATAW
1. ARECANUT AND COCONUT PALMS
2. TYPICAL DWELLING UNIT
3. DUTCH FENCING STRUCTURE
4. TYPICAL NICOBARI HUT
5. BACK WATERS (FISHING BOATS IN THE INSET), HODI (TRADITIONAL BOAT)
6. HOLLOW BRICK CIVIL STRUCTURE UNDER CONSTRUCTION
7. COMMUNITY KITCHEN (BIOMASS BEING USED FOR COOKING)
8. COMPOSITE COOK STOVE

SWADESHNAGAR
1. DENSE, GRADED FOLIAGE PROFILE
2. COCONUT, ARECANUT AND BANANA PLANTATION
3. ARECANUTS BEING DRIED ON A TRADITIONAL MAT MADE OF PALM LEAVES
4. DWELLING UNIT
5. PRIVATE WATER POND (TYPICAL FEATURE IN THE VILLAGE)
6. KITCHEN SHED (COOKING IN PROGRESS)
7. COOK STOVE IN USE (MIX OF FUEL WOOD)

PROFULLYANAGAR
1. GEO-CULTURAL SETTING WITH FOLIAGE PROFILE
2. DWELLING UNIT WITH OCCUPANT
3. INTERIOR OF A DWELLING UNIT
4. STACKS OF FIRE WOOD FOR USE AS COOKING FUEL
5. PIDHI ON MUD-PLASTERED FLOOR (FOR SITTING)
6. LIQUOR BOTTLE USED AS A LIGHTING LAMP, (DHIBRI) 500 ML CAPACITY
7. UTENSILS
8. COOK STOVES (BENGALI CHULLAH AND RANCHI CHULLAH

(SOURCE: AUTHOR, 2016)

Fig. 2.20 Ultimate recipients of the power supplied. The photo mosaics reflect the general life style of the residents in the three villages of Lataw, Swadeshnagar and Profullyanagar (*Source* Author, 2016)

2 CASE STUDIES AS AN IMMERSIVE APPROACH ... 101

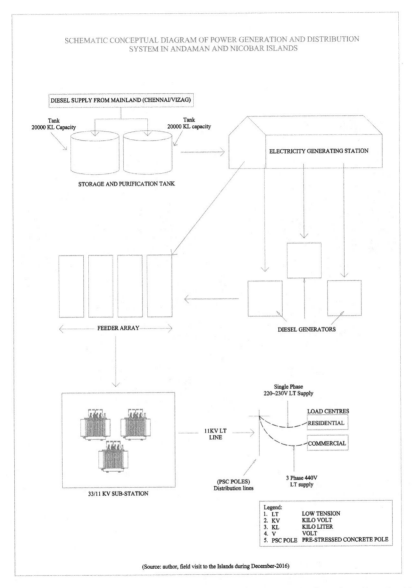

Fig. 2.21 Schematic snapshot of the contemporary HSD based conventional power supply system in Andaman and Nicobar Islands

Fig. 2.22 Oldest power sub-station at Phoenix Bay, in Port Blair (*Source* Author, 2016)

2 CASE STUDIES AS AN IMMERSIVE APPROACH ...   103

b

1. STORAGE AND PURIFICATION OF DIESEL
2. GENERATOR SETS
3. COOLING STATIONS
4. TIE LINES AND GANGWAYS
5. COOLING TANK
6. DOCK IN THE BACKDROP FOR DIESEL IMPORT FROM THE MAINLAND

(SOURCE: AUTHOR, 2016)

Fig. 2.23 Storage, purification and power generation process (*Source* Author, 2016)

1. ENERGY MANAGEMENT CENTRE
2,3,4. ARRAY OF SOLAR PANELS (FIXED TO THE GROUND)
   NON-CONVENTION POWER GENERATION SYSTEM GRID CONNECTED, SOLAR PV GENERATION SYSTEM (5 MW CAPACITY)
   COURTESY : (NATIONAL THERMAL POWER CORPORATION, NTPC)

(SOURCE: AUTHOR, 2016)

Fig. 2.24 5 MW capacity SPP of NTPC in Port Blair (*Source* Author, 2016)

1. POWER SUB-STATION
2. DISTRIBUTION SET UP
3. TRANSFORMER
4. INVERTOR (EXTERIOR)
5. INVERTOR (INTERIOR VIEW)
   (THE POWER GENERATED IS FED INTO DEDICATED SOLAR FEEDERS AT GHARACHARMA SUBSTATION)

(SOURCE: AUTHOR, 2016)

Fig. 2.25 Transmission set-up of solar power generated (*Source* Author, 2016)

106 M. K. SINGH

1. ARRAY OF FEEDERS
2. SOLAR FEEDERS
3. DISTRIBUTION LINES

FEEDERS SUPPLYING POWER TO DIFFERENT AREAS IN PORTBLAIR

(SOURCE: AUTHOR, 2016)

Fig. 2.26 Power sub-station with feeders transmitting power from conventional and non-conventional sources of generation

REFERENCES

Central Electricity Authority. (2016a). *Draft national electricity plan (generation)* (Vol. 1, pp. 1.1–6.33). Ministry of Power, Government of India.

Central Electricity Authority. (2016b). *Draft national electricity plan (transmission)* (Vol. 2, pp. 1.1–3.22). Ministry of Power, Government of India.

Central Electricity Authority. (2017). *Growth of electricity sector in India from 1947–2017* (pp. 1–86). Ministry of Power, Government of India.

Dhingra, K. (2005). *The Andaman and Nicobar Islands in the 20th century, a gazetteer*. Oxford University Press.

Electricity Department, Andaman and Nicobar Administration, Port Blair. (2008). *Guidelines for power generation through new and renewable energy sources in Andaman and Nicobar Islands* (pp. 1–21).

Electricity Department, Andaman and Nicobar administration, Port Blair. (2012). *Policy for power generation through new and renewable energy sources in Andaman and Nicobar Islands* (pp. 1–19).

Electricity Department, Andaman and Nicobar Administration, Port Blair. (2016). *Study for integration of renewable energy and other products in Andaman and Nicobar Islands* (pp. 1–49).

Ghosh, A. (1994). *A study on the development strategy for the Andaman and Nicobar Islands*. Classical Publishing Company (cross reference, Dhingra, K, p. 210).

Joint Electricity Regulatory Commission (JERC). (2018). *Determination of retail supply tariff for FY 2018–19 for electricity department, Andaman and Nicobar administration* (Petition No. 248/2017, pp. 1–78).

Kumar, M. (2016 and 2017). *Field visits undertaken in the Andaman and Nicobar Islands*.

Sinha, C. S. (1952). Resettlement of East Pakistan refugees in Andaman Islands, report on survey of further possibilities of resettlement: January–May 1952, Government of West Bengal, Regional Centre, Anthropological Survey of India, Port Blair, Acc. No. 6022/41, pp. 1–39.

2.4 THE STORY OF SOLAR PUMP IRRIGATORS' COOPERATIVE ENTERPRISE (SPICE), FROM A VILLAGE: DHUNDI, GUJARAT

2.4.1 Introduction

The IWMI-TATA water policy programme (ITP) was launched in the year 2000 as a co-equal partnership between IWMI, Colombo, and Sir Ratan Tata Trust (SRTT), Mumbai. The focus areas of this collaborative collective were sustainable groundwater management, water scarcity, and rural poverty, with an overarching theme centred around water resources management. These projects were funded with support from IWMI, Tata trusts, CGIAR programme on water, land and ecosystems (WLE), and CCAFS. IWMI-TATA, Anand, and its partner institutions have been engaged ever since, promoting solar irrigation pumps (SIPs) amongst Gujarat farmers by creating a cooperative or a farmer producer company to sell their surplus solar power to the grid (a public utility) at a remunerative price. IWMI, Anand, under IWMI-TATA water policy programme submitted a proposal to MGVCL regarding solar irrigation pumps for 'off-grid' farmers. The said proposal was approved by Gujarat Urja Vikas Nigam Limited (GUVNL). The interested farmers in the village Dhundi, Thasra taluka, Kheda district formed a cooperative society named Dhundi Saur Urja Utpadak Sahakari Mandali (DSUUSM). The members of this cooperative society were assisted by IWMI, Anand, to procure solar photovoltaic (SPV) irrigation pumps.

2.4.1.1   Claims of the Project Proponent

> The Dhundi Solar Pump Irrigators' Cooperative Enterprise (SPICE) provides the proof of concept for promoting solar power as a remunerative crop (SPaRC). We argue that SPaRC presents the best chance of taming western India's groundwater anarchy, of improving the finances of power distribution companies, of curtailing the carbon footprint of our agriculture and of creating a new, risk-free source of serious cash income for India's farmers. (Shah et al., 2016)

2.4.1.2   Envisaged Outcome
DISCOMs and farmers (both off-grid and on-grid) can mutually benefit by promoting and adopting solar irrigation pumps respectively, provided

the scheme strikes a balance between the interests and priorities of the two stakeholders.

2.4.2 Dhundi Village—The Action Arena

The revenue village of Dhundi is located in Thasra taluka of Kheda district, in the state of Gujarat (Fig. 2.27, Annexure B). The village has a total population of around 1500 (census 2011, https://villageinfo.in/gujarat/kheda/thasra/dhundi.html). There are 309 households in the village. The total area of the village is about 181.82 hectares, with a total of 250 farmers in the entire village. The dominant religion is Hinduism, and the dominant caste being Kshatriyas (rajputs) with such surnames as Parmars, Solankis, Darbars, and Chavdas. The village has a majority population engaged in agriculture. Members from about four to five families are employed with the Indian Railways. Around 35 to 40 numbers of persons are engaged with the private sector functioning as either security personnel or cab/lorry drivers.

Apart from these avocations, a large section of the working population is engaged as daily wage casual labourers under MGNREGS. Some of them also work as casual mill hands (dihadidaars) in the neighbouring villages. Agriculture is the mainstay of the village economy and the most important source of livelihood. The size of land holdings ranges from half a bigha (one bigha is equivalent to 5/8 acres or 0.25 hectares) to about eight to ten bighas of land. The major crops that are grown in the village are rice (during monsoons), wheat (during winters), tomatoes, and red millet (Amaranthus; rajagra: local name), also known as 'ramdana' in Hindi. Vegetables are also grown in sizable proportions of cultivable land (Fig. 2.28, Annexure B).

2.4.2.1 The SPICE Narrative Through Its Curator

Pravinbhai Punjabhai Parmar is the single point of contact for a general tour of Dhundi, as he happens to be the 'MANTRI' (secretary) of the 'mandali', the solar pump irrigators' cooperative enterprise (SPICE) or (DSUUSM). 'Once chosen by a popular choice, the position is almost permanent, says Pravin, nonchalantly'.

Pravinbhai Parmar has an individual landholding measuring 5 bighas (1 bigha = 2100 square yards approximately). He grows rice, wheat, red millet, tomato, and bajra during a calendar year. The water level normally stays around 40 feet below ground level (bgl); however, it further declines to about 50 feet during peak summers. He spent around 15,000 INR for boring, and thereafter, he installed a diesel pump (10 HP for 4 inches of bore diameter) for irrigating his field in 2007. For irrigating one bigha of land, around 5 litres of diesel would be required per day. The unit cost of diesel in 2007 was 40 INR, which was purchased from the neighbouring village of Dakor. Pravinbhai says that from a bigha of land the yield is around 50–60 *mann** (1 mann = 20 kg) of rice, about 40 mann of wheat, 300 crates of tomatoes (1 crate is equal to 26 kg), and around 35–40 mann of bajra in one calendar year (agricultural year).

He did not have a conventional agricultural connection from the state utility, as he did not have clear title of his land in his exclusive possession as reflected in the revenue record. On being asked about the genesis of this idea and the conception of the project, he narrated the background of this project. There were two social organizations working in the village. One of them was exclusively concerned with tree plantation on 'gauchar land' (grazing land) with the help of the locals in Dhundi. This work was taken up under the erstwhile national rural employment guarantee scheme (NREGS). The active partner for the plantation project was foundation for ecological security (FES).

Pravinbhai worked as NREGA mate under this scheme in close association with FES. The other organization was the international water management institute (IWMI). It was IWMI which collaborated with FES which mooted the novel idea of use of solar energy for irrigation in Dhundi during 2015. Pravinbhai's contract as NREGS mate was about to end. The idea of an alternate source of irrigation that runs on a non-conventional source of energy was going to be difficult, and therefore, to sell the idea to the locals (the community) was not going to be easy by any means. FES had the only option to bank upon the rapport it had built with Pravinbhai. Therefore, it was Pravinbhai who was convinced first to believe in this novel method of pumping by harnessing solar energy.

Dhundi and Pravinbhai, thus, became natural choices for IWMI-FES to test their fortunes with a technology that was to be demonstrated as a pilot. The two organizations approached around 50–60 farmers in the village; however, only 5–6 farmers were interested. The cooperative consisted of 6 farmers to begin with. As on date, it has a total of nine farmers as its members, says Pravinbhai.

The details of the members of the DSUUSM are depicted in the Table 2.5 (Courtesy: Sh. H. V. Shah, nodal officer for solar interventions, Madhya Gujarat Vij Company Limited (MGVCL).

Table 2.5 Details of the capacity of the solar plant and the owner cum consumer

S. No.	Name of system owner/captive users	Survey no., land area, village	Capacity (kW)
1.	Pravinbhai Punjabhai Parmar	88, .925 Acre, Dhundi	8
2.	Kiritbhai Budhabhai Solanki	167, 1.35 Acres, Dhundi	8
3.	Ramabhai Salambhai Chavda	243/2, 1.025 Acres, Dhundi	8
4.	Udabhai Vagjibhai Chavda	405-3, 0.55 Acres, Dhundi	10.8
5.	Laxmanbhai Savjibhai Parmar	407-1, 1.975 Acres, Thasra	10.8
6.	Fudabhai Savjibhai Parmar	175, 1.2 Acres, Jalanagar	10.8
7.	Parmar Bhagvanbhai Bhemabhai	156, 1 Acres Dhubdi	5
8.	Chavda Govindbhai Parvatbhai	150-P3, 1.63 Acres, Dhundi	5
9.	Chavda Hathibhai Mangalbhai	239-P, 0.5 Acres, Dhundi	5
10.	**Total**		71.4

Source Fig. 2.30, Annexure B; MGVCL, RE division, Vadodara

2.4.2.2 DSUUSM Becomes a Reality

In its first general meeting dated the 9 January 2016, the name of the society (mandali) was proposed and accepted. Thereafter, the following definitions were accepted: (a) 'mandali' meant DSSUUSM, (b) 'units' meant electricity units measured in kilo-watt hour (kWh), (c) 'member' meant the member of the said mandali, (d) 'general meeting' meant member of the said mandali, (e) 'evacuation point' meant the point at which the pooled-in surplus power of the members of the mandali is injected into the grid of MGVCL, and (f) 'mandali control room' meant the room where all the energy meters were installed for metering and recording the energy supplied by each farmer and also energy sold by the mandali to MGVCL (Figs. 2.31 and 2.32, Annexure B).

The objectives of the mandali are as follows: (a) the **fundamental objective** of the mandali shall be to *maximize the sale of power* by pooling in surplus power, (b) mandali would carry out activities to promote solar powered irrigation, (c) mandali would promote such water and power saving technologies as drip irrigation that shall translate into higher income for members, and (d) mandali would experiment with different types of crops and farming practices not just to increase income from agriculture *but also to increase the amount of surplus power* that is to be evacuated.

2.4.2.3 Snapshot of Dhundi Project: The Role of the Local, the Panchayat of Dhundi Village (as Recorded During Discussions)

The project right from the phase of conception, design, and commissioning witnessed two panchayats. There was a phase of transition. The project witnessed a phase of local elections to the gram panchayat in December 2016. The new panchayat was in office the next month. The strength of the panchayat is eight. Being a Rajput community dominated village, the panchayat is given a mix of Solankis, Parmars, and Darbars. The discussions regarding the solar-based irrigation pumping system were on since May 2015. The initial installation of pumps for the first group was completed in December 2015. However, the final commissioning of the project was done during May 2016. The commissioning was post-paper clearances and signing of power purchase agreement (PPA) with the state utility (MGVCL). The old and the new panchayat members were extremely open and receptive to this alternative method of irrigation. The panchayat communicated its consent to the project in writing, promising facilitation in terms of laying cables, cross-over of lines, laying down of transformers, passage through government (GAUCHAR: common grazing land) land as well as private land parcels.

2.4.2.4 Policy Support from the State-Tripartite Agreement for Installation of Solar Agriculture Pumping System

The government of Gujarat (GoG) notified the solar policy notified by the department of energy and petrochemicals. The policy announced a scheme of providing solar agriculture pumping systems to the farmers of the state. The objective of this notification was to promote energy savings in the agriculture sector and for generating awareness about solar energy usage (Gujarat Solar Power Policy, 2015). The implementation of this scheme was entrusted to Gujarat Urja Vikas Nigam Limited (GUVNL) and its subsidiary companies.

The solar agricultural pumping system was to be procured through suppliers, through a process of tendering. It necessitated the execution of a tripartite agreement between the power distribution company, the applicant/farmer, and the supplier/contractor. The DISCOM (state utility, MGVCL in this case) became the first party, the farmer/landowner/beneficiary (as detailed in the Table 2.5) was the second party, and the contractor/supplier (Shaswat Cleantech Private Limited) became the third party.

2.4.3 De-construction of Events and the Outcomes

IWMI and foundation for ecological security (FES) were already engaged in land improvement, preservation, and water conservation activities in the village. Both the organizations have adjacent offices in Anand. Since Pravinbhai was already working with them, it was through him the farmers were approached. It can be inferred that the farmers were approached directly without the involvement of the local panchayat. The initial project proposal therefore comprised six willing farmers. The proposal with a capacity cap of 100 kW had a timeline of two years, which was extended once on account of the proposed expansion of the society, but finally ended in May 2018. The rate at which the PPA was signed with the first group was 4.63 INR/kWh. With the second group, the PPA was done at 3.24 INR/unit.

However, both the groups get green energy bonus (@1.25 INR/unit) and groundwater conservation bonus (@1.25 INR/unit). This amounts to 7.13 INR/kWh to the first group and 5.74 INR/kWh to the fresh batch of three farmers. Interestingly, this notional incentive has a time frame of two years only. So, the first group gets 4.63 INR/unit for the remaining 23-year period and the late comers get 3.24 INR/unit for the remaining period of their PPA with MGVCL. The farmers have surrendered their rights for a conventional power-based agricultural connection. The new group began its power evacuation from August 2017 (Fig. 2.29, Annexure B). Coming to the role of Gujarat energy research and management institute (GERMI) and Gujarat energy development agency, it appears that the involvement of the former was in the form of technical support and there was no clarity as to the role of the latter in the capacity of the state nodal agency (SNA). GERMI is largely involved in training and skill development programmes across the energy sector.

GEDA being the state nodal agency (SNA) issued a registration certificate in respect of the application (SPPR&D26052016-348) of the cooperative. The major role for site appraisal and installation was the responsibility of the contractor/supplier, M/S Shaswat cleantech private limited (the third party and the signatory to the tripartite agreement discussed above). The office of the chief electrical inspector (CEI) is the sole authority for inspection of entire installation and certification of technical and regulatory conformity of the 'proposed system' to the norms of the central and state regulator (CERC and GERC), along with the grid supply codes and specifications. Subject to the evaluation of the technical team of the CEI, commissioning of the project was formally declared.

On being specifically asked about the nature of role of the contractor/supplier, Pravinbhai elaborated that the contractor was under no obligation to offer technical support. Hand Holding to a farmer was only for some initial days till he/she attained familiarity with the system. *'In case a technical glitch is encountered, a call is given to the supplier and the response time normally is 10–15 days on an average; remarks Pravinbhai'*. The contractor/supplier is based in Ahmedabad (there is no local support whatsoever).

2.4.4 *Commercial Interest of the Member Farmer*

The current rate of sale of water is 250 INR per bigha. It is not linked to the hours of supply. It is rather linked to the number of times irrigation services are required by a needy farmer. So, every time you require water, you shell out 250 INR, remarks Pravinbhai. This earning is the personal earning of an individual farmer by way of commercial sale of water. Thus, a farmer has three major sources of income: (a) income from sale of water, (b) income from sale of surplus power being evacuated during the day to the state utility, and (c) income from sale of agricultural produce.

2.4.5 *Technical Issues Related to Discharge*

On being specifically asked about the quantity of discharge from the pump throughout the day, it was reported that the discharge is less during mornings and evenings, but remains good and steady once the sun is out. However, the farmers pleaded ignorance about specific values and variations throughout the day in terms of litres per minute (lpm). The maximum discharge on a given clear sunny day is about 800 lpm, says Mr. Mitesh Prajapati, junior engineer (MGVCL).

2.4.6 Analysis and Discussion

The onslaught of technology creates social disruption. Concerns of the state utility (in terms of forced procurement and on-grid evacuation) may nullify the short- and long-term incentives linked to demonstration projects. The Dhundi action arena remains isolated and is now left on its own to bear the socio-economic cost of an alternate technology in the form of solar energy-driven irrigation pumps. The policy 'proposed' by interested actors did not have the sufficient thrust to see the light of the day to push the entire farming community in Dhundi.

2.4.6.1 The Operative Solar-Based Irrigation Policy Dose

Before a catharsis of the social order is attempted along with the techno-economic surgery, it is pertinent to highlight the salient features of the solar power policy of the state of Gujarat (G.R.NO.SLR-11-2015-2442-B). Section (9.7) of the said policy deals with agriculture solar pumps. The following are the excerpts: 9.7.1: Gujarat has considerable deployment of irrigation pump sets. Taking this into consideration, the state government in collaboration with the central government/mnre/mop/multilateral agencies will undertake measures to provide solar powered pump sets through subsidy support. 9.7.2: In case of surplus power generation from the solar pump sets, the distribution companies may buy this surplus solar energy at average power purchase cost (APPC) rate of the year in which the solar pump set is commissioned. 9.7.3: The state government will launch schemes determining the subsidy amount and the individual as well as total capacity of the solar irrigation pump sets from time to time. 9.7.4: The solar energy generated by the irrigation pump sets shall be credited towards the Discom's renewable purchase obligation (RPO)'.

2.4.7 Interpreting the Policy Content, Relational Dynamics Between the Involved Institutions and Actors

The case is clear. There is a policy design. This is a broad suggestive indication about deployment of solar energy to drive irrigation pump sets. The interested actors arrive at the scene to create an administrative cum procedural design for execution of this policy intent. On a plain reading of the policy text (the provisions embedded in the policy design), the broad indication for promotion of an alternate irrigation system driven by means of a renewable energy source is clear (Fig. 2.38, Annexure B).

2.4.7.1 The Demonstration Project Remains at a Secluded Distance

However, the interested actors lay down the entire justification (in the form of statements of objects and reasons) for a comprehensive solar irrigation policy (proposal) for the state of Gujarat. The contents of the proposal have been discussed in detail earlier as indicated by (TATA-IWMI), the interested actors.

2.4.7.2 Socio-political Structure

At this juncture, it becomes imperative to re-visit the socio-economic and the political order in the proposed action arena, the revenue village of Dhundi. The village comprises Kshatriyas (Chavdas, Parmars, Solankis and Darbars). There is a nine-member gram panchayat. The sarpanch is Sh. Parmararvind bhai samant bhai. There are five females (solankishantaben vijaybhai, parmarbaxaben pravinbhai, chavda sitabenmela bhai, chavda rewabendasrathbhai, and senva manibenbabbubhai) and three male members (parmar mangal bhai shankarbhai, parmar dhurabhai ramanbhai, and parmar arvindbhai chaganbhai). There is a single female member from a scheduled caste (Senvamaniben babbubhai). The panchayat is dominated by parmars, followed by Chavdas and Solankis of the Kshatriya community.

2.4.7.3 Socio-economic Structure Prior to the Initiative

There are only two dwelling units belonging to the scheduled caste category. There are about 950–1000 voters in the village. The gender ratio of males to females is 60:40. There was an existent functional order (occupational structure) described as 40 (taxi drivers and security guards)/1500 (total population), 10 (railway employees)/1500, 250 (farmers)/1500, 500 (dihadidaars plus MGNREGS workers)/1500, 100 (school-going children)/1500, plus remaining (senior citizens and others).

2.4.7.4 Evidence of Disruption of the Social, Economic, and the Political

What does the new technology implant do to a natural socio-economic order? It creates an exception, a set of preferred 'policy recipients'!

The new socio-economic order amongst the farming class is: $6/250$ (the first group of farmers who consented), followed by 3 (the late consenters)$/250$. Mathematically, this socio-economic disruption can be expressed as: $(6 + 3)/250$. And, for the community as a whole, the fraction could be: $1500 - [6 + 3/250]$. Earlier, in the village, the energy neighbourhood consisted of: (a) farming community in general, and rural, domestic conventional connections.

However, post solar-based technology intervention, the composition of the energy neighbourhood changes into: (a) grid-connected (conventional agricultural connections) farmers, (b) off-grid farmers, (c) diesel-based pump users, (d) solar pump users, and (e) domestic conventional power users. The nascent genre is referred to as the 'energy croppers' with a sense of pride! The policy recipients (the farming community) get fragmented. In terms of the local political power structures, a formal solar irrigation-based cooperative is created.

SPICE/DSUUSM becomes a formal reality. A new power centre assumes shape, the 'mandali' of solar pump irrigators. The memorandum of association of SPICE has been discussed in detail in the text (supra-) . Though the mandali remains a democratic body by and large, its functional mandate is 'commercial', and in contravention to the terms and conditions established by the buyer/client (MGVCL). The society further is a congregation of croppers, and energy croppers, energy producers and sellers (within the community and otherwise), which is non-cohesive in nature.

It is important to discuss the tripartite agreement in terms of the role of the technology partner, the third party to the agreement. Though the expenditure for operation and maintenance was to be done by individual farmers and the group as a collective, the responsibility of the third party fizzles gradually once the system is installed, tested, and declared formally as commissioned by the chief electrical inspector's office. The technology partner is not 'local' and the turn-around time taken to address a technological grievance is fairly large (refer to the interactive section supra-).

The policy dynamics in Dhundi is myopic and limited in scope and purpose in terms of: (a) failure to recognize pathways to facilitate an energy transition, (b) capacity building of energy croppers, (c) not maintaining a distinction between a core activity and a peripheral activity of a rural farmer, (d) failing to take into account the fact of disruption of social order due to 'enabled migration' to an off-grid system that results in a 'technological lock-in', and (e) strongly promoting vested, self, individual, exploitative commercial interests by tinkering with an agrarian mandate. It is to be seen later whether an energy cropper feeds his need or greed by means of overdraft of groundwater.

2.4.7.5 Legal and Technical Deviations

This assertion is supported by the following statement: 'the first goal of a solar powered pump system is to store water (USDA Technical Note, 2010: 10). This is the most significant glaring flaw in the Dhundi solar-based irrigation system (Fig. 2.33, Annexure B). Having said this, one needs to ponder over certain core issues pertaining to financial incentives (policy sweeteners) in demonstration projects of this nature: (1) What could be the intended outcomes in case the polity decides in favour of abandoning subsidies in favour of conventional, grid-connected agricultural connections? Would such a scenario leave space for acceptance of an alternate technology for irrigation by allowing technology capture in favour of non-conventional energy sources? (2) 'Open access' still remains an unresolved sensitive agenda throughout the functional structure of conventional energy systems. What would happen in case there is only a short-term or a medium-term power purchase guarantee? (3) The solar policy of the state clearly dictates the purchase of power at APPC rates. The said rate for power purchased from such non-conventional energy sources as solar and wind was 3.40 INR (CERC Order, 2015). However, the contextual PPA goes beyond that to an offer of 4.63 INR/kWh for the first group of farmers (six in number).

Should this be treated as an abrupt deviation from a laid down policy? (4) The mandate of SPICE is to sell as much power for earning as much commercial gain (refer to the mandate of the cooperative society). Would there be any takers@3.40 INR/unit as mandated by the central regulator? (5) There is a fundamental technical flaw in the design of the SPICE system and that pertains to the lack of any connected provision for water storage and conservation for use in future. Still, there is an incentive offered at the rate of 1.25 INR/kWh for two years in the form of groundwater conservation bonus! Further, in the absence of any storage facility, coupled with non-sunny days, how does green energy bonus being offered at the same rate for the same time frame gets accounted for? (6) Thus, an overall incentive of 7.13 INR/unit for a two-year duration in respect of the first set of entrants creates a limited incentive in the garb of policy demonstration.

It is reflective of an agenda that is largely driven as a demonstration project. The policy appears to be disruptive as the number of farmers gets auto-frozen. For an alternative technology implant, there has to be a certain gestation period. In case there is no space for it, the result could be discouraging. The numbers in the present format of Dhundi project do not swell beyond a few. The ad hoc policy design in respect of SPICE suffers on account of instrumental rationality as well as procedural rationality (Simon, 1976). The claims made by the agenda setters are loaded with organized scepticism. It lacks universalism and communality (Alvord et al., 2004; Botes & Van, 2000; Rogerson et al., 2013). The current case creates wedges in an otherwise organized social order. It does not pass the test of legitimacy, reason, and transparency, as there is an established conflict between the interests of the buyer (MGVCL) and seller (SPICE).

The objectives of the mandali contradict the provisions enshrined in the power purchase agreement (PPA). There is a complete and concrete ban on sale of water that is being pumped by the off-grid, non-conventional energy system. Further, the water being pumped out is only meant for individual, private consumption within the given parcel of land that has been certified by an appropriate agency for which the rights, claims, and titles have been established unequivocally. The policy design is devoid of value distribution through technology, and this aspect could largely and rightly be attributed to its being of a first prototype. An evaluation of the organizations which pushed the agenda laden with a short-term financial pittance raises the following issues at the stage of closure of an incipient demonstration project in terms of observable field practices. From an empirical perspective, they reveal who does what, when, with whom, with what resources, for what reasons, and with what kind of motivating devices! There is, however, an alternative thought as well. There is definitely a context in terms of target population, but there is an innate flaw that this proposal has very few takers.

This happened simply because the next group of farmers are offered a power purchase guarantee of 3.24 INR/unit as compared to their other counterparts. Thus, there are clear benefits and burdens linked to this offer and the technology as well. The promoting organizations did not necessarily link all the elements of the target population. The assumptions were unrealistic as the rationale for self-promotion is more evident, and this has been spelt out in the overarching speculative logic put forth in the proposal related to the solar energy-based pumping systems. This system design creates unrest within a uniform social order. It promotes uncertainty in terms of short-term financial incentives and technological lock-in.

What if a farmer decides to switch over to water-intensive agriculture practice! And in the process, he pumps more (does so by increasing the number of solar panels and enhances the pump capacity)? However, under the current legal arrangement, he cannot resort to such measures as the capacity is now frozen at 71.4 kW. Further, the incentives are frozen, as the long-term financial incentives are frozen too. In case the focus shifts from agriculture to sale of water and energy, there would be a gradual decline in agricultural production. In the business as usual (BAU) scenario, there is not going to be any perceptible change in the quantum of production as there is no incentive to increase the produce or conserve water; the only incentive is to commercially gain from sale of water and power.

A few of them had borings earlier and the use of diesel-based motors was a given. That is now used to run flour mills (atta chakkis). This is another economic activity creating avenues for additional sources of income. Such practices have a significant dent on the attitudes and behaviours of the farmers. The so-called green energy bonus creates an added incentive for creating carbon footprints as it adversely impacts the sustainable climate change initiative. There is still a large scope for diesel consumption, and its usage continues, as a driver of motor and as a polluting fuel. Thus, a farmer is about to transform himself from an agriculturist into a commercial enterprise, being driven by the idea of additional revenue streams.

2.4.8 *Conclusion and Policy Implications*

A long-term perspective plan in terms of renewable energy-based irrigation systems could be primarily based on community ownership of a system of production. A fundamental element of this energy production system is linked to the construction of an overhead service reservoir (OHSR, Fig. 2.33, Annexure B). The allocation of green energy generation benefits should be linked to water conservation as a primary attribute followed by in-house consumption of any surplus power. One hundred percent capital subsidy (90:10, state-beneficiary share), on upfront expenditure on system design, equipment purchase, installation, and commissioning could also be thought of as an essential element of policy. The submersible pump shall be a direct current (DC) motor. There would not be any incentive with regard to feed in tariff (FIT) as this system shall be totally off-grid.

There would be a permissible limit of acreage to which commercial sale of pumped water shall be allowed. The limit shall be defined by the radius of influence of the drilled borewell. The extra renewable energy (so-called surplus) shall be used to run the domestic loads of DC appliances in the dwelling unit of the energy cropper. The residential (rural, domestic) connection may be given an option to apply for either a grid connection or a linked basic minimum support price for the varieties of crops grown, or there could be a committed financial incentive for diversification for less water-intensive crops.

This incentive could be directly linked to the gross cropped area or actual quantity of production. There could also be an option for the farmer to sell surplus non-conventional power (NCP) to any dwelling unit in the neighbourhood that has DC-based load. The proposed model underlines the true nature and spirit of 'PROSUMERISM' where the producer consumes and locally sells a product (Toffler, 1980). The prosumer model banks on need-based generation and pumping, with an increased impetus on water conservation that checks groundwater exploitation. A suitable mechanism could be put in place to measure rates of replenishment of groundwater through construction of piezometers (non-production wells). This shall help in measuring the depths of groundwater in different weather conditions and determine the levels of stress on subsurface aquifer systems. Installation of these full proof systems actually in principle justifies the rightful claim for green energy bonus as well as groundwater conservation bonus that is completely missing in the current design of Dhundi project (Chapter 3).

The initial proposal mooted by IWMI-TATA and other related institutions distanced themselves from the following issues: (1) farmers are unfamiliar with solar pumping technology, (2) farmers were apprehensive of losing their priority for grid connection, (3) there was a valid fear that solar pumps may not work on cloudy days, and (4) they had no secondary use for surplus solar power. It appears that none of these fears had been effectively and practically addressed. There was a huge promotional thrust with little substance. There is no denial that the technology holds promise, but the assumptions need to be laid down categorically for pragmatic decision making.

The result of this half-hearted propaganda for meeting 'research objectives' in the form of a small-scale localized demonstration project has resulted in no takers for this proposal. This project has also met with a similar fate as the government's policy in respect of solar-based irrigation pumps. The Dhundi Saur Urja Sahakari Utpadak Mandali is presently involved in a flawed policy demonstration project. The recipients are caught in a cob-web of legal, technical, socio-political, and economic. Technological lock-in creates an unhealthy situation in the village, a threat to social cohesion.

The basis on which the initial claim has been made remains an unresolved issue, as there is not much to showcase on ground in respect of addressing 'technical' fears and apprehensions on part of the nine end-users. The message that is registered with them strongly revolves around additional source(s) of income. The marriage between culture and technology has not materialized. What remains to be seen is whether the project sustains once the so-called revenue stream begins to thin, leaving the farmer with no option, but to revert back to the conventional systems of field irrigation that has been their forte for centuries together. As has been aptly said, 'You give a man a fish, you feed him for a day, you teach him how to fish, you feed him for a lifetime'.

2.5 Annexure B: Case Study 2.2 Dhundi (Gujarat)

See Figs. 2.27, 2.28, 2.29, 2.30, 2.31, 2.32, and 2.33.

2 CASE STUDIES AS AN IMMERSIVE APPROACH ... 123

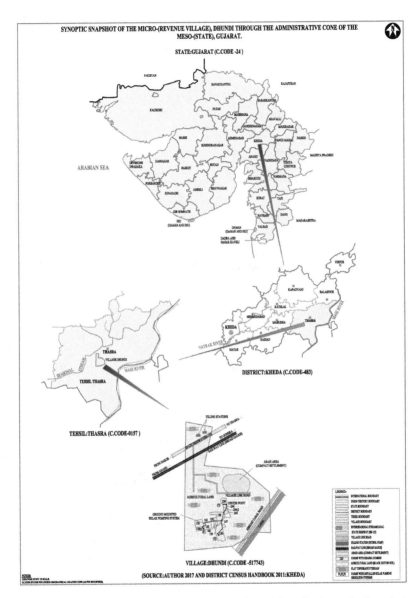

Fig. 2.27 Comprehensive snapshot of the village Dhundi, through the administrative cone of the Meso-(State)

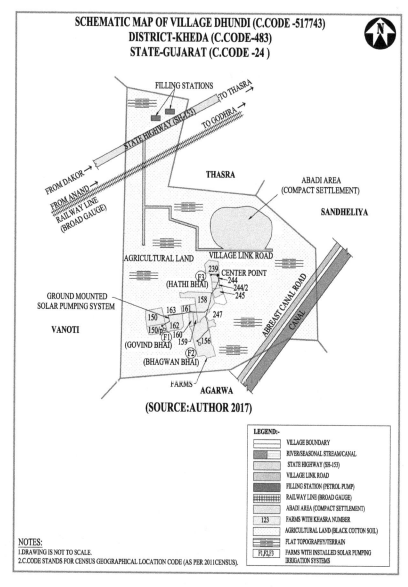

Fig. 2.28 Schematic map of village Dhundi

A CASE STUDY ON SOLAR PUMPING IRRIGATION SYSTEM, VILLAGE: DHUNDHI, TEHSIL: THASRA, DISTRICT: KHEDA, STATE: GUJARAT

c

1. THE GROUP OR CONSORTIUM OF INSTITUTIONS INVOLVED IN THE PROJECT
2. POLE MOUNTED SOLAR PHOTO VOLTAIC PANELS (CAPABLE OF BEING ROTATED HORIZONTALLY AND VERTICALLY)
3. THE SPV UNITS INSTALLED IN INDIVIDUAL FIELDS
4. INJECTION OF SOLAR POWER INTO THE GRID
5. SEPARATE ENERGY METERS FOR THE SIX FARMERS OF SPICE GROUP
6. THE INTERACTION SET UP INSIDE THE MEASURING AND CONTROL UNIT
7. ENERGY ACCOUNTING SET UP OF THE DISCOM (MGVVNL)

(SOURCE: AUTHOR, 2017)

Fig. 2.29 Energy accounting system. The borewell can also be seen

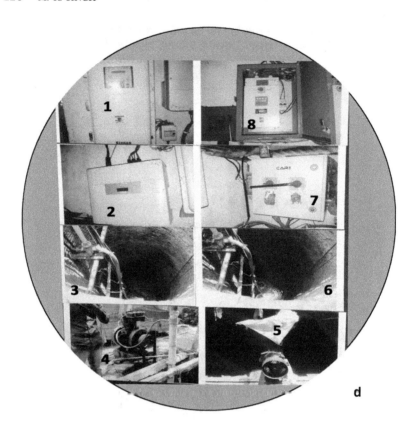

1. POWER CONSUMED BY SOLAR PUMP BEING DISPLAYED
2. SOLAR METER FOR GREEN ENERGY ACCOUNTING
3. WATER BEING PUMPED FROM THE WELL (LEVEL: 40 MBGL)
4. DIESEL GEN SET
5. FLOUR MILL (IN THE INSET), POWERED BY DIESEL GENSET
6. WATER LEVEL RISES ONCE PUMPING IS ARRESTED
7. SWITCH FOR PUMP OPERATIONS
8. ENERGY ACCOUNTING MAINS

(SOURCE: AUTHOR, 2017)

Fig. 2.30 Injection point of the solar energy into the MGVCL feeder

2 CASE STUDIES AS AN IMMERSIVE APPROACH ... 127

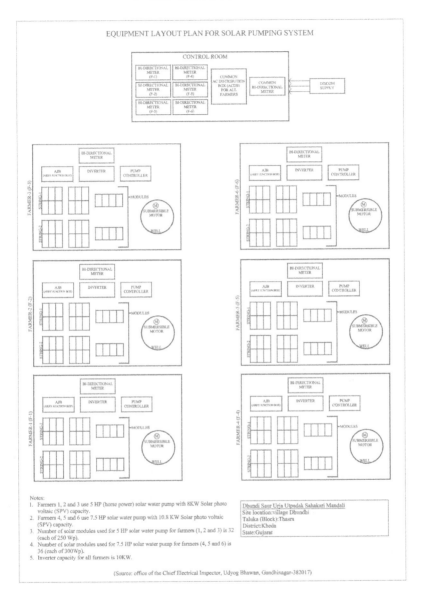

Fig. 2.31 Equipment layout plan for the solar irrigation pumps

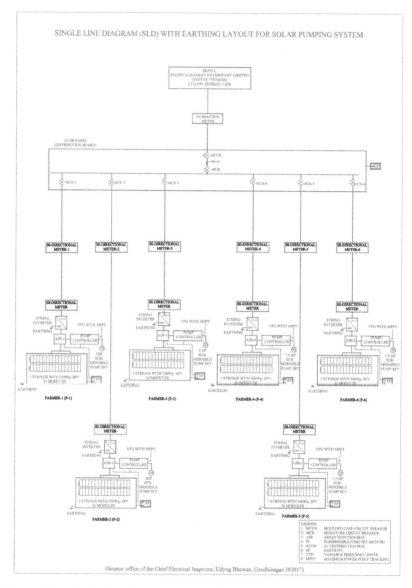

Fig. 2.32 Single line diagram (SLD) for the earthing layout plan of the installed solar pumps

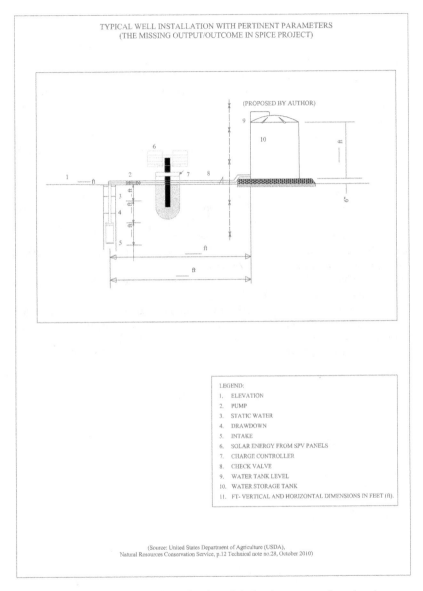

Fig. 2.33 'Ideal' well-ise of a solar based irrigation pump functional set-up. The necessary element of water conservation

References

Alvord, S. H, Brown, L. D., & Letts, C. W. (2004). Social entrepreneurship and societal transformation—An exploratory study. *The Journal of Applied Behavioural Science, 40*(3), 260–282. 10.1177/0021886304266847

Botes, L., & Van, D. R. (2000). Community participation in development: nine plagues and twelve commandments. *Community Development Journal, 35*(1), 41–58.

Central Electricity Regulatory Commission. (2015). *Determination of average power purchase cost (APPC) at the national level* (Petition no. 15/SM/2015, pp. 1–10). New Delhi.

Gujarat Solar Power Policy. (2015). G.R. No. SLR-11-2015-2442-B, dated 13/08/2015, pp. 1–22.

Shah, T., Durga, N., Verma, S., & Rathod, R. (2016). *Solar power as remunerative crop, water policy research highlight* (Vol. 10, pp. 1–6). IWMI-TATA water policy program. http://iwmi-tata.blogspot.in

Simon, H. A. (1976). *Administrative behaviour: A study of decision-making processes in administrative organization* (3rd ed.). Free Press.

Toffler, A. (1980). *The third wave* (p. 544). First published by William Morrow and Company. ISBN0688035973.

United States Department of Agriculture and Natural Resource Conservation Service. (2010). *Design of small photo-voltaic (PV), solar-powered water pump systems* (Technical note no. 28, pp. 1–71). Portland, OR. https://www.nrcs.usda.gov/internet/FSE_DOCUMENTS/nrcs142p2_046471.pdf

2.6 Unleashing Dystopia Through Technology Implant: Technological Lock-In Leads to Disruption of Social Order. A Case Study from Tayyabpur: Bihar, India

2.6.1 Introduction

Tayyabpur is a remote, revenue village lying abreast Gandak canal project. River Ganga flows in close proximity, and hence, the land is naturally blessed with fertility. The village is surrounded by pools of natural water bodies towards the south. It falls under the revenue jurisdiction of tehsil Manhar and community development (CD) block, Desri within Vaishali district of Bihar (Fig. 2.34, Annexure C). The village falls under the service (electricity distribution) jurisdiction of North Bihar power distribution company limited (NBPDCL). The village has a flat terrain, with large tracts of cultivable land. The settlement pattern is predominantly linear, but largely nucleated and compact. The overall spatial and socio-cultural attributes are shown in Fig. 2.41, Annexure C.

Tayyabpur falls under the jurisdiction of democratically elected Bhikhanpura gram panchayat. There are around 527 dwelling units in the entire village, says Mahendra Ram (mukhiya of Bhikhanpura panchayat). The ward number nine (9), which is the exclusive focus of this study, has 194 dwelling units. This ward has no access to the electricity grid. The solar mini-grid caters to 66 dwelling units as of now, says Mukhiya ji Sh. Mahendra Ram. Therefore, 128 units are without access to the solar mini-grid as well. Ward number 9 is under the exclusive occupancy of the '*nonias*', an extremely backward community, notified by the general administration department (GoB Notification, 2015).

The Nonia community figures at serial number 42 in the appended schedule one (I) of the said notification. Ward number 16 lies adjacent to this ward and has access to the central grid. Interestingly, the dwelling units sampled from ward number 16 show values to the tune of 6.5 to 7.0 kWh (units) of consumption of electricity on an average per day (source: Author). On the other hand, the residents connected to the solar mini-grid show a daily consumption of 0.042 kWh (units) of solar power per day (Fig. 2.47, Annexure C). The load demand on an average on a given day is based upon the ownership of the types of appliances, the number of units of each type of appliance, its declared usage during the day, and its power rating. All of this, however, is subject to the supply of power (reliability) either from a conventional source (grid-connected supply from NBPDCL) or from a non-conventional source (solar mini-grid). With this background about Tayyabpur, the narrative moves towards the main actor (the first direct recipient of the pilot project: Sharwan Mahato).

2.6.1.1 The Relational Dynamics Between the Protagonist and the Local Institutions

This case presents an epithetical technological crusade in the revenue village of *Tayyabpur*, remotely situated along the banks of Ganga *diara* (colloquial term for interfluve). Its local institutions: the community, the panchayat, and the energy cooperative (*that was not to be*); and the politics of the local elite that manages to not only subvert the developmental state and administration, but make it a hub of clientelism (the show stoppers), parochialism, and corruption, are to say a truism. The idealist Sharwan Mahato, a former soldier who had earlier served under the armed forces of a monolithic state, was left bewildered about the state of the nascent polity and its institutions, already mired in impolitic project execution, opportunism, and rent-seeking.

Tayyabpur prescient pitted the idealism of the patriotic soldier against the opportunism of the local elite. The varied narratives of local power struggle in *Tayyabpur* questioned the notion of an independent ideal type bureaucracy and administration. It tested the false dichotomy of the separation of politics, policy communique, and execution. It underlined with effective resonance that state institutions were little more than a source of rents for its local elite. Even after seven long decades post-independence, the unfolding politics of *Tayyabpur* underlined that even though governance was imagined as centralized, it is the *specifics of the local* that shaped everyday administrative reality and governs the fiat of a policy dose.

2.6.2 Why Tayyabpur?

During the course of discussions with the benevolent lessor Mr. Sharwan Mahato, the tale of the shoddy survey work unfolds. He narrated the shoddy nature of the survey work. It was done in a clandestine fashion, says Sharwan. The sample size was increased manifold to establish on paper the inflated demand in terms of number of takers. The numbers of intended takers reflected during the survey were actually never there in real terms.

On being asked about the actual reason about selecting Tayyabur, he smiles nonchalantly and began with an interesting narrative: '*Tayyabpur is primarily a village where about 80 percent population is engaged in various kinds of economic activity mostly in the unorganized sector primarily in Delhi, Uttar Pradesh and Assam. It has 16 wards (administrative division) in total. The major economic activity in the village is agriculture. The soil is extremely fertile, thanks to the proximity to the Ganges. The nature of individual land holdings is very small, ranging from 1–4 kathas (1 katha in Bihar = 435.56 square foot) of land. There are only 3–4 families in the entire village with holdings in the range of 1–2 acres. Further, even with a small size of holdings, the locals grow four crops in a single calendar year. Rice is the primary produce, followed by wheat, maize and vegetables.*

The produce is sufficient enough for an average family size of five, and in case there is any surplus, it is sold locally. TATA POWER had an extremely tough time to tie up for land on account of the aforesaid reasons. I was repeatedly requested by Mukhiya ji that the project is for the development of the entire community. Since my family had social credibility in the village as well as in the local market, I was asked to pitch in with support in the form of 5 kathas of my prime agricultural land. Sir, I fell into the trap 'GAON KA VIKAS', laments Sharwan. He continues further on being asked about the extreme levels of backwardness of Tayyabpur, especially ward number 9. He cites the geographical disposition of the ward in question as the prime reason for its backwardness (Fig. 2.42, Annexure C)'.

2.6.2.1 Plight of Tayyabpur and Ward No.9 in Particular

It falls at the intersection of two development blocks, Desri and Sehdoi Buzurg. With around 600 voters all together, no political leader ever gave any support to the residents. Their visibility is limited to the election season. Had this ward been geographically located in either of the two blocks centre or front (location), it would definitely have been on the radar of political representatives. There is no primary school or any other facility or support in the village. A pregnant mother has to travel 12–14 kms. one way to get herself examined. The leaders' visit is episodic and sporadic. They made tall promises about change in lives through uninterrupted power supply throughout the day.

2.6.3 Background of the Tayyabpur Solar Micro-Grid Project

Tata trusts and Massachusetts Institute of Technology (MIT), Tata centre for technology and design were working on the MIT/TATA electrification research project on the future of expanding rural electricity access in India. This initiative was being supported by Tata Power Delhi Distribution Limited (TPDDL) in its implementation. This project aimed to develop a novel solar micro-grid model with a decision support tool suitable to our Indian environment and support universal electrification. TPDDL had partnered with Tata trusts and MIT, Tata centre for technology and design for developing this model, including coordinating with utilities for information, data and understanding to develop this useful model for the Indian context.

2.6.3.1 The Utopian Conception

Implementation of this project model for installing and developing micro-grid in the country is very crucial which will be affordable and sustainable with universal applicability, helping the country to provide access to electricity in remote rural areas.

Site selection:

In the first phase of the project, the MIT/TPDDL team visited different micro-grid projects in the country, and after detailed study of possible locations for this project, two villages in Bihar in Vaishali district were shortlisted and one of them was *Tayyabpur*. This selection of location was possible with the support of the local state-run utility, North Bihar Power Distribution Company Limited (NBPDCL).

Initial phase: Broad contours of shared responsibilities

A brief study was conducted to assess demographic information. The site was found suitable for long-term sustainable and economic operation for solar micro-grid. It was decided to put up 15 kWp at the location for establishment of micro-grid in the first phase followed by additional 15 kWp capacity after one/two years of successful operation and increase in demand (Figs. 2.43–2.46, Annexure C). As a part of this project, it was planned to commission this micro-grid through investments of Tata trusts and other associated partners. Only maintenance charges for the micro-grid were to be collected from the villagers that were presumed to be nominal. The proposed tender for execution for this pilot project was floated.

Land for installation of solar projects had been identified and acquired (on lease). A self-help group/society was proposed to be formed in the village and the project would be owned and maintained by these entities (still in limbo). M/S General Electric supplied and provided for installation of all equipment related to the solar plant. TPDDL was supposed to invite bids for civil and electrical works related to 'remaining part of the micro-grid' on behalf of the self-help group/society that was supposed to be formed at the location, as specified in the tender document. TPDDL was also supposed to oversee the work as facilitator to the self- help group/society.

Bidders were therefore requested to participate in this novel project with their best offer considering long term benefit in association with this project. This pilot was supposed to demonstrate their commitment towards improvement in the Indian power sector and towards sustainable improvement of society in the developing world. Further, the notified tender document asked the bidders to quote minimum possible cost and supply appropriate products and services as per scope of work and the terms and conditions of the tender (source: interaction with Manoj Kumar Sinha, state head for PRAYAS, Bihar and Jharkhand, MIG-42, behind Shalimar sweets, Kankarbagh, Patna-800020, and tender enquiry ref: TPDDL/ENGG/ENQ/200000715/15-16, supply, testing, construction, and commissioning of electrical network and civil work for 15 kWp solar micro-grid).

2.6.3.2 *The Ulterior Design Led to Entrapment: Sharwan Gets Trapped!*

TPDDL tried tooth and nail to convince the local residents to provide a suitable plot of land for the project but to no avail. Several meetings with the previous mukhiya (Sh. Ranjan kumar Thakur) in order to sort things out produced no results. There was a lot of distrust in the minds of people, and further, there was a general uneasiness in the village, as they were sceptical about the designs of the parties involved and their good intentions of providing reliable services.

Parting with 5 kathas of agricultural land in lieu of a solar grid did not appear to be an interesting proposition at all to the locals. Elections to the gram panchayats were due across the state of Bihar. New panchayat took over. Sh. Mahendra Ram was elected as the Pradhan/Mukhiya of the Bhikhanpur panchayat. The officials of TPDDL started doing the rounds of the new power centre. Multiple meetings were held, and at last, Sh.

Mahendra Ram was successful in convincing *Sharwan mahato* to provide a portion of his land holding for the solar project. And that was how the work began on the said plot of land and the grid was formally inaugurated on 24.01.2017.

2.6.3.3 Sharwan Executes the Lease Deed: The Rules of the Utopian Design

There was a general feeling of reluctance to part away with almost 8500 square feet of agricultural land even on lease, for a time frame of 25 years. Finally, the panchayat convinced Sharwan to sign a lease agreement with the Delhi-based power distribution company (TPDDL). And, this led to the finalization of the lease agreement between Sharwan and TPDDL for a time frame of 25 years. The details of the plot are as follows: (1) plot number: 531; (2) boundary details—N (self), S (self), E (road), and W (Raghu rai's plot); (3) area—8500 sq. feet; and (4) thana (police station): 630. The annual rent to be paid to Sharwan was 15,000 INR, a pittance.

2.6.3.4 Sharwan Reduced to the Status of an Executant

An increase at the rate of 5% was allowed every three years. This increase was supposed to be over and above the last paid rent. All cess, dues, fees, and taxes due to the appropriate government were to be paid by the lessor (Sharwan), and in case the lessor failed to clear the same, the lessee of the plot would pay the same and an adjustment to that effect would be made from the rents due to the lessor.

The date from which the lease deed came into force was the date of receipt of the material for the construction of the solar plant on the given parcel of land (Fig. 2.43, Annexure C). A default on payment of four successive dues on account of rent by the lessee to the lessor was a ground for termination of the lease deed. The lessor would serve a notice of three-month period for clearance of dues. A failure in respect of clearance of dues within the time frame of the notice period would result in termination of the lease deed. Each of the parties could serve a six-month notice to the other for dissolution of the lease agreement without assigning any reason for the same. In case of any natural calamity, riot or affray, that renders the land parcel misfit for future use, the lessee would automatically get absolved from the cause of being bound by the terms and conditions of the lease deed.

An advance rent of 4 months would be due to the lessor on the receipt of the first consignment of materials for erection of the solar plant on the land premises. Any portion of the land parcel could be sublet to a third party by the lessee (for self-gain) with the written consent of the lessor. However, the third party would be bound by the same terms and conditions as the lessee. Further, the lessor was obligated to facilitate obtaining of permits and clearances required from as many quarters, as may be necessary for proper commissioning of the solar plant. It shall be the duty of the lessor to protect the said land parcel from any encroachment or any harm. The lessor was bound to ensure smooth movement of men and material for installation and commissioning of the solar plant.

Any obstruction to any kind of work during any stage of erection and commissioning of the solar plant and further during operation and maintenance shall automatically result in the termination of the lease deed. This event shall not be construed as a violation of any of the mentioned conditions in the lease deed. No heir of the lessor or any third party shall have any right to raise any objection to any activity being carried on the said parcel of land. Further, they shall have no right to any claim whatsoever on the said land parcel during the lease period. The lessor agreed to allow the lessee for any kind of temporary or permanent improvement on the said land parcel for the purposes of the solar plant project.

The lessee could enter into collaborative activities with other private entities for the purpose of installing their equipment on the leased parcel of land. In case the lessee fails to avail any notification/order from any government or semi-government institution for the purposes of the said project at any stage of the project during the lease period, or a given permission is revoked during the lease period, then the lessee would terminate the lease agreement forthwith.

The lessor assured the lessee that the parcel of land is free from all encumbrances. There is no civil suit pending in any court of law. The lessor was competent for execution of the lease deed. It would be the duty of the lessor to get clearances and permissions from any authority for any of the purpose(s) of the project in the shortest possible time. In case any government order or guideline in respect of the project is revised and/or amended, the lessor would apprise the lessee of the same and further shall get the necessary clearances, in case they are required subject to the new regulations that have any bearing on the project. In case the lessor fails in doing so, the lessee would be entitled to terminate the lease ex-parte.

It shall be the duty of the lessee to use the said premises only for the purposes of the project. He shall cause no damage to the said parcel of land whatsoever. The lessor would not pledge or mortgage the property during the lease period. In case any of the parties violates any of the critical terms of the agreement, then the aggrieved party can terminate the lease deed by giving one-month notice in advance. However, any of the aggrieved parties may request the other party to rectify the wrong by giving a three-month notice. The lease would stand terminated in case no action is taken by the party which necessitated the wrong. Any changes, modifications, or any amendment to the terms and conditions of the deed shall be with the mutual consent of both the parties. In case, the deed gets vitiated and becomes invalid under any circumstances, the lessee would return the land parcel to the lessor.

Lastly, any dispute arising out of any document or terms and conditions of the agreement would be challenged in a court of competent jurisdiction in *New Delhi only*. The said lease deed was executed on 10.03.2016.

2.6.4 Conclusive Thoughts—Tayyabpur Solar Micro-Grid: Oblivious of Socio-cultural Moorings?

In every ecosystem, there exists a culturally cohesive, functional social order.

Tayyabpur had a previous experience of a failed solar mini-grid project of 3 kW capacity, installed by a non-government organization (NGO). The prime reasons cited for its failure were somewhat proximal in character to the current case. The introduction of a new technological artefact smells of an imperialist design to alter the extant socio-cultural and functional order of the ward, through a formal scheme of utilitarian objective as a diktat, expressed through the scheme of revenue realization from the end-users of the energy service. The technological artefact is alien to the culture of *Tayyabpur* and therefore, to say the least it is not culturally neutral. It does not reflect the local values of the context. It has not culturally evolved in this socio-cultural order through incorporation of the creative skill of the community.

Therefore, to successfully implant a technology in a 'perceived' homogenous social order was a difficult task. A noteworthy feature of this project has been the reduction in capacity of the plant. The tender document mentions the capacity at 15 kW, whereas the actual installed capacity is 12 kW (Fig. 2.48, Annexure C). A solar photovoltaic (SPV) project requires a concrete understanding of the consumers' expectations from both financial and energy perspectives. This fact appears to have been completely ignored during planning and development of the project in Tayyabpur case.

The agency hired to gauge consumer mood miserably failed to interpret the desires of the consumers. The consumers were not briefed about financial trade-offs and limitations of the promiscuous technology. This tender document appears to be devoid of the client's needs and desires, as they become the basis for preparing proposals, quotations, and construction contracts. There appears to be no thought having gone into building reciprocal relationships through establishing trust and strengthening norms of reciprocity (Putnam, 1993).

2.6.4.1 *The Role of PRAYAS in the Entire Scheme of Things: Escalating Expectations? Over Hyped Technology Capacity? Politics of Inflation and Exaggeration*

An alternative plan for extending energy service ought to be based on the wishes, cultures, and traditions of a particular community and not have a socially disruptive effect. Perhaps the organizations did not do their homework well, as there exists already an example of an unsuccessful enterprise for expanding access to electricity. Thus, the citizenry as of now does not surrender its expectation in the form of energy requirements vis-à-vis their occupational structure within the home or otherwise. There are discrete and distinct spaces within the revenue village that is a mélange of caste groups.

A striking line of thought springs up from the case pertains to cultural singularity and caste homogeneity may appear to be a cake walk but could offer the bumpiest of the rides during a project cycle that is astutely mechanical in norm and character. Does creation of visible generation infrastructure guarantee cultural acceptance by the end-users? The end-users after ages witness power generation from such proximity. Embedded generation of energy promising expansion of access in itself is an enigmatic proposition.

2.6.4.2 *Reference Electrification Model Falls Short of Expectations*

An energy production system cannot be a law unto itself and further, technology cannot play the role of a regulator. There is no 'universalism' per se in a tool or a technology that has yet to brace a passive end-user, though there are claims not only about a tool that could help to model systems for providing access to electricity but also about the robustness of the micro-grid at Tayyabpur in terms of power generation and reliability of supply. This appears to be a bit too far-fetched a belief in a tool that is still evolving and is in its phases of application in an alien culture, society, and subjects as well. There appears to be an extremely narrow understanding of the psyche of the 'local end-user'. The pilot runs into rough weather during the initial phase of construction itself. The appeal of the tenderer (TPDDL) appears to fall flat on the ears of the bidders.

There appears to be a discord between the intended philanthropic demonstration and the delivered ensemble of energy service. The public utility generally does not have consumption data at the village level (Fig. 2.47, Annexure C). In this particular case, to expect the public utility to possess figures at the resolution level of every village ward is too unrealistic. In India, the power distribution companies are yet to reach the resolution level of each revenue village, for capturing rural, domestic consumption of power on a real-time basis. Therefore, designing an off-grid plant for Tayyabpur sans any comprehensive consumer coverage involved a lot of risk ab initio.

2.6.4.3 Loopholes in the Rules of the Game—Institutional Oversights and Pitfalls

The tender document and the lease deed failed on the following parameters: (a) not being comprehensive, being unclear on responsibilities, shoddy delivery of services, and poor management of internal operations, and (b) not being internally consistent; though there was one single 'bottom line' recovery of cost through strengthening of revenue streams, there was a complete lack of coordinated action amongst the macro-actors, viz. TATA trust, TPDDL, GE, and MIT. Each of these institutions appears to be driven by a strong individualistic institutional agenda.

It was corporate social responsibility (CSR) funding for meeting standards of set targets for TATA trust, demonstration of design of an off-grid plant solar photovoltaic (SPV) plant for TPDDL, philanthropy for General Electric and testing practical robustness of reference electrification model (REM) for TATA-MIT energy centre, (c) REM software for designing micro-grids not being reliable enough; *being in its incipient stage of design and development*, the most important responsibility had to be shouldered by the social organization (PRAYAS), viz. establishment of belief, creation of faith, building of trust through cooperative and coordinated action amongst the end-users, and other mute spectators squatting at the fringes.

The efforts were not serious enough and were extremely volatile; (d) there was nothing of a sort corresponding to any set objectives and evaluations in the form of a citizen's charter for the ultimate end-users. There was no sense of responsibility or commitment towards the cause of providing energy service and expanding access through means of equity and fairness. The agenda was unilateral, top-down, and totalitarian. There was no element of value creation in the entire process-product conception, design, and execution. It has been almost one and half years since the plant was commissioned; still, there are no efforts towards the creation of an 'Oorja samiti' at the level of the ward to oversee the day-to-day affairs of the energy supply system. The costs of monitoring and enforcing agreements have escalated the 'transaction costs' and have increased the problems of opportunism and shirking.

The violators go scot free in the absence of an institution such as an energy cooperative (*Oorja samiti*), as there is a marked absence of efforts guided towards problem demarcation, defining boundaries or any graduated sanction that can be levied upon the violators (Ostrom, 1990). Tayyabpur project is a classic case where a vertical network extends on to a horizontal network of prospective beneficiaries. Though the vertical network appears to be dense on account of the larger probable speculative gains of the organizations, it could not create social trust and therefore, could not extract cooperation from the prospective beneficiaries. The information flow in the vertical format was highly unreliable, whether it was in the objective, or the capacity or the design or the practical intent in the planning and commissioning of the solar mini-grid. The horizontal flows within the community were strong and truly realistic.

2.6.4.4 *The Associated Dysfunctionalities*
The case puts forth two kinds of dysfunctions for analysis (a) behavioural and (b) technological. Behavioural dysfunction is largely attributed towards the failure of assessment of the status of the community with regard to consumption patterns of energy. The myopic vision of the project proponents was utilitarian, and therefore, they remained ideologically and functionally distant from immediate expectations and futuristic aspirations of the policy recipients. As a result, the project proponents failed to meet the tall objectives, making the whole project fiscally barren at the end.

The aspect of technological dysfunction is muted on account of information asymmetry between the provider agents and recipients. The level of information asymmetry between the service provider and the user is humongous in terms of both capacity of technology to deliver and the perceptible change it could bring about in the lives of the beneficiaries. Moreover, quality and reliability of energy service were not guaranteed. There was no far-fetched vision of transfer of technology via a handshake between the local community and the technological drivers of solar micro-grid. These two dysfunctions assume huge proportions towards the end, threatening to jeopardize the socio-technical functioning of the solar micro-grid.

The solar micro-grid envisioned to provide non-conventional power to the residents does not take into account the indispensable role of locale-specific practical realities, informal processes. There was neither any space nor scope for any socio-technical improvisation in the face of technological dysfunctionality. The injection of an off-grid source of supply of electricity altered the social structure and power relations in the action arena through creation of vertical stratification in terms of access (the haves and the have-nots). There is considerable technological stress thrust onto the socio-cultural order. Not everybody in the similar cultural set-up is an end-user. Access is not free, as there is a one-time connection cost and differential tariff structure depending on the electrical load being serviced, and the time at which it is desired. Duration of supply is unreliable depending upon the relative drawl of power by another end-user (choice framework).

Not everyone is a beneficiary—*a few are, and many are not*. This kind of a technological intervention may impoverish the local wellsprings of economic, social, and cultural self-expression (Scott, 1998). This kind of technology-driven service intent, remotely aimed to trigger some form of social engineering, leaves out the necessary elements that are essential to the harmonious functioning of the 'system' design. The entire exercise that led to the commissioning of the plant was based on extremely narrow and restrictive parameters. The design of the contract appears to be unjust and oppressive. It is driven by utopian plans and an authoritarian disregard for the values, desires, faiths, and objections of its subject (lessor).

The micro-grid is caught up in an antagonistic vector design along the three vertices of a triangle represented by community, access, and end-use: with the political nature of technology, inscribed as a circle. The guardians of technology forming a purposeful protective association of domain experts and philanthropists sitting at a distance mock the sporadic presence of a minimalist state that has ceased to be an enabler and a regulator.

The Tayyabpur solar micro-grid project clearly reflects a purely anarchic state of technological dystopia wherein project design, communication clarity and the publique' is missing- (a) who decides what is necessary? (b) for whom? (c) based on which norms and conventions? (Lasswell, 1936, 295). The pilot demonstration project fails to bridge the gap between expectations and aspirations of the locals. The missing 'socio-technical' in action and therefore local energy inaction in the ecosystem of Tayyabpur.

2.6.4.5 A Year Later: The Situation in Tayyabpur

In a detailed telephonic conversation held on 4.06.2018, Sharwan responded with great deal of enthusiasm once again. He puts me across Mr. Rana Mauoresh, the recently appointed project manager, who resides in the tehsil headquarters of Manhar. Mr. Mauoresh is an employee of PRAYAS. He has been deployed for this project to revive it as the revenue streams have almost dried. Mr. Mauoresh has a bachelor's degree in engineering and a master's degree in rural development. Sharwan puts me across to Mauoresh. After exchanging pleasantries, he begins: *'I joined three months back. The plant is in bad shape. The Theft of power supply (non-revenue power) has increased manifold. No formal record has been handed over to me since the last survey was done during 2012-13'.*

Continues further: *'A file of some 95 application forms with mistakes of all sorts, being incomplete, riddled with repetitions of names, duplication of households made things worse. It is extremely difficult to locate and recognize actual beneficiaries on the ground. During field visits to the ward, it was found that, in each house there were at least 3–4 connections under different names. In some cases, people had latched on to the connection of neighbours (illegal tapping of power). There were serious issues of erratic power supply (issues of reliability of energy service). The schedules pertaining to the supply of power were not being adhered to. It appears that huge promises were made to these people at the time of survey. Whatever promises were made, never got fulfilled. They were assured 24 hours of power supply along with provision of fans and more lights which never happened'.*

Since the plant caters to AC loads, people have purchased televisions, bulbs, and fans from the local market and have started using it, as the temperature soars to almost 46 degrees celsius at this time of the year. When the project was commissioned, there were around 100 beneficiaries, but the numbers were reduced to 60s in no time. There was an exponential decline in demand. About 90% of the beneficiaries who have opted for connection are defaulters.

As on date, the exact number of connections is 65. Out of 65, only 30 beneficiaries are regularly paying their due of 100 INR per month. The extra load on the power plant has taken a heavy toll on the battery bank. *'Out of a total number of 48 batteries, 8 are dead and the remaining are in a very bad shape functioning at almost half the levels of their capacity, though I am not very sure. I have escalated the matters to the concerned quarters through my employer, PRAYAS. I am trying to fix up the problem of extending the duration of power supply. There has been an increase in the approved quantity of load up to 25 watts for every formal connection. We have increased the duration from 3 hours to almost 12 hours, from 6.00 p.m to 6.00 a.m. daily, claims Mauoresh'.*

2.6.4.6 Policy Prescription: Take Home Message

A demonstration project can produce long-lasting impact in terms of alternative options, designs, models, and approaches to solve a symptomatic problem (Mallon, 2007). Commissioning of alternate energy systems to sustain human life should be supported by strong deterministic anthropomorphic considerations along with the locale-specific social elements. The energy consumption ecosystem appears to be benign in terms of the simple, non-energy intensive lifestyle of the rural consumers.

It has a marked individual existence in terms of its remoteness, being far from population centres, and is characterized by low load densities. These micro-rural energy ecosystems comprising a mix of caste-class structures are evolutionary co-constructions of energy consumption space that came into existence through a series of cultural, material, and social engagements over a period of time. They are still evolving. This fact renders project demonstration expertise to intense uncertainty given the complex social realities.

This case highlights the central argument that the involved actors need to take into account consequential ground truths rife with concrete, cogent evidence while conceiving a project design for an alternate power generation, transmission, and distribution system for any rural sociocultural realm. A demonstration project cannot be in the hunt for a negotiated solution, when it comes to (a) tinkering with and (b) eventual recasting of a rural, remote, and dispersed rural energy consumption ecosystem.

The policy prescription (Chapter 3) seeks to propose a course correction by seeking answers to the following questions:

- *Why Tayyabur?*
- *Was there an imperative to understand passive consumer behaviour? If yes, who should have been responsible to take it up?*
- *Was there a need to study the reasons for a failed project of a lower capacity?*
- *What entails 'demands realism?' Was load demand aggregation and profiling of a rural consumer a prime requirement? Why was this aspect overlooked?*
- *Was there a need to understand the local in terms of the social, political and economic? Was the timing right to go ahead with the installation?*
- *Was there a need to see whether a policy for an off-grid project was in place?*
- *Why was the revenue village of Tayyabur still waiting for extension of the grid?*
- *NBPDCL did not have an empirical database on local consumer dynamics and load demand. Who was supposed to create this baseline data for the philanthropic pilot?*
- *Was there an incremental increase in demand for power? Was the pilot design and installation symbolic?*

2.7 Annexure C: Case Study 2.3 Tayyabpur (Bihar)

See Figs. 2.34, 2.35, 2.36, 2.37, 2.38, 2.39, 2.40, 2.41, and 2.42.

146 M. K. SINGH

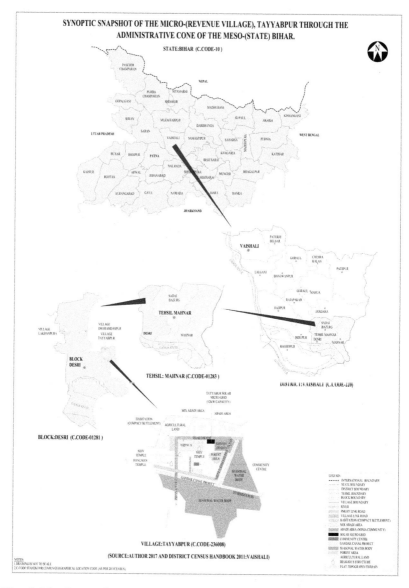

Fig. 2.34 Comprehensive snapshot of village Tayyabpur through the administrative cone of the Meso-(State)

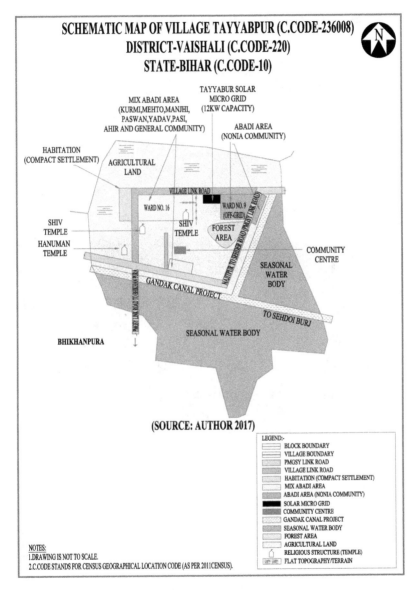

Fig. 2.35 Schematic map of Tayyabpur

A CASE STUDY ON TAYYABPUR SOLAR MICRO-GRID, BIHAR

1. ENERGY FUEL (BIOMASS AND DUNG CAKES)
2. PHYSICAL DISPOSITION OF DWELLING UNITS
3. TYPICAL STONE GRINDER (SIL-BATTA) FOR SPICES
4. PHYSICAL NATURE OF A DWELLING UNIT
5. AGRICULTURAL LAND ABREAST SOLAR POWER PLANT
   (A PATCH RENDERED UNFIT FOR CULTIVATION AS FERTILE
   SOIL HAS BEEN REMOVED TO PROVIDE FOR PLINTH OF THE SOLAR POWER PLANT SITE)

(SOURCE: AUTHOR, 2017)

Fig. 2.36 General overview of Tayyabpur village

1. LATERAL VIEW OF THE SOLAR (PV) MICRO-GRID OF 12KW CAPACITY AT TAYYABPUR
2. SOLAR PANEL ARRAY (FIXED POLE MOUNTED SYSTEM)
3. LIGHTING CONDUCTOR
4. DETAILS OF SPV MODULE MANUFACTURER
5. EARTHING FOR THE SPV PLANT

(SOURCE: AUTHOR, 2017)

Fig. 2.37 General set-up of the solar micro-grid at Tayyabpur (*Source* Author, 2017)

1. CIVIL STRUCTURE FOR HOUSING INVERTOR/CONVERTOR, BATTERY ARRAY, AND DISTRIBUTION JUNCTION
2. INVERTOR/CONVERTOR SETUP
3. BATTERY FUSE AND MPPT INPUT
4. DIESEL GENERATOR SET FOR POWER BACKUP

(SOURCE: AUTHOR, 2017)

Fig. 2.38 Electrical network of solar power generation plant

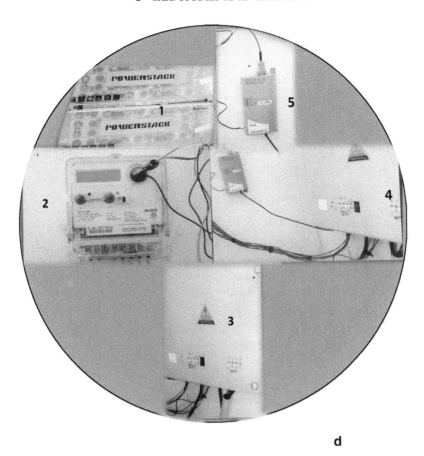

1. BATTERY STACK
2. ENERGY ACCOUNTING METER
3. DISTRIBUTION MAINS
4. MINIATURE CIRCUIT BREAKER (MCB)
5. GPS BASED ENERGY ACCOUNTING DEVICE

(SOURCE: AUTHOR, 2017)

Fig. 2.39 Set-up for energy accounting (*Source* Author, 2017)

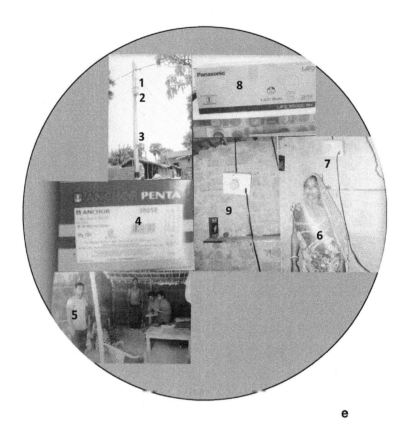

1. DISTRIBUTION LINES
2. JUNCTION BOX
3. DISTRIBUTION POLE
4. SWITCHES TO BE PROVIDED TO THE CUSTOMER
5. GROUP INTERACTION WITH THE COMMUNITY
6. A NONIA COMMUNITY BENEFICIARY OF SPV MICRO GRID POWER SUPPLY
7. SWITCH BOARD WITH AN LED BULB (7W) AND A PLUG POINT
8. CASING FOR LED (PANASONIC)
9. BRICK AND MOTAR STRUCTURE (INTERIOR)

(SOURCE: AUTHOR, 2017)

Fig. 2.40 Distribution infrastructure of the solar micro-grid along with the nature of energy service

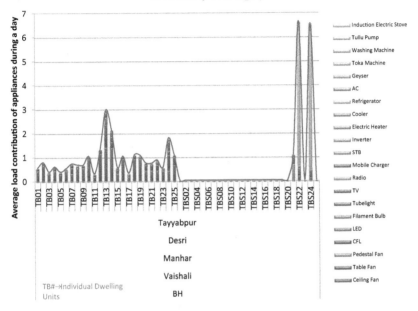

Fig. 2.41 Load profile of the village depicting actual load demand

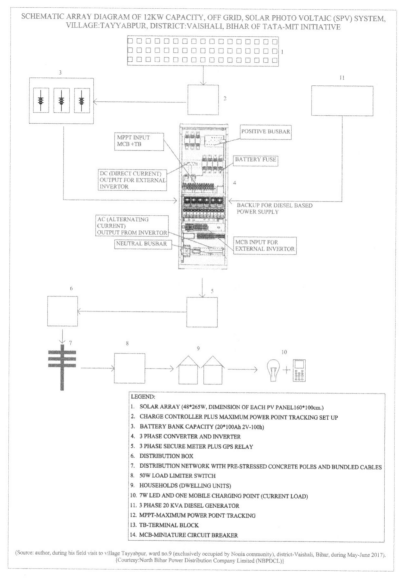

Fig. 2.42 Schematic array diagram of the solar micro-grid at Tayyabpur

References

Ellman, D. (2015). *The reference electrification model: A computer model for planning rural electricity access, submitted to the engineering systems division in partial fulfillment of the requirements for the degree of master of science in technology and policy at the Massachusetts institute of technology* (pp. 1–109).
Lasswell, D. H. (1936). *Politics: Who gets what, when and how?* Papamoa Press.
Mallon, K. (Ed.). (2007). *Renewable energy policy and politics, a handbook for decision making* (1st South Asian ed.). Earthscan, www.earthscan.co.uk
Notification of Government of Bihar. (2015). General Administration Department (GAD), Government of Bihar, letter no-11/D-2-backward and scheduled castes-6/2005-13623, dated 10 September 2015.
Ostrom, E (1990). *Governing the commons, the evolution of institutions for collective action.* Cambridge University Press. ISBN0521405999.
Putnam, D. R. (1993). *Making democracy work, civic traditions in modern Italy.* Princeton University Press, ISBN 0-691-07889-0.
Scott, C. J. (1998). *Seeing like a state, how certain schemes to improve human condition have failed.* The Yale (Institute for Social and Policy Studies) ISPS series, ISBN0-300-07016-0.

2.8 Regulating Access to Energy Through Webs of—Weak Decentralized Institutions, Meek Regulator, and Distanced Local Development and Administrative Set-Up, Case Study from Lohati Pasai, Uttar Pradesh

2.8.1 Introduction: The Constitutional Mandate for Governance of Energy Access—Pathways to Energy Service Delivery

Under the Indian Constitution, electricity is a concurrent subject, which means that both the Union and the State governments have concurrent jurisdiction to make laws in respect of the domain of energy and electricity services. However, subject to the provisions of the constitution detailing the legislative and administrative relations between the centre and the states, the enactments of the Parliament and those given effect to by the centre shall have an overriding effect on those made by the state legislatures (Constitution of India, 1950). The electricity act in vogue came into force in 2003.

Prior to the enactment of the Electricity Act 2003, attempts were made to define an electrified village (Chapter 1). However, the term 'rural electrification', for the first time, gained legal footing through this enactment. Sections 4 and 5 of the Electricity Act mandated the government at the centre to formulate a national *'Rural Electrification Policy'*, which has been since formulated and adopted in 2006, to give effect to the National Electricity Policy (2005). More importantly, under provision to section 43 of the Electricity Act 2003, the regulator (in the state) had to ensure as a part of *universal service obligations* that the national goal of providing electricity access to households is complied with. The Rural Electrification Policy (2006), set such targets as:

1. Provision of access to electricity to all households by the year 2009.
2. Quality and reliable power supply at reasonable rates.
3. Minimum lifeline consumption of 1 unit per household per day as a merit good by year 2012.

As discussed earlier, the old rural electrification (RE) programme, Rajiv Gandhi Grameen Vidyutikaran Yojana (RGGVY) has been subsumed in Deen Dayal Upadhyay Gram Jyoti Yojana (DDUGJY) (Chapter 1). This flagship programme bears the mandate for providing universal access to energy services implicit in section 43 of the Electricity Act, 2003. *The framework detailing the approach to rural electrification entails preparation and notification of rural electrification plans by respective state governments, in order to achieve the goal of providing access to all households.* This plan was supposed to be linked to and integrated with district development plans as and when such plans became available. These plans were supposed to be communicated to the appropriate electricity commission (the regulator within the state). This brief backdrop brings us closer to the belief system—*'decentralization creates institutions that are more amenable to local needs and preferences and as an ideology brings policy instrumentalities at the doorstep of its intended recipients'*.

2.8.1.1 The Core Argument: Should Distributed Application of Energy Access Be Nested in Structures Outside the Purview of Formal Institutions?

Decentralization is perceived to create conditions for a pluralistic political arrangement, in which competing groups can voice and institutionalize their interests in local democratic forums. It is argued that decentralization creates institutions that are more amenable to local needs and preferences (Clague, 1997; Manor, 1999; North, 1986). This case highlights the complexities that arise on account of virtual situatedness of decentralization dogma outside the realm of the institutions of the state. Decentralization manifests itself through varying degrees and scales of intensity across different geo-spatial and geo-cultural settings. It alters local power structures and the linked relational dynamics.

2.8.1.2 Decentralized Energy Access Grounded in the Theoretical Import of Improved Service Delivery

Assertions in favour of decentralization are founded upon a wider critique of central state planning (Weber, 1946; Wilson, 1887). Decentralization as a process of political devolution was driven by a large number of complex, yet interrelated themes. One was an ideological shift, in which the legitimacy of central state-led development has been challenged on the grounds that it propounds a culture of sub-optimal performance. A second was a political agenda, which asserts that the decentralization of systems of public and administration and the introduction of locally elected bodies are expected to produce systems and structures of governance that are better able to cater to the needs of poor and politically marginal groups in society (Giddens, 1998; Putnam, 1993). A third and related theme suggests that democratic decentralization is a political strategy that national elites have used to maintain legitimacy and control in the face of political disintegration (Ahmad et al., 2005; Cheema & Rondinelli, 1983).

To take the argument further, it is generally believed that large and centrally administered bureaucracies represent an inefficient and potentially perverse means of allocating resources within the society. Two mutually self-reinforcing assertions are generally used to substantiate this claim. The first argument is that *the central state agencies lack the time and place knowledge to implement policies and programs that reflect people's real needs and preferences*, while the second being that—*time and place gaps give the local officials, the unlimited ability to distribute resources and extract rent as they deem fit* (Chambers, 1997; Dreze & Sen, 1995; Manor, 1999). It is also suggested that greater democratization promotes economic development as decentralized structure takes into account the local variations (Chambers, 1994, 1997; Putnam, 1993).

2.8.1.3 Pre-requisite for Localized Control of Energy Access Through Active Involvement of Institutions of Local Self-Government

The subject of RE as a programme and process including distribution of electricity and non-conventional energy sources of power generation lies in the purview of the local institutions for governance of energy access (schedule 11; CoI, 1950). Despite the fact that the functional design of the energy sector is nested in the deep-seated philosophy of decentralization, it is observed that in the absence of effective devolution, delegation, communication, and coordination, the effectiveness of the design gets severely compromised (Morduch & Klibanoff, 1995; Singh, 2016).

In the absence of any framework for *demand capture* for requirements of energy services, the executional aspiration in terms of universal access to energy coupled with the daily consumption of 1 unit (kWh) of electricity still remains to be achieved (Rural Electrification Policy, 2006). This argument brings to the centre stage an inherent flaw in the contemporary policy, regulating provision for energy access. The policy estate follows a centralized trajectory of extension of policy infusion without assessing the local nature of passive consumerism. *The unilateral policy design in respect of providing energy access is bereft of an essentialist dogma based on demand collectivism through coalescence of needs of the local.*

Propelled by a standardization vacuum for assessing quality, reliability, and reasonability of rates in relation to electricity supply for a rural, domestic customer, the policy remains functionally distant from its desired objectives. Thus, there appears to be a huge gap between the policy aspirations, the policy texts, and the context (local). This case makes an attempt towards highlighting the dysfunctional functionality of energy provisioning by a non-state actor. The modus operandi of the agency (rural energy service company, RESCO) mocks the spirit of decentralized energy access through the local institutions of self-government.

Catering to expectations of the policy recipients entails creation and establishment of responsive, delivery structures as it brings in proximity to 'demands realism'. Development policies, programs and practices are now more promising than ever, and proclaim to be more pro-poor. Yet the record, for all its successes, remains dismal. It is no good recognizing obligations and meaning well if what is done does not fit the priorities and aspirations of those who want things to be done differently and as per their collective, local requirements.

2.8.2 The Race to Light Up a Dwelling Unit: Transforming Power and Relationships Through Lighting Up Lives in Motipur—A Purwa/Majara (Hamlet) of the Revenue Village, Lohati Pasai

The aforesaid backdrop about providing access to electricity (power for all) takes us to the local environs of Lohati Pasai, a revenue village in Barabanki district of Uttar Pradesh. In Lohati Pasai, grid-based supply of power varies between 12 and 14 hours during the day on an average. However, the electricity supply is erratic on a whole. The village has access to energy through formal and informal means (Fig. 2.52, Annexure D).

Motipur is an un-electrified hamlet of the otherwise electrified village, served by Jhaliya Katesar, a 200 kV substation (Fig. 2.43). An 11 kilovolt (KV) feeder from Ganeshpur provides service line connections to only four numbers of dwelling units in Motipur. The village lights up with katiya (via illegally tapped low tension lines) post-dusk and wakes up at the break of dawn, as an un-electrified hamlet. The story unfolds the experiences of the villagers, the local socio-political and administrative institutions at the hands of a non-state actor that promotes access to energy through non-conventional sources (Figs. 2.49 and 2.50, Annexure D) (Fig. 2.44).

Fig. 2.43 200 kV power substation supplying electricity to Lohati Pasai

2.8.2.1 The Local Power Relations in Motipur—Socio-political Demographic Structure at Play

Motipur contributes a total of 150 votes out of approximately 350 votes (electors) in the entire revenue village of Lohati pasai. The revenue village comprises Harijans (SCs), Muslims, Pandits (Brahmins), Koeris, Lodhs, and Malhas in order of descending population. Motipur purwa happens to be the seat of power for the Brahmin landlord, popularly known as *bhayia ji*. He is both a dreaded and a respected figure in Motipur.

His existence is ambivalent in practical terms, as he is at the mercy of the Brahmin landlord of the village, popularly known as *bhaiyaaji* (the big brother). Bhaiyaaji stays in Motipur and has a pucca mansion with a declared monthly income of 60,000 INR. His mansion comes under the notion of 'deemed electrification' but lacks a legitimate electricity meter for measuring and accounting for energy usage. The daily consumption of power for his mansion is around 10.41 units and is unaccounted for as of now.

Fig. 2.44 Photomosaic of Motipur hamlet depicting lifestyle of the local dwellers (*Source* Author, 2016)

Shhatrughan alias Lallulal, his close associate, is the gram pradhan (democratically elected village headman). Although he is a democratically elected village headman, he clearly spells out the caste-based power structure in his hamlet: *I got elected purely on account of authority that Bhaiya ji weilds, and his samman (respect) duly earned over a period of time, remarks Shhatrughan nonchalantly.*

Shhatrughan happens to be a tenant in the mansion of Bhaiyaaji. He works as a permanent khetihar kisan (farm labour) and also as a parttime driver-cum-watchman for Bhaiyaaji and his family. Shhatrughan has a family of four and resides in a mixed (kutcha-pucca) civil structure that also has an illegal power connection drawn from one of the service lines feeding Bhaiyaaji's mansion. His daily consumption of electrical power is approximately 0.525 units. The variation in the daily average consumption of power in Motipur ranges from a minimum of 0.017 units (SC beneficiary of MGP) to a maximum of 10.41 units (general category-

Brahmin consumer), with values ranging from 0.525 units to 0.96 units for *'katiya'* connections (illegally tapped service lines) for SCs and BCs, respectively, in Motipur purwa.

2.8.2.2 The Class-Caste-Wise Load Consumption Pattern in the Village

The dwelling units in Lohati Pasai were randomly sampled and physically investigated to study the nature of active usage of electrical appliances by the dwellers. A load demand profiling exercise was conducted, wherein dwelling units were randomly chosen to study their individual load demands (Fig. 2.48). LP03 to LP15 are the dwelling units which are beneficiaries of energy services provided by GGB (0.017 kWh). These dwelling units belong to Mallahs, Koeris, and Harijans. LP24 is the power consumption of the dwelling unit owned by Bhaiyaaji (10.41 kWh), and LP17 is the power consumption by Shhatrughan (0.525 kWh), the village headman. The individual load contribution throws light on the energy consumption culture and the daily chores of the rural life in the village.

All the three caste-class groups have access to energy (Table 2.6). The scheduled caste and the backward castes have two sources of supply; they are MGP beneficiaries and also tap formal supply lines illegally (Table 2.6). The range of load demand, therefore, varies from 0.017 units to approximately 1 unit in a day. The RESCO has the maximum presence in this village. The dwelling units with access to energy supply from MGP are represented as: LP01, L03-LP15 (Fig. 2.45). Interestingly, the upper caste group has a variable demand from 5 to 10 kWh (units) per day. They

Table 2.6 Showing the caste-class-wise energy access and consumption

Lohati Pasai

S.No.	Caste SC/BC/General	Access to energy service (No/Yes)	Nature of supply formal/informal/private	Load consumption in kWh
1	Scheduled Castes[a]	Yes	Informal/private	0.017–0.525 (range)
2	Backward Castes[b]	Yes	Informal/private	0.017–0.825 (range)
3	General category[c]	Yes	Formal/informal/private	>5–10.41(range)

[a]Harijans, [b]Muslim castes/sub-castes, koeris, lodhs and mallahs, [c]Brahmins
Source Author, 2017

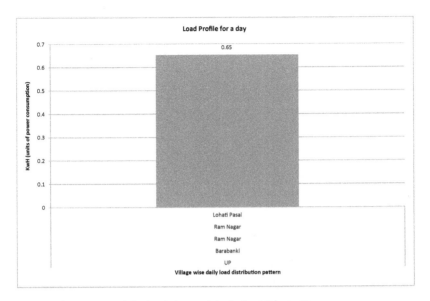

Fig. 2.45 Average daily load demand in Lohati Pasai village

have access to formal, informal, and private sources of energy supply. On an average, the daily load demand of the village is around 0.65 units (kWh). The load demand has been shown in Fig. 2.45.

The detailed individual contribution of individual load by each of the appliance types to the aggregate load demand of the village is shown in Fig. 2.46.

It is critical to our understanding that load demand (contracted demand for actual usage) is intricately linked to (a) geographical space, (b) local tastes, (c) local socio-cultural set-up, and (d) the manner in which energy access is provided for (1) through formal means, (2) informal means, and (3) through non-state agencies. Access to energy supplies is governed by proximity to local centres of political power (Fig. 2.53, Annexure D). The load demand and its contributing factors provide an incisive insight into the socio-economic and the local power structure that governs the community life in the village. It is an indication of realistic demand and complex consumer behaviour vis-à-vis supply of energy and its primary productive use. To understand the complexities of rural lifestyle further, the focus now shifts towards the actual demand for lighting.

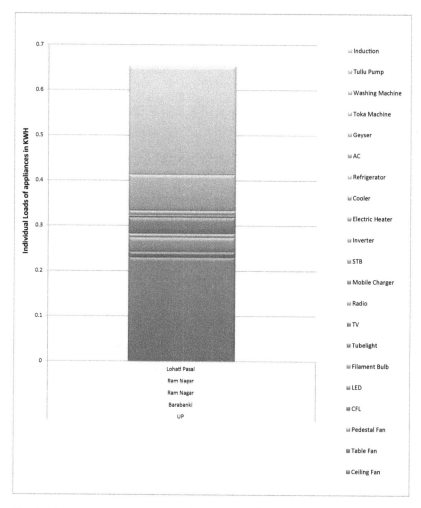

Fig. 2.46 Contribution to total electrical load by individual appliances in kWh, based on actual usage of electrical appliances

The load contribution of individual appliances in terms of lighting requirements of the village is shown in Fig. 2.47. There is a significant contribution by light emitting diodes (LEDs). There is a reason for this. LEDs were distributed as freebies to the rural folk under the (UJALA,

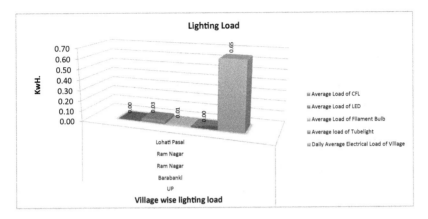

Fig. 2.47 Lighting load of different lighting appliances expressed as a fraction of total load on a daily basis across the revenue village

2015), scheme of Energy Efficiency Services Limited (EESL). There is a conspicuous absence of compact fluorescent lamps (CFLs) and tube lights. However, filament bulbs are still in use by a substantial number of households. Thus, the lighting load is about 6.15% of the total load demand (0.65 kWh) of the village. Therefore, lighting may not be the primary requirement of the rural populace in terms of primary end use of an energy service. These facts need to be taken into account while addressing local needs of energy consumption (Fig. 2.48).

The vertical, sub-divided bar graphs also show the ownership and actual usage of various appliances by different caste groups in the local cultural milieu. Therefore, it is significant to understand the local culture of electricity consumption, which is contextually embedded in the social, economic, and political structures which regulate the everyday demand for energy. *Interestingly, an energy service of 0.017 kWh (LP01 and LP03-LP15) is a pittance (supplied by MGP) as compared to the energy services offered by the state utility (formal power) or through illegitimate means (katiya).* Informal supply of power through *katiya* has a tacit sanction by the local community. However, it is the upper caste groups and the local vote bank dynamics that has the final say in resource allocation. Even the connections that are to be given on priority are also subject to similar informal rules and are, therefore, accordingly sanctioned.

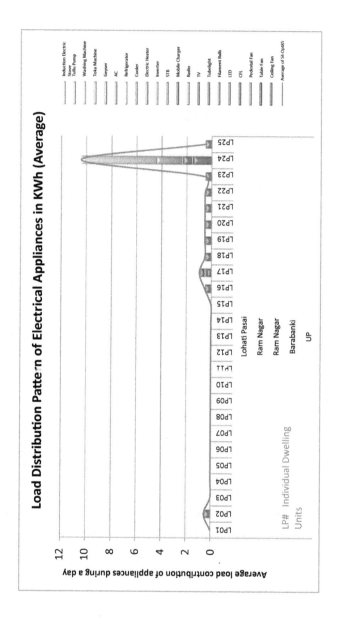

Fig. 2.48 Average diurnal (daily) load distribution pattern across the sampled dwelling units

2.8.2.3 The Operative Functionality of Non-state Actor: MGP
Not to arouse any element of unwelcome surprise and anxiety, the agency is a non-government organization (NGO) claiming to light up lives in the majara/ purwa of Motipur. The arrival of the Mishras as the agents of Mera Gao Power (MGP) introduces an interesting twist in the scenario of providing energy services in terms of altering consumer behaviour and social power relations in the local environs of Motipur. The functional extension of RESCO is through Mr. Maakhan mishra, the area manager of MGP, based in Sitapur district of UP. Mr. Buchhi mishra is based at Badosarai (a nearby locality), along with Mr. Ladoo mishra. Mr. Buchhi mishra claims to be the local site/area supervisor, whereas Mr. Ladoo mishra is the technical mill hand.

2.8.2.4 The Local Agents of MGP in the Energy Action Arena
Let us understand the modus operandi of MGP. MGP selectively chooses remote, inconspicuous, dwelling units with low-profile occupants of the purwa. Mostly, the beneficiaries of MGP belong to either scheduled caste and/or backward caste category. The ownership status of appliances is fixed. Every family gets 2 nos. of 1 W (0.25 W × 4 LED) lights and a single mobile charging point of 5 W, as claimed by the triumvirate, the Mishras. However, there is an inbuilt capability of technology (referred to as a load limiter) that regulates the quantity (duration) of power supply to six hours daily from 6.00 pm to 12.00 pm (a fact not known to the beneficiaries). Their claim to duration of supply is quite fair and transparent for DC (direct current) appliances (Fig. 2.54, Annexure D). The nature of avocation of the selected beneficiaries of MGP spans across the spectrum of self-employed entrepreneurship (Paan Ki Dukaan), casual labour (mazduri), and agricultural labour (kisani a typical term used in this part of the Hindi heartland). The nature of dwelling units is mixed (kutcha/pucca) civil structure, erected largely by government funding, as well as individual initiative.

Interestingly, none of the beneficiaries of MGP have any access either to the grid, or to the so-labelled modern energy-efficient fuels for cooking. The MGP has definitely helped them to tide over pitch darkness post-sunset by providing access to rudimentary lighting, though silent about the degree/intensity of incandescence in terms of lumens (a measure of glow). However, the manner in which the agents of MGP enter and approach a community is quite fascinating and attention drawing at the same time. Neither the de-facto nor the de-jure seat of power is taken into confidence while rolling out this energy service. Solar home lighting system (SHLS) as it is commonly known in technical parlance is installed on top of a pucca roof of a willing beneficiary, and gradually, others begin to get drawn towards the innovative method through creation of peer pressure Motipur purwa had only seven beneficiaries during July 2017. *'I have never heard of Mera Gao power (MGP), says Shhatrughan (the village headman), seemingly oblivious to their existence'*. In the current scenario, with so much thrust on extension of grid-based electricity supply to the villages, Shhatrughan feels that there is no relevance of such energy service companies as MGP (Fig. 2.56, Annexure D).

2.8.2.5 The Operational Dynamics of the Micro: The Actors, the Agents, and the Action Arena—In Terms of Resource Allocation, Access to Resource, and Its Capture

There is an inherent tussle between the private entity and the beneficiary, between beneficiaries drawing power from different sources, including MGP, between the functionaries of the ESCO and the state-backed entity (playing hide and seek), and between the democratically elected gram panchayat and the local elites. The caste issue served the immediate business interest of MGP. It fed its future aspirations as well, being close to the power centres in the village. This could help them expand their business by providing smooth access to local numbers of low-profile socio-economic groups. The so-called decentralized, legitimate, democratic three-tier institution of self-governance was practically non-existent as the real power lay with the caste groups that employed a maximum number of sharecroppers in their agricultural fields. There is also a clash of interest of an individual vis-à-vis that of the group.

The landholders in the village are primarily Brahmins and Lodhs. The remaining communities are either sharecroppers and daily rated (daily wage semi-skilled) mazdoors or self-employed entrepreneurs. The sharecroppers are at the mercy of Lodhs and Brahmins who are primarily driven by the utilitarian philosophy. Thus, they are predators and utility maximizers as well. The sum of the private interest of the tillers is subservient to the private interests of the upper castes. However, at an individual level, the interests are dissected and inclined towards self-fulfillment by means of unhindered access to freebies and other niceties in terms of unopposed, informal access to power supply lines. The clash is at two levels: horizontal and vertical. Horizontal, where similarly placed groups were embroiled with each other in terms of access, gain and control over electricity supply, and vertical, where caste hierarchies played a dominant role for ensuring access to energy on their own terms to the lesser social groupings.

At another level, the tussle assumed another dimension. At the horizontal level, the clash was between the intended beneficiaries of MGP and the unintended beneficiaries of MGP who belonged to a more or less similar socio-economic profile. At the vertical level, it was embedded in the alien socio-technical structure of the private entity (MGP) and the 'potentially demarcated' socio-political (class-caste) structure of the purwa that had formal access to state-owned power supply sources (the state power utility) and informal access to electricity service lines as well (katiya connections). MGP had never ventured into any kind of informal or formal communication method aimed towards spreading awareness about non-conventional electricity supply methods. They were thus banking totally upon the local elites for providing access to the local community. This proximity to the power centre helped the ESCO to tide over any untoward, unforeseen, unpleasant eventuality.

What seems to be unequivocally true and all pervasive throughout this narrative is the local power relationships which are prone to elite capture. The recurring periodicity of evidence on ground is indicative of the existent power dynamics that is often neglected by a centralist policy paradigm. Power is often thought and spoken of in an undifferentiated way as a good thing to possess. However, in the present context, it is marked by the conspicuous presence of power over (implying control), power to (implying the unique potential of every person), shape his or her life and the surrounding immediate world (Veneklasen & Miller, 2002: 39–41).

The conspicuous absence of the following typologies of power, viz. power with, (implying collaboration, solidarity, and collective action), and power within through self-worth and confidence. Power in the current context of Motipur purwa is either forcefully gained, seized, and captured; or lost, abandoned, and meekly surrendered. This phenomenon is not explicable through any of the forms of decentralization (a) de-concentration, (b) de-congestion, (c) delegation, or (d) devolution (Singh, 2016: 214). The relational dynamics of power and the existing social structures with its contemporary contextual complexity puts forth a complexity before the monolithic state.

The local action situation appears to be fraught with ideas of arriving at a negotiated compromise between the formal absentee actors, private agents, incongruent and opportunist polity, non-cohesive social structure, and crumbling institutions of local self-governance. The ground situation leaves one distraught over the claims of the state over energizing rural India by repudiating the unrealistic claims. It appears seemingly hard to believe that these events were occurring at the fundamental unit of functional administration (a revenue village). Where has been the ideal Weberian bureaucratic set-up?

One should pause and ponder over the absence of ideal Weberian bureaucracy in Lohati Pasai revenue village. The states' frontline institutional architecture for providing regulatory and development administration is totally amiss or is it purposefully and willingly missing? The constitutional hierarchy to oversee the functions of various elements of development administration from the level of the zila parishad (first tier) to the gram panchayat (third tier) is oblivious to the contemporary developments in Motipur purwa. Do the hard hitting and pinching ground realities of Motipur mock the spirit of ideologies, institutions, and the different theoretical constructs as well?

The access to energy in this socio-cultural realm appears to be prone to 'elite capture'. There is a reason for this. The Brahmins in the village happen to be money lenders to the majority of households. They have large landholdings (5–10 acres on an average). They control the private purse. The entire backward community looks up to them to help them tide over impinging financial requirements and during hardships. MGP is seen to exploit this situation (socio-economic dependence of the lower caste groups upon higher caste) to gain access within the community. The caste card is used by MGP to establish its business in Lohati Pasai. Further, the local gram panchayat of Lohati Pasai is controlled by upper caste Brahmins. It is this socio-economic class which allocates and regulates resource allocation including access to energy. MGP capitalizes on the bargaining power of the upper caste to gain seamless business access into the village.

2.8.2.6 Trust Deficit Between the RESCO and the Beneficiaries

The triumvirate (*the mishras*) claims to be an alternative to the state-run power supply systems. The NGO functionaries claim that they had very painful experiences with the three-tier system of the so-called grass-root democratic governance. There were blatant accusations against the *pradhan* (village headman) acting as an extortionist. Instances of employees being taken hostage, equipment being stolen, or forcibly seized were a common occurrence. On the contrary, the beneficiaries of the private power generation and distribution system had their own stories to tell.

Within the consumer group, there were voices of dissent as to quality of lighting, misbehaviour by MGP staff, lack of adherence to the weekly billing cycle, periodic/regular up-dation of bill books (Fig. 2.55, Annexure D), and the biggest woe was related to the (timely service)/promptness shown towards repair of any technical fault. There were cases of local sabotages as well. Within their closed power distribution system, there were instances of illegal tapping of power. Within the community, there were frequent altercations over sharing of distribution lines, free-riding, or rights of easement/cross-over of distribution lines. The grid-connected dwelling units, located in the close vicinity, were hostile to the beneficiaries of the private service. They used to prevent them from getting grid connectivity on one pretext or the other. They would see this service as over and above their source of electricity. Therefore, different tactics were deployed to instigate the community against the beneficiaries of MGP.

On the other hand, MGP functionaries were quite wary of the functionaries of the electricity department and would see them as their staunch adversary and as an intruder. Since the NGO is an independent entity, functioning unregulated (as an ESCO, energy service company) with impunity sans any regulation by the state or any of its agencies. It tries to establish a new unconventional, informal energy service set-up, trying to challenge the claims of the established conventional power supply system legitimized by the state. The energy service company (ESCO) sees the grid as an ardent adversary as it hurts its immediate as well as far, overt and covert, business propositions.

2.8.3 *The Non-state Actor Challenges the Formal Decentralized Institutional Mechanisms of the State that Govern Energy Access*

It appears that the organization (MGP) has institutional linkages to a cult that believes in downplaying the role of state in respect of its duties towards its citizens. There is no dispute of the fact that 'small is beautiful' (Schumacher, 1973). Technology, however big or small it may be, can never subsume or erase the might of end-users by limiting their choices by offering them pittance. A technology is a product of a given system and belief of knowledge, and it ultimately is a 'production system'. The services of MGP are noble indeed for the manner in which the entire thought of providing energy services has been constructed. However, the claims fall flat once the ground truth is captured. A direct observation of the entire system presents a picture of lock-in in terms of services, as well as technology.

When cutting costs becomes the guiding spirit, the services are bound to suffer. There comes a stage of cross-over of techno-economic consideration vis-à-vis consumer satisfaction. The claims of MGP are centred unequivocally around minimum capital expenditure and extremely low incidentals. There is no dispute about it. The institution has projected itself as the least expensive provider of an energy service across the globe. The nature of services needs to be examined in the light of the fact that 'electricity is construed as a merit good and that every household is entitled to a supply of a minimum of one unit of electricity per day, the long-term aspirational goal that was supposed to be achieved by the year 2012'. MGP has remained focused on establishing its credentials based on its minimal operation and maintenance costs. It has the innate myopic tendency similar to that of any utility maximizer. If at all the services offered in terms of luminescence are to be compared, the closest it would come to an incandescent lamp of equivalent wattage. The one-watt LED does not substitute for any other informal or formal source of lighting. A service should foster constructive engagement, cohesion, and social inclusion. However, the ground realities point towards exclusion, withdrawal, and disruption of social order.

2.8.3.1 *Energy Service Adequacy: A Far-Fetched Assessment of Demand Capture!*

An exclusively rudimentary, fixed nature of service does not result in social acceptance. MGP does not meet the smallest fraction of energy demand of the rural folk as it never studied consumer behaviour. The village has access to grid-based supply of power, barring Motipur hamlet. The arguments being put forth are not meant to cast an aspersion on the manner in which the organization has been functioning. Rather, it contends the quantum of pre-conceived and pre-designed load (DC) being serviced by means of solar energy. The load is a paltry 0.017 unit (as declared by the respondents during the field visit), usage being 6 hours of lighting by two numbers of LED (1 W each) depending on supply of power and one-hour usage of charging facility (power rating of the mobile charger: 5 W). Even if the charging facility is utilized for a full 6-hour duration, the total load comes to around 0.045 units. This nature of service (numerical value is 22 times less) mocks the national aspiration of one unit of power to be assured on a daily basis to every end-user of energy.

The claims and presumptions of MGP appear to be grossly antithetic to the conceptual frameworks and theories related to energy service. Even being an extremely small energy production system, it could be labelled as a 'closed system' operating outside the realms of participatory and representative modes of planning, making it inflexible and rigid (Sovacool, 2014). MGP as an energy service provider does not take into account any sort of stakeholder analysis that normally integrates concepts and practices from conflict resolution, business management, administration, due process, and justice (Table 2.7). The institution did not study at any stage of its journey, the relative power structures within a community, the influence and interests, and assess the broader context in which they interact (Brown & Sovacool, 2011).

The approach followed is more of an exclusivity and estrangement rather than inclusivity and engagement. This dictatorial approach led to subversion of democratic rights of the beneficiary. He/she is entitled to direct participation and effective representation in a technological decision. In this case, there is an abrupt termination of choices being limited to what is being supplied in terms of DC loads. The constraints are further exacerbated by the duration of power supply and the number of units of an appliance (2 LEDs and 1 mobile charging facility). This ideology is a readymade recipe for reducing costs on the one hand and increasing space for controversies and public disapproval (Sclove, 2010). Comparisons that have been made above with different systems of power generation and the scales at which they operate should have created fresh and exciting insights for a deeper understanding of issues that are of genuine concern across different parts of rural India.

Alternatively, it could have led to the identification of gaps in execution of any given service and could have pointed in different possible directions for better collective understanding and adoption of correctional measures (Fig. 2.51, Annexure D). Rather than indulging in criticism of other institutions and processes, there could have been an alternative thought to help sharpen the focus of energy service delivery by suggesting new perspectives (Hantrais, 1995). The section that follows further sheds light

Table 2.7 Critique on the service offered

S.No.	A. Claim	B. Presumption	C. Reality
1	Understanding a geographic entity	Viewing a rural set-up as uniform, isomorphic, and homogenous in terms of space and culture of energy consumption	Contextual domain of the rural is too complex in terms of its physical environment, individual household characteristics, and behaviour-specific disposition of a passive consumer
2	Capital expenditure per customer is lower than other micro-grid operators in India, and therefore, the operational expenses are also low	The state utilities and other private players supply energy services at a higher operational cost. The nature of energy service is akin to what is provided by MGP	Capital costs are an innate function of: (a) quality of supply, (b) quantity of supply, and (c) duration of supply. The supply-driven formula in case of MGP freezes the 'demand' of a customer to adjust to a tailor-made supply system
3	The mode of correction of user changes by MGP are identical to the functioning of a micro-finance institution (MFI)	none	The functioning of MFI is linked to the formation of self-help groups (SHGs). The groups are gradually trained, guided, and thereafter, immersed into a culture of savings, investment, and asset creation. MGP is an energy service provider. Its commercial/profit-making agenda is more visible as compared to an entrepreneur working for a social cause. There is no perceptible value addition in the life of an end-use, which is ultimately the purpose

(continued)

Table 2.7 (continued)

S.No.	A. Claim	B. Presumption	C. Reality
4	Maintenance and quality control: a dedicated team of area managers, branch managers, site supervisors deployed to address complaints from a customer	none	However, the beneficiaries are insecure about post-installation service and maintenance. The standard operational procedures for technical grievance redress are missing on ground. The beneficiaries are too remotely situated for an easy communication to take place
5	A national grid/mini-grid/ micro-grid is not financially and technically designed to cater to the needs of a small customer on account of: (a) fuel costs, (b) generation costs, (c) operating costs, (d) transmission costs, and (e) distribution costs. Therefore, daily cost of supply to small consumers cannot be realized on account of (1) billing efficiency, (2) collection efficiency on the part of large-scale generators and public/private energy service providers, and the (3) lack of willingness to pay (WTP) by the end-user as they are used to either free or subsidized energy service	MGP assumes itself to be at par with other generators and suppliers (formal and private entities) with regard to: (a) physical and technical nature of installations, (b) mode of power generation, (c) nature of energy services offered, and (d) client profile	Administrative staff college of India (ASCI) has conducted an in-depth study for standardization of capital costs for distribution business to provide last mile connectivity to every household (FOIR, 2010). This study captured data from 17 state utilities across 10 states of India The contention/claim of MGP appears to be too narrow in approach. Different energy production systems cannot be compared as the parameters on which they operate are distinctly different, viz. production design, scale of operations, tariff structures designed on utility of an available generator, etc

(continued)

Table 2.7 (continued)

S.No.	A. Claim	B. Presumption	C. Reality
6	Low cost and dependability that MGP provides cannot be provided by a grid-based infrastructure	Grid-based production system is a plug and play design and tariff setting is a simplistic process	The regulators of different states have put forth the view that each generating plant, transmission system and distribution system component is unique with two-part tariff structure comprising fixed charges and energy charges along with availability-based tariff (ABT) mechanism; each generator is to be evaluated differently based on the above parameters for arriving at a broad cost of supply by any given generator (Kumar & Chatterjee, 2012). Thus, the claim and presumption of MGP appear to be unrealistic

Note Presumptions, claim, and reality check by MGP
Source Author, 2017

on the erratic functionality of the rural energy service provider, MGP, that claims to replace grid-based power supply by the institutions of the state.

2.8.4 Conclusion and Policy Implications

The localism in governance refers to how humans make decisions and form institutions that craft rules shaping individual behaviour. The aforesaid geo-cultural setting and the narrative point towards three most pertinent areas for course correction: (a) local and regional energy governance, (b) the efficacy of the local institutions, and (c) regulatory governance. The canonical nature of energy services renders the energy action arena replete with public goods problems and externalities which may not be solved at a meso (regional)- or mega (national)-scale, as they warrant local collective action. The local collective action at the level of micro (revenue village) calls for polycentric forms of action that mix scales, mechanisms, and actors simultaneously. *The active sharing of power between numerous stakeholders, and scales can, at times, more effectively respond to energy access and services related problems than actions in isolation.*

Numerous works have argued that the presence of polycentrism enhances certain variables that can increase the likelihood of cooperation and resolution (Ostrom, 2008, 2010; Sovacool, 2011). The situation in Lohati Pasai highlights the following issues: (a) Is there a need to understand the local socio-political configurations and transformations that result from the presence of multiple institutions—in situ, familiar and outside, alien both? (b) Whether the approaches being followed at the national and the regional level are adequate or inadequate in terms of addressing issues related to fair access of energy and equitable distribution of energy services, (c) the need for broadening of roles and responsibilities of non-state actors in becoming involved in issues related to generation and distribution of energy, and (d) to which levels energy access governance can be decentralized through delegation and devolution to ensure equitable access? MGP has its own political economy rooted in authoritarianism and deep-seated centralization. The ESCO functions as an independent unit and probably believes in some sort of voluntary governance. The organization is neither recognized nor regulated by any of the institutions of the state.

The field experience presents pertinent observations with serious implications for policies and programmes overseeing quality access to energy—(a) the states' frontline institutional architecture for providing regulatory and development administration is totally amiss; (b) the '*constitutionally*' laid down hierarchical structure, to oversee and manoeuvre the elements of development administration, right from the level of the Zila Parishad (first tier), through a community development (CD) block, to the gram panchayat (third tier) is oblivious to the contemporary developments in Motipur, *reflecting institutional distancing and apathy;* (c) complete dearth of practices required for better regulatory governance of private energy service providers; (d) establishment of cannons of transparency, accountability, legitimacy, participation for effective transfer of technology; and (e) absence of established norms of promotion of equitable allocation of energy services based on local culture of energy consumption and available technology.

2.8.5 Weak Regulation Fuels Voluntarism and Monopoly by Non-state Actors Providing Energy Access

The state regulator is duly entrusted with the task of determining and notifying the standards of performance of local generators with respect to quality, continuity, and reliability of service for all consumers. The Uttar Pradesh Electricity Regulatory Commission (UPERC) was the first regulator in the country to come up with a 'mini-grid renewable energy generation and supply regulations'. These regulations were enacted with an objective to:

Supply of reliable and quality power of specified standards in an efficient manner and at reasonable rates.

The regulation recognizes the following critical constructs in respect of an electricity distribution system and supply of electricity as an essential service. The key components of the policy are: (a) identification of the key actors: (1) mini-grid operator (MGO), (2) the distribution licensee (state distribution utility), (3) the power distribution network (PDN), (4) the local generator (generation based on renewable energy sources), and (5) the consumer; (b) mutually agreed billing cycle; (c) compulsory supply hours (CSH-5.00 pm to 11.00 pm), to be notified by the regulator; and (d) standard of performance (SoP), defining the immediate hinterland for supply of energy services. The regulations lay emphasis on reliability of supply and quality of service. The domestic customers have been given priority. It casts a statutory obligation on the mini-grid operator to compulsorily supply electricity to all willing domestic consumers within a forty-metre radius.

Apart from Omni microgrid company (OMC), the leading mini-grid developer in the state of Uttar Pradesh, no other firm has furnished any document before the state electricity regulator, remarks Sh. Vikas Chandra Agarwal, director (distribution, UPERC).

Low levels of social activism and education on issues related to energy access and end use defeat the objectives of a well-conceived policy. MGP exists and functions, sans any external sanctions by any of the formal institutions of the state. Be it: (1) the state-level energy regulator (Uttar Pradesh Electricity Regulatory Commission), (2) the state nodal agency for governing power generation through renewable sources of energy

(State Nodal Agency, UPNEDA), (3) local revenue and development administration (the office of the district collector and the chief development officer), and (4) the micro-level institutions of self-government, the zila parishad (of Barabanki district), the block samiti (Ramnagar block), and the gram panchayat of Lohati Pasai; while these events were concomitantly occurring at the cutting edge of the fundamental unit of functional administration (a revenue village), the state stood in its most sublime and muted form? *Decentralization as a theoretical construct succumbs to fractured interests- when situated outside the formal structures of the state.*

An effective policy prescription for decentralized energy access from alternate sources would entail integration of social theory and cultural practices to move beyond simplistic assumptions of how individuals make choices related to energy access. Energy access to the local as a process (policy output) is embedded within a larger regional and national context. Therefore, apart from technological capacity addition at the macro-level to drive this change, energy access is also guided by complex local, sociopolitical, and cultural factors (Brown, 2010; Vaitheeswaran, 2005). The Motipur experience questions the current, centralized policy paradigm for extending energy access. Rather, it calls for an immediate change over to a comprehensive, decentralized process for planning and executing rural electrification and eventually access to energy by the local. The missing institutional architecture for overseeing quality energy access at the level of a revenue village (-micro), is indicative of (a) absence of regulatory extension of the state institution, and (b) lost development focus. The passive, decentralized systems of governance call for a relook into the modalities of energy access provisioning (Chapter 3).

2.9 Annexure D: Case study 2.4 Mera Gao Power (Uttar Pradesh)

See Figs. 2.49, 2.50, 2.51, 2.52, 2.53, 2.54, 2.55, and 2.56.

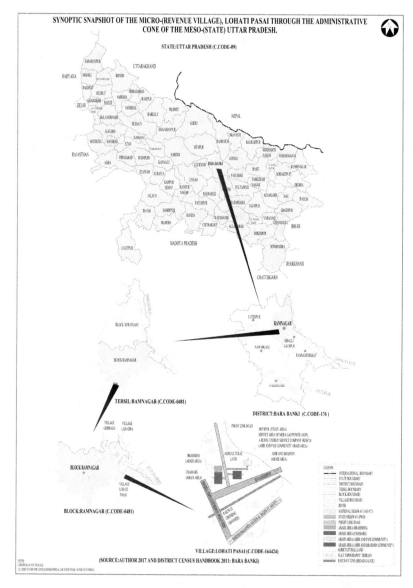

Fig. 2.49 Comprehensive snapshot of the village Lohati Pasai through the administrative cone of the Meso-(State)

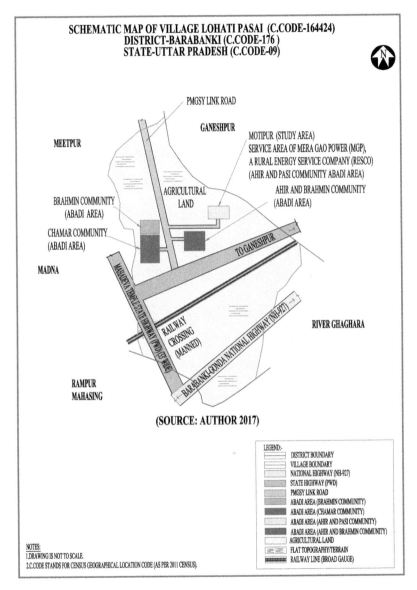

Fig. 2.50 Schematic map of the village Lohati Pasai

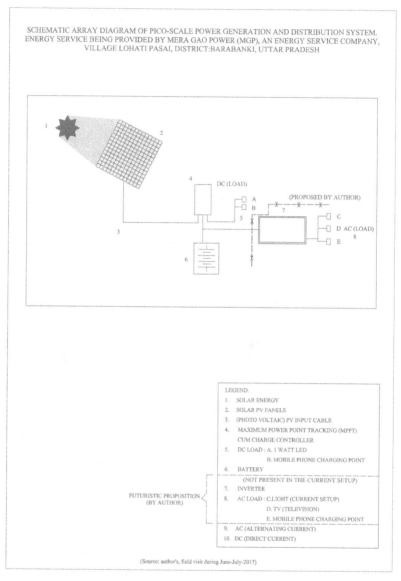

Fig. 2.51 Schematic single line diagram for the MGP energy service system. Future level 'escalation' in terms of better services has also been shown

2 CASE STUDIES AS AN IMMERSIVE APPROACH ... 183

1. FORMAL POWER SUPPLY AT BAHAU'S HOUSE.
2. INFORMAL POWER SUPPLY AT BIHARI'S HOUSE.
3. TYPOLOGY OF APPLIANCES IN NANHEY RAM'S HOUSE.
4. SARDARI LAL WITH MGP SERVICE TYPE AT HOUSE FACILITY.
5. SARDARI LAL WITH EXTENDED FAMILY AT HIS HOUSE.
6. IQBAL NARAYAN WITH EXTENDED FAMILY AT HIS HOUSE.

(SOURCE: AUTHOR, 2017)

Fig. 2.52 Energy access typology in Lohati Pasai

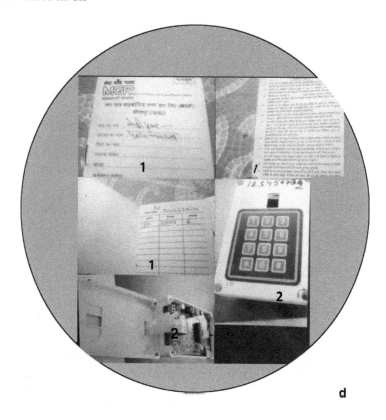

1. ENERGY ACCOUNTING (FIXED CHARGES) FOR MGP BENEFICIARIES
2. NEW INITIATIVE: PRE-PAID ELECTRICITY METERS (IN TESTING PHASE)

(SOURCE: AUTHOR, 2017)

Fig. 2.53 System of revenue collection by MGP

2 CASE STUDIES AS AN IMMERSIVE APPROACH ...   185

b

1. TYPICAL STRUCTURE OF A DWELLING UNIT 2. MUD PLASTERED TRADITIONAL COOK STOVE
3. TYPICAL KITCHEN IN A DWELLING UNIT IN MMOTIPUR
4. TRADITIONAL DIBBI FOR LIGHTING
5. COOK STOVE FOR COOKING FOOD (A DIFFERENT CONSTRUCTION)
6. FIRE WOOD AS A SOURCE OF COOKING FUEL

(SOURCE: AUTHOR, 2017)

Fig. 2.54 General life style in the village, Lohati Pasai (*Source* Author, 2017)

1. MOBILE CHARGING POINT
2. MOBILE CHARGING UNIT 4. (0.25WX4) : 1W LED (LIGHTING UNIT)
5. DISTRIBUTION MAINS
6. LOAD LIMITER
7. CHARGE CONTROLLER PLUS BATTERY
8. CONNECING CABLE
9. JUNCTION BOX
10. THE MGP SOLAR HOME LIGHTING SYSTEM (PANEL ON THE ROOF TOP)

(SOURCE: AUTHOR, 2017)

Fig. 2.55 Generation, distribution and the nature of energy service of the MGP setup in the village (*Source* Author, 2017)

2 CASE STUDIES AS AN IMMERSIVE APPROACH ... 187

1. PRADHAN (ACTUAL) DE-FACTO
2. PRADHANPATI (DE-JURE)
3. PRADHAN (ACTUAL) DE-FACTO
4. PRADHAN (ACTUAL) MOTIPUR (LOHATI PASAI)
5. INSET: BDO RAMNAGAR'S OFFICE ON NH-927
6. GRAM SACHIV (FRESH APPOINTMENT)

(SOURCE: AUTHOR, 2017)

Fig. 2.56 Village heads interviewed to assess the functioning of MGP

References

Ahmad, J. K., Devarajan, S., Khemani, S., & Shah, S. (2005). *Decentralization and service delivery* (World Bank Policy Research, Working Paper [3603]).

Brown, M. (2010). Power to the people: How the coming energy revolution will transform an industry, change our lives, and maybe even save the planet by Vijay Vaitheeswaran, sustainable development. *Law and Policy, 4*(1), Article 10.

Brown, M. A., & Sovacool, B. K. (2011). *Climate change and global energy security: Technology and policy options*. MIT Press.

Chambers, R. (1994). *Challenging the professions: Frontiers for rural development*. Intermediate Technology Publications.

Chambers, R. (1997). *Whose reality counts: Putting the first last*. Intermediate Technology Publications.

Cheema, G. S., & Rondinelli, D. A. (1983). *Decentralization and development: Policy implementation in developing countries*. Sage.

Clague, C. (Ed.). (1997). *Institutions and economic development: Growth and governance in less-developed and post-socialist countries*. The Johns Hopkins University Press.

Constitution of India. (1950). *Extracts from the constitution of India, as modified on 1st December, 2007* (pp. 1–443). Ministry of Law and Justice, Government of India.

Dreze, J., & Sen, A. (1995). *India: Economic development and social opportunity*. Oxford University Press.

Giddens, A. (1998). *The third way: The renewal of social consequences of modernity*. Polity Press.

Hantrais, L. (1995). Social policy in the European Union. *International Journal of Social Welfare, 5*(2), 113–116.

Kumar, A., & Chatterjee, S. (2012). *Electricity sector in India—Policy and regulation*. Oxford University Press.

Manor, J. (1999). *The political economy of democratic decentralization*. The World Bank.

Morduch, J., & Klibanoff, P. (1995). Decentralization, externalities, and efficiency. *The Review of Economic Studies, 62*(2), 223–224. https://www.jstor.org/stable/2297803

National Electricity Policy. (2005). *Resolution no. 23/40/2004-R&R* (Vol. II, pp. 1–17), dated 12th February 2005, the Gazette of India, Ministry of Power, Government of India.

North, D. (1986). The new institutional economics. *Journal of Institutional and Theoretical Economics, 142*, 230–237.

Ostrom, E. (2008). Tragedy of the commons. In *The new Palgrave dictionary of economics* (Vol. 2, pp. 1–5). Palgrave Macmillan.

Ostrom, E. (2010). A long polycentric journey. *Annual Review of Political Science, 13*, 1–23. www.annualreviews.org

Putnam, D. R. (1993). *Making democracy work, civic traditions in modern Italy*. Princeton University Press, ISBN 0-691-07889-0.

Report of the Administrative Staff College of India (ASCI). (2010). *Study on capital costs benchmarks for distribution business* (pp. 1–208). Centre for Infrastructure Management and Regulatory Studies, submitted to Forum of Indian Regulators (FOIR), New Delhi.

Rural Electrification Policy. (2006). Resolution no. 44/26/05-RE (Vol. II, pp. 1–17), dated 23rd August 2006, the Gazette of India, Ministry of Power, Government of India.

Schumacher, E. F. (1973). *Small is beautiful: A study of economics as if people mattered*. Vintage Books.

Sclove, R. (2010, April). *Reinventing technology assessment a 21st century model*. Science and Technology Innovation Program, Woodrow Wilson International Centre for Scholars.

Sovacool, B. K. (2011, June). An international comparison of four polycentric approaches to climate and energy governance. *Energy Policy, 39*(6), 3832–3844.

Sovacool, B. K. (2014). Diversity: Energy studies need social science. *Nature, 511*, 529–530. https://doi.org/10.1038/511529a

Unnat Jyoti by Affordable LEDs for All (UJALA), Energy Efficiency Services Limited (EESL), a Joint Venture (JV) of Public Sector Units (PSUs), Ministry of Power, Government of India. (2015). eeslindia.org

Uttar Pradesh Electricity Regulatory Commission (UPERC). (2016). *UPERC (mini-grid renewable energy generation and supply) regulations* (notification no.UPERC/Secy/VCA/Regulations/2016-020, pp. 1–18).

Vaitheeswaran, V. (2005). *Power to the people: How the coming energy revolution will transform an industry, change our lives, and may be even save the planet*. Forrar, Strauss and Girous. ISBN: 1-84407-176-6, 2003.

Veneklasen, L., & Miller, V. (2002). *A new weave of power, people and politics: The action guide for advocacy and citizen participation*. Power and Empowerment World Neighbours, PLA Notes, 43, 39–41.

Weber, M. (1946). *From Max Weber: Essays in sociology* (H. H. Gerth & C. Wright Mills, Eds.). Oxford University Press.

Wilson, W. (1887). The study of administration. First published in *Political Science Quarterly*, Reprinted in Shafritz, J., & Hyde, A. A. (1997). *Classics of public administration* (2nd ed.). Dorsey Press.

2.10 RS Farms: The Biogas Cum Dairy Farm (A Social Enterprise) That Was Not to Be: A Failed Saga of Perceived 'Collectivism, Social Innovation, and Social Enterprise'?

2.10.1 About Bahadurpur: Geography, Demography, and Socio-economic Profile

The revenue village of Bahadurpur bears a consolidation and settlement number, commonly known as hadbast no. 32., attributed to it during settlement and consolidation operations. It falls in tehsil and district, Rupnagar. It lies on the banks of River Sutlej (Figs. 2.57 and 2.58, Annexure E). The village has a total population of 425, which includes 226 males and 199 females. There is only a single family belonging to the scheduled caste category with 4 members (2 males, 2 females), as per the district census handbook (DCHB) of Roopnagar (census, 2011). The village has 85 nos. of dwelling units. The total number of registered voters is 316 (district election office, Rupnagar).

The village has a majority population of Sainis (backward caste), followed by Tarkhans (community engaged in manufacture of minor implements used by a carpenter and/or a farmer), who also belong to the backward caste category. The primary occupation of the residents is agriculture. The major crops grown are wheat and paddy. The panchayat in the revenue village of Bahadurpur comprises 5 wards (artificially created based upon territorial/physical and community contiguity). The panchayat has six members, 1 sarpanch, and 5 panches, respectively. Out of the 5 panches, 3 are females and 2 are males. No direct elections have been held in this village since the last three terms (last direct elections were held in 2003).

The sarpanch and the other members are nominated by mutual consensus of the local population, claims Dilbar Singh (RS Farms). There is a formal panchayati raj institution (PRI). However, within this formal institution, a new informal structure has been created through organized, mutual consent, presenting an altogether different construct of consensual democracy (democratization of consensus).

The basic facilities that are present in the village include a *primary school*, an *aaganwadi* centre, a milk collection centre, two *kiryana* (shops for daily needs), and other miscellaneous shops for catering to the domestic chores of the households. Apart from these, there is a bicycle repair shop as well. An interesting fact that deserves a special mention: *the village has 45 numbers of LPG connections from two different gas agencies* (Fig. 2.69, Annexure E). The village boasts of its biogas plant- a source of clean cooking fuel and green manure, known all over by the name of Ram Singh Farms (*interaction with former sarpanch: Sh. Ajmer Singh and Block Development and Panchayat Officer, Rupnagar: Smt. Rajwinder kaur, 2017*).

2.10.2 The Family Genealogical Tree and the Prenatal History of RS Farms

The third generation of late Sardar Ram Singh now manages the biogas plant and the farm, collectively known as Ram Singh Farms. The first generation was the era of Sardar Ram Singh and his wife Smt. Karam Kaur. Shri Ram Singh passed away on 7 October 2006. Smt. Karam Kaur is now 76 years of age. The second generation belongs to their three sons: (a) Sardar Sital Singh, (b) Sardar Dilbar Singh, and (c) Sardar Balbir Singh. Smt. Sukhwinder Kaur, Kuldeep Kaur, and Sarabjeet Kaur have been married to the three brothers, in the sequence of their mention. The three couples have been blessed with the third-generation siblings. Harpreet Kaur, Jaspreet Kaur, and Gurpreet Singh are daughters and son of Sital Singh and Sukhwinder Kaur. Talwinder Kaur, Rajwinder Kaur, Jasdeep Kaur, and Gursimran Singh are daughters and son of Dilbar Singh and Kuldeep Kaur, and lastly, Gagandeep Singh, Bhupinder Singh, and Preetinder Kaur (predeceased) are sons of Balbir Singh and Sarabjeet Kaur.

The third generation has been mostly out on account of attaining higher education in such fields as dental studies, computer applications, information technology, business administration, commerce, and other engineering disciplines. The education has been mostly in the state of Punjab. The only far-off place has been district Solan in the state of Himachal Pradesh (source: Balbir Singh and Gagandeep Singh, during fieldwork, September–October, 2017). The biogas farm is the brainchild of Sardar Balbir Singh (belongs to the second generation), the middle son of Late Shri Ram Singh. The operations and maintenance are overseen by Gagandeep who has completed his graduation and stays with the family in the village. The family is a joint, collective unit.

The second-generation siblings are non-resident Indians (NRIs), based in Dubai running a scrap business. One of the three brothers, Sital

Singh is also engaged in real estate business in the tehsil (sub-division) of Shri Anandpur Sahib, about 35 kms, from Bahadurpur. Gagandeep also manages field visitors from different parts of the country as he is fairly conversant with the concepts and functions of the biogas plant, the history behind its conception, and therefore, handles visitors and media (Fig. 2.65, Annexure E).

2.10.2.1 The Early days of Conception of the Biogas Plant
'We three brothers have been exposed to different kinds of good practices in foreign lands'-remarks, Dalbir Singh. It was that exposure to some good practices in terms of improvement of basic civic amenities that motivated us to do something creative for our native village. Shifting to Chandigarh, nearby union territory, was a thought at one point of time, remarks Dilbar Singh'. Though the family shares an exceptionally strong affinity towards the village, however, at one point of time a unanimous call had been taken by the second generation of men to shift base. It was the third generation that wanted to stay back. It is the third generation which kept the elders motivated and made them do something purposive, creative, and constructive for Bahadurpur.

2.10.2.2 Creation of Trust—Investing in Human Capital, Accumulating Social Capital: The Beginning
Dalbir Singh had abandoned his higher studies (pre-engineering course), with the thought of creating some kind of innovative community-centric resource/asset in the village. *'I chose to drop out not because I could not cope with the curriculum, but because I had to do something for my birthplace, Bahadurpur-remarks Mr. Singh'.* Thus, the first collective thought was related to creation of urban facilities and basic civic amenities in the village. The biogas plant was a much later mental offspring and a delayed plan. It was in the year 2007–2008 that a village assembly was convened and a uniform resolution was passed with regard to the agenda of 'hygiene and cleanliness'. The aim was (a) conversion of all surface drains into subsurface drains, (b) creation of porous structures in the form of rectangular punctured manholes to arrest rain water flow and arrest surface water run-off, (c) no dumping of any kind of solid waste by any household into the subsurface drainage, and (d) prevention of water logging on any of the streets and drainage network in the village.

The Singh family took the onus upon themselves to look into the issues of levelling, gradient, lining of the drainage, and other technical issues. They were the front runners of the campaign in letter and spirit. This was a complete community-driven project. Labour and material were locally arranged. Each household contributed a minimum sum of 5000 INR towards this cause. Some paid more, and the remaining amount was paid by the Singh family. The total length of the sewage network was around two kilometres. A sum of 30 lakhs INR was incurred for this project including rain water harvesting structures and sump construction. Therefore, the first community mission for hygiene, cleanliness, and rain water harvesting was achieved through community involvement.

This project established goodwill and trust of the family in the tiny community set-up of the village. The next thought was handling of animal waste in the village that was the prime reason for clogging of drains and resulted in overflowing drains. It was now that the idea of a full-fledged biogas arrived. The Singh family had a small unit in their house for meeting their cooking fuel requirements. They had 3 milch cattle then. The biggest issue was cleansing of the waste pit, *'gobar nahi uthana'*, as no labour would be ready to handle animal waste manually (a huge mental block, a socio-psychological barrier). Animal waste handling was the biggest challenge. Since it was difficult to run a family size unit, how would it be possible to run a community size biogas plant? This was a prime concern for all of us during 2009–2010, when we first thought of giving this project a first shot, says Dilbar Singh. The tiny village of Bahadurpur had by then garnered a lot of print and electronic media attention due to its earlier success story.

2.10.2.3 Issues, Fears, and Anxieties Eroded Trust

Therefore, this fear of adverse reporting and loss of self-repute were also seated in the subconscious mind of the family (presumptuous extraneous influence). Earlier discussions were centred around conception and development of a biogas cooperative. However, the fear of individual number of animals held by a single household, size of the family (number of mouths to be fed), and door-to-door collection of waste, followed by its transportation and dumping till the processing point (digester) led to the abandonment of this idea. There was a fear that this idea will find very few takers, and even if some agree, the project could lead to the disruption of social fabric in the village on account of the fact—who shall get how much and for what duration? On what parameters is the decision going to be based? These fears/dilemmas point towards the established theoretical constructs of the rationale and logic of individual action, collective community action, collective action of a few, the individual better-off option, or a collective win–win situation. Interestingly, waste is an individual item produced in each household. In terms of its potential to produce biogas through a collective unit (a common anaerobic digester), it becomes a community resource.

As an individual household, it only qualifies to remain as a waste waiting to be dumped somewhere, under cover. Therefore, cattle refuse in the form of urine and solid refuse at an individual level remains a waste, while in collective terms it could be labelled as a 'promising' source of cooking fuel, farmyard green manure, and electricity as well. Although, the fact that collective action shall produce better and greater outcomes as compared to individual inaction or inertia, still the idea of a cooperative biogas system had to be abandoned in Bahadurpur. The biggest fear being that there were some households, who did not have anything to contribute, as they did not have any domestic animal; therefore, they were not entitled to the supply of biogas as they were non-contributors towards this particular collective action.

2.10.2.4 *The Humble Beginning as an Individual Enterprise*

The Singh family, however, decided to give this project a try on their own. They applied for a loan of 1.25 INR for this project. It was sanctioned in two tranches. The first tranche was a sum of 75 INR and the second was 50 INR. The loan was sanctioned by the Oriental Bank of Commerce (Roopnagar branch). The family has small collective landholding of 4 acres as of now. However, the family has a scrap business abroad (Balbir Singh metal trading company limited), based in Dubai.

Apart from this, they are active in the real estate sector as well registered as promoters (with Punjab Urban Development Authority, PUDA) by the name Twenty First Century Buildcon Private Limited. As a first step, cattle shed was prepared (a sum of around 20 lakhs were spent @ 100 INR per square feet), thereafter, the second major expenditure was incurred towards purchase of 65 cows (an expenditure of 30–35 lakhs was incurred), a sum of 8.5–9.0 lakhs was incurred on the milking parlour, and further an expenditure of 8.5–9.0 lakhs INR was incurred on the construction of chilling plant and a diesel generator set. The least cost was incurred on the construction of fixed dome, subsurface digester, and the entire unit, which was around 2.50 lakhs, in which around 1.5 lakh was labour component and the material (sand, cement, brick plus reinforcement) cost was around 1 lakh INR. As of now, the strength of cattle is 160, including calves.

2.10.2.5 The Biogas Unit Becomes a Reality

The biogas plant was commissioned during April 2011. The distribution network runs around a radius of 30 m. The total cost of the gas supply network is around 45,000 INR. A one-time connection cost for every household is 600 INR. The connected household has to purchase the biogas *chullah* (stove) on its own which costs somewhere between 900 and 1200 INR. The main regulator (the nozzle) that connects the tertiary (final) inlet to the challah is also purchased by the end-user. The supply of biogas was initially for a full 24-hour cycle, but subsequently reduced to three slots of two hours each during the day, morning (7.00 am–9.00 am), afternoon (12.00 pm–2.00 pm), and evening (5.30 pm–7.30 pm). The timings, however, vary during different seasons (Figs. 2.66–2.68, Annexure E).

2.10.2.6 The Recurring (Operation and Maintenance Costs)

The monthly operation and maintenance costs of the entire unit along with the maintenance of the animal farm (milch cattle management) comprising feed and fodder (the maximum: 6.0–6.5 lakhs), diesel consumption (around 25,000 INR), medicinal treatment (10,000), electricity bill on an average (12,000–15,000 INR), gas production system, slurry pumping system, and gas distribution network till the last point of supply come to around 7.5–8 lakhs INR. This sum also includes the establishment costs in terms of wages that are paid to Mr. Gurnam Singh, accountant (8000 INR per month), Mr. Inderjit Singh, operation and repairs (10,000 INR per month), Mr. Kuldeep Singh, Mr. Hardev Singh, and Mr. Bhola, sweepers and cleaners (11,500 INR each per month). The details are placed in Table 2.10, Annexure E.

2.10.2.7 Expansion and Diversification—From a Biogas Unit Providing Free Cooking Fuel Supply, into a Dairy Farm and a Sweet Meat and Confectionary Unit

Ram Singh Farms supply free biogas across Bahadurpur village (Figs. 2.59–2.63, Annexure E). The dairy farm has a herd of around 160 cows including calves, both indigenous and mixed breeds. The primary product is milk that is processed for commercial gains after substantial value addition and sold through the local sweet outlet at the revenue boundary between Bahadurpur and Lodhi majra (shut down during 2016). The secondary residues generated (post-anaerobic digestion) from animal waste (cow dung and urine), biogas is supplied free of cost via aerial distribution network to individual households, and the bio-slurry that is left as an end product after the digestion and fermentation process is sold as green organic manure to the farmers in the neighbouring villages. *'We had developed a sewage system in our village during 2009-10. On account of this endeavour, the entire village has undergone a radical transformation into a village that is up to mark and standards to match any developed countryside globally, remarks Dalbir Singh'.*

The subsequent step was to put up a biogas plant to produce clean cooking gas. *'We asked the local populace to deposit cow dung at the plant, in case they wish to get clean cooking fuel (biogas), free of cost-remarks Balbir singh, the youngest in the second generation of siblings. This was the real challenge- to keep waiting for raw material (cattle waste), and therefore, we started our own dairy farm; continues Dilbar Singh'.* The farm was set up as a small initiative to produce free cooking gas but later it had grown and expanded into a food-processing unit producing milk and sweet meats along with other milk products. *'We got the plan and design of the plant from Mr. Sarabjeet Singh Sooch (senior research engineer, school of energy studies for agriculture, college of agriculture engineering and technology), Punjab agricultural university (PAU), Ludhiana. Thereafter, the plant was erected with the help of construction workers from Panipat district of Haryana, says Dilbar Singh'.*

2.10.2.8 The Physical and the Technical Details of the Unit

The biogas plant is 130 cubic metres in size and installed in an area measuring 2400 square feet (the shed area). The quantum of waste is humongous (10,000 litres); cumulative solid waste and urine is fed into the digester daily. After fermentation and digestion, the organic biofuel is generated. The process is almost synchronized functionally and requires minimal human intervention (Figs. 2.66–2.69, Annexure E). The biogas is supplied to almost 75 plus households in the village with its primary, secondary, and tertiary aerial distribution systems (Fig. 2.63, Annexure E). *'About 8–10 cylinders can be filled daily without much effort, remarks Mr. Singh'.* The plant remains operational throughout the year. The lean period in terms of digester functionality is during winters when the temperatures are low. The supply is scheduled in terms of three slots during the day: morning, afternoon, and evening commensurate with the meal timings of the Punjab households (breakfast, lunch and dinner).

The reason for free supply of biogas is attributed towards adding social value through service towards the community, being natives of this village. The waste/slurry left after the biogas enrichment process is a rich source of green farm manure. The slurry is sold to the farmers at the rate of 500 INR per tanker. The capacity of a single tanker is around 5000 litres. In a day, around 3–4 tankers of manure are filled and sold to the farmers of nearby villages (Fig. 2.62, Annexure E). The dairy cattle are given nutritious feed like silage of maize, hay, binola cakes, seeds, dry fodder, etc. The farm has a 'state of the art' feed plant that comprises a pulplizer unit, a grinding unit, and a mixing unit. This feed processor is imported. The Singhs also do on-farm breeding. There is a standard method of gradation of cattle. They are graded into three batches of (a) early lactation and high yield grade, (b) milk yielding grade, and (c) nascent 3- to 6-month–old calves. The vaccination of calves begins from the seventh day and continues up to 3 months.

Having made a humble beginning from around 3 cows, the herd strength has swelled to more than 150 cows plus calves. The total number of active mill hands is just four to manage the entire operations (Figs. 2.59–2.63, Annexure E). The machinery deployed at the farm is a mix of the best technologies across the globe, especially Germany—the pioneers/front runners in clean, green technology. The dairy farm produces around 1000 litres of milk on a daily basis. Around 30–40% of the milk produced is processed to be sold as raw milk, while the remaining is used to manufacture a range of milk products including sweet meats.

The milk processing plant produces a range of around 200 items, which are produced in batches depending upon the demand from the market. A total of 5 mill hands are deployed at the milk processing centre as of now (Author, 2017). The family takes pride in proclaiming that they never sought any opinion from any food-processing expert. The growth was only by means of self- and experiential learning. The regular challenges had been mostly linked to state apathy, cattle management, maintaining standards of products, and increasing the shelf life of processed raw milk. The family venture wishes to expand into an indomitable food chain franchisee and thereafter transforming itself into the most popular food chains in the country. The prime reason behind this aspiration is the 'joint family structure', that has withstood hardships together to stand up as a single, homogenous, cohesive unit standing tall and strong (*Source* Personal interaction with Sardar Dilbar Singh, Balbir Singh and Gagandeep Singh s/o Balbir Singh, 2017).

2.10.2.9 Interaction with the Mason (the Chief Architect) and the Principal operator—The Real Heroes

Sh. Ram Kumar is a trained mason, who has undergone around two and a half months of specialized training at Punjab Agriculture University (PAU), Ludhiana, for construction of Janta model of biogas plants. As of now, he is primarily engaged in the business of construction of biogas plants. He was especially deployed by Dr. Sooch on personal request of Sh. Dilbar Singh. Sh. Ram Kumar is a native of Nawatar village, tehsil: Bapoli, district: Panipat (Haryana). This plant was constructed during 2010–2011 by him and 2 trained masons. Around 6–7 labourers assisted him in the project. It took around 60 days to accomplish the task. *We had to create two digesters of 10 feet diameter and 10 feet vertical depth, as the village is very close to the river Sutlej and the groundwater depth is shallow, around 14 feet below ground level (bgl), remarks Ram kumar.* The floor of the digester is about four feet above the water table. The plant is entirely a subsurface structure, made of bricks, sand, and cement. It is a robust structure, a lot of hard work went into plinth strengthening to prevent any leakage/seepage of groundwater, proclaims Ram Kumar. Initially, everyone used to say that this plant shall not last for more than a year, but it is working fine with no complaints till date (Figs. 2.59–2.62, Annexure E).

Mr. Baljeet Singh, aged 42 years, is a native of village Alampur, tehsil and district: Rupnagar. He is the man responsible for operations and maintenance of the entire biogas distribution network. His job profile includes such tasks as attending to complaints of valve repair, repair of burners, clearing of pipes and valves of carbon soot, and dewatering of the primary and secondary distribution system. He earns around 4000–5000 INR per month on account of the services rendered to the end-users. The payment from the individual households is on a voluntary basis in the form of tokenism.

He is an extremely committed worker and is available on call. Since the supply is unmetered and is totally free, he survives on his one goodwill for his living. He does not receive any emolument from the Singh family. Apart from this job, he is a trained plumber and a pump operator as well. He also maintains the water supply distribution system of the village. He earns an additional 5000 INR per month from the households. Since the water supply is metered, he receives on an average 100–150 INR per household. He maintains the metering and billing history of every household. However, *9000 INR is too meagre a sum to support a family*, remarks Baljeet.

2.10.3 Theoretical Imports Applied to Deconstruct RS Farms as a Social, Economic, Cultural, and Political Entity

Theoretical review comprises of three aspects as applied to RS Farms: (1) social economy, social enterprise, and social capital; (2) governance issues relating to common property resources (CPR) and dilemmas related to collective action (Ostrom, 1990), and (3) institutional dynamics (North, 1990). However, in the process of understanding the social economy and associated social activism, reliance has also been placed on the established concepts of social capital (Putnam, 1993). The following subsections touch briefly upon each of the theoretical concepts in relation to the unit of study—RS Farms.

2.10.3.1 Social Enterprise

The definition of social enterprise/entrepreneurship (SE) is much debated in the literature (Table 2.8). Filtered through the lens of public interest, one tends to focus on a relatively narrow definition of the term: 'an organization intended primarily to pursue social impact, which is also financially viable (Rogerson et al., 2013; Zacharakis et al., 2012)'. The definition presented is asymmetric, combining the intent on the social dimension with fact on the financial one. Social impact is the objective here and achieving minimum financial viability the constraint (Rogerson et al., 2013).

Social impact for a social enterprise in a development context has two dimensions. (a) *Reach:* if a social enterprise is to achieve important social impact, its target group should be large and social enterprise should focus on supporting the most disadvantaged groups, and (b) *Depth:* the second dimension relates to the idea of a SE helping generate substantial, rather than marginal, social, or environmental value for all they serve (Rogerson et al., 2013). Social enterprises have developed from and within the social economy sector, which lies between the market and the state and is often associated with concepts such as 'third sector' and 'non-profit sector'.

Social enterprises have emerged as an effective tool to deliver policy objectives in two key areas of social and economic policy: service delivery

Table 2.8 Showing selected definitions of social enterprise/entrepreneurship

Year	Author	Definition
2001	Dess	'Play the role of change agents in the social sector, by: (1) Adopting a mission to create and sustain social value (not just private value), (2) Recognizing and relentlessly pursuing new opportunities to serve that mission, (3) Engaging in a process of continuous innovation, adaptation, and learning, (4) Acting boldly without being limited by resources currently in hand, and (5) Exhibiting heightened accountability to the constituencies served and for the outcomes created' (p. 4)
2000	Fowler	'Social entrepreneurship is the creation of viable (socio-)economic structures, relations, institutions, organizations and practices that yield and sustain social benefits' (p. 649)
2004	Alvord, Brown and Letts	'Social entrepreneurship that creates innovative solutions to immediate social problems and mobilizes the ideas, capacities, resources, and social arrangements required for sustainable social transformations' (p. 262)
2006	Austin, Stevenson and Wei-Skillern	'We define social entrepreneurship as innovative, social value creating activity that can occur within or across the non-profit, business, or government sectors' (p. 2)
	Mair and Marti	'We view social entrepreneurship broadly, as a process involving the innovative use and combination of resources to pursue opportunities to catalyse social change and/or address social needs' (p. 37)

Year	Author	Definition
	Peredo and McLean	'Social entrepreneurship is exercised where some person or group; (1) aim(s) at creating social value, either exclusively or at least in some prominent way; (2) show(s) a capacity to recognize and take advantage of opportunities to create that value ("envision") (3) employ(s) innovation, ranging from outright invention to adapting someone else's novelty, in creating and/or distributing social value; (4) is/are willing to accept an above-average degree of risk in creating and disseminating social value; and (5) is/are unusually resourceful in being relatively undaunted by scarce assets in pursuing their social venture' (p. 64)
	Weerawardena and Mort	'We define social entrepreneurship as a behavioural phenomenon expressed in a NFP organization context aimed at delivering social value through the exploitation of perceived opportunities' (p. 25)
	Sharir and Lerner	'To apply business strategies for the purpose of more effective confrontation with complex social problems' (p. 16)
2009	Zahra, Gedajlovic, Neubaum and Shulman	'Social entrepreneurship encompasses the activities and processes undertaken to discover, define, and exploit opportunities in order to enhance social wealth by creating new ventures or managing existing organizations in an innovative manner' (p. 522)

Source Ferri and Urbano (2011)

and social inclusion. (a) *Service delivery:* SEs may operate in the provision of welfare services to specific groups of individuals or within a spatially defined community. The participatory nature of social enterprises presents distinctive advantages in its capacity to engage stakeholders in the design and delivery of services, contribute non-monetary resources, identify gaps in service provision, and pioneer new services leading to social cohesion; (b) *social cohesion:* recent forms of social enterprises facilitate social inclusion through workforce integration of marginalized people (e.g. long-term unemployed, disabled, minorities, etc.) by combining training and skills development through temporary and/or permanent employment in a business with social dimension that trades in the market.

Another view of social entrepreneurship is to understand SE: '*a process that contributes to social wealth, explores the opportunities for social change and leads to social ventures* (Öztürk, 2013)'. SEs have addressed essential human needs that have been ignored and forgotten by the current institutions and businesses (Öztürk, 2013). Conducted studies and researchers have emphasized the social entrepreneurial nature by expressing their particular behaviours and characteristics. *Empirical findings to this effect have been analysed to revolve around five themes of—(a) skills, (b) background/experience, (c) discourse, (d) demographics and (e) motives (Hoogendoorn et al., 2010).*

2.10.3.2 Summing Up the Theoretical Framework for SEs

To sum up the discussion, post-creation of a framework for RS Farms, it can be construed that social entrepreneurs are the people whose new ideas centralize the appearing social problems, who will force each opportunity in order to sustain their vision, and who simply will not give up unless they obtain their framed goals (Bornstein, 2004, 2005). Dees (1998: 4) defined the baselines of social entrepreneurial dimension as follows: 'social entrepreneurs play the role of change agents in the social sector, by: (a) adopting a mission to create and sustain social value (not just private value), (b) recognizing and relentlessly pursuing new opportunities to serve that mission, (c) engaging in a process of continuous innovations, adaptation, and learning, and (d) acting boldly without being limited by resources currently in hand'.

2.10.3.3 The CPR Framework and the Related Institutional Dynamics

The framework looks at the problem of collectively managing shared resources. Ostrom uses the term 'common pool resources' to denote natural resources (waste in the current case is naturally produced) used by many individuals in common, such as fisheries, groundwater basins, and irrigation systems. Such resources have long been subject to overexploitation and misuse by individuals acting in their own best interests. The proposed theoretical construct of Ostrom has been used in the present scenario as an effort to: (1) *critique the foundations of policy analysis as applied to natural waste generation systems*, (2) *present concrete basis of successful and unsuccessful efforts to govern and manage such resources by the community in Bahadurpur*, and (3) *make an effort to develop better local policy frameworks/tools to understand the capabilities and limitations of self-governing institutions for regulating such special category of bio-resources.*

Ostrom outlines in detail the fundamental logic in respect of 'three models' most frequently used to provide a foundation for recommending state or market-centric solutions. Ostrom provides alternate theoretical and empirical alternatives to these models, with a purpose to illustrate the diversity of solutions that go beyond states and markets. Towards the closure, the framework attempts to explain, as to how communities of individuals fashion different ways of governing the commons. Could this work in a situation like Bahadurpur?

The central question in this case study is to examine how a group of principals who are in an interdependent situation fail to organize and govern themselves to obtain cumulative joint benefits when all face fears of free-riding (households with no animals or with fewer animals), shirk (do not collect and transport waste to the plant site), or otherwise act opportunistically. The core theme of the classic has been deployed to decipher this case.

2.10.3.4 The Three Influential Models

a. *The tragedy of the commons:*
   Since Garrett Hardin's challenging article in Science (1968), the expression 'the tragedy of the commons' has come to symbolize the degradation of the environment to be expected whenever many individuals use a scarce resource in common. Similar logic is clearly

expounded in another classic: *'The economic theory of a common property research: The fishery'*. There appears to be some truth in the conservative dictum that everybody's property is nobody's property (the Bahadurpur waste disposal site is a standing example).

b. *The Prisoner's dilemma game:*
Hardin's model has been formalized as a prisoner's dilemma game. The prisoner's dilemma game is conceptualized as a non-cooperative game in which all players possess complete information.

The paradox that individually rational strategies lead to collectively irrational outcomes seems to challenge a fundamental faith: *'rational human beings can achieve rational results'*. There is a very strong possibility in the village of Bahadurpur where every household is aware of the collective benefits. This can easily see the light of the day in case they take a collective resolve as a unanimous body through a negotiated settlement. This compromise can be evenly struck by an institutional mechanism of direct nomination of members to the governing body of the village (already existing and functional since the last 15 years), the gram panchayat (the local democratic institution of self-government). Thus, an institution can pitch in to reduce uncertainties by reducing complexities of human behaviour (North, 1990: 25). Thus, rational, Pareto-optimal outcomes could be a definite possibility.

c. *The Logic of Collective Action:*
A closely related view of the difficulty of getting individuals to pursue their joint welfare, as contrasted to individual welfare, was developed by Mancur Olson (1965). The grand optimism as expressed in group theory was challenged: *'If the members of some group have a common interest or object, and if they would all be better off if that objective is achieved, it has been thought to follow logically that the individuals in that group would, if they were rational and self-interested, act to achieve that objective* (Olson, 1965: 1)'.

2.10.3.5 Summing Up CPR and Institutional Issues

The tragedy of the commons, the prisoner's dilemma, and the logic of collective action are closely related concepts in the models that have defined the accepted way of viewing many problems that individuals face when attempting to achieve collective benefits. Given the above contextual background, the given case of Bahadurpur presents the following options of policy prescriptions available for ensuring effective, common, collective compliance for attainment of larger public good in real terms by ironing out the *'individualistic'* kink of the Singh family.

2.10.4 Theoretical Imports Applied to Ram Singh (RS) Farms

RS Farms (a biogas unit) is an informal institution. It is geographically indigenous, but exogenous in character based on informal rules, individual and/or collective needs, and the prevalent social structure in the village, Bahadurpur. The farm is, however, a social, economic, political, and an apolitical enterprise as well. Does it infringe upon the right of self-determination of the end-users of biogas? Free service (supply of biogas) guarantees wastage. It does not guarantee abstinence from usage of other competing fuels (free and charged) such as liquefied petroleum gas (LPG) charged and wood (biomass, free). The unit is trapped in the limited intellectual web of its serendipitous creation.

2.10.4.1 Governing and Managing Animal Waste—Does a Refuse/Reject (End Product of Biological Metabolism) Qualify to Be Treated as a Common Property Resource?

Waste/refuse has been categorically construed as animal generated bio-waste for the scope of this case. The dilemmas of collective action relate to waste management by means of an informal mechanism which is non-institutional in character. Initially generated at the level of individual households, the private owners of milch cattle, assumes humongous 'collective' proportions when dumped at any given site in the village. The public action of collective dumping of individually generated (private) waste on account of ownership of domestic animals generates 'community scale waste quantum' that is a serious threat to the local community environment. As of now, every individual household has a self, temporary, individual interest in getting rid of the bio-waste. However, collectively all of them are under constant threat of any serious epidemic outbreak. Further, the waste that lies in the open is nothing more than an eyesore.

It adds to the problem of clogged drains and sewers by finding its natural course into them on account of natural or man-made action. The proportion of this perennial collective threat is much larger than the ephemeral individual relief earned by unregulated dumping. A private individual at the initial stages gains by immediately getting rid of the bio-waste generated by his privately owned animals. Thus, there is a potentially strong case for a win–win situation for the residents of Bahadurpur as a whole in case they decide to deposit all of this bio-waste at RS Farms (the biogas plant). Collectively, the community is in a more well-off position in case they agree to do this, than they are individually. However, this never happened in Bahadurpur! Why does individual, private, self-interest prevail over the larger 'public interest'?

This agenda gets the narrative back to the theoretical proposition of: *'governing the commons- the evolution of institutions for collective action'*. The nature of bio-waste is a bit different. There is no dispute to the fact that it is a resource in terms of its multiple end usages. However, it is under the private ownership of individuals before it is dumped. The site of dumping in the village is a common property earmarked for dumping of all sorts of village wastes ever since the last settlement and land consolidation operations happened. In local parlance, such a dumping site in a revenue village is referred to as *'hadda-rudi'* meaning, waste/refuse dumping site. Thus, the access at this site is open for all. Though bio-waste is a resource and is subject to open access, the private rights of the individuals have not ceased to operate.

This fact potentially gives rise to the dilemma of collective action in Bahadurpur! It can be construed as a special instance where the potential of the waste is generally known, and the benefits are also known in case it is harnessed by the enterprising Singh family; however, there is a trust deficit as to the even and equitable distribution of the benefits post-processing of the bio-waste. Thus, the local actors do not suffer on account of information asymmetry, but there is a strong sense of fear of not being equitably compensated and hence, refuse to act as a group. Therefore, the commons continue to be at a loss individually by rejecting the collective public good.

2.10.4.2 Social Enterprises, Institutions, Structures: Processes and Outcomes in Bahadurpur

I would introduce institutions first and thereafter the need for civic engagements that are critical for institutional architecture, processes, and service delivery. North offers the following definition: 'Institutions are the rules of the game in a society or, more formally, are the humanly devised constraints that shape human interaction (North, 1990: 3)'. Three important features of institutions are apparent in this definition: (1) that they are humanly devised, which contrasts with other potential fundamental causes, like geographic factors, which are outside human control, (2) that they are the rules of the game setting constraints on human behaviour, and (3) that their major effect will be through incentives. Institutions can differ between societies because of their formal methods of collective decision-making (democracy versus dictatorship) or because of their economic institutions (security of property rights, entry barriers, the set of contracts available to businessmen).

They may also differ because a given set of formal institutions are expected to and do function differently; for example, they may differ between two societies that are democratic because the distribution of political power lies with different groups or social classes, or because in one society, democracy is expected to collapse while in the other it is consolidated. Without delving deeper into institutional taxonomy and architecture, let us try and understand why social networks and social trust might relate to good governance. There is an algorithm proposed by Putnam. Social trust establishes social networks. Once a social network gets established, civic engagement occurs. This results in the creation of an accountable, representative, democratic institution.

The larger question that remains unanswered is whether that leads to building of political trust as well, eventually leading to better policy outcomes. The social structures of cooperation and engagements outside such affiliations as village-level education committees, village-level sanitation committees, progressive farmers' cooperative, the Gurudwara, and religiosity neutralized solidarity, trust, and tolerance by countering each-others' designs in Bahadurpur. This led to the creation of political inequality with weakened civic engagements, and the civic community remains in a state of precarious suspension on account of weakened norms of reciprocity, passive communication with unclear flow of information, and weak collaboration.

What could have alternatively happened in the village, had not the Singh family indulged into its imperialist cum capitalist designs? There would have been some takers of their social innovation against the current odds. What are essential ingredients for the creation of a robust, well-meaning, and well-intended institutional framework? Social norms based on trust, balanced (specific), and generalized (diffuse) norms of reciprocity through creation of dense networks of social exchange with improved, open, and extensive interpersonal communication (horizontal, vertical and mixed) boost social capital, the life and blood of any given institution whether formal or informal, or social, economic, or political.

This could be the strongest take home message by the founding fathers of the RS Farm biogas cum dairy unit.

2.10.5 Role of State and Its Policy Instruments and Instrumentalities

The central sector scheme on National Biogas and Manure Management Programme (NBMMP) was mainly created to set up family type biogas plants. This scheme has been under implementation since 1981–1982. The programme was implemented by State Nodal Agencies (SNAs)/State Nodal Departments (SNDs) like agriculture department, District Rural Development Agencies (DRDAs) and Khadi and Village Industry Commission (KVIC) centres.

2.10.5.1 Mandate of NBMMP

The mandate as outlined for the effective execution of the NBMMP is very clear in terms of its outlined objectives: (1) to provide clean biogaseous fuel mainly for cooking purposes and also for other applications for reducing the use of liquefied petroleum gas (LPG) and other conventional fuels, (2) to meet 'lifeline energy' needs for cooking as envisaged in 'Integrated Energy Policy', (c) to provide bio-fertilizer/ organic manure to reduce use of chemical fertilizers, (d) to mitigate drudgery of rural women and reduce pressure on forests and accentuate social benefits, (e) to improve sanitation in villages by linking sanitary toilets with biogas plants, and lastly, (f) to mitigate climate change by preventing black carbon and methane emissions (NBMMP, GoI, MNRE, 2009).

2.10.5.2 Incongruent, Self-Contradicting Policy Designs for Creating Delirium

The state recognizes the latent potential of biogas as a cooking fuel in kitchens and therefore, makes an attempt to push through the agenda of optimal utilization of biogas across regions. Would agenda setting only suffice, without creation of operational structures and frameworks for capacity building at the cutting edge (in the action arenas)! The answer is a definite and certain 'no'. Going further, very recently, the central government acting in contravention to the laid down mandate of NBMMP (the only programme in the country for effective management of animal refuse, domestic animals in particular), as discussed above, rolled out the Pradhan Mantri Ujjwala Yojana (PMUY) on 1 May 2016 in Ballia district of Uttar Pradesh (PIB Release, 2016a).

The main mantra of this scheme is Swacch Indhan, Behtar Jeevan (clean fuel, better life)—Mahilaon ko mila samman (upholding respect for women). The scheme is aimed at replacing the unclean cooking fuels in the most underprivileged households with clean and more efficient liquefied petroleum gas (LPG). The identification of eligible below poverty line (BPL) families was made on the basis of socio-economic caste census (SECC) data which was provided by the union ministry of rural development.

In the very first year of the announcement of the said scheme, a sum of 2000 crore was allocated for the financial year 2016–2017 (PIB Release, 2016b). To take things further, the cabinet committee on economic affairs (CCEA) has approved an enhancement of the target of PMUY from five crore to eight crores with an additional budgetary allocation of 4800 crores. The revised target is proposed to be achieved by 2020 (PIB Release, 2017). After loading the policy arsenal with a tilt towards LPG supplies, taking an unprecedented policy trajectory, very recently, the government of India, through the nodal ministry of MNRE has set up an ambitious annual target of establishing 65,180 biogas plants under NBMMP during the fiscal year 2018–2019 (*Source* Press Information Bureau [PIB Release, 2018]), for ensuring compliance towards clean development mechanism (CDM) showcasing its commitment towards mitigation of climate change by adopting alternate measures for energy consumption.

2.10.5.3 Biogas Takes a Hit Despite Its Potential as a Resource
However, the policy stance in either of the cases by two different central ministries is inherently contradictory and antagonistic to one another. The aim of the state appears to create euphoria amongst the rural populace in the garb of aggressive policy marketing without substantive execution in the policy arena. The institutions of the macro are in cut-throat, aggressive competition with each other without realizing the long-term policy outcomes of such policy parallelism and pluralism that is unequivocally in contravention to one another ab initio.

Biogas has multifarious uses and it has the innate potential to create the maximum amount of social, economic, political, and environmental impact (Fig. 2.70, Annexure E). However, the above narration clearly underlines the degree of policy undercutting the policy actors (the central ministries) resort to, while acting in isolation, in their respective isolated policy estates. A dichotomy of such nature and scale leaves a long-lasting lethal impact in the policy arena (Fig. 2.64, Annexure E). The myopic view adopted at the highest level of an active polity creates distrust amongst similarly placed institutions at the macro-level. The contradicting directives are passed on at the regional level (meso-), where the capacity to resolve such dichotomy is extremely limited or even non-existent. The structures and functions of the regional institutions are governed by duality in terms of control by the centre and the diktat of the regional power centres as well.

The policies at the national level stand in contravention with one another. The ramifications of such cryptic pluralism result in the premature death of such social innovations and initiatives as Bahadurpur.

A perusal of the MNRE report establishes the degree of institutional apathy towards biogas as a resource (IREDA, 2015: 13–23). There is no mention of any kind about this specific resource. The entire report is tilted in favour of solar energy and wind energy policies of the different states (regional centres). A lesser proportion is occupied by small hydel projects followed by biomass power generation policies.

Biogas is a huge source of combined heat and power (CHP). However, it has never received the policy attention it deserves even when the costs involved are a pittance. For example, in contrast to solar and wind energy, it is possible to control the production of biogas because it is dependent on the volume of bio-waste input per unit of time. Further, as said earlier, the utilization of biogas is versatile, for example, for electricity, for heating, and for cooking as clean cooking fuel (Fig. 2.70, Annexure E). Despite these indisputable advantages, the biogas energy system has been translated and made to be perceived as an extremely complex system on account of ulterior interests of different actors, each with their own view and reasoning on reality, interests, motivations, and expectations. The greatest irony being the fact that it receives the least attention from its own renewable energy sources' fraternity that is further exacerbated by reductionist, myopic, and monolithic policy designs.

The scale and the intensity of such kind of policy oversight speaks volumes about the preferential 'private' interests of public and private actors who dominate the policy framing estate being close to centres of power, dictating policy design.

2.10.5.4 The After Effects of the Macro-policy Design on a Micro-Entity

There is a very strong sense of disillusionment and disenchantment of the family towards the agencies of the state, as they squarely blame the state for trouncing their initiative that led to the exponential decline of their business interests. *'Around 150–160 people had to be thrown out of jobs who were gainfully employed in the food processing unit, and an additional work force of 30–40 persons who were deployed at the biogas plant as well, were also retrenched-laments Mr.Dalbir Singh'.* What remains as of now in Bahadurpur village is an operational biogas plant, a dairy (milk production unit), and a bio-slurry (leftover waste from the digester) unit. The self-esteem and morale of the Singh family are at its lowest ebb.

The Singh family is fundamentally against the state-led model of development as they perceive state as a brutish evil doer armed with its plenary powers. Throughout the course of interaction, the family blames the line departments of renewable energy, industries, and the pollution control board. The state does more harm than good to humankind across histories and cultures as they exemplify their stance through profound and repetitive usage of such terms as excessive regulation, enforcement, coercion, and totalitarianism.

2.10.5.5 Seeing Like a State, Scott Re-visited—Understanding Events and Fallouts

Collectively, the family sees the modern state together with its modern policy construct, as a harbinger of dystopia. In spite of their covert commercial designs, the family is of the firm and considered opinion that the modern state armed with its legal and regulatory prowess has unleashed a systemic design that ravished the local nature of their process design, and the adversarial attitude of the line departments resulted in creation of such structures and systems that mutilated the local knowledge (Scott, 1998).

'Metis' understood as local, traditional, folk wisdom should be the substructure and the fundamental structural framework on which the superstructure of any institution or enterprise be based (Scott, 1998: 309). The family proposes that rather than erosion of indigenous diversity through application of state-led blind models of sectoral centralization, an institution or an enterprise should take much of its shape from the continuously evolving metis of the people engaged in it. This process shall not only enhance the range of experience and skills of the people engaged but shall vehemently boost the quality of the said institution and its product on account of the enthusiastic and constructive engagement of its people.

There is a strong undercurrent driving towards decentralization, collectivization, collective action, people's participation, and creation of democratic institutions to usher holistic, all-inclusive development (Singh, 2016). A cultural system of some thought is found in all human societies and Bahadurpur is no exception. The society here is a close-knit structure, being homogenous in terms of caste composition and economically as well. It has its defined networks of values and attitudes, customs and behavioural patterns. It appears that the biogas unit appears to be a product of a very remote noble thought to redefine the way of life in the village and thus provide a new world order guided by an alternate energy system that would provide a secure supply of clean cooking fuel satiating the daily domestic cooking needs of a household.

Though the social set-up approved of the earlier initiatives of the Singh family, this initiative somehow could not gain currency with the residents. For the first time, it appears, they become a variation of the strong individualistic and paternalistic designs of the Singh family. There are only three kinds of social formations in the village, viz. Tarkhans, Sainis, and a single family of scheduled castes. The majority decisions are normally taken by consensus. However, there was no effort put in by the Singh family in respect of this initiative.

The attitude of the family was different. They were also pretty unsure about the fact whether this biogas unit could be run as a community-driven initiative. The biogas plant, as a social and economic unit of structure and function, never became a source of active communication and engagement amongst the local beneficiaries. Though the distribution network was established and the supply began in April 2011, there is still an uneasy calm in the village, even after seven years of commissioning of supply of biogas. The final dent to mutual trust and cooperation was perhaps provided by the blind expansion of the plant into a full-fledged dairy farm followed by a commercial food-processing unit. This action established the fact of singular benefit to a single family, simply because 'biogas is a waste product'. It is an altogether different matter that it has the power to drive electronic devices and run kitchens. These benefits were perceived as remote and tertiary benefits of this production system.

The villagers perceived that the real immediate benefits in terms of the dairy and food-processing unit go to the Singh family. This line of thought shook the belief systems of the villagers, as they construed themselves as receivers of a remote benefit that does not impart any substantial economic gain. The Singh family miserably failed to communicate the shared benefits of the plant, perhaps, knowing fully well that saving on LPG, firewood, and dung cakes would not find any takers. Communication that is central to civic engagements temporally and spatially was altogether missing in this particular venture of the Singh family. It remains as an individual, self-driven, private venture of the family bearing the tag of Sh. Ram Singh.

The Singh family faces its first dilemma—whether knowing how, why, and what leads to better institutional arrangements can solve all the common problems? Perhaps not! There are certain unanticipated challenges that crop up one after the other. Firstly, one of the big challenges in a traditional society with a newly created outlook is the scale of problems they are facing. Their second dilemma revolves around how does one stimulate cooperation even in populations of small sizes. Thirdly, new problems shall always emerge. Fourthly, it is often not in everybody's interest to solve a problem. Different people have different positions and interests. A problem for one participant can be an opportunity for another. Hence, not everybody has an incentive to solve a problem. Problems do not exist in a vacuum, there is already an ecological (social and economic in the present case) context for every problem. There is a very strong sense of alienation in the village. Even though the family tries to make up for the loss by supplying free gas to about seventy households in a desperate attempt of appeasement of the fellow residents, it does not help in any manner in bridging the trust deficit created.

The rest of the village feels to be nowhere near to the Singh family, as the family has been in the limelight in print, electronic, and social media ever since the day of commissioning of the unit. There exists a situation of mutated competition (North, 1990: 24). 'The family background and past working experiences construct the nature of future initiatives of a social entrepreneur' (Bornstein, 2005: 13). It may be inferred from Bornstein's statement that experience factor has high importance of the created characteristics of social entrepreneurs as much as the innate skills have (Öztürk, 2013: 47).

Nevertheless, the background of social entrepreneurial activity mostly subsumes the experience of social entrepreneur. This fact is applicable to the Singh family running the RS Farms. This discussion is further bolstered by a study (Perrini & Vurro, 2006) that lays emphasis on the following aspects: (a) personal experience has impact on the social ventures which are developed by social entrepreneurs. In the present case, two of the second-generation siblings are non-resident Indians (NRIs), which broadens one's outlook in terms of expansion of alternative approaches on social aspects, (b) previous experience: this phrase refers to experiences that have lived in the past and shaped the social entrepreneurs' activities. Significance of previous experience is that it helps to understand the backdrop of the personality of a social entrepreneur.

The previous experience could be the trajectory taken by the ideas of a social entrepreneur to be deployed in the current spatial and temporal context. Thus, it integrates the existing reality and social gaps along with innovative ideas for creating social impact. This study almost perfectly fits in the present case of the Singh family. Having been exposed to the excellent civic amenities in Dubai and other foreign lands, they came up with an idea of subsurface sewage system, covered drains, and rain water harvesting structures to be created in their native village of Bahadurpur.

Further, ever since the early eighties, the second-generation siblings had been exposed to the functioning of an individual family size biogas plant. This idea was, therefore, later conceived as a biogas unit cum dairy farm to be run on a commercial scale. There was an expansion in the form of a full-fledged food-processing plant in the neighbouring village of Lodhi majra. However, these expansions bolstered civic estrangement as these were purely driven by business interests. The expansion was covertly done without seeking the necessary approvals as warranted by the institutions of the state. Such independence of actions and the sole motive of earning profit triggered the arrival of the 'regulatory' state and the result was forced shut down of the ulterior economic enterprise of the RS Farms.

2.10.6 Conclusion, Policy Implications, and Prescription—Does the Case Exemplify a Paradigm of Negotiated Compromise for Pursuing an Economic Interest Sans Creation of any Social Value?

The time is ripe to raise questions about the responsibility dimension of the 'perceived' social enterprise. The first step towards clarity in examining the doctrine of social responsibility of business is to ask precisely what implies for whom (Friedman, 1970: 1). The business interests and intentions of the family overran the intent of creation of any sort of social value. The ulterior design driven by the sole motive for amassing personal economic gains suppressed the initial thought of social innovation aimed to create a social impact through creation of social value based on the trust and solidarity of every single user in the village.

It was purely on the account of this fact that the system of direct elections to the gram panchayat was replaced by nomination of members to this democratic institution of self-governance. However, the family took a shot in the arm the moment the idea of a singular biogas plant along with a dairy was conceived, knowing fully well that this initiative could alter power structures in the village and disrupt the social fabric. And finally, sometimes 'consensus-based' democratic institutions like the one that exists in Bahadurpur (nominated gram panchayat) make it difficult to amend or change rules. However, the remote possibility of achieving an attempt to manage 'organized consent' cannot be ruled out in the present scenario.

Negotiated settlement in Bahadurpur was achieved through the supply of 'free' gas to about seventy dwelling units, thereby confirming to the norms of the 'majoritarian' principle. It could be construed as- purchase of subdued consent in the face of an outright economic enterprise'. The latent threat of disruption of the visible distribution infrastructure could have been a precursor of the idea of free supply.

The questions that emerge from a careful perusal of the theoretical constructs applied the endeavour to deconstruct and decipher as to what went wrong for RS Farms. (1) Is there a political economy of a biogas plant? (2) Does Bahadurpur exemplify a business interest, a social interest, or a political interest? (3) On an individual level, is the Singh family driving a social economy? (4) Is there a boundary problem with respect to the Bahadurpur case being at the tri-junction of a social entrepreneurship, a social enterprise, and an individually driven (self-centred) economic initiative? (5) Does the Bahadurpur project qualify to be classified as social innovation? (6) A formal democratic institutional structure (PRI) undergoes transformation on account of alternatives offered in terms of mutually agreed developmental goals? (7) Does social choice hinge upon economic incentive only? (8) How does an informal institution interact with a formal structure in an environment of trust deficit? (9) Why does this enterprise fail to create social value? And, lastly (10) Would there be any takers of biogas in case the rationed supply is measured and charged (post-metering) on actual usage, or in terms of duration of supply? An attempt is made to answer the aforesaid queries in terms of theoretical abstract models as discussed below.

2.10.6.1 Policy Prescription
The policy options are as follows:

a. *LEVIATHAN as the only way*:
Because of the tragedy of the commons, environmental problems cannot be solved through cooperation and the rationale for a government with major coercive powers is overwhelming. The presumption that an external Leviathan is necessary to avoid tragedies of the commons leads to recommendations that central governments control most natural resource systems. The question therefore arises—whether Bahadurpur is a fit case wherein the state presses all its regulatory, enforcement, and legal institutions into action in order to achieve social, political, and economic efficacy in respect of the gas production system by ensuring fair distribution of access to tangible gains created as a result of this intervention?

b. *PRIVATIZATION as the only way*:
'The only way to avoid the tragedy of commons is to end the common-property system by creating a system of private property rights'. The legal nature of bio-waste undergoes immediate change the moment it is dumped at a collective public place earmarked for the purpose. There could be a possibility of creating private rights of ownership in case a collective mechanism is evolved for waste collection, transport, and deposit at the plant site. Or, the private rights remain operational in case there is a door-to-door mechanism of waste collection post-quantification of the same. This could either be done within the village community or through engagement of an external private enterprise. This could eventually be a reality, however, with an added cost.

c. *External Actor—The only way*:
The theoretical framework further cautions against the thought of presuming that the individuals sharing commons are inevitably caught in a trap from which they cannot escape depends upon the capacity of individuals to extricate themselves from various types of dilemma situations. Ostrom categorically emphasizes on the meaning of successful institutions, defining them as ones that enable individuals to achieve productive outcomes in situations where

temptations to free ride and shirk are ever present. These thoughts provide interesting options before the Bahadurpur villagers!

In case they surrender their private interest, the individual, self-driven entrepreneurship of the Singh family could be converted into a community-driven institution of collective entrepreneurship, thereby creating huge social impact by harnessing social capital, through risk elimination, or its dispersal thereby eliminating trust deficit. This changeover from individual to collective could substantially increase economic gains through minimizing input costs in terms of saving on daily energy needs and increasing farm output by use of green, organic bio-slurry. This could eventually lead to the disappearance of the '*demarcation*' problem related to the current structural, functional, and social disposition of the biogas plant in Bahadurpur. What appears to be a remote possibility that seems applicable in the current situation in Bahadurpur is provided by Olson. He challenges the presumption that the possibility of a benefit for a group would be sufficient to generate collective action to achieve that benefit.

This import appears to be directly applicable to Bahadurpur, a tiny village with around 85 households. The nature of settlement is dense and nucleated. Therefore, there could be a possibility of individual households getting together and contributing towards a common interest. Does a naturally generated bio-waste waiting to be identified as a CPR, provided it is harnessed with the action of the collective, which strengthens the institutions of self-governance in Bahadurpur? The theoretical framework provides clear and concrete information about the processes involved in (1) governing long enduring CPRs, (2) transforming existing institutional arrangements, and (3) failing to overcome continued CPR problems.

There is a strong possibility of similarities between different CPR problems. Therefore, given the similarity between many CPR problems and the problems of providing small-scale collective goods, the theoretical framework contributes to the understanding of factors that can enhance or detract from the capabilities of individuals to organize collective action related to providing for public goods. Bahadurpur, a biogas plant is definitely a closed system devoid of collectivism in thoughts, beliefs, and actions. The production system as of now does not add either to epistemic value or to the social value by any means. It has become static and surrounded by a monolithic agenda of basic survival on account of overhyped and accidently solicited public glare.

2.10.6.2 Proposed Role of Social Capital in Developing Consensus for Acceptance of Progressive, Local Energy Systems as an Alternate Source of Clean Cooking Fuel from the Biogas Unit in Bahadurpur (Table 2.9)

2.10.6.3 Concluding Thoughts

Towards the closure of this case, I am left with this thought: *'How do we build the rationality for collective action for decentralized energy systems in Bahadurpur- being uniform and symmetrical in terms of socio-economic outcomes and creating social value?'* *What would be the elements of such rational institutional frame-work? What kind of specific design elements would be required to be put in an institutional framework to achieve a Pareto-optimal efficiency for even and equitable distribution of clean cooking fuel along with fair access towards other ancillary by-products of the production system- bio-slurry, and gas-based power! How do we build partnerships in a pursuit meant for economic gain in a community set-up? The individual entrepreneur is neither incentivized by the local community, competing interest groups or the state through its institutions.*

Neither the private entrepreneur is on the hunt for any mediating institution, nor the policy of the state institutions allow for any stability under the current circumstances to this economic enterprise. The conflicting interests have no intersection even though there could be a possibility of potentially large gains through resolution of disagreements. The policy state is replete with directives that smack of parallelism and pluralism. It does not create a segregated niche for biogas for its distinctiveness especially with respect to its closest sitting alternative- biomass. The central focus for a policy on biogas should be hinging upon animal, human and kitchen refuse, and not beyond this. And in case the programme has to be given a new life, alternate structures and local institutions need to be created for effectively running this self-sufficient energy production system. However, the degree of disengagement on the part of the local entrepreneur appears to be on the higher side which limits his bargaining freedom (North, 1990: 90). The entrepreneur feels that there is a directed institutional apathy towards the 'enterprise' which further creates a deadlock between the parties.

Table 2.9 Developing consensus by enhancing social capital for local energy entrepreneurship

Obstacles in Bahadurpur village	Sources of problems	Purposive functions of Social Capital (what ends can social capital meet in eliminating the existent obstacles?)
Lack of participation by: • Homogenous community • Remote stakeholders	Passive task specific in-action	Could alter the incentives for active participation
Lack of will in: • Similarly placed groups • Differently placed groups • Fence sitters	All the three groups fail to accept that alternate fuel supply system is in their best interests	Could provide a common platform for horizontal communication between groups through active demonstration of benefits (short term and long term)
Turf war over claims relating to conception, design, and expansion of the active multifunctional system within/between:		
• Local and regional institutions of the state (State Nodal Agency, Punjab Pollution Control Board and Industries department) • Line departments at the district level (dairy, agriculture, and animal husbandry) • Local institutions such as gram panchayat, village education development committee, village water supply, and sanitation committee, other farmer cooperatives (economic institutions)	Conflicting views, perspectives, and perceptions emerging from different functional structure, such as licensing, regulation, enforcement leaving no incentive for social innovation There is an element of subdued competition, with strong conflict of interest. The biogas unit is seen as a private economic enterprise without any community service agenda	Could help iron out differences with regard to the differences in views about the nature of innovation and its futuristic trajectory

(continued)

Table 2.9 (continued)

Obstacles in Bahadurpur village	Sources of problems	Purposive functions of Social Capital (what ends can social capital meet in eliminating the existent obstacles?)
Lack of resources and capacity in: • Punjab Energy Development Agency (PEDA, SNA) • PPCB and industrial policy promotion and planning • Rural development department and other allied line departments	Stakeholders lack the will and the capacity to act on their own on account of information asymmetry, remoteness from the field realities, and exercise of regressive sanction provided by statute	Could bring together the local knowledge, the local resource base and the local social enterprise model into the active realm of policy process to develop synergy between stakeholders in order to uniformly apprise the affected stakeholders and build creative capacity
Lack of cooperation between: • political and apolitical institutions • state and local institutions • local institutions and economic enterprise • local institutions, economic enterprise, and governance structures	The incentivizing structures available to stakeholders do not foster constructive engagement through collective action	Could alter the rules of the game to create incentives to encourage cooperation in order to facilitate acceptance of alternative ideas as a uniform construct

Source Based on Kim and Lim (2017: 6)

2.11 Annexure E: Case Study 2.5 Bahadurpur (Punjab)

See Figs. 2.57, 2.58, 2.59, 2.60, 2.61, 2.62, 2.63, 2.64, 2.65, 2.66, 2.67, 2.68, 2.69, and 2.70 and Table 2.10.

222 M. K. SINGH

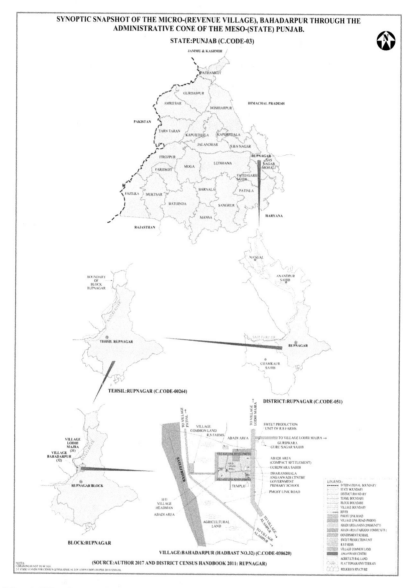

Fig. 2.57 Comprehensive snapshot of the revenue village, Bahadurpur, through the Meso-(State)

2 CASE STUDIES AS AN IMMERSIVE APPROACH ... 223

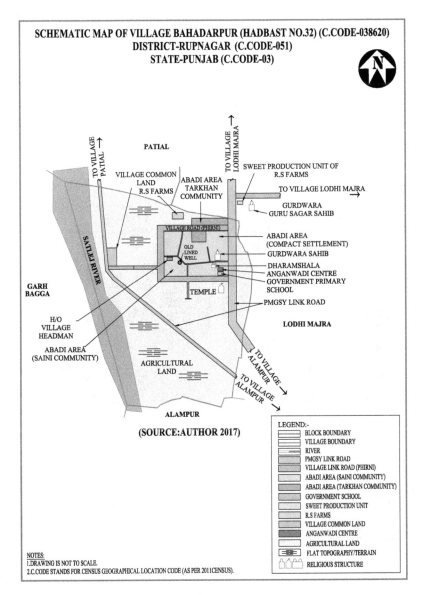

Fig. 2.58 Schematic map of the village

1. MAIN ENTRANCE TO THE BIO-GAS AND DAIRY FARM
2. THE "ARRAY", (LONGITUDINAL) "FEEDING ZONE"
3. CATTLE FEED PROCESSING MACHINE
4. FINE, PROCESSED CATTLE FEED
5. RESTING AREA FOR MILCH CATTLE
6. THE (SHED) DIMENSIONS AND BIO-WASTE TRANSFER PLAN

(SOURCE: AUTHOR, 2017)

Fig. 2.59 Synoptic view of R S farms

1. CATTLE FEED MIXER
2. BIRD'S EYE VIEW OF THE FEEDING AREA
3. SLIT THROUGH WHICH CATTLE WASTE IS PUSHED INTO THE DIGESTER THROUGH SLOPING LINEAR TRENCHWAYS.
4. THE CATTLE ASSEMBLY ZONE
5. RAW, COARSE CATTLE FEED

(SOURCE: AUTHOR, 2017)

Fig. 2.60 Complete cattle assembly zone card the feed area

Fig. 2.61 Slurry churning unit and the exterior controls of the sub-surface digester

2 CASE STUDIES AS AN IMMERSIVE APPROACH ... 227

d

1. PUMPING SYSTEM FOR UPLIFTING BIO-MANURE SLURRY
2. DRIED BIO-MANURE (SILAGE PIT)
3. BIO-MANURE COLLECTION POINT (TANKER BEING FILLED)
4. THE END RESULT OF BIO-MANURING (ORGANIC FARM)

(SOURCE: AUTHOR, 2017)

Fig. 2.62 Bio-slurry (a by-product) being filled into a tanker

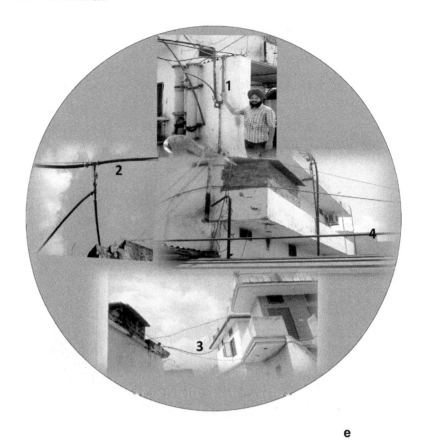

1. BIO-GAS EVACUATION AND SUPPLY RELEASE SYSTEM
2. DISTRIBUTION MAINS
3. AN INSULAR BEND (SAG) TO BOOST GAS PRESSURE DURING DISTRIBUTION
4. SECONDARY DISTRIBUTION SYSTEM (DISTRIBUTION NETWORK FOR SUPPLY OF BIOGAS)

(SOURCE: AUTHOR, 2017)

Fig. 2.63 Complete aerial distribution system of biogas supply within the village

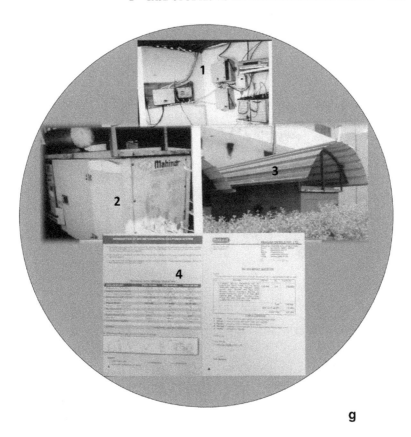

1. CONVENTIONAL POWER SUPPLY AND POWER BACK UP SYSTEM TO THE FARM
2. DIESEL GENERATOR SET
3. BIO-GAS POWER GENERATION UNIT UNDER EXAMINATION TO "POWER" BAHADURPUR FROM BIO-GAS
4. SPECIFICATIONS OF THE BIO-GAS GENERATOR

(SOURCE: AUTHOR, 2017)

Fig. 2.64 Un-utilized (idle) biogas-based power generation system

1. INSIGNIA
2. TRADEMARK
3. SWEETMEATS AND CONFECTIONERY PRODUCTS
4. CLIP FROM A VERNACULAR PRESS
5. HOLISTIC COVERAGE OF THE VILLAGE
6. AWARD TO THE FOUNDERS

(SOURCE: AUTHOR, 2017)

Fig. 2.65 'Public attention' and accolades earned over a period of time post commercialization

2 CASE STUDIES AS AN IMMERSIVE APPROACH ... 231

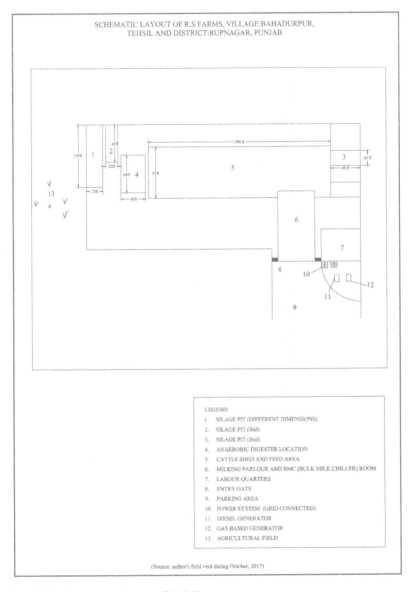

Fig. 2.66 Schematic layout of R S Farms

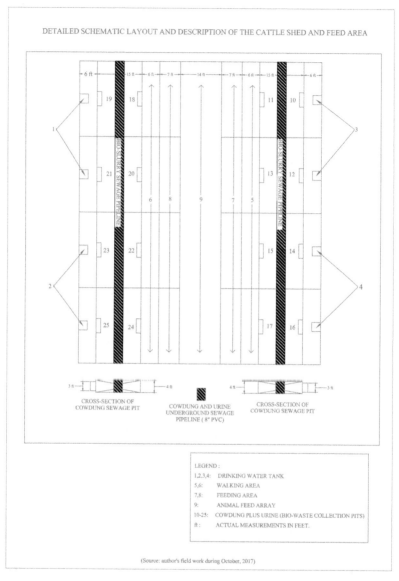

Fig. 2.67 Schematic disposition of the cattle shed and feed area

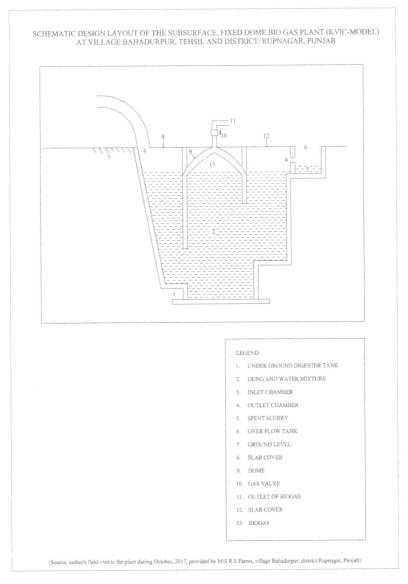

Fig. 2.68 Actual layout of the biogas plant at Bahadurpur (sub-surface)

ਵੱਲੋਂ

ਜ਼ਿਲ੍ਹਾ ਕੰਟਰੋਲਰ,
ਖ਼ੁਰਾਕ ਸਿਵਲ ਸਪਲਾਈਜ਼ ਅਤੇ ਖਪਤਕਾਰ ਮਾਮਲੇ,
ਰੂਪਨਗਰ।

ਸੇਵਾ ਵਿਖੇ

ਮਾਨਯੋਗ ਡਿਪਟੀ ਕਮਿਸ਼ਨਰ,
ਰੂਪਨਗਰ।

ਮੀਮੋ ਨੰ:ਨਿ.ਸ.-2018/ 2617   ਮਿਤੀ: 19/06/2018

ਵਿਸ਼ਾ:- ਗੈਸ ਕੁਨੈਕਸ਼ਨ ਸਬੰਧੀ ਮੰਗੀ ਸੂਚਨਾ ਬਾਰੇ।

ਉਪਰੋਕਤ ਵਿਸ਼ੇ ਦੇ ਸਬੰਧ ਵਿੱਚ।

2.   ਆਪ ਜੀ ਵੱਲੋਂ ਮੰਗੀ ਗਈ ਸੂਚਨਾ ਦੇ ਸਬੰਧ ਵਿੱਚ ਦੱਸਿਆ ਜਾਂਦਾ ਹੈ ਕਿ ਪਿੰਡ ਬਹਾਦਰਪੁਰ ਅਤੇ ਲੋਦੀਮਾਜਰਾ ਵਿਖੇ ਕੋਈ ਵੀ ਗੈਸ ਏਜੰਸੀ ਨਹੀ ਹੈ। ਪਿੰਡ ਵਾਸੀਆ ਨੂੰ ਹੇਠ ਦਰਸਾਈ ਡਿਟੇਲ ਅਨੁਸਾਰ ਗੈਸ ਏਜੰਸੀਆਂ ਵੱਲੋਂ ਗੈਸ ਦੀ ਸਪਲਾਈ ਦਿੱਤੀ ਜਾਂਦੀ ਹੈ:-

ਲੜੀ ਨੰ	ਪਿੰਡ ਦਾ ਨਾਮ	ਕੁਨੈਕਸ਼ਨਾ ਦੀ ਗਿਣਤੀ	ਦੂਰੀ	ਗੈਸ ਏਜੰਸੀ ਦਾ ਨਾਮ
1	ਬਹਾਦਰਪੁਰ	15	9 ਕਿ.ਮੀ ਲੱਗਭਗ	ਜੱਸ ਗੈਸ ਏਜੰਸੀ (ਇੰਡੇਨ),
2	ਲੋਦੀਮਾਜਰਾ	92	9 ਕਿ.ਮੀ ਲੱਗਭਗ	ਰੂਪਨਗਰ
3	ਬਹਾਦਰਪੁਰ	30	8 ਕਿ.ਮੀ ਲੱਗਭਗ	ਘਨੌਲੀ ਗ੍ਰਾਮੀਣ ਵਿਤਕਰ (ਇੰਡੇਨ),
4	ਲੋਦੀਮਾਜਰਾ	50	8 ਕਿ.ਮੀ ਲੱਗਭਗ	ਘਨੌਲੀ

ਇਹ ਆਪ ਜੀ ਦੀ ਸੂਚਨਾ ਹਿੱਤ ਪੇਸ਼ ਹੈ ਜੀ।

ਜ਼ਿਲ੍ਹਾ ਕੰਟਰੋਲਰ,
ਖ਼ੁਰਾਕ ਸਿਵਲ ਸਪਲਾਈਜ਼ ਅਤੇ ਖਪਤਕਾਰ ਮਾਮਲੇ,
ਰੂਪਨਗਰ।

Fig. 2.69 Office memorandum showing the details of LPG connections in Bahadurpur

2 CASE STUDIES AS AN IMMERSIVE APPROACH ...   235

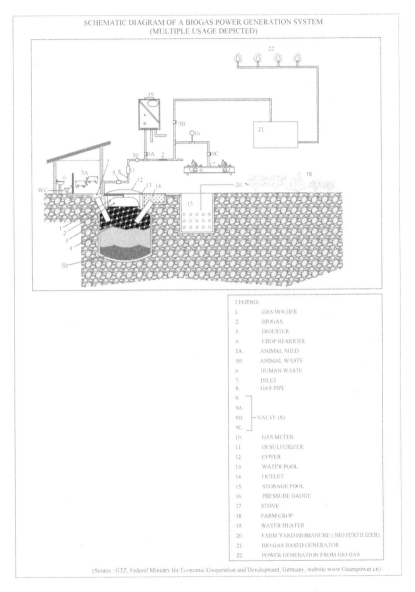

Fig. 2.70 Actual potential of a biogas-based power generation system

Table 2.10 Equipment/instrumentation details of the generation and distribution system of biogas from RS farms along with unit costing and/or expenditure incurred

Equipment/Instrument	Expenditure in (INR)
A. *Waste generation*	
(Source of Waste)	50000–60000
1. Unit cost of one cattle	6.00–6.5 lakhs
2. Animal feed and fodder	7.5 lakhs per month
3. Animal feed processor (GEA)	50,000 per month (recurring)
4. Establishment cost, as on date salaries and wages	
B. *BIOGAS generation system*	
Generation System : (gas)	2.00–2.50 lakhs
Digester (capacity as declared : 120 cubic metres)	
C. *Distribution system with last mile service connection*	
Distribution System : Total pipe line length: 6150 feet	40,000–45,000
a. 1" PVC pipe: 2050 feet	
b. 3/4" PVC pipe: 3550 feet	
c. 1/2" PVC pipe (40 mm dia.): 550 feet	
Power supply system (lying unused)	
1. Diesel based generator set (Mahindra) 30 KVA capacity	3–3.25 lakhs
2. Diesel cost per month	10,000–15,000
Cost of equipments for providing, last mile connectivity to provide service to the end-user	
a. One time connection cost	600
b. Biogas stove	900–1000
c. Clips/clamps	5
d. Burners	100
e. Valves/regulator	110–115
D. *By products*	
a. Milk/Dairying	
Bulk Milk Chiller (BMC)	4.00 lakhs
b. Bio slurry pump unit (mud pump + diesel based engine)	25,000–30,000
Biogas generator set (Prakash) (white elephant for biogas based power, lying defunct generation system (30 KVA capacity)	6 lakhs
Total	30.26–31.76 lakhs

Source As declared by Sh. Gagandeep Singh, RS Farms during the field visit, September 2017

REFERENCES

Bornstein, D. (2004). *How to change the world: Social entrepreneurs and the power of new ideas* (2nd ed.). Oxford University Press.

Bornstein, D. (2005). *So, you want to change the world? The emergence of social entrepreneurship and the rise of the citizen sector*. The Hart House Lectures.

Compendium of State Government Policies on Renewable Energy Sector in India. (2015). *Compiled by Central Board of Irrigation and Power on behalf of Indian Renewable Energy Development Agency Limited* (pp. 1–271).

Dees, J. G. (1998). *The meaning of social entrepreneurship, draft report for the Kauffman Centre for Entrepreneurial Leadership*. Stanford University.

Ferri, E., & Urbano, D. (2011). *Social entrepreneurship and environmental factors: A cross country comparison, research work, international doctorate in entrepreneurship and business management, department of business economics and administration*. Universitat Autonoma de Barcelona.

Friedman, M. (1970). The social responsibility of business is to increase its profits. *New York Times Magazine.*

Hardin, G. (1968). The tragedy of the commons. *Science, 162*(3859), 1243–1248.

Hoogendorn, B., Pennings, E., & Thurik, R. (2010). What do we know about social entrepreneurship: An analysis of empirical research. *ERIM Report Series Research in Management and in International Review of Entrepreneurship, 8*(2), 71–112.

IREDA. (2015). *Compendium of state government policies on renewable energy sector in India* (pp. 1–271). Compiled by Central Board of Irrigation and Power (CBIP) on Behalf of Indian Renewable Energy Development Agency Limited (IREDA).

Kim, D., and Lim, U. (2017). Social enterprise as a catalyst for sustainable local and regional development. *Sustainability, 9*(8), 14–27. 10.3390/su9081427.

National Biogas and Manure Management Programme, NBMMP. (1981). OM no. 5-5/2009-BE, Government of India, MNRE, bio-energy technology development group, dated 27th November, 2009 (pp.1–35).

North, D. C. (1990). *Institutions Institutions, Institutional change and economic performance*. Cambridge University Press.

Ostrom, E. (1990). *Governing the commons, the evolution of institutions for collective action*. Cambridge University Press. ISBN0521405999.

Olson, M. (1965). *The logic of collective action: Public goods and the theory of groups*. Harvard University Press. ISBN 0-674-53751-3.

Öztürk, F. (2013). Understanding social entrepreneurship and features of it. *Studia i Materiały, 16*, 43–55. https://doi.org/10.7172/1733-9758.2013.16.3. ISSN1733-9758

Perrini, F., & Vurro, C. (2006). Social entrepreneurship: Innovation and social change across theory and practice. In J. Mair, J. Robinson, & K. Hockerts (Eds.), *Social entrepreneurship*. Palgrave Macmillan.

Press Information Bureau (PIB) Release. (2016a). *Pradhan Mantri Ujjwala Yojana: A giant step towards better life for all*. Press Information Bureau (PIB), Government of India (GoI). http://pib.nic.in/newsite/printrelease.aspx?relid=148971, dated the 17th August, 14:49 IST.

Putnam, D. R. (1993). *Making democracy work, civic traditions in modern Italy*. Princeton University Press, ISBN 0-691-07889-0.

Press Information Bureau (PIB) Release. (2016b). Press Information Bureau (PIB), Government of India (GoI). http://pib.nic.in/newsite/printrelease.aspx?relid=148971

Press Information Bureau (PIB) Release. (2017). Press Information Bureau (PIB), Government of India (GoI). http://pib.nic.in/newsite/printrelease.aspx?relid=176351

Press Information Bureau (PIB) Release. (2018). Press Information Bureau (PIB), MNRE. http://pib.nic.in/nesite/printrelease.aspx?relid=177871. Government of India (GoI), 22nd March 2018, 17:11 IST.

Scott, C. J. (1998). *Seeing like a state, how certain schemes to improve human condition have failed*. The Yale (Institute for social and policy studies) ISPS series, ISBN0-300-07016-0.

Singh, S. (2016). *The local in governance: Politics, decentralization, and environment*. Oxford University Press.

Stake, E. R. (1978). *The case study method in social inquiry* (pp. 5–9), written at the Centre for applied research in Education, University of East Anglia, as part of assignment for the Organization for Economic Cooperation and Development (OECD), Paris. http://www.jstor.org/stable/1174340

Rogerson, A., Green, M., & Rabinowitz, G. (2013). *Mixing business and social- what is a social enterprise and how can we recognize one?* (Working paper, shaping policy for development, pp. 1–17). ISSN 1759-2917.

Yin, K. R. (2003). *Case study research: Design and methods*. Thousand Oaks, California: Sage.

Zacharakis, A., Beckmann, M., Dees, J. G., Krueger, N., Khanin, D., Mueller, S., Murphy, J. P., Santos, F., Scarlata, M., Walske, J., & Zeyen, A. (2012). Social entrepreneurship and broader theories: Shedding new light on the 'bigger picture'. *Journal of Social Entrepreneurship*, iFirst, 1–20, http://dx.doi.org/10.1080/19420676.2012.725422

CHAPTER 3

Collectivization of Local Demand Through Localized Energy Needs and Resource Assessment—Understanding Demands Realism

3.1 THE LOCAL ENERGY INACTION: THE MISSING ANTHROPOGENIC DIMENSION

This section of the text draws liberally from the results/observations obtained from the mixed-method investigative paradigm, deployed as a research tool to investigate and explore: the subjects, objects, and phenomenon both tangible and intangible comprising (geo-climatic zones, physiographic divisions, human beings, societies, cultural spaces, patterns of energy consumption, institutions, structures, and frameworks, local non-conventional energy resource base evaluation) that are an integral part of this study. The subjects were studied through a mixed approach that involved huge element of physical interaction with the elements of this study and use of physical instrumentation in order to quantify the potential of each geographical region in terms of its local energy resource base to effectively service its local energy requirements, in case it is harnessed. Visual ethnography was used as a tool to capture the energy consumption related lifestyle of different cultural spaces spread across the length and breadth of the sampling universe (the geo-climatic zones and physiographic divisions).

The essence of this work pertains to creation of empirical data in respect of assessment of potential of an alternate source of energy (specifically solar and rural bio-degradable waste) and to unravel and decipher the anthropological dimension of energy consumption patterns in the rural heartland of the Indian subcontinent.

3.1.1 Polysemy Around Rural Flavour of Energy Poverty

Identification of symptoms of rural energy poverty is a herculean task given the different metrics for measuring its magnitude. The issue gets exacerbated on account of the varied approaches adopted by individuals and organizations to establish this phenomenon. To ascertain whether a community is energy poor or prone to becoming energy poor is difficult, as it is purely contextual in terms of lifestyles, habits, tastes, preferences, and the levels of community engagement. Since there appears to be a problem in terms of defining vulnerability (becoming energy poor), it becomes even more difficult to operationalize the existent definition of energy poverty as discussed in Chapters 1 and 2.

The fieldwork undertaken by the author in five different geo-climatic zones and six physiographic divisions villages of the Indian subcontinent bears a testimony to the fact of 'energy poverty' being strongly endemic and local in character. The states that have been covered are Himachal Pradesh, Punjab, Gujarat, Rajasthan, Uttar Pradesh, and Bihar along with one union territory, Andaman and Nicobar Islands. The contextual grounding features different physiographic divisions: (*the Himalayas, the great plains, the west coast plains, the central highlands, the islands, and the peninsular plateau*), and the geo-climatic zones (*montane, humid sub-tropical, tropical wet, semi-arid, and arid*). The study is completely immersed in the physical terrain (geo-spatial features, both natural and man-made), the local culture of energy consumption within the overarching socio-economic-political context.

The local weather conditions have an important bearing on tastes and preferences as well, especially in terms of usage of any given energy service. The problem of recognition of signs and symptoms of energy poverty gets aggrandized particularly when there is a range of options available to choose from for an end-user, in terms of an energy basket carrying varieties of services. Moreover, the concept presents enormous ambiguity when regular/reliable power supply of more than fourteen to eighteen hours per day is encountered as evidence as declared by the respondents—the actual end-users (Tier 3 and 4 category states, Fig. 3.1 at Annexure).

Driven by this reliability of supply a dwelling unit, therefore, may have the best of the modern electronic multipurpose gadgets, along with the most primitive forms of solid and liquid fuels for cooking and occasional lighting as well. This is a common feature witnessed across a majority of cases (dwelling units–sampling unit), showing simultaneous usage of a primitive fuel type for cooking, along with modern electrical appliances for other need-based usages. Energy poverty could, therefore, be, episodic, local, contextual, relative, and symptomatic. Hence, there is an imperative to probe this phenomenon with unorthodox diagnostic tools for an alternate understanding and conceptualization from a rural context. The evidence from the field is strongly suggestive of the fact that it is paradoxical as a conceptual construct.

3.1.2 What Does the Evidence Bring on the Table?

Physical inspection of socio-cultural spaces and creation of photomosaics helped in immersion into the context for developing an understanding of the most essential and central element of this study, the human dimension in energy usage. In the discussion that follows, due impetus is laid upon the signs and symptoms [ethnographic (visual), and quantitative] related to creation of an empirical database from across the sampling universe in respect of: (a) ownership and usage pattern of electrical appliances, (b) assessment of average diurnal load of a dwelling unit (assessment of demand for power), (c) typology of cooking fuels being used, (d) expenditure on cooking fuels, (e) energy budgeting of individual dwelling units expressed as a sum of electricity bill, cooking fuel expenditure and expenditure on lighting needs in case of power outages, (f) lighting load of a dwelling unit in terms of contribution by individual lighting devices powered by electricity, (g) assessment of quality and quantity of solar insolation during the day from sunrise till sunset for a real-time estimation of solar resource potential, (h) waste quantification for biogas resource from three different sources of waste: (a) human waste (census 2011 data, local survey, and physical interaction), (b) animal waste (self, animal husbandry and veterinary department, revenue administration), and (c) kitchen waste plus other bio-degradable waste from the dwelling unit (physical assessment through inspection and participant response). This exercise aided in the evaluation of quantity and quality of fuel assessment for biogas generation on a real-time basis.

The evidence that has been collected aids in establishing baseline energy demand within a dwelling unit in terms of electrical loads which includes the demand for daily lighting and the requirement of fuel types that are used in cooking. The study has purposively restricted itself to a civil structure and the focus is on rural, domestic needs. The second feature in terms of creation of empirical data is the assessment of potential of two renewable sources of energy, solar, and biogas (based on the quantum of human refuse, animal refuse, and kitchen refuse). And most importantly, the composite and schematic maps along with the photomosaics of socio-economic and cultural spaces help in adequate understanding of the human dimension related to consumption of energy in differently situated, rural areas, spread across different terrains and cultures. Thus, the study creates a robust empirical database to map the baseline energy flows across geographical spaces and cultures with a central 'anthropogenic' dimension. The culture of energy consumption (energy demand) is discussed hereafter, based on database created from different parts of rural India.

3.1.2.1 The Island Ecosystem (Village: Profullyanagar, Tehsil and Community Development (CD) Block: Mayabunder, District: North and Middle Andaman, Union Territory (UT))

Profullyanagar is longitudinally spread along the Andaman Trunk Road, situated at a distance of 26 kms from the tehsil headquarters of Mayabunder (Fig. 3.2, Annexure). The topography is undulating. The nature of settlements is dispersed, though grouping of dwelling units is not uncommon. The total area of the village is about 397.03 hectares (Table 3.2, Annexure). The plantation primarily consists of areca nut, coconut, palm, and banana. Rice fields are also a common sight. The detail of the schematic map (nazari naqsha) of Profullyanagar in terms of its man-made and natural features is depicted in Fig. 3.3 (Annexure). The photomosaic depicting the terrain features, general lifestyle, and other collective elements of socio-cultural features is shown in Fig. 3.3 (Annexure).

The mosaic depicts in detail the cultural space, the social space, the economic space, and the human space of energy consumption. It lays down the context of this ethnographic work. The daily chores of a rural household situated in the tropical wet geo-climatic zone and island-based physiographic setting relies on traditional methods of cooking. The utensils used are those suited for open mouth mud plastered cook stoves. Fuel used for cooking is largely forest produce. Kerosene lamp (dhibri) is occasionally used for lighting. However, the oil is used as an igniting aid for the firewood. A typical 'gatha', a stack of collected wood weighs around 10–12 kgs. A gatha lasts for 3–4 days on an average depending on the size of the household, the number of meals being cooked and the kind of delicacy that is being cooked. Storage of firewood is very common, on account of the geo-climatic realm in which the village is physically situated. Though the village comprises both settlers and non-settlers, it is the Ranchi community, primarily consisting of Bengalis that is found in majority. Locally grown rice, fish, and local vegetables are the common feature of an eat-well plate here.

In terms of availability of non-conventional energy sources, Profullyanagar is comfortably placed with a solar insolation potential of about 2.33 kWh on an average, on a daily basis (Author, 2016–2017). Further, it has huge potential for biogas-based power generation. The daily quantum of power that can be generated from biogas produced comes to around 98 kWh, which is almost one hundred times the average daily load demand of the entire village. The village has an average daily load requirement of around 0.81 kWh as shown in Fig. 3.4a (Annexure). The lighting load of this village is around 23.4% of the total electrical load, on an average on a daily basis (Fig. 3.5, Annexure).

Though, the village receives around 22 hours of conventional, grid-based power supply (Fig. 3.1, Annexure), which is more than enough to cater to the current electrical load demand of the village, however, as the collective evidence suggests, the green and clean future lies in the hands of bio-methane based power generation system. The detail of actual loads contributed by individual appliances is depicted in Fig. 3.4c, at (Annexure). The annual per capita consumption of power is 67.8 kWh. The annual per capita demand for lighting is 15.9 kWh. Though, solar potential is also good enough to meet the current demand however, it may not service any additional load that is created on account of either change in the ownership status of the appliances by the end-users or a change in behaviour captured through increased duration of usage of a higher load, for example, extensive use of electric induction stove. An attempt has been made to study the monthly expenditure on items pertaining to energy consumption in an individual dwelling unit.

A major chunk of expenditure goes towards meeting of cooking fuel expenditure that includes all sources as LPG, kerosene, and forest produce. Forest produce dominates the cooking fuel mix in the households. Electricity dues are nominal on account of the fact that the subsidy is to the extent of 80%. The positive feature is fairly regular and reliable supply of power that is reflected in a minimal expenditure on kerosene oil consumed for the purpose of lighting (0.37%). On an average every dwelling unit spends around 12% of its total income on meeting its domestic energy requirements as shown in Fig. 3.4b (Annexure). Thus, the data speaks of pluralism and the inherent ambiguity that surrounds the definition of energy poverty.

There is reliability of power supply, the lifestyle is in sync with the current power generation and distribution system and there is fairly reasonable ownership of electrical gadgets. Therefore, the first thought that comes to the mind is whether Profullyanagar is energy poor. The median income criteria of 10–15% of monthly or annual income expenditure on energy requirements may not hold good to label it as energy poor. Secondly, in case it qualifies to be energy poor, how can energy poverty in Profullyanagar, be ameliorated? Definitely, the current power generation system based on high sulphur diesel (HSD) generator sets is not the answer. The answer lies in the base load energy demand data (demand) and the resource potential assessed for solar and biogas (the supply through alternative means of energy). There could be a dual fuel grid to run the entire village that could run on hybrid sources of power, solar, and biogas.

Therefore, the local evidence depicts that—(a) the average load demand of an individual dwelling unit is less than a unit of power—0.81 kWh, (b) that annual per capita consumption of power is 67.8 kWh, and the annual per capita demand for meeting the requirements for lighting is a paltry 15.9 kWh. The village falls in the first level of basic human needs (50–100 kWh, HDR, 2010), and the lighting load is far below the annual per capita criteria of 120 kWh (Tennakoon, 2009), (c) the grid-based power supply is reliable in terms of quality and duration of supply, and (d) there is tremendous potential for biogas-based power generation system.

Hence, the policy prescription for an alternate energy system needs to be guided by empirical, context-based evidence for addressing local needs and meeting long term requirements of mitigating climate change (Do such low load demands warrant the extension of the central grid?). The evidence from Profullyanagar presents a strong case pointing towards a re-look into the basic criteria for defining 'energy poverty'. There is a need to look for mechanisms and alternatives through a series of microanalysis that is grounded in the actual context of energy consumption in a typical rural Indian setting based in an island ecosystem.

3.1.2.2 The Mainland Black Cotton Soil Rich Ecosystem (Village: Moti Varnoli, Taluka: Desar and District: Vadodara, State: Gujarat)

Moti Varnoli is radially spread between the perennial stream, Mahi and Vadodara-Desar-Timba state highway. The village has a centrally aligned PMGSY link road as the main source of rural connectivity. The terrain is flat with a fairly dispersed linear settlement pattern of dwelling units (Fig. 3.6, Annexure). The settlement is primarily aligned along the link roads running across the village. The village has a single 11 KVA distribution transformer (DT) connected to 11 kV feeder system for supply of electricity. The entire village has a thick veneer of fertile, black cotton soil. There are huge tracts of agricultural plots under individual as well as collective ownership (Fig. 3.7a, Annexure). The village is situated at a distance of 5 kms from the block headquarter. The total area of the village is about 470 acres (Table 3.3, Annexure).

The cropping pattern comprises cotton, toor (lentil, pulses), and occasional tendu leave plantation (in small patches). The detail of the schematic map (nazari naqsha) of Moti Varnoli in terms of its anthropogenic and natural features is depicted in Fig. 3.7a (Annexure). The photomosaic depicting the physical terrain features, general lifestyle, and other collective elements of socio-cultural features is placed in Fig. 3.7b (Annexure). The mosaic depicts in detail the cultural space, the social space, the economic space, and the human space of energy consumption. The photomosaic depicts the temporary nature of settlement, the quality of access link roads to the main PMGSY link road, animal fodder, and the beautifully decorated entrance to a temporary dwelling unit.

An important feature is shown towards the top, right-hand quadrant of the mosaic. The *'desi divo'*, as it is commonly referred to in Gujarati language, is the traditional lighting lamp that is used in case of power supply disruption for meeting lighting needs. Most of the dwelling units had only female presence as the males are out to work as casual labourers in the village itself or in the neighbouring villages of Chitlav, Rajpur, Manekla, etc. Those having agricultural plots in the village are engaged in primary agricultural activities. The village is situated in the west coast plains (physiographic identity) and semi-arid geo-climatic zone.

In terms of local resources of non-conventional energy, Moti Varnoli is comfortably placed with a solar insolation potential of about 6.95 kWh on an average, on a daily basis shown in Fig. 3.8a (Annexure). Further, it has fairly high potential for biogas-based power generation. The daily quantum of power that can be generated from biogas produced comes to around 49 kWh, which is almost fifty times the average daily load demand of the entire village. The village has an average daily load requirement of around 1.20 kWh shown in Fig. 3.8a (Annexure). The annual per capita consumption of power is 95 kWh. The annual per capita lighting demand is 26 kWh. The lighting load of this village is around 27.5% of the total electrical load, on an average on a daily basis (Fig. 3.9, Annexure).

The village receives around 14–18 hours of conventional, grid-based power supply (Fig. 3.1, Annexure), which is more than enough to cater to the current electrical load demand of the village, however, as the collective evidence suggests, the green and clean future lies in the hands of solar as well as bio-methane based power generation system. The detail of actual loads contributed by individual appliances is depicted in Fig. 3.8c (Annexure). The solar potential is also fairly high, approximately seven times the current demand of the village, good enough to meet the current demand. However, it may not service any additional load that is created on account of either change in the ownership status of the appliances by the end-users or a change in behaviour captured through increased duration of usage of a higher load, for example, extensive use of submersible pumps meant for drawing water for meeting daily household needs.

An attempt has been made to study the monthly expenditure on items pertaining to energy consumption in an individual dwelling unit. A major chunk of this expenditure goes towards meeting the expenditure on cooking fuel that includes all sources: LPG, dry wood, and kerosene. Liquefied petroleum gas is the primary source of cooking fuel. The positive feature is fairly regular and reliable supply of power that is reflected in terms of almost negligible expenditure on kerosene oil consumed for the purpose of lighting (0.09%). Thus, on an average, every dwelling unit spends around 9.79% of its total income on meeting its domestic energy requirements in Fig. 3.8b (Annexure).

Thus, the data presents a contrarian view towards the general way of understanding energy poverty in terms of spending towards energy needs. The evidence is contradictory. There is good enough reliability of power supply, though 6 hour-cuts are normal on an average on a daily basis in this village of Vadodara (Fig. 3.1, Annexure). The lifestyle is in sync with the duration and reliability of power supply when placed along with the ownership typology of electrical gadgets by individual dwelling units. Further, in terms of the energy ladder hypotheses, the entire village has access to high efficiency cooking fuel, LPG also.

Similar situation crops up here as well whether Moti Varnoli is energy poor. The median income criteria of 10–15% of monthly or annual income expenditure on energy requirements do not hold good as an indicator of energy poverty. Is there a need to switch over to an alternate energy generation system? The switch over is supposed to be driven by needs actualization in terms of understanding community needs and their aspirations. The switch over not only requires a change in energy production design but more importantly, it needs to be based on the prevalent culture of consumption in Moti Varnoli. Yes, a part of the answer lies in the base load data (1.20 kWh) that underlines the present actual demand for power. However, this demand is currently driven by the supply side conditions. The resource potential assessed for solar and biogas can cater to the community needs in totality provided the community owns up mandate to run, maintain, and distribute energy as per their requirements on a day to day basis. There is no dispute to the fact that solar and biogas both hold good promise for the village could be a dual fuel grid to run the entire village that could run on hybrid sources of power, solar, and biogas.

Thus, the local evidence shows that—(a) the average load demand of an individual dwelling unit is a little above 1 kWh (1.20 kWh), (b) the annual per capita demand for power is 95 kWh, and (c) the per capita annual demand for lighting is 26 kWh. Both the values put Moti Varnoli in the first level bracket of basic human needs (HDR, 2010) and another study that requires a certain basic minimum requirement for lighting (120 kWh per annum per person, Tennakoon, 2009). However, the same village has access to most modern, highly efficient fuel for cooking as reflected in the energy budget. Such mixed nature of evidence further adds to the ambiguity and complexity of the metrics adopted to define 'energy poverty'. The larger question remains to be answered—whether the thrust on extension of the central grid for servicing such small quantum of loads which are largely dispersed, a feasible option.

3.1.2.3 The Nature of Evidence from the Great Plains (Village: Bhikuchack, CD Block: Belchi, Tehsil: Barh, District: Patna, State: Bihar)

Bhikuchack is a very small revenue village. It has an area of 148 acres. The total population of the village is 714 (Table 3.4, Annexure). The village is a remote entity located along the upcoming national highway (NH)-30A that is under construction. It shall provide better connectivity between Barh and Fatuha tehsils/subdivisions of Patna district. The village has a densely packed, nucleated settlement pattern. There is no general segregation of dwelling units on the basis of caste or sub-castes. The population comprises kurmis, mahatos, manjhis, paswans, yadavas, pasis, ahirs, and the general community (Fig. 3.11a, Annexure). Geographically, the scheduled caste hamlets are located at some distance (around 50–75 meters) from the mixed populace (Fig. 3.11b, Annexure). The terrain is totally flat. The village is a low-lying area and is protected by newly constructed embankments.

It is extremely prone to flooding from the Ganges (Fig. 3.10, Annexure). The majority of the population is engaged in agriculture that is primarily rain-fed. However, isolated tube-wells are not uncommon. The village falls under the humid sub-tropical geo-climatic zone and classified as a geographic entity under the 'great plains' category (physiographic division). The village has a single link road that constructed under the state government scheme—Mukhya Mantri Gram Sampark Yojana. The link road provides access to the villagers to the national highway. Almost the entire population is engaged in agriculture (Fig. 3.11a, Annexure). The entire belt in Belchi block including Bhikhuchak is known as the vegetable belt of Patna district, prime reason being the geographical proximity to Nalanda and Patna districts.

This belt is also known for growing green chilies. Being exposed to fluvial influence, fresh veneer of alluvium adds to the soil fertility every year. A small proportion of the population is also engaged in casual, semi-skilled labour work either in Barh or Fatuha. The NH-30A project also provides gainful employment to the villagers. The photomosaic (Fig. 3.11a, Annexure) gives the complete glimpse of the terrain features, spatial disposition of dwelling units and the overall socio-economic profile of the context defined in terms of the revenue village of Bhikhuchak. The nature of land holdings in terms of average size falls under small and marginal category. The photomosaic depicts the mixed nature of dwelling units along with the sources of energy within a dwelling unit for catering to human and animal needs (Fig. 3.11b, Annexure).

The village has recently been the beneficiary of extension of the central grid and has achieved the status of being electrified. The entire village of Bhikhuchak has an average daily load of 0.65 kWh shown in Fig. 3.12a (Annexure). The load distribution pattern has been shown in Fig. 3.12c (Annexure). The annual per capita demand for power is 42 kWh (access can only help meeting basic needs), as spelt out by the universal criteria on energy services and access levels (HDR, 2010). The annual per capita demand in terms of lighting load is about 11.6 kWh (much lower than the minimum requirement of 120 kWh, Tennakoon, 2009). The ownership status of electrical appliances along with their individual contribution to the daily load has been shown in Fig. 3.12c (Annexure).

The primary contributors to the daily average load are such appliances as, ceiling fan, bulbs (primarily filament/incandescent), television, and set top boxes. The village has parched green cover. It is almost devoid of green cover. The solar insolation potential is around 6.55 kWh per day, almost ten times the current demand for power. The resource potential in terms of energy production from biogas is a huge promise almost 197 kWh per day. It can be generated by tapping the latent energy of human, animal, and household refuse. The average expenditure on cooking fuels is about 15.70% of the total earnings (Fig. 3.12b, Annexure). LPG takes the lead followed by kerosene and thereafter, dung cakes. *'The expenditure on electricity bill is paltry as meters have not been installed in the units that have been connected to the grid remarks- Bhupendra Umrao, assistant electrical engineer, HQ and Samarjeet kumar, assistant electrical engineer, Barh'*. The energy budget of the entire village is slightly higher than the median income criteria of 15% to be labelled as energy poor (15.70%)! The lighting load is 28% of the total electrical load of the village (Fig. 3.13, Annexure). The village has an average supply of power for 14 hours on a daily basis (Fig. 3.1, Annexure).

The rate of revenue realization is extremely poor. The single-phase connection wires run along pre-stressed cement concrete (PSCC) poles which do not withstand dust storms during peak summers. Since the poles are not properly bound to earth on account of shoddy plinth work, they get uprooted or become tilted easily. This results in frequent disruption of supply and adds to the unreliability of grid-based power supply in this part of the CD block. The village of Bhikhuchak presents strong evidence of low electrical loads, non-revenue power, usage of high efficiency cooking fuel in the form of LPG though kerosene and dung cakes are also common. The question arises whether Bhikhuchak qualifies to be energy poor? The usage is mixed in terms of fuel mix used for cooking, and the energy consumption related expenditure is also on the higher side a discussed above. The signals cannot be individually assessed.

Evidence strongly suggests that the terrain characteristics and the consumption culture along with local resource potential point strongly towards distributed, embedded generation of power. The future of Bhikhuchak lies in biogas-based power generation system that shall not only help in improving addressing power demand at all times but also provide clean cooking fuel supply apart from other ancillary advantages that are inherently linked with such an energy production system. The solar potential is also fairly good in terms of servicing daily load requirements of the households. However, the benefits are restricted in terms of diversity of uses it can be put to vis-à-vis biogas production unit. Bhikuchack does qualify to be labelled as 'energy poor'. *This piece of evidence also questions the centralized policy paradigm of extending the central grid to address needs of rural electrification, even when the local energy resource base (the empirical evidence of resource assessment potential) puts up a strong case in favour of embedded generation of power through biogas and solar as a combination of sources!*

3.1.2.4 The Evidence From (Village: Ghanghaol, Tehsil: Fatehpur Sadar, CD Block: Haswa, District: Fatehpur, State: Uttar Pradesh)

The revenue village of Ghanghaol is contextually situated in the central highlands as a physiographic entity and humid sub-tropical geo-climatic zone (Fig. 3.14, Annexure). The area of the village is about 678.64 hectares. It has population of 2201 (Table 3.5, Annexure). It is about 20 kms from the district headquarters. The village has a totally flat topography. It has an elongated, lensoidal geographical extent. The link road of the public works department (PWD) runs across the village (Fig. 3.15a, Annexure). The village has all weather ponds which have been revived under MGNREGS recently. The pattern of settlement is linear and dense. A distribution system of canal network of minor irrigation department runs though the village which supports the farmers whose lands are situated towards the tail end of the canal distribution network.

Agriculture remains the mainstay of the village as an economic activity. The major crops that are grown here comprise wheat, paddy, and lentils. The interior connectivity of the village is provided through interlocked paving of bricks, locally known as *'khadanjas'*. *'The caste groups are a mix of upper castes comprising Brahmins, Thakurs and kayasths, and the backward groups include lodhs, nais and malhas remarks C. Indumathy, Chief Development Officer (CDO), Fatehpur'*. Another noteworthy feature of this village is that it has a large area under mango orchards. 'Dasahri' happens to be the local variety of mango that is grown here.

A large number of dwelling units in this village have been constructed under the state government housing scheme known as 'Lohia Awas Yojana (LAY)' under the political mandate of the Samajwadi party government. It is an important scheme for the reason that it has an inherent component for standalone, solar home lighting system (SHLS). The street lighting has been also recently been taken up for revamping to switch over to solar energy. The photomosaic depicts a composite snapshot of the socio-cultural features of the village (Fig. 3.15b, Annexure). It depicts the manner in which energy is consumed in a typical dwelling unit in this part of rural India. The mosaic also shows the interiors of a LAY house with its SHLS (Fig. 3.18, Annexure). The average electrical load on a daily basis is slightly less than half a unit—0.48 kWh as shown in Fig. 3.16a (Annexure). The annual per capita consumption of power is 30 kWh. The annual per capita lighting load is about 2.50 kWh. The solar potential appears to be extremely promising standing at 5.14 kWh at this time of the year. However, the capacity of power generation from biogas overrides all the estimates, standing at a colossal figure of 310.05 kWh (Fig. 3.16a, Annexure). The demand for electricity is characterized by extremely low loads of power consumption. Tube lights and ceiling fans dominate the contribution made to the overall electrical load.

As discussed above, that this village has a large number of LAY beneficiaries, the electrical loads of those dwelling units is similar—0.525 kWh representing 2 nos. of light emitting diodes (LEDs), one ceiling fan (Fig. 3.47, Annexure). The village gets on an average 10–12 hours of grid-based power supply (Fig. 3.1, Annexure). On an average, a family spends around 20% of its monthly earnings towards meeting its energy requirements as shown in Fig. 3.16b (Annexure). A substantial chunk of this percentage goes towards expenditure for meeting the cooking fuel requirements shown in Fig. 3.16b (Annexure). The cooking fuel mix is dominated by usage of firewood, followed by LPG and thereafter kerosene plus dung cakes. Lighting load is about 8.33% of the average electrical load of 0.48 kWh (Fig. 3.17, Annexure).

Interestingly, the lighting load is dominated by the usage of LED lights. This fact can be explained on the basis of the higher number of LAY houses in the village. The average load profile is around half a unit of power as shown in Fig. 3.16c (Annexure). Thus, the evidence strongly points towards the universal fact that has been spoken about earlier pertaining to energy poverty. Ghanghaol can be aptly labelled to be energy poor in terms of its—(a) low electrical power consumption, (b) dominance of fire wood in its fuel mix used for cooking, and (c) almost exceeding the median expenditure limit (10–15% of the monthly income is spent on meeting energy needs), as an average dwelling unit spends almost 20% of its monthly earnings towards meeting its energy requirements (Fig. 3.16b, Annexure).

However, an exception is created here on account of the policy dose that has been administered on sectarian lines in the form of a rural housing scheme, LAY. This state-specific scheme provides efficient lighting devices, and ceiling fans along with plug in points to charge communication devices such as mobiles. This endemic policy dose distorts the average demand for grid-based conventional power supply, being higher. Thus, a standalone, off-grid, solar energy-based lighting system creates an aberration in terms of application of the borrowed concept of energy poverty. Conversely, this policy dose is also suggestive of the fact that in case there are strong endemic signs and symptoms of 'rural' energy poverty, then an appropriate policy design can help address the same provided, no slippages occur at the stage of execution in the action arena. However, it is also important to take into account the quantification of the resource potential of the two sources of renewable energy viz., solar and biogas because the happenings in the remote village of Ghanghaol underpins the need for decentralized, embedded, distributed generation to boost demand for energy by increasing supply through active involvement of the community through existing formal and informal networks in the village.

Thus, Ghanghaol is a fit case to be considered for embedded, decentralized power generation to service such low loads as 0.48 kWh (30 kWh is the annual load per capita) on an average and the annual per capita lighting needs of 2.5 kWh. The centralized power generation and grid extension for addressing the needs for rural electrification finds itself in the dock in the light of the empirical evidence presented in terms of local demand for energy and the assessment of the potential of two RE (renewable energy) sources, solar, and biogas (5.14 kWh and 310 kWh), respectively.

3.1.2.5 Evidence From (Village: Amargarh, CD Block and Tehsil: Sadulshahar, District: Ganganagar, State: Rajasthan)

The revenue village of Amargarh lies in the 'great plains' as a part of the physiographic classification and falls in the 'arid' geo-climatic zone of the Indian subcontinent (Fig. 3.19, Annexure). Amargarh has an area of 490 hectares. It has a total population of 2145. The village is about 44 kms away from the district headquarters of Sriganganagar (Table 3.6, Annexure). It is located along the Sadulshahar-Sangaria state highway (SH) of the public works department of the government of Rajasthan (Fig. 3.20, Annexure). The village has almost a perfect square disposition. The topography is extremely flat. There are neatly carved out rectangular agricultural holdings. The agricultural holdings are fairly large the average size, normally ranges from 5 to 8 acres. The holdings are held together as a composite unit. Every land parcel has an access in terms of water supply for irrigation along with an approach for tilling. The village has a huge chunk of village common land, locally known as '*shamilat*'.

Natural water bodies have been preserved in the village. The pattern of settlement is linear extending along the phirni of the village. The nature settlement is dense (nucleated) with a mixed population from different caste groups. Jat Sikhs, bagdis, majhabi Sikhs, meghwals, and Jats are common as a caste group in this village. The village link road is commonly known as 'phirni' and it encircles the entire village (Fig. 3.20a, Annexure). The major crops grown in the village are cotton, cluster beans, mustard, and wheat. Though the village has predominantly an agrarian flavour, a sizeable number of the population is engaged in skilled labour in Sriganganagar. A sizeable majority are teachers, lawyers, and self-employed entrepreneurs. The schematic map gets depicted through the photomosaic that gives a collective snapshot of the otherwise 'rural' lifestyle of Amargarh. 'Tandoors' are at the heart of individual and community living in Amargarh. The photomosaic depicts the general lifestyle in the village and the manner in which energy is traditionally consumed in the village (Fig. 3.20b, Annexure).

The village is 'electrified' and the average duration of grid-based power supply on a daily basis is almost greater than 18 hours (Fig. 3.1, Annexure). The lifestyle in terms of consumption of electrical energy is highly energy intensive. The ownership status in respect of electrical appliances along with their contribution to the daily load is shown in Fig. 3.21c (Annexure). The average daily demand for power in terms of electrical load comes to about 9.58 kWh shown in Fig. 3.21a (Annexure). The annual per capita consumption of power is 688 kWh. The annual per capita demand for lighting is 21.5 kWh. There are dwelling units in the village with air-conditioners as well. Vast majority of dwelling units have almost every single electronic gadget that provides comfort and saves time as shown in Fig. 3.21c (Annexure). The dwelling unit labelled as AM12 deserves special attention in terms of its load demand.

It happens to be the residence of one of the most influential entity in the village, belonging to the Jat Sikh community. The energy budget in terms of expenditure on electricity charges and cooking fuels presents an interesting story. The charge on electricity consumption along with expenditure on cooking fuels comes to around 8.70% of the total average monthly earnings of a dwelling unit as shown in Fig. 3.21b (Annexure). The expenditure on any other alternate source of lighting is nil. The lighting load is about 3.13% of the daily average electrical load demand of the village (Fig. 3.22, Annexure). The mix of cooking fuel presents an interesting dichotomy that necessitates the reason to understand the traditional and cultural concept of energy consumption in a typical rural Indian setting.

Though every household in the village has double domestic LPG connection, the dependency on firewood does not decrease. There is on an average, almost an equal consumption in terms of monthly expenditures on the twin fuel mix. The data in terms of visual aid and quantification reflects that the pattern of energy consumption is not a function of any given energy efficient technology or the varieties of cooking fuels placed very high on efficiency. Rather, it is the local, micro, traditions, practices, customs that define the overall culture of energy consumption. It is fundamentally linked to the food habits, tastes, and local preferences that have evolved over centuries to show up in its present form. Thus, Amargarh presents itself as a 'strong binary' with diametrically opposite and strongly contradicting patterns of dependence on energy systems. The electrical loads speak of a very high energy intensive lifestyle in terms of daily power demand, whereas the cooking needs present a diametrically opposite 'traditional' lifestyle that is not at all energy intensive. Moreover, Amargarh also falls short of the median income criteria of a minimum of 10–15% of the monthly expenditure on meeting energy consumption requirements.

Therefore, the empirical, contextual, locale-specific, endemic evidence again raises the same question—whether Amargarh is energy poor? What could be a probable answer? Coming back to the resource assessment potential in terms of solar and biogas—the results obtained at this point of time of the fieldwork establish that solar insolation alone shall not be able to service even 50% of the current power demand of the village. The solar insolation potential comes to be around 5.48 kWh. Biogas potential is immense, figuring around 245 kWh on an average per day. This empirical evaluation of power generation potential clearly stamps the solid promise it holds to service any kind of electrical loads on a given day. Given, the socio-cultural fabric of Amargarh and the lifestyle of energy consumption, the evidence suggests that a biogas based micro-grid can effectively meet all domestic and other requirements of the community. The policy needs to take into account the inherent element of 'robust' evidence for a fair assessment of the hidden potential of any given renewable energy resource. Biogas is 'indigenous' and should be socio-culturally acceptable technology to the local community as an 'alternative design' of a local, community centric energy system.

3.1.2.6 Evidence from Himalayan Foothills (Village: Kakira, CD Block: Bhattiyat, Tehsil: Chowari Khas, District: Chamba, State: Himachal Pradesh)

The revenue village of Kakira falls abreast the Dalhousie cantonment. It lies in the 'Himalayan zone' of the physiographic divisions. The village represents the 'montane' geo-climatic zone of the Indian subcontinent. The census village has an area of 5 hectares. It has a total population of 769. It is situated at a distance of 76 kms from the district headquarters of Chamba (Table 3.7, Annexure). Kakira is primarily a physiographic high. It is situated at an elevation of 1136 meters above mean sea level (MSL). It has an undulating, rolling topography (Fig. 3.23, Annexure).

The lush green Himalayan slopes are traversed by terrace farming activity (Fig. 3.24a, Annexure). Kakira is primarily a local bazaar, a tiny market abuzz with economic activity. The caste composition of the village comprises Gorkhas followed by the mahajans (banias). The Gorkhas are primarily retired army personnel, whereas the Mahajans have an absolute control over the Kakira bazar. They are self-employed local entrepreneurs. Scheduled castes comprise 6–7% of the total population who are primarily employed with the state government and based in Shimla. Kakira bazar is the nodal centre of the community life of the village. The activities on a daily basis are based on personal relations within the members of the community. *Bartan bhandars* (utensil shops), *kiryana shops* (for daily needs), electronics, local tailor, cobbler, etc. are a part and parcel of the socio-cultural fabric of the village (Fig. 3.24b, Annexure).

The village is 'electrified' with an average supply of almost 20–22 hours on a daily basis (Fig. 3.1, Annexure). The average load of the village comes to around 10.22 kWh per day at this time of the year as shown in Fig. 3.25a (Annexure). The ownership status of appliances by individual households along with their actual contribution to the daily load demand is depicted in Fig. 3.25c (Annexure). The annual per capita demand for power is 1026 kWh. The annual per capita demand in terms of lighting load is about 27 kWh. The major contributors to the overall electrical load are such appliances as electric induction stoves and geysers. The photo-mosaic provides a composite glimpse of a modern kitchen in a dwelling unit in Kakira.

The lighting load is a paltry 2.64% of the total electrical load of 10.22 kWh (Fig. 3.26, Annexure). LED use dominates the lighting load (Fig. 3.26). The energy budget of Kakira presents an interesting picture. The average monthly expenditure on an average on energy services comes to about 5.22% of the total monthly earnings as shown in Fig. 3.25b (Annexure). Out of this, 71% of the expenditure is towards clearance of electricity charges. This fact explains the energy intensive lifestyle of the residents of the village. LPG dominates the cooking fuel expenditure in Kakira. The other appliance that contributes towards meeting the needs of cooking is the induction stove that contributes to the electrical load and the related energy charges. The village does not use any other source of fuel for cooking.

The resource assessment in terms of potential for solar and biogas is on the lower side. The solar potential for the village has been assessed at 4.88 kWh at this time of the year. Thus, in spite of the fact that the village is at an elevation of 1136 MSL, it does not receive the required intensity of solar radiation to service the current electrical load demand of the village that has been assessed at 10.22 kWh per day. Solar insolation potential falls short by a huge margin of 5.34 kWh (52%). Further, the potential for power generation from biogas has been worked out to be around 10.09 kWh as shown in Fig. 3.25a (Annexure). Kakira village presents an interesting set of empirical evidence in terms of the quality and quantity of energy consumption, and the related expenditure on energy services. The culture of energy consumption is governed by physiography, climate, local weather conditions and the socio-economic profile of the local residents. Apart from this the state-specific policies in respect of power tariff for the rural domestic connections also affects energy materialism to an appreciable extent.

The state of Himachal Pradesh is endowed with huge hydro-electric potential. The electricity board makes huge sales of power at the power exchange, at very competitive prices. The consumption is extremely lower in the higher Himalayan reaches. Thus, the state is regarded as a 'power surplus' state. For residential, domestic connections, there is a subsidy to the tune of almost 60% per unit of power consumed by a rural, domestic consumer. However, this subsidy decreases progressively as the units of power consumption increase. The ratio falls to almost nil, starting from 2/3:1/3 (state share: consumer share) for different ranges of power consumption in terms of kWh (units). The rates at which power subsidy is disbursed for residential, domestic Supply in Himachal Pradesh across socio-economic strata are detailed in Table 3.1 (*Source: Smt. Urimla Devi, senior revenue assistant, O/o Sub divisional Officer, electricity sub-division, Rait (district, kangra, Himachal Pradesh, during personal interaction with the researcher during September 2017)*).

Table 3.1 For BPL families (per month)

Unit	Rate payable by HPSEB per unit	Subsidy given by Govt. per unit	Rate paid by consumer per unit
0–60 units	2.85	1.85	1.00
Above 60 units	Same rates as of APL families		

For APL families (per month)

Unit	Rate payable by HPSEB per unit	Subsidy given by Govt. per unit	Rate paid by consumer per unit
0–125 units	3.70	2.20	1.50
126–300 units	4.60	1.70	2.90
301 and above	5.10	0.75	4.35

Kakira is a village where the families do not normally have domestic animals. The village comprises of working class and locally employed entrepreneurs. Therefore, the potential for biogas from waste is on the lower side. Further, at higher elevations, the insolation becomes erratic as local weather conditions are turbulent, which increase the intermittency of the incoming solar radiation. These are very local, micro-scale phenomena which ought to be taken into account while considering deployment. Evidence from the village of Kakira strongly suggests that the loads cannot be serviced individually by any of the two renewable sources of energy.

Further, the village has attained 100% electrification. Every dwelling unit has a metered power supply. The power supply is reliable in terms of quality and duration (consistent). The village presents a peri-urbane picture on account of the local socio-economic fabric that is largely created on account of the communities that reside there. 'The village should be considered eligible to be upgraded as a nagar panchayat, on account of its proximity to the cantonment board of Dalhousie and also by the general living standards of the locals-remarks smt. Santosh Kumari, the gram Pradhan of panchayat Kakira'. The presence of almost all the civic amenities that make life comfortable could be witnessed in Kakira.

Thus, the evidence from this local setting requires a different thought process for enhancing the levels of other services. The general living standards did not change on account of access to modern energy service rather it is the demographic cultural composition that has a concrete bearing on the living standards. It is the nature of gentry that has settled in this village that has given rise to the contemporary social and economic structure of the village. Thus, Kakira village, although being a part of rural India, is not energy poor. The problems are of a different nature here viz., poor road infrastructure, poor waste management, and scarcity of water that require a very different kind of policy intervention. Coming back to the requirements of energy and the pattern of consumption, evidence presents a strong case in favour of grid-based power supply in the light of high demand for energy reflected through higher load demands. Moreover, the lower and erratic promise of biogas and solar dependent renewable energy systems may not address the immediate or futuristic demands of the Kakira community as their lifestyle is energy intensive on account of the socio-economic structure that exists there.

3.1.2.7 Evidence from the Piedmont Zone of the Lesser Himalayas (Village: Anher, CD Block: Pathankot, Tehsil: Pathankot, District: Pathankot, State: Punjab)

The revenue village of Anher lies at the border of the two districts of Pathankot (Punjab) and kangra (Himachal Pradesh). The village lies at the intersection of two physiographic divisions—the 'Great plains and the Himalayas', lying at the toe of the lesser Himalayan ranges (Fig. 3.27, Annexure). Further, it falls at the intersection of two geo-climatic zones as well—'the montane and the humid sub-tropical'. The village has an area of 785 acres along with a total population of 1223. The distance from the block headquarters is about 24 kms (Table 3.8, Annexure). The village is predominantly occupied by the 'baazigars'.

They belong to the scheduled caste category, though Rajputs and Jat Sikh families are also present. The village has a riparian economy. The primary crops that are cultivated here are wheat, paddy and animal fodder. Anher has sufficient area under 'litchi' and 'kinnow' (citrus) orchards. The village has a triangular geographic outline. The road infrastructure is good, a PMGSY link road that runs across the village. The topography is generally flat with a rising slope towards north (Fig. 3.28a, Annexure). The photomosaic depicts the general lifestyle of the residents of the village. It presents an amalgamation of the general culture in terms of living standards, amenities and overall social bearing (Fig. 3.28b, Annexure). The village has a very old lined well that is a perennial source of potable drinking water.

The village is completely electrified and it receives on an average, around 19–20 hours of grid connected power supply (Fig. 3.1, Annexure). The average daily load demand of the village is about 7.36 kWh as shown in Fig. 3.29a (Annexure). The ownership status of various electrical appliances along with their individual contribution to the total load, based upon their actual usage is depicted in Fig. 3.29c (Annexure). The annual per capita consumption of power is 461 kWh. The major contributors to the average demand are refrigerators, coolers, tube lights, and filament bulbs. The peak load is about 14 kWh for dwelling unit labelled as AN18, while the lowest load quantum is a little less than 2 kWh, AN02 and AN22 as shown in Fig. 3.29c (Annexure). The lighting load is about 7.6% of the total load (Fig. 3.30, Annexure). The annual per capita demand for lighting is 35 kWh. The major contributor to the lighting load is tube light followed by incandescent filament bulbs. The village deploys twin cooking fuels for meeting their kitchen requirements. Firewood dominates the cooking fuel mix followed by LPG. The average monthly expenditure on energy services (energy related needs) comes to around 12% of the average monthly income, Fig. 3.29b (Annexure). Within this, the lion's share is towards expenses on cooking fuel requirements (7.56%) followed by expense on electricity bills (4.52%).

Therefore, Anher falls within the range of the universally accepted median income criteria of 10–15% expenditure on access to energy services to qualify as 'energy poor' Fig. 3.29b (Annexure). The village holds substantial promise in terms of assessed potential of power generation from biogas that comes to about 53.48 kWh. This potential is more than six times the current average power (load) demand of the village. Solar insolation potential is on the lower side, coming to about 5.33 kWh. Thus, on its own a solar energy-based micro- or mini-grid cannot service the current daily average load demand of Anher.

The question that remains to be answered is whether Anher is energy poor? The answer is unclear. If one goes by the income criteria and the domination of firewood in the cooking fuel mix, the answer would be a 'yes'. On the other hand, in terms of 100% grid connectivity and an average annual consumption of 461 kWh of electricity, it falls somewhere between level one and two of energy access (in terms of meeting basic needs and productive uses) on the universal scale pertaining to the use of energy services and access levels (HDR, 2010). The amount of average annual energy consumption in Anher falls across the bracket of the 'basic human needs and productive uses'—50–100 kWh and 500–1000 kWh per person per year, respectively (HDR, 2010). However, this village gets on an average more than 18 hours of reliable grid-based power supply. This important fact cannot be overlooked. Still further, the average annual consumption of lighting load is 35 kWh which is much below the basic minimum criteria with regard to annual requirement of lighting per person—120 kWh (Tennakoon, 2009). There are different types of evidences that have been encountered in Anher: (a) high daily average load demand (7.36 kWh), (b) firewood usage exceeds use of LPG for meeting cooking requirements, (c) reliable grid-based power supply, and (d) lighting needs are met by use of tube lights and filament bulbs mostly.

Thus, there are contradictory evidences from a single village. One set of evidence qualifies it to be labelled as energy poor while the other completely absolves it from being considered energy poor. The culture of energy consumption in Anher is explicable in terms of the general caste structure, the nature of the local economy and the socio-cultural fabric. The 'bazigars' are primarily engaged in local, manual labour. The rural economy is predominantly agriculture based. The energy intensive lifestyle that is reflected in the load demand is primarily on account of two reasons: (1) use of more number of devices that are less energy efficient but are available locally at very low prices and (2) the families of the upper caste have access to other modern energy intensive electrical gadgets.

In terms of assessment of the local renewable energy resource potential, solar-based micro- or mini-grid (5.33 kWh) cannot meet the current load requirements of the village, where as the power generation potential from biogas on an average for a day is about 53.48 kWh, which can effectively service the contemporary load requirements of Anher. Therefore, the empirical evidence, in terms of the energy requirements and the resource potential, presents a case in favour of grid connected biogas-based power generation with the conventional power supply system as a permanent backup. Therefore, in the light of the arguments placed above, it may not be possible to define exact metrics that enables labelling a particular community, a cultural space, a geographic entity as energy poor. However, the solution is best offered by the locale-specific, culture-based collection of empirical evidence to unbundle the convoluted notion of 'energy poverty'.

3.1.3 Evidence from Case Studies Put Together

3.1.3.1 Learnings from Tayyabpur Solar Micro-grid (Fig. 3.31, Annexure)

The policy estate is contextually embedded in a complex arena—represented by philanthropic designs of business houses, domain knowledge of experts, a planning tool (in early stages of research and demonstration—the reference electrification model, software), and a local socially active organization. There are a series of discords in this project that are linked to—project planning, choice of planning tool, manner of project execution, design of the power generation source, regular operation and maintenance and lastly, need assessment of the recipients of energy service (the most essential element). The empirical evidence collected from the case puts forth two kinds of dysfunctions for analysis: (a) behavioural and (b) technological.

Behavioural dysfunction is largely attributed towards the failure of assessment of the status of the community with regard to consumption patterns of energy, as the ward does not have access to the central grid.

The project proponents fail to connect with the psyche of the ultimate end-user. The subjects were never offered to come on board for the micro-grid project to have a sense of connect with the project. Rather, they were only apprised of the quantity of energy service offers, and the amount that they shall have to pay in lieu of the services rendered, based on the latent capacity of the solar plant (this attribute is concealed). The proponents appear to be too simplistic and presumptuous in their efforts. The myopic vision of the project proponents was utilitarian, and therefore, they could not assess and appreciate the real and natural, in terms of the expectations and aspirations of the subjects involved. As a result, the implant of the project was an attempt to create only a visible infrastructure. Thus, the project proponents could exploit the subjects inefficiently and making the whole project fiscally barren. The lack of effort on the part of the actors comprising the policy estate (TATA-MIT, TATA TRUST, TPDDL, and PRAYAS) led to estrangement of the ultimate end-users.

The aspect of technological dysfunction is latent as it is remotely dependent on a design capacity of a 'software planning tool, REM'. It dictates the capacity of the solar plant but does not take into account on a daily basis, the practical issues pertaining to plant siting (IFC, 2012) in respect of a natural source of energy (solar) and the associated natural environment parameters (humidity, wind, temperature, shade, etc.). It has been a mechanical enterprise with a limited resolve being too deterministic. There was no far-fetched vision of transfer of technology through a marriage between the community and the solar power plant. The level of information asymmetry between the service provider and the user is humongous in terms of both the 'capacity' of technology and the perceptible change it could bring about in the lives of the beneficiaries. The technological initiative was incapacitated on account of trust deficit, disillusionment, and repulsion that gradually built up in the community. The solar micro-grid and its operators presented a patriarchal arrangement in terms of their general mannerisms towards their clients (the nonia community). The dysfunctions assume huge proportion threatening to jeopardize the normal technical functioning of the solar micro-grid.

The solar micro-grid, as a source of non-conventional power to the residents of the ward, does not take into account the indispensable role of locale-specific practical realities, informal processes, and improvisation in the face of unpredictability. The injection of an off-grid source of supply of electricity has altered the social structure and relations in the ward. There is a technological stress that has crept into the community. Not everybody in the similar cultural set-up is an end-user. Access is not free, as there is a one-time connection cost and differential tariff structure depending on the electrical load being serviced and the time at which it is required. Duration of supply, however, is not guaranteed as that shall depend upon the relative drawl of power by another end-user.

This feature alters the power structure in an otherwise, culturally homogeneous ward. Not everyone is a beneficiary, a few are and many are not. This attribute of technology-driven service intent remotely aimed to trigger some form of social engineering, leaves out the essential elements that are primordial to the harmonious functioning of the 'system' design. The entire exercise that led to the commissioning of the plant was based on extremely narrow and restrictive parameters. The design of the contract appears to be unjust and oppressive. It is driven by utopian plans and an authoritarian disregard for the values, desires, faiths, and objections of its subject (lessor). The micro-grid is caught up in a pull between the three vertices of a triangle represented by community, expectations, and aspirations, with the political nature of technology inscribed. The guardians of technology forming a purposeful protective association of domain experts and philanthropists sitting at a distance mock the sporadic presence of a 'minimalist state' that has ceased to be an enabler and a regulator.

Tayyabpur solar micro-grid presents itself as a glaring example of a purposeful protective association of domain experts, philanthropists and social contractors. It is an illuminating craft that presents an otherwise latent ramification of the politics of knowledge laced with information asymmetry between the technology literates and the illiterate end-users. It also mocks the sporadic presence of a minimalist state that could never come to the rescue of its citizens for fulfilling its obligations that are codified under law. There are very strong voices of dissent within the community, presenting a collective unwillingness towards non-acceptance for solar energy-based power labelling it as '*naqli bijli*'—virtual power and not real power that is supplied through conventional grid-based generation sources—as the collective understands it locally. Therefore, it may not be an understatement to say that—Reference Electrification Model (REM)—fails to bridge the gap between heightened expectations and aspirations of the 'locals' in terms of access to 'energy service'.

3.1.3.2 Learnings from Dhundi (Solar Pump Irrigators' Cooperative Enterprise) (Fig. 3.32, Annexure)

The evidence from the field presents Dhundhi as a fit case that suffers on account of onslaught of technology (triggered by technological implant). This project is a live example of a demonstration project (a pilot) that triggers disruption of socio-cultural fabric by creating clear-cut winners (presumptuous) and losers. The policy estate is embedded in the polity and comprises—the department of energy and petrochemicals (the administrative department, government of Gujarat), the Gujarat energy research and management institute (GERMI), the joint consortium of International water management institute (IWMI) and TATA (interested actors), Gujarat energy development agency (presumed facilitator), and the technology partner (Shaswat cleantech).

The institutions of the state appear as mute spectators to contemporary happenings as outputs. The executors of the policy design are—Gujarat Vidyut Nigam limited (GUVNL), the state utility (MGVCL), and the technical arm of the state (O/o the chief electrical inspector, government of Gujarat). The policy recipients reside in the local action arena (Dhundhi village). The genuine concerns of the state utility (conditions laid down in the power purchase agreement) may reduce the effects of short-term condiments guaranteed by the interested project proponents (IWMI) and the not so-interested agent (TATA) acting in a policy estate. The case is clear. There is a public policy design nested in private institutional interests. This is a broad suggestive indication about deployment of solar energy to drive irrigation pump sets.

The interested actors (TATA-IWMI) arrive at the scene to create an administrative cum procedural design for execution of this policy intent. On a plain reading of the policy text (the provisions embedded in the policy design), the broad indication for promotion of an alternate irrigation system driven by means of a renewable energy source is clear. The policy 'proposed' by interested actors did not have the sufficient thrust to see the light of the day to push the entire farming community in Dhundi. However, the 'interested actors' lay down the entire justification (in the form of statement of objects and reasons) for a comprehensive solar irrigation policy (proposal) for the state of Gujarat (huge aggrandization of the untested potential of a policy dose-solar energy-based irrigation systems). The contents of the proposal have been discussed in detail in the chapter on case studies. Interestingly, the demands on behalf of the policy recipients have also been raised, which is far and beyond the scope and intent of the envisaged policy design.

What the new technology implant does to an established socio-economic order? It creates an exception, a set of preferred 'policy recipients'! Earlier, in the village, the energy neighbourhood consisted of: (a) farming community in general, and rural, domestic conventional connections. However, post solar-based irrigation technology intervention, the composition of the energy neighbourhood changes into: (a) grid connected (conventional agricultural connections) farmers, (b) off-grid farmers, (c) diesel-based pump users, (d) solar pump users, and (e) domestic conventional power users. The new genre of cultivators referred to as—'energy croppers' with a sense of pride! The policy recipients (the farming community) get fragmented. In terms of the local political power structures, a formal solar irrigation-based cooperative is created. SPICE/DSUUSM becomes a formal reality. A new power centre gets crystalized, the 'mandali' of solar pump irrigators. The memorandum of association of SPICE has been discussed in detail in the preceding chapter. Though the mandali remains a democratic body by and large, its functional mandate is 'commercial', and in contravention to the terms and conditions of the buyer/client (MGVCL).

The society gets denatured further into a congregation of croppers, and energy croppers, energy producers and sellers (within the community and otherwise), which is non-cohesive in nature. It is important to discuss the tripartite agreement in terms of the role of the technology partner, the third party to the agreement. Though the expenditure for operation and maintenance is to be done by individual farmers and the group as a 'collective', the responsibility of the third party fizzles gradually once the system is installed, tested, and declared formally as 'commissioned' by the chief electrical inspector's office. The technology partner is not 'local' and the turn-around time taken to address a technological grievance is fairly large (refer to the interactive section supra-). The policy dynamics in Dhundi is based on ad-hocism in terms of: (a) failure to recognize pathways to facilitate an energy transition, (b) capacity building of energy croppers, (c) does not maintain a distinction between a core activity and a peripheral activity of a rural farmer, (d) fails to take into account the fact of disruption of social order due to 'enabled migration' to an off-grid system that results in a 'technological lock-in', and (e) strongly promotes vested, self, individual, exploitative commercial interests by tinkering with an agrarian mandate.

The Dhundi action arena remains isolated and is now left on its own to bear the socio-economic cost of an alternate technology in the form of solar energy driven irrigation pumps. It is yet to be seen whether an energy cropper feeds his 'need or greed' by means of overdraft of groundwater. There appears to be a marked personal stake in terms of interestedness. The Dhundi experiment creates wedges in social order and does not pass the test of legitimacy, reason, and transparency, as there is an established conflict between the interests of the buyer (MGVCL) and seller (SPICE). The objectives of the mandali contradict the provisions enshrined in the PPA.

The policy design is devoid of value distribution through technology, and this aspect could largely and rightly be attributed to its being of a first proto-type. Thus, there are clear benefits and burdens linked to this offer and the technology as well. The promoting organizations did not necessarily link all the elements of the target population. The assumptions were unrealistic as the rationale for self-promotion is more evident, and this has been spelt out in the overarching speculative logic put forth in the proposal related to the solar energy-based pumping systems. This system design creates unrest within a uniform social order. It promotes uncertainty in terms of short-term financial incentives and technological lock-in.

This approach to alternate technology implant within a very short span of time sans any robust policy apparatus promotes technological imperialism. It creates a class of bourgeois (energy croppers) and proletariats (non-energy croppers). Therefore, there is a very strong binary that is created within a similar functional (occupational) order, in a given socio-cultural context. Dhundi is a glaring example of this phenomenon. The marriage between culture and technology has not materialized, rather there is an entrapment driven by the lure of multiple revenue streams. The demonstration of this practice has indoctrinated 'capitalist' ideology in the minds of users of off-grid, solar irrigation pumps.

What remains to be seen is whether the project sustains once the 'so called' revenue stream begins to thin, leaving the farmer with no option, but to revert back to the conventional systems of field irrigation that has been their forte for centuries together. Policy sweeteners may not be as sweet as they appear to be. Therefore, the evidence from Dhundi suggests that exceptions created on account of a reductionist mandate based solely on economic considerations may not guarantee any 'multiplier effect' as there can be seen that there are no takers of the proposed technology. The demonstration is not driven by the dictum of technology diffusion.

What the polity does—it uses its coercive power using the policy design—and forces its institutions to purchase the so-labelled 'green power' at prices, that are exorbitantly higher than the average power purchase cost (APPC rate) as laid down in the notified policy (Chapter 2). The evidence suggests that the demonstration project has neither an element of natural resource preservation (groundwater conservation) nor it has the capacity to create an enabling environment for triggering an attitudinal cum behavioural change at the level of end-users' rather, it appears to create acrimony between users and non-users.

3.1.3.3 *Learnings from North and Middle Andaman District (Demand for Local Renewable Energy Systems: Evidence from North and Middle Andaman District) (Fig. 3.33, Annexure)*

The centralist model of HSD-based power generation system in these islands is based on the fundamental premise—'I know what I supply in bulk, and I presume that is the demand'. This is a typical guiding philosophy of a top-down approach that underlines supply side management (SSM). Consumers are functionally too remote from this centrist paradigm of supply of power. The actual load centres (spaces and cultures of energy consumption) are scattered and dispersed in terms of being singular or isolated clusters of dwelling units. *A very strong feature in these islands is—low load demand. Low loads in these terrains are on account of moderate effects of equatorial climate that keeps the need for energy services on the lower side. As it exists, a rural energy system has very strong, innately generic micro-features in terms of habits, tastes, preferences of the largely passive consumers it nurtures. A cautious aggregation of such attributes creates the overall demand based on the listed cultural sub-attributes. There is a purposive, demarcated existence of typically energy intensive community, and energy non-intensive communities in the island-based rural ecosystem.*

The load demand in this physiographic division is driven by needs of comfort, communication and entertainment (CCE). Thus, the evidence highlights 'CCE' as the drivers of energy demand. The local needs point towards the shifting of 'nodes' in terms of local energy resource base evaluation. The twin resources that have been assessed in terms of their potential to service the load created by the drivers, have their respective advantages and disadvantages. Evidence strongly highlights the promise that each of these resources hold, solar, and biogas.

Solar as an energy resource is 'free' from raw material requirements, whereas a biogas plant would be dependent on raw material in the form of—waste from—(1) household, (2) animals, and (3) human beings (Chapter 2). Thus, solar has an edge over biogas. However, the constraints that are placed on solar are a function of—local weather conditions (erratic), topography, vegetation, and equatorial climatic regime. All of these factors vehemently add to the intermittency and non-reliability of solar insolation. Moreover, power generation through harnessing solar energy cannot be regulated through manual intervention. When these constraints are cited, the balance of convenience strongly tilts in favour of biogas. The potential in the present case has been assessed for the category of wastes that can easily be tapped to generate bio-methane with locally available technology. Tropical climates shall help maintain the most critical parameter that governs the efficiency of the anaerobic digester—hydraulic retention temperature (HRT). The end uses to which the biogas can be put to could be endless in terms of their multifarious uses as—clean cooking fuel, heating, power generation, and bio-slurry (green, organic manure). These are immediate end-products of the process of waste digestion and fermentation which have huge potential to support the entire rural ecosystem, apart from meeting the small requirements of a dwelling unit.

The empirical evidence collected points towards a large pool of untapped potential for individual home based or small cluster-based (geographical/physiographic contiguity must be considered) biogas driven power generation systems. A thoroughly professional and thoughtful approach should necessarily avoid policy oversights and myths. What is required at this stage is dotting of the inhabited islands with swarm energy applications based on biogas, followed by solar and then with a diesel based back up plan. Further, the gathered evidence suggests deployment of a different energy systems model for every village depending upon the nature of spatial disposition first, thereafter taking into consideration the socio-economic profile of the residents within a dwelling unit.

The strength of any production system lies precisely in its unique sociocultural values: its wealth of empirical know-how and in a seemingly attention to detail. One should cautiously refrain from routine meddling and regular manipulation of rural energy landscape. The evidence strongly moves a strong case for a robust, well-informed policy design, which could be as labile for immediate demonstration. One should consciously refrain from setting up megawatt-scale systems leading to loss of land, deforestation on a mega scale, and creation of new transmission and evacuation corridors without demand. The dwellers in the interior villages do not have an energy intensive lifestyle, and therefore, any plans of a switch over to mega-modern, alternate energy systems change would be counterproductive for this special geographic and cultural realm on account of the observations and arguments cited above.

The study shows that a mix of existing conventional fuel (HSD)-based energy generation system along with an energy alloy-based (biogas and solar, non-conventional fuels) hybrid power generation system would be socially and culturally in sync with the prevalent culture, climate, and physiography. This model shall be economically more feasible as compared to what is being currently mooted akin to central grid build-outs that provide exceptionally subsidized electricity supplies. Diesel-based generation should stay for some time, before it can be completely weaned off. The hybrid system based on an alloy of renewable sources of energy should heavily rely on biogas, followed by a remote possibility of solar and definitely diesel as the 'evidence' suggests.

These small-scale rural ecosystems are embedded in a social order that dictates the manner and intensity in which primary energy shall be generally consumed, irrespective of the manner in which it is generated. A rural energy niche is a cultural landscape, and its natural environment is influenced and altered by elements of human action, a fact and a reality that cannot be afforded to be overlooked by myopic conceptions of techno-economic evaluations. The demand forecasting needs to understand the rural psyche of a remote consumer in terms of duration of supply and the time of use. That entails a completely decentralized approach towards rural energy management that is site specific, very micro—in scale that is of the community, by the community, and for the community. The rural energy services aspirations should be mapped and addressed locally as the consumption is endemic and contextual. The evidence hints towards pragmatic demand side management, which is required for these remote, isolated, scattered centres of energy consumption with low load densities.

3.1.3.4 Learnings from the Functional Experience of Mera Gao Power (MGP) (Fig. 3.34, Annexure)

The present case highlights the inefficiencies of the state in terms of absenteeism of electricity regulator and passive (locally inactive and therefore, inefficient) decentralized systems of governance. Governance, broadly conceived, refers to how humans make decisions, and form institutions that craft rules shaping individual behaviour (North, 1990). The constitutional mandate of localization of energy governance bears a subdued existence. The micro (the village) as an action arena appears to be too remote and distant from the regulatory framework for energy access. Decentralization succumbs to a painful death when assessed in relation to its active role in—governing energy access, allocation of energy resources and redistribution of energy services. Local renewable energy resource potential evaluation is neither a regional nor local agenda marked by its conspicuous absence from any systemic agenda. The nature of energy services witnessed indicates—(a) the energy access arena is replete with public goods problems and (b) externalities are too localized to be solved at a meso (regional)- or mega (national)-scale, as they warrant local collective action.

The local collective action at the level of micro (revenue village) calls for polycentric forms of action—those that mix scales, mechanisms, and actors simultaneously—imply that the sharing of power between numerous stake holders and scales can, at times, more effectively respond to energy access and services related problems than actions in isolation. A number of studies drawing from the lifetime works of Ostrom have argued that the presence of polycentrism enhances certain variables that can increase the likelihood of cooperation and resolution (Ostrom, 2008, 2010; Sovacool, 2011).

The preceding discussions point towards three most pertinent areas for analysis and discussion: (a) local and regional energy governance, (b) the efficacy of the local institutions, and (c) regulatory governance of localized independent generation and distribution. The situation in the action arena (villages) highlight the following issues—(a) is there a need to understand the local socio-political configurations and transformations that result from the presence of multiple institutions (familiar and alien both)? (b) whether the approaches being followed at the national and the regional level are adequate in terms of addressing issues related to fair access of energy and equitable distribution of energy services, and (c) the need for broadening of roles and responsibilities of non-state actors in becoming involved in issues related to generation and distribution of energy?

These issues highlight the incompetency of the existing institutional framework to regulate the rural energy sector. This requires a re-look into the existing energy governance architecture at all levels, including the operational architecture especially at the regional level. A key ask could be the creation of a totally separate architecture for rural energy governance. MGP has its own political economy rooted in authoritarianism and deep-seated centralization. MGP functions as an independent unit and probably believes in some sort of 'voluntary governance'. The organization is neither recognized nor regulated by any of the institutions of the state.

MGP is a private limited company that is engaged in the business of generating and supplying electricity from renewable energy sources. The firm does not qualify for exemption under Section 12 of the central electricity act, 2003. It is active and operational, functioning with impunity, avoiding the mandate of the electricity act and the authorities created under it. It has assumed upon itself the responsibilities of the state for guaranteed energy service and assumes to be at par with the states' institutions, their structures and functions. It does not qualify to be labelled as a micro-grid, given its technology design, capacity and the nature of service it renders.

The Uttar Pradesh Electricity Regulatory Commission (UPERC) was the first regulator in the country to come up with a mini-grid renewable energy generation and supply regulations (refer to the preceding chapter on case studies for details). These regulations were casted pursuant to the pronouncement of the National Tariff Policy (NTP) 2016. The state is represented through its 'regulatory institution' and its 'design' notified as a policy. It is disheartening to note that the state along with its regulatory institutions, structures, and processes appear to be passive, dormant, functionally defunct, and sessile. MGP is a pygmy organization vis-à-vis the might of the state.

The rural energy service provider (RESCO) appears to be too robust on paper and is functionally meek at the level of action arena when it comes to servicing clients' energy needs. Having said all this, it appears to be a fact that MGP is beyond the reach of the 'state'. Low levels of social activism and education on issues related to energy strengthen the resolve of MGP to exist and function sans any external sanctions by any of the formal institutions of the state. Be it the state level energy regulator (UPERC), or the state nodal agency for governing power generation through renewable sources of energy (SNA, UPNEDA), or local revenue and development administration (the office of the district collector and the chief development officer), and above all the micro-level institutions of self-government, the Zila Parishad (of Barabanki district), the block samiti (of Ramnagar block), and the gram panchayat of Lohati Pasai. It appears seemingly hard to believe, while these events were concomitantly occurring at the cutting edge of the fundamental unit of functional administration (a revenue village); where has been the ideal Weberian bureaucratic set-up?

The evidence from the field mocks the ideals and the objectives of the national rural electrification policy that strongly speaks of active and constructive interlacing of local self-government with the national policy objective of rural electrification. It appears to be a plain rhetoric, as realities exhibited as 'ground truths' present altogether a different picture. Moreover, the evidence strongly underlines the need for integration of collective functions of the meso—(the regional state) and the micro—(the revenue village) with a shared objective of improving energy access through a check on the activities of non-state actors in the field of energy governance, rather than indulging in a turf war leading to compartmentalization of functions.

3.1.3.5 *Learnings from Bahadurpur Biogas Plant—Ram Singh (RS) Farms: The Biogas Cum Dairy Farm (A Social Enterprise) That Was Not to Be (Fig. 3.35, Annexure)*

The evidence from Bahadurpur is primarily centred around two foci: (a) the local misgivings that result from the project and (b) policy parallelism infusing a conflict situation at the macro- and meso-level. Beginning with the first sub-category—the conception of the biogas unit had an individualistic design right from the very beginning. Since, it was a family driven project, and therefore, did not find support from the community. The biogas plant did not infuse a sense of common purpose to drill down the element of collective common good in the village. The dwelling units in the village already have an assured access to liquefied petroleum gas (LPG). The rationale for an alternative in terms of cooking fuel does not register with them, even if it is being provided free of cost. There is a missing element of social value creation and that pervades across—similarly placed groups, differently placed groups and the fence sitters that are common to both the groups. The similarly placed groups are those with a similar socio-economic profile. Interestingly, fence sitters who do not opt for the service in spite of the act that it is free, comprises members from both profiles.

The feeling of alienation stems from the fact of isolated, independent decision making by a single family on every aspect right from the conception, design, and functional operation of the biogas unit. The otherwise cohesive society in Bahadurpur in terms of informal structures that determines and dictates social and political engagements chose to distance itself from collective action. The prime reason for such an eventuality was the fear of 'unfair compensation' sans principles of equity. Thus, resources that generate raw material in terms of refuse from different sources for the production of biogas gets reallocated and redistributed in the end. And, resource allocation and redistribution of a 'commodity' are a political process.

Thus, a new debate opens up and fuels a dichotomy related to the nature of biogas-should it be construed as a service or a commodity? This complicates political decision making in a small socio-cultural set up comprising two to three communities. However, consensus building appears to be a remote possibility. The fear that was deep-seated in the mind of the project proponent was related to collection, transportation, and storage of refuse on a daily basis. However, this fear was never disclosed before the village community.

Bahadurpur is replete with trust deficit that prevents attainment of a collective equilibrium directed towards a potentially win–win situation between the social elements and the action situation (grounded in an economic enterprise driven by a subdued social objective). When people interact in action situation, they make decisions based on the choice rules associated with the position they occupy in an action situation. Therefore, how does one build the rationality for collective action for decentralized energy systems in Bahadurpur! The rules that decide action as a collective could be uniform and symmetrical in terms of actual socio-economic outputs as an immediate measure.

What process tweaking in all likelihood creates perceptible social value in this project which happens to be an individual centric action. What would be the elements of such rationality that could be incorporated in an outcome oriented institutional framework that needs to be created in such an action situation where interests sit apart. To add to the complexities further, what kind of specific design elements would be required to be put in an institutional framework to achieve a Pareto-optimal efficiency for even and equitable distribution of clean cooking fuel along with fair access towards other ancillary by-products of the production system—bio-slurry, and gas-based power! The misgivings of the community and a skewed state policy are discussed hereafter.

(a) How do we build partnerships in a pursuit meant for economic gain in a community set-up? The individual entrepreneur is neither incentivized by the local community, nor by the competing interest groups or the state, through its institutions which bear the mandate for promoting such innovative practices. The conflicting interests have no intersection even though there could be a possibility of potentially large gains through resolution of disagreements. However, the degree of disengagement on the part of the local entrepreneur appears to be on the higher side which limits his bargaining freedom (North, 1990: 90). The entrepreneur feels that there is a directed institutional apathy towards the 'enterprise' which further creates a deadlock between the parties. *Thus, the evidence from Bahadurpur presents a failed saga of perceived 'collectivism, social innovation, and social enterprise'*. It exemplifies a model of negotiated compromise for pursuing an economic interest sans creation of any social value that renders the project socially unacceptable.

(b) Contaminated policy conception results in asymmetric policy design—the state recognizes the latent potential of biogas as a cooking fuel in kitchens and therefore, makes an attempt to push through the agenda of optimal utilization of biogas across regions. Would this agenda setting only suffice, without creation of operational structures and frameworks for capacity building at the cutting edge (in the action arenas)! The answer is a definite and certain 'no'. Biogas is a huge source of combined heat and power (CHP). However, it has never received the policy attention it deserves even when the costs involved are a pittance.

In support of a strong case in favour of biogas, it is argued that— 'in contrast with solar and wind energy it is possible to control the production of biogas as it is dependent on the volume of bio-waste input per unit of time. Further, as said earlier, the utilization of biogas is versatile in terms of its potential for electricity generation, for meeting heating requirements, and for cooking as clean cooking fuel (Chapter 2). In spite of these indisputable advantages, the biogas energy system has been translated and made to be perceived as an extremely complex system on account of ulterior interests of different actors, each with their own view and reasoning on reality, interests, motivations and expectations'.

Bahadurpur is a typical case where, neither the private entrepreneur is on the hunt for any mediating institution to help him sustain the enterprise, nor the policy of the state institutions allow for any stability under the current circumstances to this economic enterprise. The policy estate is replete with directives that smack of parallelism and pluralism. There is conflict between polity and the policy conception. This conflict perpetuates through the policy design element, leading to unclear policy mandates towards the end (Chapter 2). The central focus for a policy on biogas should be hinging upon animal, human and kitchen refuse, and not beyond this. It does not create a segregated niche for biogas for its distinctiveness especially with respect to its closest sitting alternative-biomass. And in case the programme (national biogas and manure management programme, NBMMP) has to be given a shot in the arm, alternate structures and local institutions need to be created for effectively running this self-sufficient energy production system. The greatest irony being the fact, that it receives the least attention from its own renewable energy sources' fraternity that is further exacerbated by reductionist, myopic, and monolithic policy designs.

3.1.4 Summing Up: The Empirical Evidence from the Fieldwork in Different Geo-Climatic Zones and Physiographic Divisions Establish That at the Micro-level

The evidence from the field strongly suggests that the local three tier rural institutional architecture of self-government, is too 'remote' in terms of their placental linkages to energy driven actions and the related ramifications in terms of skewed nature of supply and impoverished local demand. The community development philosophy is severed from the tangible benefits that can be achieved through well-organized local constituents, in case local energy resource assessment is attempted. This aspect of non-conventional energy resource inventory has to be given its due now. Energy linked activities that sow seeds of energy transition in terms of generation and consumption at the micro-level, however, do not get any support at the local level, in spite of the fact that it has the capability to bring about social change. An effective aggregation of energy demand and its local profiling shall aid in effective redistribution of local resources with the help of existent local institutions. This initiative shall help in taming powerful business (economic) interests and guard the interests of small, local consumers who would want to hold reigns of generation at some point of time. This could further help in reduction of any kind of organized opposition.

The local institutions along with the active involvement of the community could draw up their local energy action plans based on local resource base inventory and the local energy demand. There is a need for an effective energy literacy campaign in favour of resource assessment, local demand capture and endemic, distributed generation. This could be done at the micro-level through the support and involvement of local institutions or the third sector, a social, community-driven enterprise through political bargaining at the local level with the help of such intermediaries that can help create and build capacities for effective energy governance at the micro-level. There is an immediate need to collate and club the interests of rural consumers, based on their socio-cultural moorings and energy demands. These initiatives could create conditions to make local energy planning more participatory and reduce conflicts. Evidence also cautions towards adoption of economic stringency. This procedure should be selective and not prescriptive to begin with, as it could create trust deficit and thus narrow the local energy options irrespective of the huge promise it holds. Further, energy management entails redistribution of an end product, which is politically difficult, as distribution is limited by resources. Thus, this discussion brings us back again towards the overarching, imperative directed towards evidence-based policy prescription for an effective demand side management (DSM).

3.1.5 *The Case Studies That Have Been Discussed in the Preceding Section Suggest That the Policy Conception and Construct in Terms of Structural Design Require an Immediate Course Correction*

Policy outcomes are not just a function of the distribution of resources or power amongst social forces as political or economic actors, such as feudal or capitalist elements, but also of the distribution of preferences or interests amongst the institutions themselves as social, economic, and political actors—a claim that holds across macro and micro levels. Different institutional arrangements lead to different outcomes. An action arena consists of people as participants and an action situation in which they participate. When people interact in action situation, they make decisions based on the choice rules associated with the position they occupy in an action situation. Also, people may hold different positions in any given action situation and therefore, may not be able to make the same decisions. Human decision making is about making rational choices and thus involves social dilemmas. Institutional taxonomy and architecture shall govern decision making and therefore, resource allocation, distribution, and redistribution between political, social, and economic actors operating at national (macro-level), regional (meso-level), and the village level (micro-level) shall be an arduous task.

Institutions can differ between social groups and communities at various scales because of their formal methods of collective decision making (democracy versus authoritarianism) or because of their economic institutions (security of production systems, entry barriers in terms of restricted open access, a set of contracts available to private entrepreneurs). They may also differ because a given set of formal institutions are expected to and do function differently; for example, they may differ between two social frameworks that are democratic because the distribution of political power lies with different groups or social classes, or because in one society, democracy is expected to collapse while in the other it is consolidated. Thus, energy governance is too complex a process in terms of its political, economic, and social engagements at all the three levels in the contemporary 'too centralized' operational structure of policy framework. Further, it strongly points towards the missing dimension of 'human' element in the realm of energy generation, and distribution that is much desired at the level of micro. The 'local' element needs to be proactively recognized and the 'capacity building' process in terms of design elements of technology be imparted to fortify the community in order to take care of their local needs. Information asymmetry needs to be eradicated completely.

There is a dire need to adhere to the cannons of the national electrification policy. There exists a huge gap between the macro-institutions (federal level), the regional institutions at the state level, while the institutions are largely 'incapacitated' at the level of districts in terms of general awareness about issues related to energy generation, transmission, and distribution. There exists an absolute institutional vacuum at the level of the village where policy demonstration does take place. What is warranted at this stage is an in-depth study of failures rather than success to help design better policies, preferably in terms of human engagement at the site of energy demand and the micro-culture that underpins the pattern of energy consumption.

Decentralized energy governance entails proliferation of small scale, localized, on-site, embedded, distributed, standalone, power generation that are off-grid. And for this to happen, empirical resource evaluation for different sources of renewable energy in terms of their locale-specific potential needs to be assessed for an effective, collaborative, and real-time demand side management without compromising on the twin essentials of reliability and affordability of any given energy service. The models (flow diagrams) appended to the section on learnings from case studies bear a strong testimony to the fact that the local is complex. There cannot be a generalist and universal approach to policy formulation in the rural electricity sector as—energy access and energy end use exhibit non-universal character. Policy needs to be placed at the heart of the context to render it acceptable for realistic and practical outcomes.

Annexure

See Fig. 3.1.

3 COLLECTIVIZATION OF LOCAL DEMAND THROUGH LOCALIZED ... 279

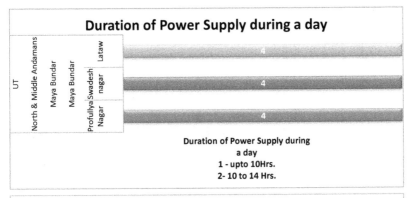

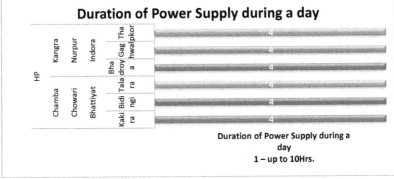

Fig. 3.1 Duration of power supply in the states and one union territory studied

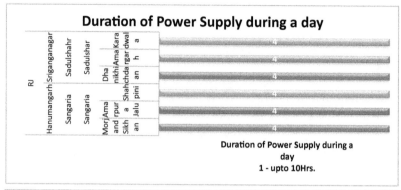

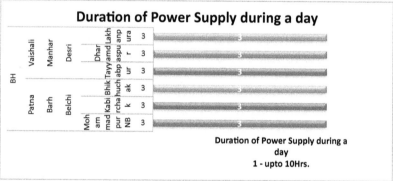

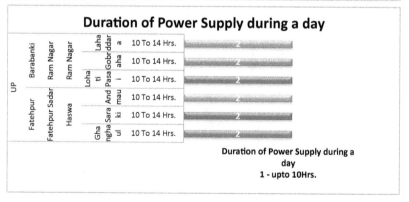

Fig. 3.1 (continued)

3 COLLECTIVIZATION OF LOCAL DEMAND THROUGH LOCALIZED ... 281

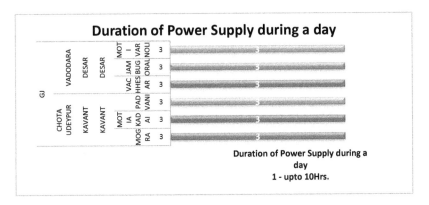

Fig. 3.1 (continued)

Profullyanagar

See Figs. 3.2, 3.3, 3.4, 3.5, and Table 3.2.

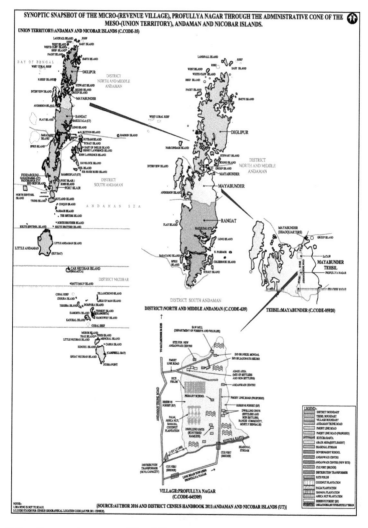

Fig. 3.2 Composite map of Profullyanagar

3 COLLECTIVIZATION OF LOCAL DEMAND THROUGH LOCALIZED ... 283

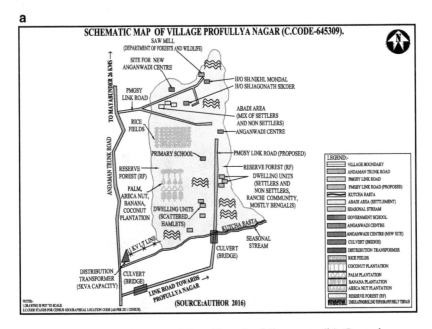

Fig. 3.3 (a) Schematic map of the village Profullyanagar; (b) General pattern of energy consumption and lifestyle in the village

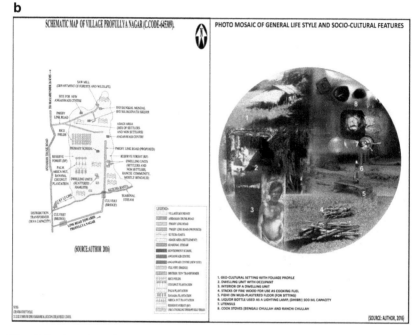

Fig. 3.3 (continued)

3 COLLECTIVIZATION OF LOCAL DEMAND THROUGH LOCALIZED ... 285

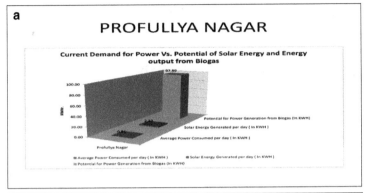

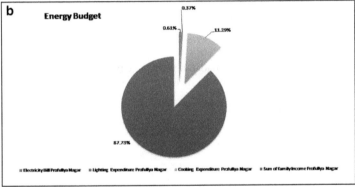

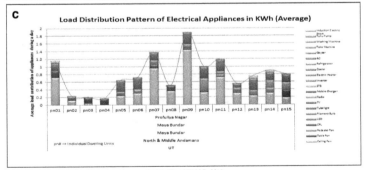

(SOURCE: AUTHOR, 2016)

Fig. 3.4 (a), (b), and (c) Renewable energy resource potential vis-à-vis the load demand, energy budget, and the load demand on account of appliance usage

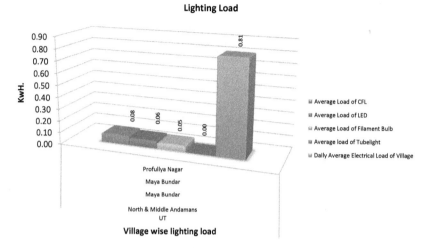

Fig. 3.5 Fraction of lighting load demand as a percentage of the total load demand contributed by use of different lighting devices

Table 3.2 Basic details of village Profullyanagar

Village: Profullyanagar, Tehsil: Mayabunder, Block: Mayabunder, District: North & Middle Andaman

S.No.	Particulars	
1	Name of Village	Profullyanagar
2	Name of Revenue Village	Profullyanagar
3	Population	458
4	Scheduled Caste	Nil
5	No. of Total Household	105
6	Area of Village	397.03 hectares
7	Irrigated area	0.00 hectares
8	Non irrigated area	69.82 hectares
9	Primary School	01
10	Anganwadi School	02
11	Co-operative Society	01 (14 kms away at Billiground)
12	Veterinary Hospital	29 kms away at Webi village
13	Primary Health Centre	01 (around 14 kms away at Billiground)
14	Post Office	01 (sub post office situated around 8 kms away at Nimbudera) (main post office is situated around 25 kms away at Mayabunder)
15	Police Station	01 (around 14.5 kms away at Pinakinagar village)
16	Railway Station	00
17	Nearest Bank	SBI & CO-operative Bank situated 14.00 kms away at Billiground village
18	Distance from Block Headuarter	24 kms

Village: Profullyanagar, Tehsil: Mayabunder, Block: Mayabunder, District: North & Middle Andaman

S.No.	Particulars	
1	Name of Village	Profullyanagar
	Name of Revenue Village	Profullyanagar
2	Nagar Panchayat	Gram Panchayat: Basantipur
3	Area of Village	
	A- Total	397.03
	B-Irrigated	0.00
	C-Non Irrigated	69.82
4	Ponds	
	A-Number	24
	B-Area	2.10 hectares
5	Population	
	A-Total	458
	B-Female	225
	C-Male	233

Number of Animals								
Cows	Buffalo	Sheep	Goats	Pig	Horse	Poultry	Dogs	Total
25	00	00	60	15	00	1500	30	1630

Moti Varnoli

See Figs. 3.6, 3.7, 3.8, 3.9, and Table 3.3.

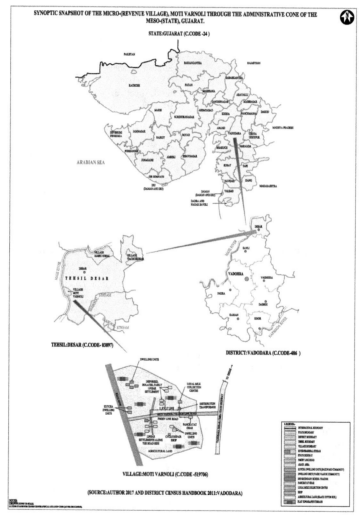

Fig. 3.6 Composite map of Moti Varnoli

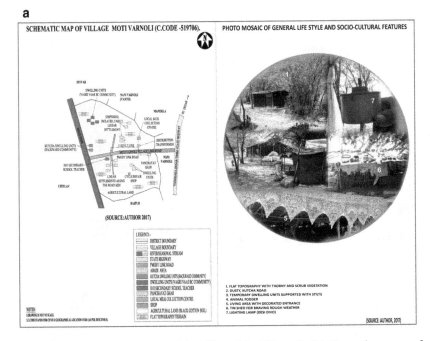

Fig. 3.7 (a) Schematic map of the village Moti Varnoli; (b) General pattern of energy consumption and lifestyle in the village

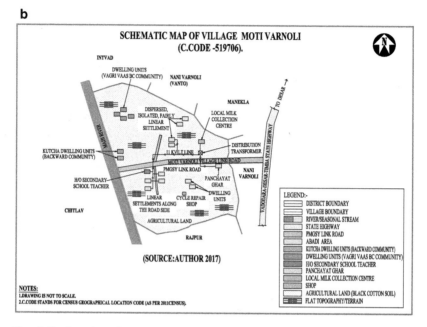

Fig. 3.7 (continued)

3 COLLECTIVIZATION OF LOCAL DEMAND THROUGH LOCALIZED ... 291

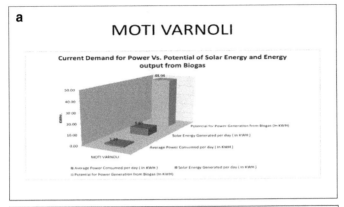

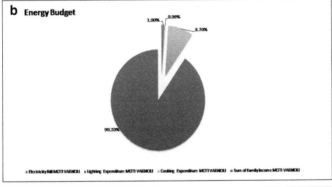

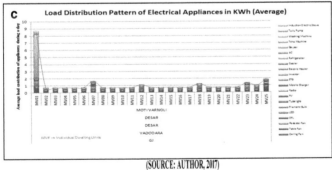

(SOURCE: AUTHOR, 2017)

Fig. 3.8 (a), (b) and (c) Renewable energy resource potential vis-à-vis the load demand, energy budget, and the load demand on account of appliance usage

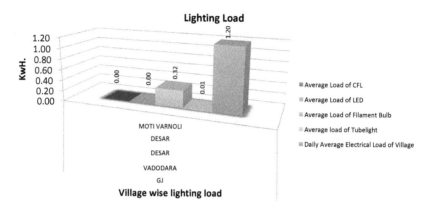

Fig. 3.9 Fraction of lighting load demand as a percentage of the total load demand contributed by use of different lighting devices

Table 3.3 Basic details of village Moti Varnoli

Village: Moti Varnoli, Block: Desar, District: Vadodara

S.No.	Particular	
1	Name of Village	Moti Varnoli
2	Name of Revenue Village	Moti Varnoli
3	Population	1388
4	Schedule Caste	137
5	No. of Total Household	301
6	Area of Village	470 Acre
7	Irrigated area	350 Acre
8	Non Irrigated area	120 Acre
9	Primary School	01
10	Anganwadi centre	02
11	Co-operative Society	01 (Milk Co operative Soc)
12	Veterinary Hospital	00
13	Primary Health Centre	01 (5 km Desar)
14	Post Office	00 (Moti varnoli)
15	Police Station	01 (5 km Desar Village)
16	Railway Station	30 km (Timba)
17	Nearest Bank	02 (5 km SBI, BOB Desar)
18	Distance from Block head Quarter	05 km

Village: Varnoli, Block: Desar, District: Vadodara

S.No.	Particular	
1	Name of Village	Moti Varnoli
	Name of revenue Village	Moti Varnoli
2	Nagar Panchayat	0
3	Area of Village	
	A-Total	470 Acre
	B-Irrigated	350 Acre
	C-Non Irrigated	120 Acre
4	Ponds	
	A-Number	1
	B-Area	1 Acre
5	Population	
	A-Total	1388
	B-Female	660
	C-Male	728

Numbers of animals

Cow	Buffalo	Ship	Goats	Pig	Horsee	Poultry	Dogs	Total
55	193	20	250	0	2	0	0	520

Bhikhuchak

See Figs. 3.10, 3.11, 3.12, 3.13, and Table 3.4.

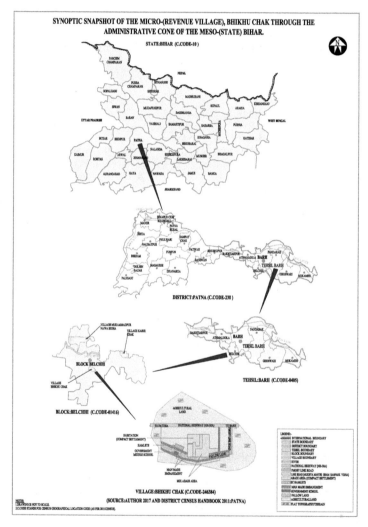

Fig. 3.10 Composite map of Bhikhuchak

3 COLLECTIVIZATION OF LOCAL DEMAND THROUGH LOCALIZED ... 295

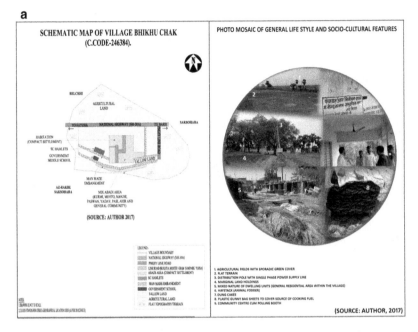

Fig. 3.11 (a) Schematic map of the village Bhikhuchak; (b) General pattern of energy consumption and lifestyle in the village

b

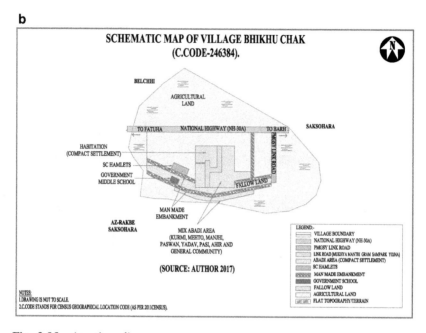

Fig. 3.11 (continued)

3 COLLECTIVIZATION OF LOCAL DEMAND THROUGH LOCALIZED ... 297

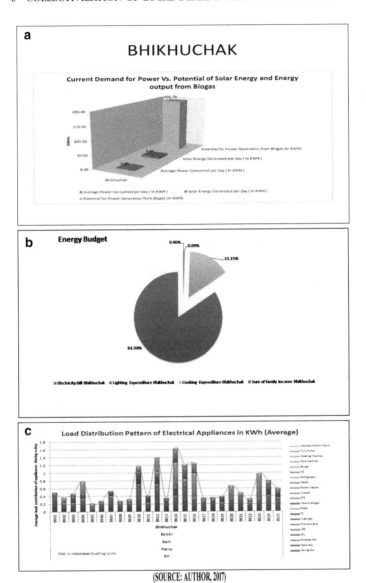

(SOURCE: AUTHOR, 2017)

Fig. 3.12 (a), (b), and (c) Renewable energy resource potential vis-à-vis the load demand, energy budget, and the load demand on account of appliance usage

298 M. K. SINGH

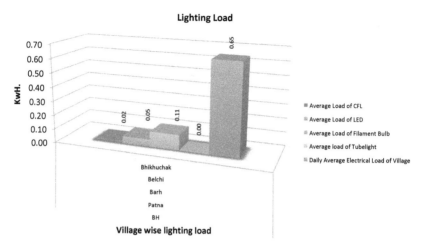

Fig. 3.13 Fraction of lighting load demand as a percentage of the total load demand contributed by use of different lighting devices

Table 3.4 Basic details of village Bhikhuchak

Village: Bhikhuchak, District: Patna

S.No.	Particular	
1	Name of Village	Bhikhuchak
2	Name of Revenue Village	Bhikhuchak
3	Population	714
4	Scheduled Caste	140
5	No. of Total Household	126
6	Area of Village	148 Acre
7	Irrigated area	133 Acre
8	Non Irrigated area	15 Acre
9	Primary School	2 (1 Primary School) (1 Upgraded Middle School)
10	Anganwadi Center	1
11	Co-operative Society	Nil
12	Veterinary Hospital	1 km
13	Primary Health Center	Belchhi, 3 km
14	Post Office	Belchhi
15	Police Station	Belchhi
16	Railway Station	Barh 25 km
17	Nearest Bank	Bank of Baroda 1/2 km
18	Distance from Block Head Quarter	1 km

Village: Bhikhuchak, District: Patna

S.No.	Particular	
1	Name of Village	Bhikhuchak
	Name of Revenue Village	Bhikhuchak
2	Nagar Panchayat	Belchi
3	Area of Village	
	A-Total	148 Acre
	B-Irrigated	133 Acre
	C-Non Irrigated	15 Acre
4	Ponds	
	A-Number	0
	B-Area	0
5	Population	
	A-Total	714
	B-Female	339
	C-Male	375

Number of Animals								
Cows	Buffalo	Sheep	Goats	Pig	Horse	Poultry	Dogs	Total
286	952	0	246	0	0	0	0	1484

Ghanghaol

See Figs. 3.14, 3.15, 3.16, 3.17, 3.18, and Table 3.5.

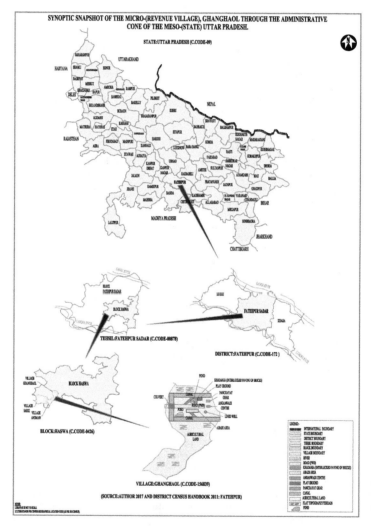

Fig. 3.14 Composite map of Ghanghaol

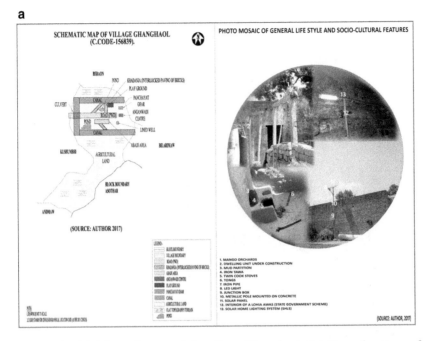

Fig. 3.15 (a) Schematic map of the village Ghanghaol; (b) General pattern of energy consumption and lifestyle in the village

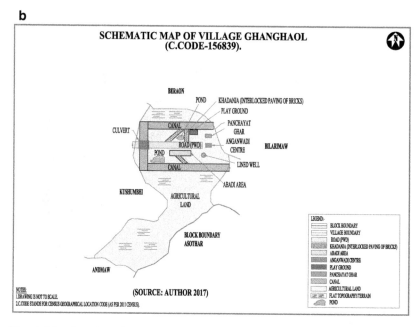

Fig. 3.15 (continued)

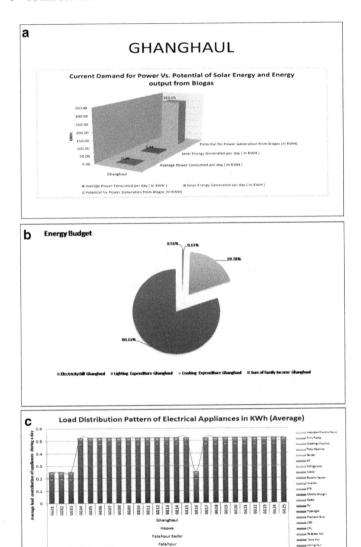

Fig. 3.16 (a), (b), and (c) Renewable energy resource potential vis-à-vis the load demand, energy budget, and the load demand on account of appliance usage

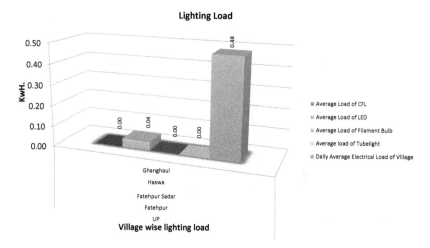

Fig. 3.17 Fraction of lighting load demand as a percentage of the total load demand contributed by use of different lighting devices

SOLAR HOME LIGHTING SYSTEM FOR A DWELLING UNIT CONSTUCTED UNDER LOHIA AWAS YOJANA (LAY), (UTTAR PRADESH)

Fig. 3.18 Ghanghaol LOHIA AWAS YOJNA SHLS

Table 3.5 Basic details of village Ghanghaol

Village: Ghanghaol, Block: Haswa, Fatehpur

S.No.	Particulars	
1	Name of Village	Ghanghaol
2	Name of Revenue Village	Ghanghaol
3	Population	2201
4	Schedule Caste	729
5	No. of Total Household	378
6	Area of Village	678.64 hectares
7	Irrigated Area	4.98 hectares
8	Non Irrigated Area	180.64 hectares
9	Primary School	01
10	Anganwadi Centre	02
11	Co-operative Society	04 km
12	Veterinary Hospital	12 km
13	Primary Health Centre	12 km
14	Post Office	03 km
15	Police Station	07 km
16	Railway Station	20 km Fatehpur
17	Nearest Bank	12 km Barouda UP Gramin Bank, Gajipur
18	Distance from Block Head quarter	15 km
19	Distance from District Head Quarter	20 km

General information

1	Name of Village	Ghanghaol
	Name of Revenue Village	Ghanghaol
2	Nyaya Panchayat	Kushumbhi
3	Area of village	
	A-Total	678.640 hectares
	B-Irrigated	498 hectares
	C-Non Irrigated	180.640 hectares
	D-West Land	0.640 hectares
4	Ponds	
	A-Number	34
	B-Area	9.3 hectares
5	Population	
	A-Total	2201
	B-Female	1021
	C-Male	1180
6	A-Dr. Ram Manohar Lohiya Awas (LAY)	05
	B-Indra Awas Yojna / PMAY (G)	22

Number of Animals

Cattle	Buffalo	Sheep	Goat	Pig	Horse	Poultry	Dog	Total
843	1174	606	568	35	2	58	22	3308

Amargarh

See Figs. 3.19, 3.20, 3.21,3.22, and Table 3.6.

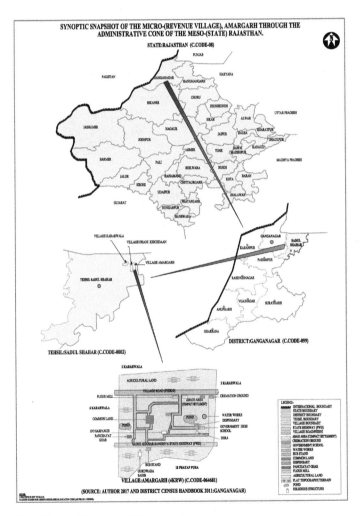

Fig. 3.19 Composite map of Amargarh

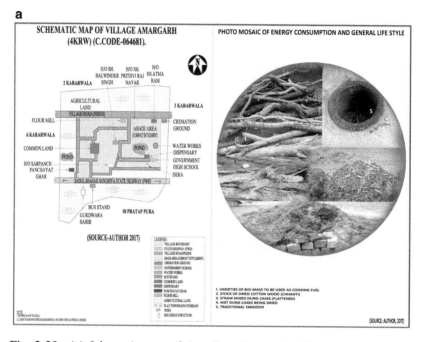

Fig. 3.20 (a) Schematic map of the village Amargarh; (b) General pattern of energy consumption and lifestyle in the village

3 COLLECTIVIZATION OF LOCAL DEMAND THROUGH LOCALIZED ... 309

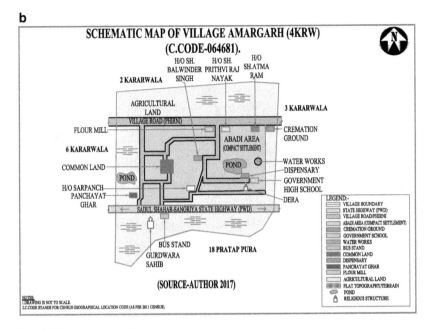

Fig. 3.20 (continued)

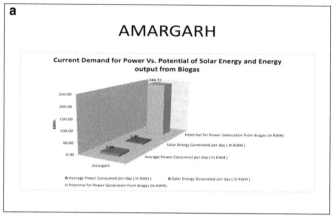

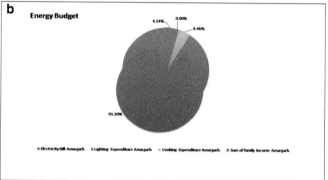

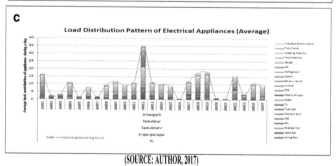

Fig. 3.21 (a), (b), and (c) Renewable energy resource potential vis-à-vis the load demand, energy budget, and the load demand on account of appliance usage

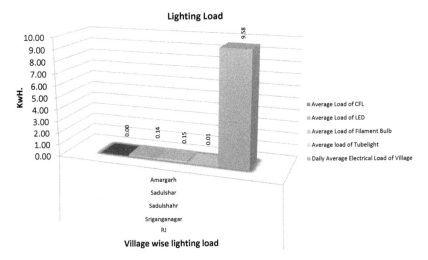

Fig. 3.22 Fraction of lighting load demand as a percentage of the total load demand contributed by use of different lighting devices

Table 3.6 Basic details of village Amargarh

Village: Amargarh, Tehsil, Block: SadulShahar, District: Sri Ganga Nagar

S.No.	Particulars	Details
1	Name of Village	Amargarh
	Name of Revenue village	4 KRW
2	Nyay Panchayat	Kardwala
3	Area of village	
	A-Total	489.6250 hectares
	B-Irrigated	440.8230 hectares
	C-Non Irrigated	2.3400 hectares
	D-West Land	–
4	Ponds	
	A-Number	–
	B-Area	–
5	Population	
	A-Total	2145
	B-Female	1003
	C-Male	1142
6	A-Dr. Ram Manohar Lohiya Awas	–
	B-Indra Awas Yojna/Pmay(G)	15

Number of Animals

Cattle	Buffalo	Sheep	Goats	Pig	Horse	Poultry	Dogs	Total
245	1203	242	338	–	5	–	177	2210

Village: Amargarh, Tehsil, Block: SadulShahar, District: Sri Ganga Nagar

S.No.	Particular	Details
1	Name of Village	Amargadh
2	Name of Revenue Village	4 KRW
3	Population	2145
4	Scheduled caste	787
5	No. of Total Household	422
6	Area of village	489.625 hectares
7	Irrigated area	440.823 hectares
8	Non Irrigated area	2.3400 hectares
9	Primary School	1
10	Anganwadi Center	2
11	Co-operative Society	6 km Kardwala
12	Veterinary Hospital	9 km Sadul shahar
13	Primary Health Center	9 km Sadul shahar
14	Post Office	4 km Kishanpura Urradha
15	Police station	9 km Sadul shahar
16	Railway Station	9 km Sadul shahar
17	Nearest Bank	9 km Sadul shahar
18	Distance from Block Head Quarter	9 km Sadul shahar
19	Distance from District Head Quarter	44 km Shri Ganganagar

Kakira

See Fig. 3.23, 3.24, 3.25, 3.26, and Table 3.7.

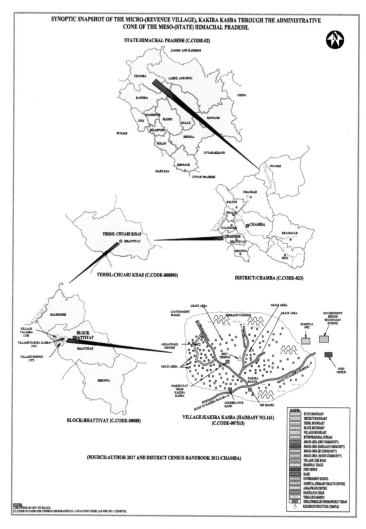

Fig. 3.23 Composite map of Kakira

3 COLLECTIVIZATION OF LOCAL DEMAND THROUGH LOCALIZED ... 315

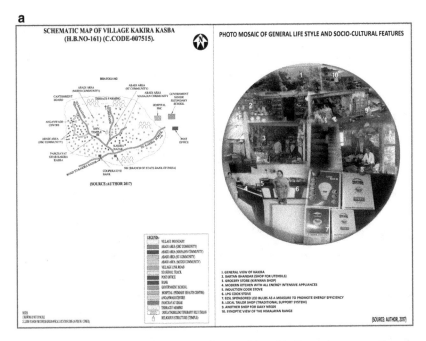

Fig. 3.24 (a) Schematic map of the village Kakira; (b) General pattern of energy consumption and lifestyle in the village

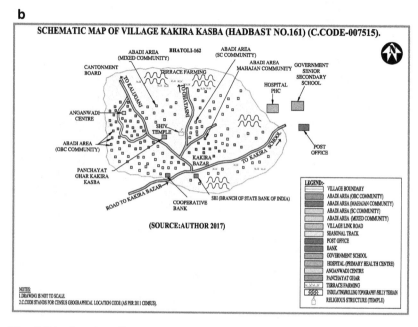

Fig. 3.24 (continued)

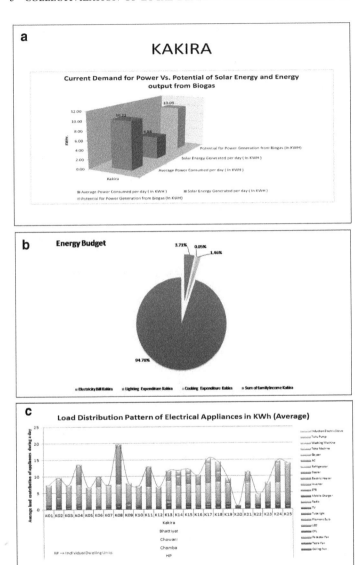

Fig. 3.25 (a), (b), and (c) Renewable energy resource potential vis-à-vis the load demand, energy budget, and the load demand on account of appliance usage

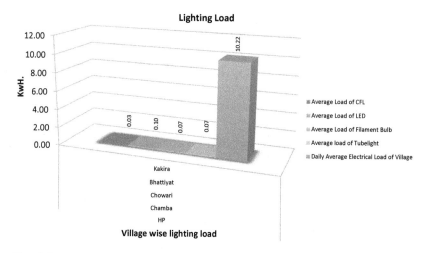

Fig. 3.26 Fraction of lighting load demand as a percentage of the total load demand contributed by use of different lighting devices

Table 3.7 Basic details of village Kakira

S.No.	Particular	
1	Name of Village	Kakira Kasba (Village Code = 007515)
2	Name of Revenue Village	Kakira Kasba (161)
3	Population	538 (as per 2011 census)
4	Scheduled Caste	13
5	No. of Total Household	148
6	Area of Village	5 hectares
7	Irrigated area	0
8	Non irrigated area	5 hectares
9	Nagar Panchayat	Kakira Kasba
10	Area of Village	
	A-Total	5 hectares
	B-Irrigated	0
	C-Non Irrigated	5 hectares
11	Ponds	
	A-Number	NIL
	B-Area	NIL
12	Population	
	A-Total	538
	B-Female	290
	C-Male	248
13	Primary School	2 (1—GPS Kakira, GGPS—at kakira Jarei near 0.5 km)
14	Anganwadi School	01—Anganwadi at Kaluganj
15	Co-operative society	NIL
16	Veterinary Hospital	Kakira Jarei 1.5 kms
17	Primary Health Centre	Kakira Bazzar 1 km
18	Post Office	Kakira Bazzar 1 km
19	Police Station	Bakloh 1 km
20	Railway Station	Pathankot—80 kms, Jassur—52 kms
21	Nearest Bank	SBI Kakira, HP State Co-operative Bank Kaira, PNB Bakloh 1 km away at Bakloh
22	Distance from Block Headquarter	21 kms

Anher

See Fig. 3.27, 3.28, 3.29, 3.30, 3.31, 3.32, 3.33, 3.34, 3.35, and Table 3.8.

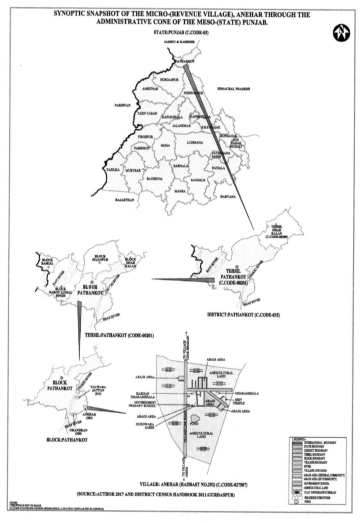

Fig. 3.27 Composite map of Anher

3 COLLECTIVIZATION OF LOCAL DEMAND THROUGH LOCALIZED ...   321

a

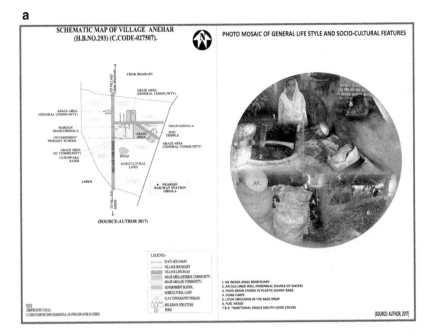

Fig. 3.28 (a) Schematic map of the village Anher; (b) General pattern of energy consumption and lifestyle in the village

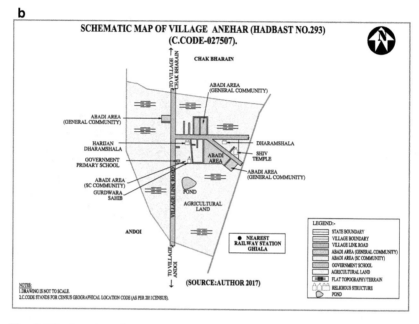

Fig. 3.28 (continued)

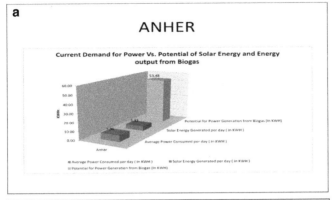

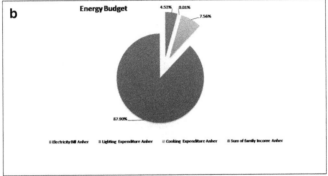

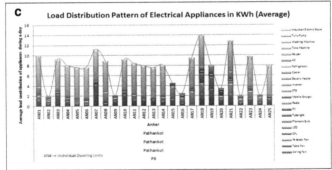

(SOURCE: AUTHOR, 2017)

Fig. 3.29 (a), (b), and (c) Renewable energy resource potential vis-à-vis the load demand, energy budget, and the load demand on account of appliance usage

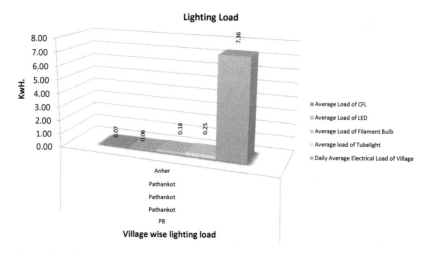

Fig. 3.30 Fraction of lighting load demand as a percentage of the total load demand contributed by use of different lighting devices

Table 3.8 Basic details of village Anher

Village: Anher, Block Pathankot, District: Pathankot Hadbast No. 293

S.No.	Particular		
1	Name of Village	Anher	
	Name of Revenue Village	Anher	
2	Nagar Panchayat	1	
3	Area of Village		
	A-Total	785 Acre	
	B-Irrigated	220 Acre	
	C-Non Irrigated	565 Acre	
4	Ponds		
	A-Number	1	
	B-Area	1 Kanal	
5	Population		
	A-Total	1223	
	B-Female	598	
	C-Male	625	

Number of Animals								
Cows	Buffalo	Sheep	Goats	Pig	Horse	Poultry	Dogs	Total
65	215	21	30	0	18	700	60	1109

(continued)

Table 3.8 (continued)

Village: Anher, Block Pathankot, District: Pathankot Hadbast No. 293

S.No.	Particular	
1	Name of Village	Anher
2	Name of Revenue Village	Anher
3	Population	1223
4	Scheduled Caste	733
5	No. of Total Household	210
6	Area of village	785 Acre
7	Irrigated area	220 Acre
8	Non irrigated area	565 Acre
9	Primary School	1
10	Anganwadi Center	1
11	Co-operative Society	0
12	Veterinary Hospital	0
13	Primary Health Center	0
14	Post Office	1 (1 km in Ghiala village)
15	Police Station	1 (5 km Nangal Bhoor)
16	Railway Station	1 km (Ghiala Railway Station)
17	Nearest Bank	5 km (SBI Nagal Bhoor)
18	Distance from Block Head Quarter	24 km

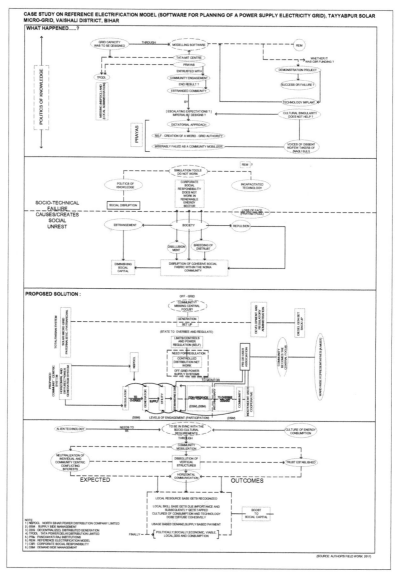

Fig. 3.31 Policy prescription for Tayyabpur

3 COLLECTIVIZATION OF LOCAL DEMAND THROUGH LOCALIZED ... 327

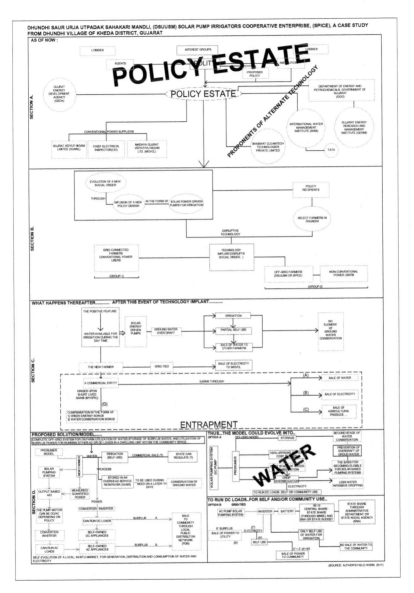

Fig. 3.32 Policy prescription for Dhundhi

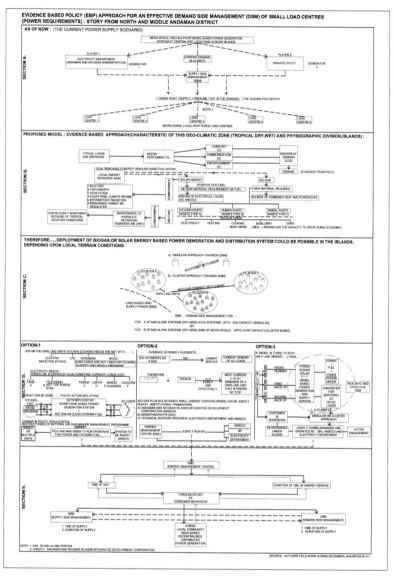

Fig. 3.33 Policy prescription for Andamans

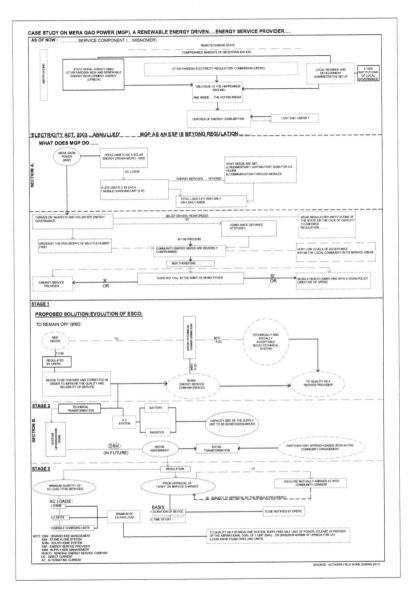

Fig. 3.34 Policy prescription for Lohati Pasai

330   M. K. SINGH

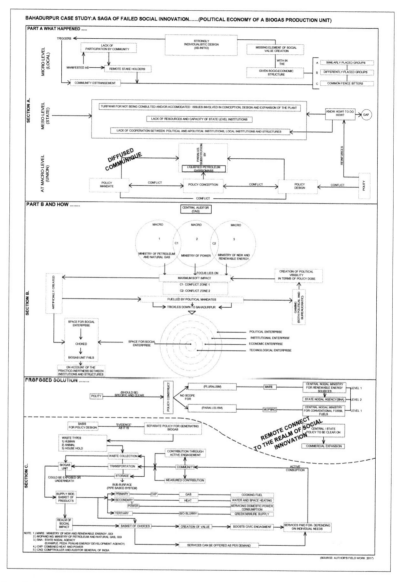

Fig. 3.35 Policy prescription for Bahadurpur

REFERENCES

Human Development Report (HDR). (2010). *The real wealth of nations: path ways to human development*. 20th century edition, published for the United Nations development programme (UNDP). New York: Palgrave Macmillan.

IFC. (2012). *Utility scale solar power plants: A guide for developers and investors*. International Finance Corporation, the World Bank Group.

National tariff policy. (2006, January 6). *The gazette of India, extraordinary, Ministry of Power* (Resolution No. 23/2/2005-R and R, Vol. 3, pp.1–21).

National tariff policy. (2016, February 28). *The gazette of India, extraordinary, Ministry of Power* (Resolution No. 23/2/2005-R and R, Vol. 9, pp. 1–38).

North, D. C. (1990). *Institutions, institutional change and economic performance*. Cambridge University Press.

Ostrom, E. (2008). Tragedy of the commons. *The New Palgrave Dictionary of Economics, 2*.

Ostrom, E. (2010). A long polycentric journey. *Annual Review of Political Science, 13*, 1–23. www.annualreviews.org

Sovacool, B. K. (2011, June). An international comparison of four polycentric approaches to climate and energy governance. *Energy Policy, 39*(6), 3832–3844.

Tennakoon, D. (2009). *Energy poverty: Estimating the level of energy poverty in Sri Lanka*, report prepared by practical action south Asia. http://www.practicalaction.org.uk/energy/south-asia/docs/region_south_asia/energy-poverty-in-sri-lanka-2008.pdf

Utility scale solar power plants. (2012). A guide for developers and investors. *International Finance Corporation*, 1–201.

Uttar Pradesh Electricity Regulatory Commission (UPERC). (2016). *UPERC (mini-grid renewable energy generation and supply) regulations* (Notification No. UPERC/Secy/VCA/Regulations/2016-020, 1–18).

CHAPTER 4

Decentralized Energy Systems Entails: Evidence-Based Policy Approach

Undulating Topographies of Energy Governance

A journey through differential policy designs representing impolitic execution, time to engage with praxis through EBP!

4.1 THE PRISTINE BEDROCK: THE FOUNTAINHEAD OF ASPIRATIONAL WELFAREISM

I begin with an extract from Part IV of the Indian constitution—'The state shall strive to promote the welfare of the people by securing and protecting as effectively as it may a social order in which justice, social, economic and political, shall inform all the institutions of national life [article 38 (1)]. The state shall, in particular, strive to minimize the inequalities in income, and endeavour to eliminate inequalities in status, facilities and opportunities, not only amongst individuals, but also amongst groups of people residing in different areas or engaged in different vocations [article 38 (2)]'.

The state shall, in particular, direct its policy towards securing—(b) that the ownership and control of the material resources of the community are so distributed as best to sub-serve the common good; (c) that the operation of the economic system does not result in the concentration of wealth and means of production to the common detriment [article 39 (b) and (c)]. The state shall endeavour to organize agriculture and animal husbandry on modern and scientific lines and shall, in particular, take steps for preserving and improving the breeds, and prohibiting the slaughter, of cows and calves and other milch and draught cattle [article 48]. And further, the state shall endeavour to protect and improve the environment and to safeguard the forests and wildlife of the country [article 48A] (Constitution of India, 1950)'.

4.2 The Aspirational Core—The Constitutional Mandate for Governance of Energy Systems: A Critique of Pathways to Energy Service Delivery

In Dr. Ambedkar's well-known description, the constitution 'is a federal constitution in as much as it establishes what may be called a Dual Polity (which)...... will consist of the union at the centre and the states at the periphery each endowed with sovereign powers to be exercised in the field assigned to them respectively by the Constitution'. Yet the Constitution, said Ambedkar, avoided the 'tight mould of federalism' in which the American Constitution was caught, and could be 'both unitary as well as federal according to the requirements of time and circumstances (Constituent Assembly Debates, 1948)'. *'By independence we have lost the excuse of blaming the British for anything going wrong. If hereafter things go wrong, we will have nobody to blame except ourselves- B.R. Ambedkar'.*

Article 243(G) lays down the powers, authority, and responsibilities of panchayats (institutions of self-government). The eleventh schedule with the entries as rural electrification including distribution of electricity (serial No. 14) and non-conventional energy sources (serial no. 15) iterates the constitutional mandate of the 'micro' or the local institutions of energy governance. Electricity as an entry figures at serial no. 38 in the concurrent list of the seventh schedule in the Indian Constitution.

Under the Indian constitution, electricity being a concurrent subject means that both the union and the state governments have concurrent jurisdiction to make laws, in respect of the domain of energy and electricity services. In the light of the provisions of the constitution discussed above, it becomes expedient to briefly re-visit the legislative and administrative relations between the Centre and the States under the existent framework of energy governance architecture (Chapter 1). The enactments of the Parliament and those given effect by the Centre shall have an overriding effect on those made by the state legislatures. The contours of power dynamics between the centre (federal level) and the states (regional level) are explicit in Part XI of the Indian Constitution.

Chapter 1, *Part XI of the constitution deals with the distribution of legislative powers between the Union and the States. Article 245 spells out the extent of laws made by Parliament and by the Legislatures of the States. Article 246 spells out the subject-matter of laws made by Parliament and by the Legislatures of States. Article 248 spells out the residuary powers of legislation of Parliament. Article 250, Article 251 and Article 254 tilt the balance of convenience in favour of the Union.* Chapter 2, *Part XI of the Constitution deals with the administrative relations between the Union and the States. Article 256 and Article 257 act in furtherance of the objective of Part I of the constitution that spells out the mandate of administrative relations between the centre and its constituent states* (Constitution of India, 1950).

These articles emphatically establish that the centre shall have a leading edge in situations where a clash of interest arises in respect of a subject that falls under the shared purview of the Union and the state. This preceding discussion is an attempt to situate the 'politics of energy provisioning' within the ambit of federalism. It also calls for a clinical analysis and impartial catharsis of the impolitic policy execution of providing access to energy services. This eventually follows a centralized trajectory of extension of the central grid, and the so designed rural electrification schemes. All of this emanates from the fact that electricity is a concurrent subject.

The subject of governance of energy access is to be evaluated in terms of the existing institutional architecture, and concomitant frameworks as well as the organizational structure spread across various vertical levels (macro-centre, and meso-state level) responsible for providing energy access to rural India. The legitimacy of the meso-(regional-state) structure of energy governance vis-à-vis residuary and overriding powers of the macro-(federal) in respect of the concurrent list appears to be under continuous challenge as dual control breeds distrust and infuses dichotomy in terms of prioritizing agendas in terms of providing for energy access in rural areas.

4.3 The Burden of Aspirations—As Spelt Out in the Rural Electrification Policy, 2006

The term rural electrification, for the first time gained legal footing through the enactment of the central electricity act, 2003. Sections 4 and 5 of the Act make it mandatory for the government at the centre to formulate a national Rural Electrification Policy, which has been since formulated and adopted in 2006, to give effect to the national electricity policy (2005). More importantly, under provision to Section 43 of the electricity act 2003, the appropriate regulator would need to ensure as a part of universal service obligations, that the national goal of providing electricity access to households is complied with.

The rural electrification policy, 2006, set such targets as—(1) provision of access to electricity to all households by the year 2009, (2) quality and reliable power supply at reasonable rates, and (3) minimum lifeline consumption of 1 unit per household per day as a merit good by year 2012. Although the macro—(federal government) contends that the aspiration at serial number 1 stands fulfilled on 28th of April, 2018, the burden of the remaining aspirations still remains unfulfilled. Catering to expectations entails creation and establishment of responsive, delivery structures that appreciate 'demands realism' in terms of the local.

Extent policies, programs and practices in respect of rural electrification are now more promising than ever. Yet the record, for all its successes, remains dismal. The ground realities witnessed in the context of providing energy access to rural and remote geographies present a different picture. It is no good recognizing obligations and meaning well if what is done does not fit the priorities and aspirations of those who want things to be done differently. The collective voice of the rural requires all eyes and ears of the institutions entrusted with the task of ensuring reliable and quality access to energy. The fallacy of electrical base load (a certain basic minimum level of guaranteed energy service) showcases concrete evidence questioning the claims of the policy design and the mushrooming schemes purporting to cater to 'demands realism'.

4.3.1 The Rural Load Demand Variability

Figures 4.1 and 4.2, at Annexure, reflect the variability in terms of the load demand across similar socio-economic profiles throughout rural India. These dwellings situated in different parts of rural India, in different politico-administrative units reflect diverse mannerisms of energy end use. These units differ in the manner in which energy is accessed-access to power (electricity) in these units happens to be on account of a variety of mechanisms—(a) formal state intervention, (b) informal self-intervention by the end-user, and (c) energy service being provided by private energy service companies.

The formal state intervention is in terms of—(1) access to the central grid, and (2) standalone, off-grid solar power packs, both the services are being paid for by the state, and the beneficiary pays a certain minimum amount commensurate with the supply. The formal intervention of the state in two dwelling units constructed under the erstwhile rural housing scheme, *Indira Awas Yojana* (known as *Pradhan Mantri Awas Yojana [grameen], PMAY [G] now*) have been compared. *The scheme does not have a provision for access to energy.* One of the dwelling units constructed under IAY has a formal, accounted for, connection to the grid. The daily load demand of the unit is 0.525 kWh that is largely a function of usage of such electrical appliances as ceiling fan(s) and tube light(s). The other IAY civil structure also has an access to the grid and has a daily load demand of 1.825 kWh. The appliances that contribute towards this load are ceiling fan(s), cooler(s), television, and tube light(s) (Fig. 4.2, Annexure). This energy usage is not formally accounted for labelling it as a non-revenue (un-metered) earning energy service. Both these dwelling units were constructed under a similar rural housing scheme. The socio-economic structure of the occupants is similar. They are contextually situated in a similar geo-climatic zone and physiographic division, yet have different demands in terms of power consumption.

Coming to another example of state intervention (by two-state governments) in terms of providing standalone solar power packs (SPPs), wherein two formats of SPPs are shown (Figs. 4.1 and 4.2, Annexure). One of them is provided by the state of Gujarat, and the other by the state of Uttar Pradesh. *In the latter case, the standalone system is an inbuilt component of a rural housing scheme, popularly known as Lohia Awas Yojana (LAY).* The solar power pack (SPP) of LAY provided by Uttar Pradesh New and renewable energy development agency (UPNEDA) can service a direct current (DC)-based appliance load of 0.253 kWh. The appliances that can be run by the SPP comprise ceiling fan, a mobile charging unit, and LED lighting devices.

On the other hand, the SPP provided by Gujarat energy development agency (GEDA, SNA for Gujarat) can service a DC load of 0.437 kWh which comprises usage of ceiling fan, portable table fan, and LEDs, apart from provision of mobile charging points. An important feature of the SPP in the case of Gujarat is that the institutional responsibility has been entrusted to distribution utilities. The off-grid dwelling units are entitled to this facility. GEDA is too remote to even oversee the objective functioning of the SPP. The SPP in the state of Gujarat is to be provided only in rural areas that cannot be connected to the grid on account of adverse terrain characteristics.

The applications for the SPP are to be moved in the electricity sub-divisional offices in whose jurisdiction the eligible end-user resides (Author, 2017). Thus, the off-grid power supply system in Gujarat services almost twice the amount of load as compared to SPPs provided by UPNEDA (SNA for UP). Thus, there are similar institutions performing dis-similar functions. This happens on account of lack of capacity and unclear mandates, the policy framework does not account for well-defined institutional roles in the action arena. Therefore, GEDA suffers from latent dysfunction on account of institutional capabilities and capacity as well. However, the SPP scheme of UPNEDA was a scheme nested in a clear-cut policy directive linked to a rural housing scheme, *Lohia Awas Yojana (LAY)*.

4.3.2 Act Utilitarianism by Self-Interested Actors

An important feature of the grid-based conventional power system in northern India is illegal access to energy supply non-revenue power. These informal connections are commonly referred to as '*katiya*' (illegally tapped power service lines). It contributes to huge revenue losses to the local distribution utilities of the state government. The load demands of these informal (illegal) connections are shown as non-electrified dwelling units (*NEDUs*). The dwelling units have been categorized into three types labelled as NEDU1, NEDU2, and NEDU3 depending upon their load demand and energy use (Figs. 4.1 and 4.2, Annexure). These units consume alternating current (AC) loads of 0.515 kWh, 0.525 kWh, and 0.725 kWh, respectively (Author, 2017). The devices that run on '*katiya*' connections are largely ceiling fans and bulbs or tube lights, their numbers differ depending upon the income and family size.

The aforesaid events across local energy access arena highlight a plethora of issues that are hinged upon the following aspects of energy provisioning—(a) supply akin to systems of production, (b) legitimacy of actors in the action arena, (c) technical character of energy demand, (d) consumer capability, and (e) institutional asymmetry. These aspects can be further explicated in terms of experience and evidence—(1) different energy production systems (grid-based, conventional and off-grid, non-conventional sources of power supply), (2) the involvement of state actors and the individual, non-state actors, (3) the different nature of loads

(AC or DC), (4) the different varieties of demanded loads (in terms of ownership status of various electrical appliances), (5) the different institutional structures of providing access to energy service (s) viz., distribution companies (state utilities) and state nodal agencies (SNAs), (6) regional political moorings, and (7) local power structure reflected through illegal tapping of service lines to service load(s).

4.3.3 *The Static Interventions of the Non-state Actors in Providing Energy Services*

It is important to highlight the misgivings of the so-called demonstration projects. These interventions were largely driven by a lethal combination of research funding and fulfilling corporate social responsibilities, which was not desirable for want of time and place knowledge. The private energy service companies run on their own whims and fancies, independent of any obligation towards the *energy regulator* (meso-level) or the local institutions of self-government (micro-level). The first case of an energy service based on solar energy comes from Tayyabpur village, in Vaishali district of Bihar. The solar grid in *Tayyabpur* (Fig. 4.2, Annexure) is a demonstration project of TATA power (Chapter 2). The grid services DC loads to the tune of 0.042 kWh. This load comprises one LED and a mobile charging point (Fig. 4.2, Annexure).

Another private energy service company that is being discussed is MGP (Chapter 2). The company provides a pair of LEDs (1 W each) and a mobile charging unit. The DC load that the SPP of MGP services comes to is about 0.017 kWh (Fig. 4.2, Annexure). The quantum of electrical load demands calculated by taking into account a usage duration of 6–8 hours in every single case. It is noteworthy to mention that the private operators supply power only for a fixed timeframe of 5–6 hours post sunset from 6.00 pm to 11.00 pm. The aforesaid empirical evidence calls for a relook into the policy framework that lays down the roles and responsibilities of appropriate regulator's and the local institutions.

4.3.4 *Passive Consumerism and the Extent Policies of Rural Electrification*

Understanding passive consumerism is a daunting task in rural, remote, and complex cultural settings. The aforesaid dataset questions the executional aspiration in terms of the daily consumption of 1 unit (kWh) of electricity. How much is that in terms of the number and type of electrical appliances that it can run? Is that enough? Or, something else warrants attention. Perhaps we do not have a conclusive response at the moment. Even more complex and severe is the conception of the second executional aspiration pertaining to *'quality and reliability of supply at reasonable rates'*. In the absence of any robust empirical database for assessing quality and reliability of energy supply, how can reasonable rates be arrived at? And more so, in relation to a rural, domestic category of a consumer, who is too remote to be measured in terms of his usage and preferences. And such low, sporadic load signatures are not accounted for at the level of a majority of designed power sub-stations. It becomes a fatal aspiration existing in a vacuum. The functionality of centralized power generation systems cannot be either definitive or deterministic in terms of the executional aspirations as they operate under complex networks of institutional mechanisms.

Practically speaking, supply-side management (SSM) is dictated by polity and effervescent policy determined by the nature and structure of political engagements at the macro-(centre) and meso- (regional) levels of energy governance. The contemporary policy still favours centralization that entails creation of mega-size visible infrastructure and remote generating technologies (Bolton & Foxon, 2015; Kelly & Pollitt, 2011). This policy concentration on remote-centralized sources of energy, renewable or non-renewable increases the vulnerability of the rural, remote end-users, and the local institutions as well. In the process, it distances the end-user further from the energy generating process. This adds to the arsenal of information asymmetry already existing, that is minimal in terms of understanding of energy and power systems. The end-user remains an indifferent, insensitive, passive consumer of an electricity or energy service. The local institutions also remain inactive and functionally distant from the centrist policy design.

4.4 The Missing 'Local' in Energy Action and the Associated *Polysemy* with *Endemic, Episodic* Texture of Rural Energy Poverty (EP)

The baseline energy demand appears to be profusely driven by passive consumerism, active political engagement, and self-aggrandizing alienation at times. There are instances of complete abstinence from usage of a particular electrical appliance in spite of physical possession. Such behaviour sends out strong signals in respect of consumer behaviour. The nature of empirical evidence in respect of use of cooking fuels strongly contends the 'energy ladder' hypotheses. The mix of cooking fuels appears to be governed by these thought processes—(a) what is available for free? (b) What is available for less (involves a lower expenditure)? (c) What can be had for relatively less (cost comparison becomes the guiding spirit of decision making)? This choice matrix comprising a triad of free, subsidized, and cross-subsidized cooking fuel supply options gets even more complicated when a policy dose of free or highly subsidized supply of electric power is administered. The choice option to a passive consumer further opens up. *The evidence from the field shows a marked positive shift towards passive consumerism sans any thought pertaining to collectivism towards prudent need-based usage or conservation.*

4.5 Evidence-based Policy Approach to Address Energy Poverty

The 'rural' nature of energy poverty has a variegated cultural flavour in different parts of the Indian subcontinent. The evidence created on account of deployment of mixed-method investigative paradigm (Chapter 1) accentuates and/or attenuates the signs and symptoms of energy poverty as exhibited across the rural landscape. There are mixed pieces of evidence that resulted from an empirical investigation and contextual assessment of electrical load demand and related consumption of cooking fuels. The observed electrical load demand is largely a function of—(a) variations in ownership status of different electricity-driven appliances, (b) temporal span of usage that in turn is a function of flexibility and scalability of usage, (c) seasonality, local weather conditions, and the levels of community engagement, (d) source of electrical energy (state actor or a non-state actor), (e) grid-based supply or an off-grid system, (f) the design of the energy production system (whether based on renewable or non-renewable source of energy), and (g) local socio-political engagements in terms of access to nodes of influence controlling access to energy.

The rural energy policy arena does not give the right thrust and the rightful place to evidence in terms of—(1) a nuanced understanding of energy poverty phenomenon, (2) locale-specific energy demand profiling in the rural parts of the Indian subcontinent that entails an in-depth understanding of spaces and cultures of energy consumption (*the inherent human element related to energy consumption*), and (3) micro-level, renewable energy resource profiling (assessment of potential that is ready to be harnessed) to service local, small, micro-demands. Evidence in terms of qualitative and quantitative empirical databases can be instrumental in rightly and adequately informing the policymaking process. This approach stands in contrast to opinion-based policy, which relies heavily on either the selective use of evidence or on the untested views of individuals or groups, which are often inspired by ideological standpoints, prejudices, or speculative conjecture of lobbies and interest groups (Segone & Pron, 2008).

Empirical evidence from the field expressly points towards an imperative for—(1) relying on context-based evidence and (2) understanding the micro-culture of energy consumption in the rural Indian subcontinent. There is an imperative for a comprehensive assessment of renewable resource potential across geo-climatic zones and physiographic divisions, and this needs to figure in very strongly in the policy design. This study has marked a humble beginning in this direction by taking up a comprehensive local resource base evaluation (for solar energy and biogas) at the lowest unit of administration, a revenue village (for civil structures). The energy policy estate needs to take into account the qualitative nature of demand in the rural areas of the country for achieving the desired outcomes.

4.6 The Missing Dimension of Energy Systems Decentralization in the Policy Estate as Well as the Action Arena

Decentralization as a paradigmatic construct provides an emancipatory framework ameliorating the local from a centralized governance structure. However, its muted passive, and inconsequential expression in terms of its role in regulating access to energy. Its efficacy is put to stringent scrutiny in the broader context of contemporary participatory energy governance at the most remote, micro-level of energy consumption. The passive flavour of decentralized energy governance manifests itself through varying degrees and scales of failure across different geo-spatial and geo-cultural settings. The ground truth of rural energy access provisioning is marred by institutional distancing, vexed priorities of the actors, and extremely low levels of awareness about technology and its effects. There is no formal institutional mechanism giving the beneficiary even an episodic authority to impose either an economic or social sanction on the service provider. The decentralized structures of energy governance exist at best as aspirations too distant from its' executants' and beneficiaries.

4.7 The Missing Contextual (Scale, Scope, Time, and Place) Dimension in Local Energy Access action

The complexity and heterogeneity of the socio-cultural context are not taken into account, either during policy conception (problem definition stage) or during implementation stage, which often results in unanticipated challenges during stages of implementation. There is an imperative for understanding the human dimension in a rural energy ecosystem, as there is a pressing need for demand assessment, understanding choices and preferences, and behaviour of a passive consumer of electricity. The policy arena has remained at a secluded distance from the thought of 'localism' in energy action, and the innate human element that occupies the centre-stage of this novel thought. The human dimension in localized energy action is driven by the guiding philosophy of *prosumerism* (Toffler, 1980), wherein the producer is a consumer as well and is an active element of the design and production system.

4.7.1 Localized Action for Active Engagement with Energy Access Framework

Local energy action conceived as community driven, small-scale energy production and consumption systems display the local potential to engage actively with the centralized policy framework of energy generation, transmission, and distribution. Local energy action would require active engagement of local resources that would eventually boost social capital, build local capacities, and enhance the resilience of local communities. The existing structures of energy governance at various vertically integrated levels have a general sympathy towards the idea of popular control of institutions.

There could be strong voices of dissent based upon these arguments—(a) whether local control of energy systems has the potential to be more efficient or flexible, and (b) would it find any takers at the lowest level of formal democratic institutions, the gram panchayats. A very strong argument in favour of local energy governance could be the limited capability of the large and distant institutions to recognize local energy needs, local demands, and its specifics at the level of a dwelling unit. Thus, such large and distant institutions are oblivious to the local energy consumption trends, that are steered unequivocally by the local socio-economic cultures and general preferential trends.

A localized, human centric, community-driven energy action would make optimum use of local resource base and capabilities, thereby promoting active participation at the level of energy end-users. In the process, this would help foster stronger norms of reciprocity, reduce trust deficit, and intensify community engagement. Localism of energy action at the level of micro shall promote diversification of resources and promote diversity in terms of garnering additional local support in terms of skill and resource in normal times as well as during emergencies. Diversification at the level of community could result in deployment of alternate approaches to service their immediate needs for energy, thereby leaving a lot of scope for social innovation at the local level.

4.7.2 *Positivist Approach for Building Capacities*

Such initiatives could help reduce community vulnerability by infusing resilience. Such positivism can lead to creation of growth poles that can act as potential positive catalysts for drawing other private-energy entrepreneurs for collaboration to build up an alternative, sustainable techno-economic model that is driven largely by social concerns and community objectives. However, this could give rise to conflict situations as well. Therefore, the bargain in terms of resource harnessing and distribution of an energy end-product could be regulated by an existing formal or informal institution, or a new institution could be created that shall act as a one stop 'ombudsman' for locally addressing such issues should they arise. However, there is a strong case of pessimism driven by the fear of exaggerated claims of success stories about community-driven renewal energy systems. Still, there is a need for migration towards addressing demand side priorities while designing energy access policies.

The evidence from the field suggests that initiatives undertaken without community involvement were not received well by the local end-users of energy services (Chapter 2). Notwithstanding the aggressive propaganda highlighting the stories of successes of the project has been vehemently pursued by the organizations with utmost impunity. The success of a localized initiative in any given local area is a function of favourable presence of a certain set of conditions. These local sets of conditions may not be adaptable in any other local area that may be geographically contiguous or separated by an appreciable distance. More than the local resource potential and innate capacities (*in terms of human and social capital*), even when the energy demands of two communities could be identical, the local political realities may differ so much that what works in one socio-cultural space may not be even considered by the other community culture (*case studies on Tayyabpur solar grid and Mera Gao Power demand an impartial scrutiny*).

4.7.3 Argument in Favour of a Socio-technical Approach

The dominant notion of electricity is that it is merely a technical input. Empirical evidence very strongly underlines the political and emphasizes the importance of both politics and society in understanding electricity. As emphasized earlier, that the rural energy consumption profile is variable in its expanse and complexity, there is a strong case for an alternative approach. Going beyond a technical perspective that usually ignores such nefarious complexity, the case studies make an attempt to unravel the politics that makes electricity and energy services (of varying qualitative grades) accessible to its people. Decentralized democracy, and its empowerment mandate notwithstanding, the pieces of evidence from the rural heartland present a unique picture on the issue of access to grid-based supply of electricity, off-grid non-conventional supply and amalgamated use of various cooking fuels. It is the local power relations that ultimately govern the fiat of policy.

The quantum of electricity consumption does not rest entirely on load demand estimation. The feasibility of access is decided at first by the political, and thereafter by the socio-cultural dynamics at the micro-level. Under the present set of socio-economic conditions, the local energy needs cannot be serviced to the satisfaction of the rural populace. A simplistic and universal approach in terms of understanding of local issues of energy demand (and its management) by the level of central and the state-level institutions shall lead to fragmentation of local interests and which could further give birth to nascent dominant interest groups that can alter the basis of resource allocation and its subsequent redistribution. The evidence from the field argues for a shift from the narrow, restrictive conception of electricity, towards a broad-based approach that incorporates political as well as socio-cultural dynamics at the local level that can be better appreciated by decentralized structures of governance.

The challenge being, understanding local power and creating more equitable institutional mechanisms as well as new structures of electricity governance. The rural ecosystem needs to be energized in ways that differ from standard uniform urban prototypes. An alternative energy production design shall necessarily entail a sound understanding of the local ethos, and the micro-processes that operate at the socio-cultural and the political level. The narrow, inconclusive, reductionist techno-economic approach that is normally being followed on the basis of limited awareness about local energy systems shall disrupt the social fabric and eventually fail on account of non-acceptability by the community.

4.8 The New Decentralized Energy Systems Paradigm Based on EBP—Evidence Exposes Latent Tension All Along Vertically Integrated Institutions, Structures, and Processes

Administrative efficiency and efficacy require administrative astuteness in terms of practically making a policy work. How about executing a policy that is largely bereft of the constitutional mandate! The Wilsonian paradigm states that administration lies outside the proper sphere of politics. It further asserts that the administrative questions are not political questions. Although politics sets the task for administration, it should not be suffered to manipulate its offices. The field of administration is a field of business, and therefore, should distance itself from the hurry and strife of politics (Wilson, 1886, pp. 11–12).

The art of administration is linked to the constitutional mandate of separation and distribution of powers. And, that the most formidable challenge for federalism (cooperative or competitive) is to be able to identify the appropriate levels of government for the exercise of certain functions. Therefore, segregation, separation, distribution, and dispersal of power between the Centre, State, and the local three-tier institutions becomes a vitally important matter as it is characterized by extreme socio-cultural polarity. There could be two rules of interpretation that often feature in federalism cases: the federal character of legislative power and the doctrine of liberal construction (Khosla, 2012, p. 55).

The doctrine of plenary power confirms that once the construction of an entry does not upset any other constitutional provision, it knows no bounds. The liberal principle banks upon the shared purview of legislative authority on a given subject. However, the entry no. 97 and article 248 tilt the balance in favour of the centre and undermine the latent spirit of horizontal separation of powers and the doctrine of harmonious construction. The entries in the lists could bear causality between them, and therefore, the vertical distribution of power that hinges upon the legitimacy of legislative competence, of the centre or the state precariously balances itself when confronted with a conflict of territorial and administrative interests.

The best way to divide authority is—(a) without hampering it, and (b) by adopting a course that does not obscure administrative responsibility. How it is to be done is best left to be decided by the instrumentalities of government. There could be a few alternatives that would require a deviation from the conventional architecture, towards a radical shift in terms of designs, processes, and functions that are more progressive, open, and non-conventional. Since the need as it appears, has arisen, it should capitalize on its potential of the local resource base, the *metis* (Scott, 1998). *In the aforesaid context of the provisions emphatically laid down in the constitution, how do institutions created under aegis of a written, sacrosanct text repeatedly flounder—(a) when it comes to skillful craftsmanship in terms of conception and design of a policy, and (b) in working out processes and procedures for actual delivery of services related to something as fundamental as access to energy.*

What ails the action arena in terms of contextual definition of a policy problem, in effective communication of a robust policy prescription and lastly, in demonstration of policy outputs and evaluating outcomes. Institutions can impact policy design in different ways. They can regulate its subsequent efficacy through exercise of coercive measures in the larger interests of general welfare or they can appropriate the design to suit and satiate latent interests that are covertly private, but overtly public.

4.8.1 Conventional, Institutional Frameworks Are Not Good Enough

Institutions often flaunt powers of regulation through exercise of eminent domain as well, justifying the unequivocal 'public good' nature of a policy framework. There has been with passage of time, an eventual blurring of the lines between the exercise of police power and the power of eminent domain especially when it comes to addressing of a general public welfare objective., say e.g. providing access to primary energy meant for satiating needs that are basic and fundamental for a vast majority of the rural Indian populace (Burke et al., 2017; Rehman et al., 2010, 2012; Victor & Heller, 2007). State-driven development (Kohli, 2009) can derail the policy process as institutions at the federal and the state level are wrangled in asymmetric pluralism in terms of processes and procedures.

Institutional heterogeneity has the potential to unleash itself as a brutish evil doer when armed with conflicting agendas. The state, it appears, has distanced itself from its core philosophy of allocating resources in a manner that serves the common good of communities through creation of an enabling environment for participatory energy governance at the lowest level in order to transform the rural energy landscape of the Indian subcontinent.

High-end, mega, and massive non-conventional power generation systems across cultures and societies without acculturation of technology could be a perfect recipe for unleashing dystopia on an otherwise passive consumer of power, as a consequence of the big push in terms of high modernism. The modern state with its nascent power production design has resulted in the creation of such disruptive socio-technical structures that mutilate local resource bases. Sector-specific centralization of sources of energy and their subsequent amalgamation under coercion into such production systems could ruin the extant systems of transmission, distribution, and actual consumption. The constitution spells out the mandate for the layered institutional architecture in terms of decentralization, collectivization of local resource base, collective community action, and creation of robust democratic institutions of energy governance at the micro level.

However, the unitary federal construct (the macro-) squatting atop centralized institutions runs down its writ of command through exercise of its dominant position in terms of a formidable and resistant unitary bias challenging the notion of cooperative federalism in respect of decentralized energy systems at the micro level. Is the notion of 'shared responsibility' reflective of pragmatism in the context of Indian polity? Does it mean individual responsibility or is it really collective? In case it refers to the latter, then the context appears to be clearly defined in terms of political allegiance rather than policy demonstration, or at best restricted to policy communication.

4.8.2 Conventional Structures Addressing a Symptomatic Issue Appear to be Lacking in Cohesive Action—Sector Characteristics Need to be Appreciated and Tackled

Rural electrification is a process that cannot be thought only in terms of being a technical input. Rather it is a socio-technical input affecting the cultural and socio-economic ecology of a rural landscape. The logjam with regard to data inconsistency and variability in execution levels across regional politics can be at the best understood in terms of amalgamation of policy conception and design at different levels across horizontal central institutions, though stratified in terms of vertical hierarchies. Modes of delivery and the quality of delivery of different public services vary in the forms of politics and governance they adopt (Mcloughlin & Batley, 2012; Wild et al., 2012). However, certain political and governance-related opportunities and constraints frequently recur around the delivery of energy services in particular (Brown & Mobarak, 2009, Oda & Tsujita, 2011).

It is extremely difficult to infer whether sector characteristics influence the politics and governance of the delivery of energy services or the static, structural institutional typology adversely affects the efficacy of energy service delivery. The nature of general relationship between different institutions, actors and agents that make up the policy estate dictates the outcomes in an action arena (field of policy execution). It further determines the degree to which accountability and enforcement mechanisms are brought into play while affecting outcomes (Cox et al., 2010). Where the relationship between the 'trio' (institutions, actors and agents) is skewed towards imperfection, the effectiveness and efficiency of energy service delivery gets severely undermined and further results in the skewed allocation of resources.

Provisioning for an energy service entails investment in grid extension or protection from load shedding to secure the support of particular groups, the diversion of resources for patronage or rent-seeking, emphasis on visible infrastructure rather than reliability of service, suboptimal resource allocation coupled with weak regulation and enforcement (Badiani & Jessoe, 2012; Golden & Min, 2012). The hallmark of Indian polity is its plurality along with regional and cultural polarity. Since political accountability in respect of providing for energy services is strong, it results in skewed supply of service to particular groups and further, towards effective targeting of groups for providing subsidies as well (Greacen, 2004; Jain, 2006). Local socio-cultural dynamics and stratified political structure play a key role in controlling access to the distribution network. Energy service access is extremely prone to elite capture as well (Chapter 2). Issues of territorial and administrative jurisdictions, policy in-congruence, lack of coherency in roll-out processes and variegated delivery pathways adopted, coupled with performance oversight has jeopardized effective energy service delivery. An inherent feature of the electricity sector is that it suffers from monopolistic tendencies, information asymmetries, and political returns particularly in the 'distribution chain' (Dixit et al., 2007).

Policy in this sector is plagued by political market imperfections and preferences for allocation of business to particular groups over others (Mcloughlin & Batley, 2012). Weak institutions, poor enforcement, lack of accountability further promote mounting of non-revenue power on account of theft and non-payment of bills (Smith, 2004). Poor social and physical infrastructure ensures an unreliable supply subject to proximity to local power centres (Sovacool, 2012). It takes more than a driver to conceive, design, and deliver a healthy renewable energy policy. Depending on the technology or energy source in question, a range of policy instruments or adjustments are required for actual integration of projects based on renewable sources and the energy they produce into the pre-existing brown conventional power generation systems.

4.8.3 *Shaking Up the Archaic Energy Governance and Planning Structural Frame*

An integration of a new energy production system entails a comprehensive overview of where the current and futuristic potential obstacles are, and therefore, the interventions are designed accordingly. For altering the design of the monolithic, age-old conventional power system of India, there appears a requirement for a massive overhaul of the existing architecture of energy governance (Chapter 1). Although the current policy framework appears to be overarching in terms of targets, set for a comprehensive mix of power generation from renewable sources, with an exclusive thrust on solar energy followed by wind, it cannot be construed to be the policy objective that shall serve the purpose of a talisman to guide all policymaking in respect of different energy production systems.

Coercive federalism manifests itself either through arm twisting a regional power centre, or garnishing a policy platter with *sweeteners*. This measure does not help much, as this sector is characterized by institutional voids at the micro-level, poorly defined network of civic engagements at the meso-level (intermediate, regional level of state), and a myriad of parallel power structures at the macro-level. Compartmentalization of functions adversely affects the spirit of competition, and rather promotes oligopoly and oligarchy as well.

4.8.4 The Need for New Policy Based on Cohesive Integration of Conventional and Non-conventional Energy Production Systems

A national, comprehensive, and overarching energy policy objective asks for—(1) uniform, cohesive long-term growth and development of renewable sources of energy, (2) its seamless integration into the existing power production design, and (3) its overall mandate to be in sync with international obligations on climate change. Such a policy should rest on a tripod of foundations that provides for—(a) an incentive for a much-needed constitutional amendment followed by a positive legislation in favour of each of the renewable energy sources (*specific to the Indian subcontinent*), (b) reliance on context-specific evidence to review existing legislation, and policies that may be acting as a barrier, and (c) an insurance against obstructive legislation being put in place thereafter to ensure confidence in the upcoming renewable energy sector. Once an overarching national policy objective is in place (based on the tripod of foundations), alternate structures and frameworks can be established that are in sync with the overarching national objective of energy generation and eventual consumption (Rural Electrification Policy, 2006).

This should be effectively done in two fundamental ways—(a) a policy framework can be sliced and diced from the perspective of an individual, locale-specific project (Chapter 3), and (b) drill down through the entire architecture of energy governance at all levels of the government including their legislative (territorial, administrative, and regulatory) jurisdiction (Chapter 1). In order to effectively address the problem highlighted at (a), there is an imperative to step in the shoes of the renewable energy project proponent and traverse the entire path from project conception to project completion that comprises ten stages—(1) site identification, (2) site acquisition and assessment, (3) project feasibility, (4) social impact and environmental impact (assessment), (5) design and technical development, (6) commercial engineering, (7) construction, (8) project commissioning, (9) operation and maintenance, and lastly (10) decommissioning and reinstatement.

Each of these critical tasks vertically spread across a number of stages, under three overarching categories—(a) technical and commercial, (b) social and environmental, and (c) dialogue and consultation. This is true of any given renewable energy generation project. Every single sub-task needs to be evaluated in terms of policy risks/burdens so that it becomes clear that the frameworks put in place are conducive and not obstructive to the said project.

In order to initiate procedures for scoping a correct policy for addressing (b) above, we need to ask two fundamental questions—(1) have all the laws that affect renewable energy projects been analyzed to ensure that they are conducive and not obstructive, and (2) are the policies and measures at all tiers of the government consistent and self-reinforcing?

4.9 Complex, Multi-stage Policy Formulation in the Renewable Energy Sector

The policies at the level of the state and the centre spanning across the value addition chain of energy/electricity, primarily visualize *source of energy* as a primary, vital input. Therefore, the policies need to be symmetrical and congruent. And, as broad based as possible. Given the need for policy changes, it has to be borne in mind that the implementation shall not be a simple, fair, and straightforward exercise. Policy and legislation could be either reinforcing or may be antithetic at some stage towards each other (Chapter 2). These processes could be mutually independent and exclusive or they could be mutually dependent and inclusive, thus spanning across regimes of actors guided by elements of positive and negative rationality depending upon their epistemic training and domain knowledge. In real terms, political decision making is often far from rational, and policy cobwebs of the rural energy sector exhibit numerous real expressions of such political misgivings (Chapters 2 and 3). Thus, energy policies at some stage may appear to be devoid of rationality for they become opinionated, influenced, guided, and captured by elite designs.

The current trend of high end modernistic designs for the non-conventional energy sector shall promote growth of dual societies consisting of *energy haves* (elites in terms of access to ultra-modern energy services) and *energy have-nots* (battling for access to the rudimentary energy services as in case of Lohati Pasai, in Barabanki district of Uttar Pradesh or Tayyabpur village in Vaishali district of Bihar).

It appears that the policy proposal before a rural end-user is either a traditional, orthodox, conventional approach, or an erratic, ad-hoc, discontinuous jump towards a modern alien (exogenous, imported) technological approach. A rational policy approach would be modernism of a lower form that hinges upon a self-learning approach of a beneficiary. The rural energy policy design should enable to build capacities and enhance the potential of different communities with an intent to gradually infuse technology as a booster dose for a smooth transition. An assessment of local renewable energy potential shall progressively build trust and generate enormous levels of comfort that shall further help in the creation of an alternate energy production, distribution, and consumption style. It shall enhance community skills being local and micro, and predominantly rural economy based as compared to its urbane prototypes. A rural energy system change should necessarily provide for amalgamation of the social and the technical, for a smooth transition to an alternate production and consumption design.

This shall depend on a number of principles underpinning a resilient energy system, namely—(1) appropriateness based on utilization of locally available renewable resources, (2) capacity enhancing, (3) adaptable and upgradable production systems, and (b) easy to repair and maintain locally (O'Brien & Hope, 2010). There has to be a rural approach driven by *'community-centric prosumerism'* while designing policy frameworks for renewable energy-driven micro-ecosystems. It should take care of community vulnerability to internal shocks such as fluctuating load demand, systems disruptions, and pricing issues based on actual consumption, and other local factors.

Through deployment of distributed renewable energy technologies (RETs) coupled with building capacities for local resource management, an active engagement gets initiated between the social and the technical that could eventually evolve as a panacea for addressing the symptomatic effects of rural energy poverty in different parts of the Indian rural energy landscape.

Therefore, to move on to good policy, we need to witness a paradigm shift from the target based policy [TBP: 20 GW of solar power (by 2019) to 100 GW (by 2022) and from an additional 15 GW of wind power (during 2012–17) to an additional 40 GW (by 2019) approach, NITI Aayog, 2017] to evidence based policy (EBP) approach for better understanding of social, cultural and political realities that govern and affect daily lives of a passive consumer of electricity and thereafter, recasting the targets for green energy source deployment.

A good and reasonable polity is one that avoids opinion-based and evidence-influenced policy. These frameworks translate into sub-standard policy formulation and equally disruptive demonstration in the action arena. The need of the present times is a policy process that helps planners make better-informed decisions by putting the best possible evidence at the centre of the policy process (Segone & Pron, 2008). An effective policy prescription has an element of effective communication as its essential design element. It should be based on contextual realities supported by a robust database to help in setting up an informed agenda. Therefore, the guiding spirit of a human-centric rural energy access policy should be an evidence-based approach projecting the needs and preference of the ultimate policy recipients. This approach shall help effectively in bridging the design-reality gap in terms of both supply and demand-side issues in the rural electricity sector.

Annexure

See Figs. 4.1 and 4.2.

4 DECENTRALIZED ENERGY SYSTEMS ENTAILS … 355

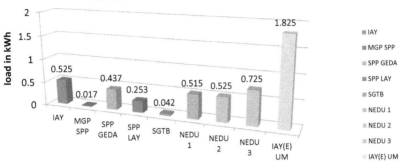

IAY	Indira Awas Yojana
MGP SPP	Mera Gao Power Solar Power Pack
GEDA SPP	Gujarat Energy Development Agency Solar Power Pack
LAY SPP (UP)	Lohia Awas Yojana Solar Power Pack
SGTB	Solar Grid Tayyabpur (TATA Power)
NEDU 1 - BH 2 - UP 3 - GJ	Non-electrified Dwelling Unit Illegal Tapping of Power (कटिया), Non-revenue Power
IAY(E) UM	Indira Awas Yojana (Electrified), Unmetered Power Supply

Fig. 4.1 Variations in base load demands from different sources in different parts of the country from different sources and formal/informal arrangements. What should be a base line minimum electrical load to take a call for addressing demand realism?

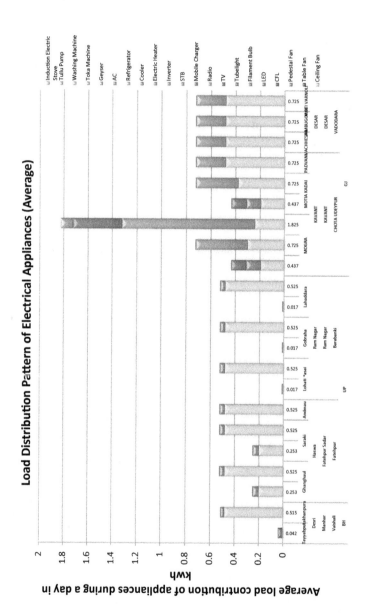

Fig. 4.2 Individual contribution by each of the functional electronic appliance (AC or DC) to the aggregate load demand

REFERENCES

Badiani, R., Jessoe, K. K., & Plant, S. (2012). Development and the environment, the implications of agricultural electricity subsidies in India. *The Journal of Environment and Development, 21*(2), 244–262. https://doi.org/10.1177/1070496512442507

Bolton, R., & Foxon, T. J. (2015). Infrastructure transformation as a sociotechnical process-implications for the governance of energy distribution networks in the UK. *Technological Forecasting and Social Change, 90,* 538–550, ISSN 0040-1625. https://doi.org/10.1016/j.techfore.2014.02.017

Brown, D., & Mobarak, A. (2009). The transforming power of democracy: Regime type and the distribution of electricity. *American Political Science Review, 103*(2), 193–213.

Burke, M., Sovacool, K. B., Baker, L., Kotikalapudi, C. K., & Holle, W. (2017). New frontiers and conceptual frameworks for energy justice. *Energy Policy, 105,* 677–691. ISSN 0301-4215. This version is available from Sussex Research Online: http://sro.sussex.ac.uk/id/eprint/67183/

Central Electricity Act. (2003, May 26). *The gazette of India, part-II, registered no. DL-33004/2003.* Legislative Department, Ministry of Law and Justice, Government of India (pp. 1–134).

Constituent Assembly Debates. (1948, November 23). *Constituent assembly debates, volume VII, no. 1* (pp. 33–34). https://cadindia.clpr.org.in/constitution_assembly_debates/volume/7/1948-11-23

Constitution of India. (1950). *Extracts from the constitution of India, as modified on 1 December, 2007.* Ministry of Law and Justice, Government of India (pp. 1–443).

Cox, M., Arnold, G., & Villamayor Tomás, S. (2010). A review of design principles for community-based natural resource management. *Ecology and Society, 15*(4), article 38.

Dixit, S., Dubash, N. K., Maurer, C., & Nakhooda, S. (2007). Benchmarking best practice and promoting accountability in the electricity sector. *Electricity Governance Initiative (EGI)* (pp. 1–176). http://electricitygovernance.wri.org

Golden, M., & Min, B. (2012). *Theft and loss of electricity in an Indian state, working paper 12/0060.* International Growth Centre (IGC) (pp. 1–38). https://www.theigc.org/wp-content/uploads/.../golden-Min-2012-Working-Paper.pdf.

Greacen, C. E. (2004). *The marginalization of small is beautiful: Micro-hydroelectricity, common property, and the politics of rural electricity provision in Thailand,* Ph.D. Dissertation, University of California at Birkeley.

Jain, V. (2006). *Political economy of the electricity subsidy: Evidence from Punjab.* Munich Personal RePEc Archive (MPRA) (paper no. 240, pp. 1–10). http://mpra.ub.uni-muenchen.de/240/

Kelly, S., & Pollitt, M. (2011). *The local dimension of energy, Electricity Policy Research Group* (EPRG Working Paper 1103, Cambridge Working Paper in Economics 1114, pp. 1–34), University of Cambridge.

Kohli, A. (2009). States and economic development. *Brazilian Journal of Political Economy, 29*(114) (n) 2, 212–227.

Khosla, M. (2012). *The Indian Constitution.* Oxford University Press.

Kumar, M. (2017). Field investigations conducted by the author.

Mcloughlin, C., & Batley, R. (2012). *The effects of sector characteristics on accountability relationships in service delivery* (Working Paper 350, pp. 1–35), Overseas Development Institute (ODI), London. www.odi.org.uk

National Electricity Policy. (2005, February 12). *The gazette of India, resolution no. 23/40/2004- R and R, volume 2* (pp. 1–17).

National Rural Electrification Policy. (2006, August 23). *The gazette of India, Part-1-Section-1, Ministry of Power, Resolution No. 44/26/2005-RE, volume-II* (pp. 1–17).

O'Brien, G., & Hope, A. (2010). Localism and energy: Negotiating approaches to embedding resilience in energy systems. *Energy Policy, 38*(12), 7550–7558. ISSN 0301- 4215.

Oda, H., & Tsujita, Y. (2011). The determinants of rural electrification: The case of Bihar, India. *Energy Policy, 39*(6), 3086–3095.

Rehman, I. H., Kar, A., Banerjee, M., Kumar, P., Shardul, M., Mohanty, J., & Hossain, I. (2012). Understanding the political economy and key drivers of energy access in addressing national energy access priorities and policies. *Energy Policy, 47*(S1), 27–37. ISSN 0301–4215. https://doi.org/10.1016/j.enpol.2012.03.043

Rehman, I. H., Kar, A., Raven, R., Singh, D., Tiwari, J., Jha, R., & Mirza, A. (2010). Rural energy transitions in developing countries: A case of the Uttam Urja initiative in India. *Environmental Science and Policy, 13*(4), 303–311.

Scott, C. J. (1998). *Seeing like a state, how certain schemes to improve human condition have failed, the Yale* (Institute for social and policy studies) ISPS series, ISBN0-300-07016-0.

Segone, M., & Pron, N. (2008). *The role of statistics in evidence-based policy making.* UNECE Work Session on Statistical dissemination and communication (pp. 1–7).

Smith, T. B. (2004). Electricity theft: A comparative analysis. *Energy Policy, 32*(18), 2067–2076.

Sovacool, B. K. (2012). The political economy of energy poverty: A review of key challenges. *Energy for Sustainable Development, 16*(3), 271–282.

Toffler, A. (1980). *The third wave.* First published by William Morrow and company, ISBN0688035973 (p. 544).

Victor, G. D., & Heller, T. C. (Eds.). (2007). *The political economy of power sector reform: The experience of five major developing countries*. Cambridge University Press.

Wild, L., Chambers, V., King, M., & Harris, D. (2012). *Common constraints and incentive problems in service delivery* (Working Paper 351). Overseas Development Institute, London. www.odi.org.uk

Wilson, W. (Writer). (1886, November 1). *The study of administration*. TeachingAmericanHistory.org. http://teachingamericanhistory.org/library/document/the-study-of-administration. Retrieved on 29 October 2017, at 8:36 AM IST.

CHAPTER 5

Conclusion: Overcoming Barriers to Decentralized Energy Systems in India

Bridging the Design-reality Gap; Bringing Policy Closer to Praxis—Overcoming Challenges While Addressing Concerns

5.1 THE WORLD VIEW ON ENERGY ACCESS AND END USE OF ENERGY

Access to energy services is critical for advancing human development, furthering social inclusion of the poorest and most vulnerable in society, and to meet many of the sustainable development goals (SDGs). The International Energy Agency (IEA) defines energy access as '*a household having reliable and affordable access to both clean cooking facilities and to electricity, which is enough to supply a basic bundle of energy services initially, and then an increasing level of electricity over time to reach the regional average* (www.iea.org/energyaccess/methodology*)*'.

For the first time, the SDGs included a target focused specifically on ensuring access to affordable, reliable, and modern energy for all by 2030 (SDG 7.1). It recognizes the importance of access to modern energy services in its own right, and of the centrality of energy in achieving many of the other goals (World energy outlook, IEA, special report, 2017).

A basic bundle of energy services means, at a minimum, several light bulbs, task lighting (such as a flashlight), phone charging, and a radio. Access to clean cooking facilities means access to (and primary use of) modern fuels and technologies, including natural gas, liquefied petroleum gas (LPG), electricity and biogas, or improved biomass cook stoves (ICS) as opposed to the basic biomass cook stoves and three-stone fires used in developing countries. This energy access definition serves as a benchmark to measure progress towards goal SDG 7.1, which includes two specific indicators to measure progress: 7.1.1—proportion of population with access to electricity and 7.1.2—proportion of population with primary reliance on clean fuels and technology (IEA special report, 2017, p. 21).

5.2 Re-collecting Experiences of the Microculture of Energy Demand and the Rural Dimension of EP

As discussed earlier, the rural dimension of energy poverty broadly exhibits the following attributes—(a) it is local in scale, micro- in socio-economic context, strongly multi-dimensional, and depicts asymmetrical symptoms of energy poverty (the pieces of evidence are scattered and are self-contradictory), (b) it bears strong adherence and exhibits deep-rooted contextual grounding in any given socio-cultural space, (c) the demand for an energy service is strongly dis-similar for different rural ecosystems, (d) there are strong and mixed signals in terms of access to different types of energy service(s) in different geo-spatial settings, (e) it is marked by mixed attributes of active and passive consumerism depending on the means and the ends to be met in the context of an energy service. This study brings forth an alternative view—the rural lifestyle may or may not be energy intensive, and therefore, rural ecosystems need not be energy poor. The 'rural' flavour of energy poverty sheds light on the relationship between the needs of a rural household and the consumption pattern of energy services. It is this relationship that becomes the driver of demand for energy access.

The established systemic policy design which provides for energy access ignores the manner in which societies and cultures perceive a resource allocation and their behaviour towards their political and socio-cultural surroundings which controls distribution of an allocated resource. Every single programmatic dose of energy access alters the character of the local socio-cultural, socio-economic, and socio-political order.

5.3 India Needs to Recognize the Importance of Local Nodes of Energy Consumption for an Effective Engagement with SDGs

Access to energy supplies is the centre stage, being given its due for the first time, as a driver for other sectors that contribute to improvements in services delivery. However, this framework captures the macro-perspective of energy access at the level of a nation as a geo-political entity. In the absence of a framework for data capture at the minutest level of rural India, the essence of evaluation of energy access remains insignificant. Another important element that longs for due recognition is linked to the end use to which an energy service is put. This aspect by and large depends upon the consumer base. And therefore, strongly subjective in character given the plurality and the cultural heterogeneity of rural India. More so, it is extremely important to explore and factor in these elements for a real time, effective management of small loads that exhibit the real flavour of the 'local' energy demand solely driven by consumer behaviour as an end-user.

5.4 Challenges Before India—Balancing Growth and Sustainable Development

India's energy consumption has almost doubled since 2000, and the potential for further rapid growth is enormous. The debate surrounding energy access has become a key one in rural energy policymaking over the last few years, an acknowledgement of the important role of energy in development. The electricity sector in India is one of the most diversified in the world. Sources of power generation range from commercial sources like coal, lignite, natural gas, oil, hydro, and nuclear power to other non-conventional sources like wind, solar, and biomass. The demand for electricity in the country has been growing at a rapid rate and is expected to grow further in the years to come. India is set to contribute more than any other country to the projected rise in global energy demand, around one-quarter of the total: even so, energy demand per capita in 2040 is still 40% below the world average.

India's urbanization is a key driver of energy trends: an additional 315 million people—almost the population of the United States today—are expected to live in India's cities by 2040. Taking population growth into account as well as the high policy priority to achieve universal electricity access, India adds nearly 600 million new electricity consumers over the period 2040. Keeping pace with the demand for electricity requires nearly 900 GW of new capacity, the addition of a power system four-fifths the size of that of the United States today (India Energy Outlook, IEA, 2015). The Indian energy system is concentrated around the conventional system of power generation relying heavily on coal-based thermal power plants and hydropower. Coal is by far the most important fuel mix, but India's recent climate pledge underlined the country's commitment to a growing role for low-carbon sources of energy, led by solar and wind power. India's power system needs to almost quadruple in size by 2040 to catch up and keep pace with electricity demand that—boosted by rising incomes and new connections to the grid—increases at almost 5% per year (India Energy Outlook, IEA, 2015).

Balancing a power system in which variable renewables meet one-fifth of power demand growth requires flexibility from other sources and a much more resilient grid. India thus emerges as a major driving force in global trends, with all modern fuels and technologies playing a part. Oil demand increases by more than any other country, approaching 10 (million barrels) mb/day (d) by 2040. India steps up its deployment of renewables, led by solar power, for which India becomes the world's second-largest market. Natural gas consumption also triples to 175 billion cubic metre (bcm), although at 8% in 2040, it still plays a relatively limited role in the overall energy-mix.

Solid biomass, comprising primarily fuel-wood (the mainstay of the rural energy economy) the primary cooking fuel for some 840 million people in India today, does not see a large increase (India Energy Outlook, IEA, 2015). This primarily happens on account of increase in incomes and supportive policies; these include one of the world's largest cash transfer programs, which subsidizes the purchase of liquefied petroleum gas (LPG) cylinders via payments to individual bank accounts (PIB release, 2016).

With these huge challenges in terms of ever-increasing numbers and alternatives for tackling exponential increase in energy demand, it is desirable that alternate energy production designs based on unconventional resources should proliferate locally. Till such time, local demand for energy has been assessed, and the potential of locally available renewable resource base is ascertained, deployment of small-scale energy production systems should be gradual in the rural electricity sector. Another important concern is creation of relevant formal/informal institutions and structures that could bear the social and economic cost of integration of alternate energy production systems with the conventional ones.

5.5 Energizing Rural India—Rural Electrification: Context, Relevance, Issues, and Concerns

This section aims at understanding the various approaches to systematically analyse the main themes central to the planning and progression of rural electrification approach for energizing rural India. There appears to be a gap in conceptualization and design of programs on account of failure to understand the drivers of rural energy demand. Why a centrally decided, singular practice of extension of the central grid gets primacy over other means and mechanisms to achieve RE targets?

India is an overwhelmingly rural country, approximately 70% of the total population lives in rural areas (Srivastava et al., 2012). For this reason, India's economic and social development is inherently linked to growth in the rural sector (Aggarwal et al., 2014). In order to contribute to India's overall development, the rural sector must have access to modern electricity and fuel sources (Palit et al., 2013). Rural electrification has been in the focus of policy makers for the past several decades. The need for extension of the electricity system to rural areas was felt quite early, immediately after independence.

The rural electrification programs had twin objectives; (a) village electrification and (b) pump energization for irrigation. However, this policy priority has rarely translated into effective schemes on the ground. Farm output still remains the focus, ever since the days of green revolution in the mid-1960s (NDC report, 1994). Village electrification remained on slow and unclear track, hovering between different definitions and unclear outcomes aimed at mere extension of electricity lines to a particular area (Samanta, 2015). India, home to 18% of the world's population, uses only 6% of the world's primary energy.

There is an ocean of literature pressing upon the fact that sustainable and affordable supplies of energy are critical to alleviating poverty, improving public health, enhancing education, and generally facilitating economic and societal growth (Chakrabarti, 2002; DFID, 2002; ESMAP, 2010; GNESD, 2006; Kemmler, 2007a; Sovacool, 2012). Energizing rural India is thus crucial to promoting the country's broader economic and social development (Clarke et al., 2013; Kemmler & Spreng, 2007b). Notably, India has made significant strides in improving access, now claiming achievement of 100% RE as on 28.04.2018—all inhabited

5,97,464 villages as per census data 2011 stand electrified (Economic times, 2018, the 1st of May).

Universal household electricity access by 2022 is the new mantra driving various programs. Apart from launching DDUGJY to cater to the commitment of electrifying villages, the government of India has recently launched SAUBHAGYA—Pradhan Mantri Sahaj Bijli Har Ghar Yojana has been announced. This scheme aims at achieving universal household electrification in the country by March, 2019 (ministry of power, annual report: 2017–2018, p. 3). However, the claims have been subject to critical scrutiny on account of two reasons—(a) the fundamental criterion based upon *deemed electrification concept* does not ensure quality and reliability of service, (b) grid access does not define the type of end use of an energy service, by a passive consumer of electricity.

The reason appears to be substantially strong and clear—the real drivers of demand for energy, nested in rural areas, are yet to be comprehensively studied and understood throughout the expanse of rural India. Rural ecosystem of energy consumption is a distinct cultural space where local demand resides (Calvert, 2016). The real context (*necessary demand driver*) does not find a mention in any of the policies or programs aiming at energizing the rural Indian landscape. The maze of institutions and the associated instrumentalities of energy governance need to address critical concerns. These concerns can be broadly categorized as: (a) Governance and planning related, (b) Policy and design related, and (c) Institutional.

5.5.1 Governance and Planning-Related Concerns

It is an accepted fact that the development of a sub-sectoral policy on rural electrification is a policy matter for the MACRO (the union; the control centre of the planning framework). Whereas the responsibility for effective implementation of the policy returns to the MESO (the state; the operational framework). The role of the MICRO (the III-tier architecture of local governance) is marked by its conspicuous absence at any of the stages. The local goes missing from the design and execution scene. Rural electrification has been, for decades, the sole imperative and prerogative of the central government. The electricity act, 2003 has been instrumental in overhauling the '*mega-picture*' of the electricity sector, however, a lot remains to be done with regard to the approach towards rural electrification, especially decentralized distributed generation (DDG) based on non-conventional sources of energy including off-grid, stand-alone systems.

There is a pressing need for an enabling environment for active community partnership, both as generators and consumers of electrical energy. A greater precision is required in the enabling provisions of regulatory policies and programs of rural electrification as a whole (Fig. 1.1, Annexure A in Chapter 1). The contemporary institutional set-up, agencies, and their structures need to adopt a more nuanced approach in terms of engaging with the MESO—and its functional energy governance architecture. This shall involve a closer association with the MICRO—the three-tier local governance structure.

Local understanding of the basic needs of any given geo-spatial terrain, in terms of demand aggregation and its subsequent profiling should be effective through the MICRO—a non-existent entity at present vis-à-vis energy governance framework. There is a strongly felt need for decentralization, delegation, and devolution at the level of 'MESO' towards 'MICRO' along the different phases of a sub-sectoral strategy, (a) designing, (b) detailing, and (c) localizing programming and execution. Thus, there is a much-desired need in terms of the unequivocal sharing of responsibilities between the entities (polycentric nodes) proposed to negotiate this paradigmatic manoeuvering (Ostrom, 2008, 2010).

There is a need to build capacities in terms of boosting human capital to allow local communities to have a greater choice in terms of localized energy generation and planning its distribution. This ought to be commensurate with the general tendency at the top towards multi-sector collaboration in terms of energy-mix. However, this attempt may not progressively lead to de-compartmentalization in electrification (energy) planning and execution of small projects at the MICRO-level in absolutely certain terms. This shall depend upon the quality of—(a) norms of reciprocity established, and (b) the intensity of active networks of civic engagements (Putnam, 1993) between the key actors and rural development sectors of the local economic space. These soft features have their own time frame of attaining maturity and getting accepted.

5.5.2 Policy and Design-Related Concerns

Although the overall intent of the national electricity policy and the rural electrification policy stands explicated through the approaches to energize rural India, the overall energy policy approach still remains far from being socio-technical. It remains *techno-economic*. This is usually a somewhat sophisticated economic criterion in terms of (discounted kWh cost, cost–benefit ratio, internal rate of return, net discounted value) operating within a set of constraints that can be political, technical, financial, and strategic.

Of late, the macro-trajectory of energy policy has been altering its course. A new element of the production design is energy generation mix from various sources, thereby reducing reliance on brown fuels. The policy approach marks a gradual shift towards bringing in an energy system change with increased deployment of mega-scale solar energy-driven plants on our landscapes. There has been an indiscriminate attempt to compensate for the decreasing plant load factor (PLF) that leaves the thermal plants idle (CEA report, 2017). This policy design of alternation of generation mix unfortunately ignores twin principalities—(a) the promise that a local area may hold in terms of its RESP, and (b) the patterns and intensities of energy demands across local geographies and associated cultures (Chapter 3).

A non-conventional energy generation system cannot be pressed into action without any assessment and evaluation of resource assessment. There is a necessitated basic requirement for taking into account the primordial need for on-site, embedded generation, and local consumption. This is essential for fulfilling systemic needs for better energy management being nearer/proximal to the small, rural micro-load centres. The varied terrain characteristics which are situated in different geo-climatic zones are interwoven with the spaces and culture of energy consumption. This reality still longs for recognition and placement in our energy policy framework. However, it does not figure in the policy horizon as of now.

The nature of energy demand distribution remains largely unaccounted for: in terms of space and time (when and where) in rural electrification programs. Where do we plan (territorial extension and expansion)?— The rural energy consumption landscape of the Indian subcontinent is littered with distinct 'spaces' of collective identities, variegated patterns of energy-centric life styles (intensive and non-intensive), and riddled with complexities of relational attributes of local culture, traditions and practices. The spatial nature of settlements makes it even more complex. Further, the context of energy transition in terms of generation (transmission and supply) and distribution (consumption) is functionally located in different physiographic divisions and geo-climate zones. These have a marked impact on the locale-specific demand profiles across seasons and even during any given day.

A rural electrification process must take into account the signs and symptoms of cultural loads. Ultimately, a process design is designed to address a specific need. There appears a need for a course correction in policy and design as well, in the context of rural electrification! What are the short-term outputs and long-term outcomes that are intended to be achieved? We need to re-think rural electrification in the light of the local needs both in terms of energy demand and the local resource potential to address need-based realistic demand (demand side management).

We normally follow mainly two distinguishing approaches for planning of rural electrification with a given time horizon, given the objective (generally bound to the creation of visible infrastructure in any given territory) and which aims only to optimize an economic criterion (objective function) by allowing narrow investment choice.

This investment choice is based on maximized generation of energy produced by limited non-comparative technologies. It is commonly referred to as the multi-sector approach. This also entails an economic optimization identical to the previous one. This approach is vehemently skewed towards one particular energy source within the framework of the non-conventional energy sector; driven largely by the reductionist quantitative dimension of attaining massive (Gigawatt scale) targets. This approach is strongly symbolic in nature, structural in scope and distances itself yet again from the innate, anthropogenic dimension of energy. What is required is an altogether different systems approach to convert human (local) energy inaction to local (human) energy in action by tapping/harnessing the local resource base. The focus needs to shift to localized production and consumption, driven by the concept of *prosumerism* (producer becoming a consumer: Toffler, 1980).

It is a fact that rural electrification is prohibitively costly. It has a lot of scope for recurring revision on account of the fact that '*the context has been missing*'. There is not enough thrust on the creation of ground-based data in respect of the consumer base. Once this is done, it becomes easy to perform simulations as the only method currently being followed is the extension of the central grid. However, a switchover to alternate energy systems and technologies-contextually grounded, and smaller in scale, would entail local deployment of disparate simulation tools for effective DSM. It is further necessary that the policy and design process must be adaptable to the local realities to highlight the local needs appropriately.

5.5.3 Institutional Concerns

The power system has grown rapidly in recent years, but the poor financial health of many local distribution companies remains a key structural weakness. Low end-user tariffs, technical losses in the network, and high levels of non-payment for electricity consumed, mean that distribution company revenue often fails to cover the costs owed to generators. This has created a cycle of uncertainty for generators and held back much-needed investment in network infrastructure. A combination of factors ranging from low tariffs, high cost to serve, poor efficiency levels, and inappropriate organizational frameworks have led to the continued neglect of rural India, in so far as electricity services are concerned (forum of Indian regulators, 2007).

It is important to note that one-third of India's population still does not have access to electricity. Most of the utilities are struggling to provide the minimum lifeline supply of one unit per household per day to the rural areas. The supply of electricity to rural areas has been attempted almost exclusively through conventional grid supply by the state utility. There is a significant disincentive on the part of state utilities to extend either better service to the rural consumer or provide extended hours of supply. This in turn results in low collection efficiency and high distribution losses (Planning commission annual report, 2013–2014).

There is a vicious circle encapsulating poor supply, low tariffs, and poor demand that magnifies the per unit average cost of supply to a rural consumer. To add to all of this, there are consistent efforts/attempts in various states to rationalize user tariffs, on lines other than techno-economic considerations. The attempts for cross-subsidization of one category of customer against the other have also been met with significant hurdles. Any attempt to charge an agricultural consumer has inevitably been politically thwarted (Jain, 2006). Though the situation varies from state to state, stimulating the necessary grid strengthening and capacity additions requires pressing ahead with regulatory and tariff reforms and a robust system of permitting and approvals for localized smaller projects. In the meantime, regular load-shedding in many parts of the country obliges those consumers who can afford it to invest in costly back-up options, and results in poor quality of service for those who cannot.

The state utilities are at the heart of the power system. The generation systems, even while increasing the absolute level of generation, have not been able to keep pace with the demands of the expanding customer base. There is a crisis of production on account of gradual and progressive reduction of plant load factor (PLF) of thermal plants, which constitute three-quarters of the generation mix (CEA, 2017). Uncertainty over the pace at which new large dams or nuclear plants can be built means strong reliance on solar and wind power. However, there is an enormous need for a realistic estimation of the potential of renewable energy resources. And, therefore the policy design should not be just driven by the high ambition to deliver on the pledge to build up a 40% share of non-fossil fuel capacity in the power sector by 2030 while ignoring the local.

5.6 Summing Up Challenges to Implementation of Rural Electrification Projects

The aim of rural electrification planning, design, and policy is to fulfil the general objectives defined under the national electricity policy 2005. The overall purpose was to extend access to electricity within a given territory, and within a given time horizon. However, this single sovereign approach was bereft of the essential aspect of integration of spatial planning across meso- and micro-, in order to strengthen the social and economic impact of rural electrification.

As a result, this program did not infuse confidence in the private sector. Though it was visible, it had no takers apart from the state utilities. As Lahimer et al. (2012) put it—*'rural electrification is a complicated issue because of user affordability, rural in accessibility and remoteness, low population densities and dispersed households, low project profitability, fiscal deficit, scarcity of energy sources, population growth, lack of professionalism and over-dependence on subsidies'*. A summary of challenges (barriers) to the successful implementation of rural electrification projects is discussed below.

> *Financial*: High upfront cost requiring savings over time; unavailability of capital and lack of initiative through dependency on subsidies (ESMAP, 2010; Friebe et al., 2013; Lahimer et al., 2012; Loka et al., 2013; Narula et al., 2012).
> *Infrastructure*: Access to market through lack of local infrastructure and other market-based factors (e.g. competition and marketing) (Ashley & Maxwell, 2001; Hirmer & Cruickshank, 2014; Lahimer et al., 2012; Painuly, 2001).

Technical: Low technical skill levels and access to quality materials, products (Ashley & Maxwell, 2001; Hirmer & Cruickshank, 2014; Painuly, 2001).
Social: Local ownership and acceptance (Benecke, 2008; Bhattacharya, 2013; Botes & Van, 2000; Simpson et al., 2009; Yadoo & Cruickshank, 2010).

5.7 Addressing Issues and Concerns: Re-aligning the Lost Policy Focus

The existing framework is closed for any lateral substitution for accelerating the process of rural integration especially in terms of openings for alternate sources of energy, open access to the distribution network, alternate tariff structure, etc. and developing a niche rural market for renewable energy sources. Consequently, in the interest of optimizing access to electricity for all, the need is to first identify and establish the sufficient and good reasons for this policy. What should have been the drivers of such an alternative policy thought process? Electricity has the potential to create user-value by broadening the perception of a product experience rather than just object interaction (passive consumerism). However, the Indian experience of rural electrification is reflective of the fact that development work typically focuses on economic and physical aspects of development. It often neglects the needs of the local communities that are affected by it.

Rural electrification programs have been myopic in terms of vision, and regressive in terms of planning and execution. The thrust has always been on creation of visible distribution infrastructure along a given time horizon. The concept of the process has been bereft of the larger perspective of energy service. The programs of the yesteryears including the existing RE program are grounded in a vulnerable framework of loose definition of an electrified village. The current planning and design approach should into account the following (*the CAP algorithm*):

(a) Coverage rate: expressed as a percentage of the number of dwelling units (civil structures) with electricity supply to the total number of dwelling units in a revenue village,
(b) Access rate: expressed as a percentage of the number of households in dwelling units (civil structures) with electricity supply to the total number of households in a revenue village. The level of

access thus indicates the actual proportion of households potentially having access to electricity, and
(c) Penetration rate: expressed as a percentage of the number of households per dwelling unit to the total number of households/total number of dwelling units. The level of penetration consequently indicates the proportion of households and/or dwelling units effectively having access to electricity.

Moreover, the concept of energy services discussed above (Bazilian et al., 2011, 2012; Birol, 2007; Pachauri, 2011), referred to as useful energy refers to a user value construct (end use of energy) that the energy supply allows to fulfil is absent in our conception of access to energy service approach. The value-based concept pertaining to end use shall not find its rightful place in a policy agenda for want of empirical data about rural, domestic energy consumption patterns. Another reason for its conspicuous absence from any RE agenda is related to the extension of the central grid that only promotes passive consumerism.

Consumer satisfaction, user value of an energy service is still an alien concept for dogmatic RE policy conceptions in Indian context. Further, not all technologies are valued in terms of the quality of service rendered (service reliability, number of hours per day, cost per user, possibility of productive uses, etc.). This approach renders units of consumption (in kWh) less valuable vis-à-vis end usage. It is high time that a parallel transition takes place in terms of this understanding as well.

5.8 The Dilemmas of Energy System Transition

(1) Viable technological options in connection with an energy production mix based on brown and green fuels.

Mega systems are not designed to cater to local, small, and sporadic demands (loads or load centres). This policy framework is antagonistic to the philosophy of creation of local energy guilds effectively (presumably) run by prosumers (Toffler, 1980). As a result, the rural electrification process still remains an unfinished agenda in India, being completely oblivious to the basic needs of the rural societies in terms of quantity and quality of service in their domestic lives. The issues related to the ability and willingness to pay in respect of rural, domestic consumers, require an in-situ, longitudinal study.

The provision of state subsidies stand on a slippery ground as there is lack of concurrence on demand profiling of rural, domestic demand, regressively constructed in terms of electricity distribution network extension. The fact of having a balanced, optimized supply within a given territory falls within the concept of an embedded local generation, and distribution system that could possibly run on energy alloys (mixed sources of power generation). The determining factor in the composition of this mix shall primarily be the availability of local resource supplies. Further, this shall be governed by the techno-economic conditions for production, transport, and distribution of the energy produced. The current energy generation paradigm is very typical of an orthodox, top-down, target-based approach resulting in mass proliferation of mega-watt (MW) scale gigantic energy systems necessitating creation of energy-intensive societies by boosting supplies.

(2) Re-thinking cross-subsidization of one category of consumer against the other.

Rural domestic, individual, and community clusters, including productive-sector users are all of equal importance with regard to human development through improvements in social welfare, towards a gradual progression towards *commodious living* in space and time,

(3) Linking of up-stream (energy supply) and down-stream (end use) to each other.

Although new and innovative concepts relating to energy services lead to greater consideration of end-service provision and the meeting of human requirements, rather than the energy (as indicated by the components of human development index, HDI) source or production, transport or distribution technologies, it would be inopportune to arbitrarily compare the upstream (which refers to system of production, transport, and distribution) with downstream (the energy end-service). Inasmuch as the upstream can exist without a relevant downstream. There cannot be a culturally, economically, socially sustainable downstream (rural domestic consumers) without incorporating the need for the development of an acceptable (locally) and economically viable, socio-technical upstream. Furthermore, different sources of production cannot be compared with each other in terms of quantity of generation, and reliability of supplies, and lastly,

(4) Financial arrangements amongst generators: big and small based on production design

The scope of providing financial incentives between functionally similar, but operationally dis-similar categories of generators are intrinsic to the techno-economic balance of energy (electricity) systems. The financial transfers need to be regulated in accordance with the provisions adopted in the national tariff policy (NTP, 2006; 2016). Availability-based tariff (ABT) based on the availability of a generator to immediately ramp-up production or make available the shortfall in generation should not be considered a dogma in the absence of a robust database for renewable energy source; solar, wind, biogas, etc. (the other category of generators). Further, there could be either single or multiple tariff structures depending on the locale-specific generation and consumption pattern resulting in effective and real demand side management (DSM) of energy supply (Kumar & Chatterjee, 2012).

Moreover, these transfers can be made depending upon the scale of 'horizontal spread' in terms of access to local load centres, and 'vertical integration' with conventional energy (electricity) systems run by various network of operators (state run utilities and private entities).

5.9 Summing Up—Transcending Barriers and Closure of Design-Reality Gap

Economic paradigms, together with assessments of the potential contributions of new and existing technologies shall continue to provide the basis for the analysis of alternative public policies relating both to energy production and consumption. At the same time, there is considerable evidence to suggest that the noneconomic behavioural and social sciences can contribute significantly to such analysis in at least four major areas- (1) increasing the accuracy of predictions of behavioural responses to economic incentives, (2) increasing our knowledge of non-economic approaches to behaviour change, (3) increasing the capacity of the public to make choices about new and existing energy technologies, and (4) anticipating the consequences of alternative energy policies. (Elliot Aronson, Chair, committee on behavioural and social aspects of energy consumption and production, 1984, pp. vii–viii)

The future lies in deployment of distributed energy resources (DERs) through use of renewable energy technologies (RETs)—The immediate requirement is an amendment in the three lists appended to the Indian constitution viz., the union, state, and the concurrent list. This should eventually be followed by a comprehensive assessment of locally available resources for onsite power generation and distribution, understanding of local needs in terms of availability and reliability of energy service, creation of regional nodes of indicative technology, and ranking of individual projects in terms of economic viability. The rural energy landscape of India should eventually be dotted with decentralized energy systems promoting micro-level energy governance, and localized energy access in terms of direct community control over generation and consumption (Fig. 5.1, Annexure). The need of a rural occupant residing in a dwelling unit has to be understood first. The nature of shelter (temporary or permanent) must be taken into account. How the present energy requirements met, whether as a self-help measure or through a policy conduit (a scheme, an apparatus) provided by the state.

Therefore, the policy initiative must take into account the stage of development a community is in. Identifying these requirements is a complex problem and there lies no simple solution. Different solutions would be required for different areas. The nature of problems shall also be different—some could be political, while others could be social or cultural or could be some combination of all three in varying proportions. Therefore, an appropriate policy cannot be conceived and designed in the absence of social will and the right political climate (Dunn, 1978). The extant policy must realize that the need for a rural energy system can only be met by way of 'gradualness' as opposed to 'big push'. Subsistence socio-economic, cultural ecosystems have minimum risk-taking abilities.

The aim of policy for such communities should never be aimed at return maximization but rather to avoid policy inflicted disaster. A policy communique or a policy demonstration that is not socially desirable can cause disruption in the community practices and values (case studies on Dhundhi and Tayyabpur). An added aspiration could demand flexibility in its deployment by the community with minimum expert intervention. A very important 'human' dimension that ultimately defines the limits of social acceptability and optimum functionality of a technical system lies in local capacity building.

Local expertise development is a prime concern as renewable energy technologies (RETs) involve technologies whose operational traits are rarely self-evident. Unequivocally, the evidence suggests that the nodal institutional structures are silent about such issues and as a consequence, the policy prescriptions generally remain quiet on the relative costs and benefits of such technologies. The experience from Tayyabpur (Vaishali district of Bihar) and Lohati Pasai (Barabanki district of Uttar Pradesh) shows that the local circumstances are characteristically unique. A lack of appraisal of local realities can derail the intended outcomes.

Expertise must be made available locally and capacities have to be created in-house, for the simple reason that the rural populace would want to gain utmost familiarity with regard to the usage in the given set of local specifications of society, culture, economy, and politics. A closely related understanding from village Dhundhi (Gujarat) and village Bahadurpur (Punjab) relates to an external influence in terms of organizational goals and aspirations. A private organizational 'interest' in terms of research and demonstration projects coupled with a philanthropic perspective may not be successful, as the community may intend to choose actions that they believe in, which could be either self-driven or gartered with specific state actors that exist for capacity creation at the local level.

A related aspect that requires serious introspection and understanding is related to institutionalizing technology in the community lifestyle, which would necessarily entail detailed and in-depth engagement with the community at the primordial stage of conception of a decentralized, community driven, renewable energy production system. The rural energy landscape of India is replete with diversity on account of local, endemic pluralities, therefore, any sort of universal generalization in terms of further research and policy communication and demonstration would produce unintended and least expected outcomes. The empirical dataset in terms of energy consumption culture, resource potential assessment, and the failed (or partly successful) initiatives of myopic policy culture, warrants a rigorous understanding of the social processes (the innate anthropogenic dimension) that facilitated, jeopardized, or transformed the local, alternative renewable energy design systems.

5.10 Scope for Further Research

This work opens the door for a plethora of research themes related to—(a) understanding drivers and impediments that govern the behaviour of a passive consumer of energy placed in different socio-political spaces, (b) understanding and acceptability of policy dose by the policy recipients situated in different geo-spatial settings, (c) evaluating value-behaviour gap amongst different socio-cultural spaces of energy consumption in different terrains, (d) assessment of effects of judgments and decision biases on renewable energy-related behaviour of communities placed in similar context and those placed otherwise, (e) pluralism and parallelism in policy design showcasing clear-cut prejudices and biases in favour of one knowledge system over the other, (f) effects of social norms, local traditions, energy consumption culture, and civic engagements on use of alternate designs of sustainable energy systems, (g) policy communication and effective demonstration to develop collective community action towards promotion of energy literacy in respect of non-conventional sources of energy, (h) understanding psychological and behavioural effects of practices by non-state actors that work on the self-assumed principle of voluntary energy governance, (i) understanding the true potential of renewable energy sources in terms of extremely localized assessment of potential of individual resources for a robust resource profiling across geo-climatic zones and physiographic divisions, (j) evaluating the need for creation of separate policy think tank and related institutional frameworks for governing non-conventional energy sources, controlling and regulating different production systems for different sources of non-conventional energy at various levels of energy governance architecture, (k) understanding the need for risk profiling in respect of—(1) source of renewable energy, (2) technology purported to be used for harnessing it, (3) local weather conditions, (4) siting, design, and planning of a production, distribution, and consumption renewable energy system, (5) scaling of local renewable energy systems in terms of economies of 'scale and scope', and (6) understanding factors that enhance the acceptance of a non-endemic alien technology, lastly, (l) understanding rural nature of energy poverty in Indian context, re-defining matrix for its assessment in terms of its incidence across cultures and spaces of energy consumption that are situated in different terrains and climatic zones.

Further, one single method shall not be adequate to meet the requirements of the suggested research themes. The heterogeneity and asymmetric design of programs and schemes creates a sort of multicultural consumption pattern which remains to be probed as a separate and independent research project. The methods shall have to be multi-disciplinary for a concrete and comprehensive evaluation of a research theme. The complex nature of rural energy poverty is subject to further detailed cross-cultural verification and validation. There is a need for recognition of exceptions in contrast to the contemporary world-view about energy poverty.

We need a strong and robust framework to clearly define the identifiable boundaries of energy poverty in the exclusive context of rural India. Not one approach of methodological individualism, or one based on an exclusive instrumentalist method, can on its own solve this demarcation problem. Rather an interdisciplinary approach with a method triangulation framework shall be required to provide some concrete answers to help in the conception of an 'appropriate policy' for the rural energy sector, to make a rightful dent to a heterogeneous, rural socio-cultural landscape. The evidence-based approach that forms the backbone of this study contends the contemporary evaluation and description of energy poverty in India, being largely based on census and NSSO data inadequate in terms of problem identification and description.

There is a need for a detailed probe in order to comprehensively evaluate the true 'relativist' nature of the phenomenon in rural Indian context. Once this is achieved, it shall be easy to place a policy design in the context of a symptomatic problem which could be relative energy poverty of varying intensities in different parts of rural India. The polity thereafter can take a call based on a set of data to design a context-specific policy for roll out of renewable energy technologies (RETs) to decentralized energy systems in rural India.

However, this would hinge strongly upon an evidence-based policy approach that shall effectively lay down the site-specific policy prescription, in terms of which source of renewable energy is to be harnessed with the available technology in a given geo-spatial setting based on the local nature of demand for energy. On the basis of a sound understanding of the local nature of demand, the polity can take a call on tackling relative energy poverty through distributed (energy system/distributed energy resources) DES/DER by the aid of RETs. Thus, EBP paradigm shall help in designing effective policies for the rural energy sector (Fig. 5.1,

Annexure) that shall have an essential 'anthropogenic' dimension in the form of an active consumer. This shall eventually pave the way for cohesive diffusion of technology in the socio-culture regime of energy consumption in different plural societies residing in the rural Indian landscape.

5.11 Renewable Energy Technologies (RETs)—Alternate Pathways to Power Generation, Holding a Promise to Service Culture-Specific Demands, Exhibited Through Distributed Loads

For decades, as demand for power has grown, India has added large-scale conventional power supply resources. Now, with solar and wind power and other renewable energy resources becoming commercially viable in the marketplace, there are additional choices available the policy makers and stakeholders concerned with the technical, economic, and environmental characteristics of a future power system that keeps pace with economic growth (narrow and myopic vision), the social goes missing, there is no local in the policy arena or the constitutionally obligated local actors (Schedule 11, Constitution of India, 1950).

Mega systems promote passive consumerism and shall distance the consumer further from the policy process. Such policy processes shall never allow the locals to understand national or international obligations as there shall remain no differentiation between green power and brown power (oil and gas-based power generation), whatsoever. Further, the current agenda for pushing across mega renewable power generation, exclusively based on harnessing solar energy does not help much in promoting the cause of other renewable sources of energy (Planning commission reports, 2006, 2011). There needs to be a fair balance between all the sources of alternate power generation (wind, biomass, biogas, small hydro, tidal, waste, etc.) which should be exclusively guided by local resource availability and local demand based on empirical evidence.

There is no good reason to create exceptions in favour of one renewable resource without taking into account the demerits. Businesses with interests in fossil fuels exploit popular sentiments to stifle policy change. While polity promotes renewables at international forums, domestic policymaking has not been framing the right required policies (Planning

Commission reports, 2006, 2011; UNDP, 2010). Although the electricity act, 2003 and the national action plan for climate change and the Paris accord-conference of parties, (NAPCC/COP21) provide for a roadmap for promoting/increasing renewable share. It is a harsh reality that 'renewables' are still extremely un-evenly deployed and differentially distributed for want of data on locale-specific resource potential to match local energy demand.

One of India's major advantages today and going forward is that its RE potential is vast and largely untapped. Recent estimates indicate that India's solar potential is greater than 10,000 GW and its wind potential could be higher than 2,000 GW (NITI Aayog, RE roadmap 2030, 2015, p. 4). Seeing the relevance in the current scenario, government of India has enhanced its aspirations multi-fold: amending the same from 20 GW of solar power (by 2019) to 100 GW (by 2022) and from an additional 15 GW of wind power (during 2012–2017) to an additional 40 GW (by 2019). The targets are huge and would therefore require herculean efforts in terms of laying down viability and operational standards. The demand for power is largely met through coal and hydro. Switching over to mega, non-conventional power systems would entail a major shift in production, transport, and distribution systems (TERI, 2018).

Creation of additional capacities for evacuation of additional power would inter-alia involve massive land acquisition for creation of transport corridors, that would in turn threaten green cover along with permanent loss of land to any futuristic productive engagement. Further, all of these non-conventional production systems are proposed to be grid-tied, which would necessitate shut down of conventional power generation systems running on coal or water. On one hand, we are thinking about alternate technology but we have completely ignored the local needs.

What calls for this switch over is not an intrinsic requirement but our international commitments to contribute to the global cause of climate change. However, we have seriously missed out upon the basic requirement: renewable resource assessment in different parts of the country. We do not have a robust historical database for any of the renewable sources. There is still a long way to go. We need to focus on a wide array of system designs available—local, small-scale, off-grid, mini-grid, or grid-tied energy production systems that can be run locally. The national policy agenda is not in sync with the mandate of the electricity act, 2003 that calls for promotion of decentralized, distributed generation.

There remains a huge gap that needs to be filled in terms of optimizing potential realization of renewable resources that are available locally, although differential potential still needs to be assessed. This energy form in its current format is strongly looked upon as an alien element by the conventional energy sector, which dictates and dominates policy formulation. Renewable energy technologies are best and ideally suited to distributed applications.

5.12 Tweaking with the Principle and the Institutional Framework

The polity and the contemporary policy construct appear to be too distant from any kind of 'social learning' that enables germination of an alternative understanding in terms of—what was good, what was bad and why, for the rural electrification programs. The contemporary policy of energy access is laced with moral and ethical dilemmas of a 'compromised' action (not doing enough). It is further crippled with a subdued, passive existence of rural consumers (policy recipients), who bear the burden of policy being too remote functionally and ideologically. The quadrate of rights, titles, interests, and liabilities of the associated actors are normally not acknowledged by the policy estate. The exclusive set of evidence (from Tayyabpur and Dhundhi) further corroborates the ignominy that lies entrenched in the land parcel where the plant/project has to come up. Thus, solar or biogas-based energy supply systems are not an exception to this specific set of ground truth (Tayyabpur, MGP, Dhundhi and Bahadurpur). The nuisance value of the fixed capital asset (the upfront cost) begins to reduce in proportion to the size of the energy production systems. Smaller designs could help for better comparisons of costs of production, supply and distribution of energy services in rural settings.

There is an imperative for a much-awaited amendment to schedule VII of the Indian constitution. Electricity should be re-casted as: *energy from a mix of generation sources* and placed in the union list. There should also be a distinct designated entry as—*electricity from renewable energy sources* that should be added to the list II (the state list). The old entry 'electricity' needs to be deleted as the national policies in respect of energy generation mix and tariff design have undergone substantial change very recently (CEA, 2016a, 2016b). A new entry in the form of *'decentralized power generation from renewable energy sources'* should be added to list of items in schedule XI, with simultaneous deletion of the entry no.15 that pertains to non-conventional energy sources.

Land is a state subject. Therefore, states can have a designated policy in respect of 'common lands' to be ear-marked for small-scale, locale-specific, renewable energy projects only for kilowatt scale systems. In case, there is a politically felt need to take on board the department of rural developments and panchayats, there could be a state-specific amendment to the panchayati raj act. The gram panchayats should be given a mandatory directive through the act to fulfil the objectives as detailed in schedule XI. Thus, local generation and distribution should be in sync with the overall framework of generation mix and gradual switch over to renewables. This would entail creation of local energy governance and regulation structure along with a rural energy market for an effective and realistic, demand side management (DSM).

Demands realism would entail boosting local supplies of resources, tools, skill, finances and most importantly, overall energy management. However, these state-specific amendments should be in line with the overall state and national policy objective in respect of the rural electricity sector. For the purpose of achieving singularity and uniformity, there has to be an amendment to the list I (the union list) in the form of an entry that reads as '*energy from a mix of generation sources* (an addendum)'. These are some very general, broad suggestive lists of mandatory amendments that need to be initiated without any further delay as policies need to have a crystal-clear contextual grounding in terms of these sacrosanct entries in the magna-carta of Indian political system, the Indian constitution. India lacks any sacrosanct renewable energy legislation. Though a draft has been in the public domain since 2015 (Annexure A), it would be futile exercise to even discuss it prior to the amendments indicated above. There lies a strong imperative for amendment of the principal for frameworks that can be designed based on that.

5.13 Tweaking with the Conception and Policy Design in the Rural Electricity Sector

The phenomenon of energy poverty still lies unrecognized in the Indian policy estate (sum total of polity, policymaking institutions, and policy actors) that governs the energy planning architecture. The conception of a given policy design and its resultant schemes in the context of extending energy access to the rural Indian heartland needs to find a good, sufficient, and cogent reason for its appropriate contextual grounding. The policy design in respect of providing energy access is skewed and flawed for want of clinical evidence in order to first recognize the signs and symptoms of rural energy poverty and thereafter, a good enough policy dose could be administered on the ultimate recipients (the missing 'human' element in energy action). Thus, there appears to be a huge gap between the constitutional aspirations, the policy texts, and the context defined by the action arenas. Evidence-based policy approach aims to improve relevance, efficacy, efficiency, and effectiveness of policy processes.

The evidence presents the following attributes in respect of the geo-spatial texture of rural energy poverty—(a) it is an extremely complex function of preferences, habits, and lifestyles across communities with similar or dis-similar socio-economic functionalities, (b) it is marked by variations in intensity of energy consumption (demand), (c) there is tremendous variation between the fulfilled and unfulfilled needs of energy consumption in terms of usage of electric power and cooking fuels, and (d) it presents a complex rubric of socio-cultural behaviourism that is reflected in tastes, preferences, and energy consumption lifestyles. Thus, the pieces of evidence point towards symptomatic and asymptomatic (mixed) presence of energy poverty, which has strong adherence and deep contextual grounding in the predominantly rural, local, socio-cultural spaces of energy consumption.

The EBP paradigm shall lay the foundation for a well-informed debate as to—(1) re-thinking appropriateness of grid-extension as a policy tool to resolve problems of energy access, (2) re-visit the metrics that make it difficult for EP to be universally applicable, especially when this study attempts to answer the central question—whether rural India is energy poor?, (3) conceive a composite (qualitative and quantitative) rationale for demand profiling (linked to socio-cultural profiling of communities) at the level of civil structures (centres and spaces of energy consumption) for a real-time DSM, 4) evaluation of potential of the local resource base in terms of renewable energy generation potential for decentralized, distributed, renewable energy sources (RES).

The policy needs to take into account the 'human dimension' of energy usage that has been missing ever since the conception of rural electrification programs. There has to be thoughtful engagement between the policy arena and the action arena that would entail massive tinkering with the contemporary thought process of mega-scale, modern, centralized energy production systems. The policy arena is oblivious of the need for a comprehensive evaluation of base-load energy requirements (baseline energy flows) of communities spread across different cultural spaces. The discussion based on different base-load demands on account of individual (self-driven), private (non-state actors), state actors raises a fundamental question relating to myopic, retrograde, and regressive policy designs and therefore, universal energy access still remains an unfinished agenda. Therefore, the national aspiration of power for all (PFA) shall remain an elusive dream for a longer period of time.

5.14 Translating Policy Aspirations into Praxis

As first things first—it should find a sound contextual grounding in the GANDHIAN PHILOSOPHY of SWARAJ. I prefer to call it ENERGY SWARAJ for the rural heartland of the Indian subcontinent (Fig. 5.1, Annexure). Therefore, an appropriate policy for the rural energy sector should aim at—(a) improvement of quality of life of the people, (b) maximization of the use of renewable sources, (c) creation of active consumers of energy in spaces and cultures of energy consumption through employing—local skills, local material resources, local financial resources (there is a need to link the micro-credit framework to rural energy systems), (d) compatibility with local culture and practices, and (e) satisfying local wishes and needs (Dunn, 1978).

It is expedient to raise certain basic questions and sort of try and answer them during the process of conception and designing of different policy texts for the rural energy sector that is spread across different terrains—(1) what are the ultimate goals and potential of the policy in human and economic terms, (2) what is the appropriate/possible renewable resource mix in financial/economic terms, (3) what are the domestic, indigenous, locally available appropriate technologies, (4) the probable mix of technologies and from where, (5) what is the state of the rural, domestic market, (6) what is the attitude of the local communities and the gram panchayats towards the conceived policy appropriateness, (7) what are the short term, medium term and long term risks and gains in terms of the intended outputs and outcomes, and most importantly, (8) risk grading associated with the locked promise in terms of 'energy generation potential' from different non-conventional sources under different site-specific conditions.

The future lies in deployment of distributed energy resources (DERs) through use of renewable energy technologies (RETs)—The immediate requirement is an amendment in the three lists appended to the Indian constitution viz., the union, state, and the concurrent list. This should eventually be followed by a comprehensive assessment of locally available resources for onsite power generation and distribution, understanding of local needs in terms of availability and reliability of energy service, creation of regional nodes of indicative technology, and ranking of individual projects in terms of economic viability.

A decentralized, self-sufficient, distributed local energy action shall imbibe the following five philosophical outlooks—(1) conservation philosophy implies the definition of renewable energy as a resource that does not get depleted over time, however, the proposition being mooted is in favour of their pragmatic usage leading to an effective and robust localized DSM, (2) community control philosophy upholds the ethos of the constitution by emphasizing upon the fact that the allocation and redistribution of resources (energy access based on principles of fairness and equity for promotion of social cohesiveness and cementing plural fabric) at the micro-level should be as democratic as possible in relation to the production and distribution of energy, (3) equity philosophy implies that distributed energy resources are a social and cultural necessity of a pluralistic, heterogeneous society and stresses upon the fact that the systems of energy would be of the community, for the community and by the community, strictly in sync with the constitutional philosophy, (4) community as a collective first, individuals come thereafter, thereby drilling down deep the central dogma of energy collectivism for enhancing community resilience, and lastly (5) appropriate technology philosophy entails that the harnessing tool is indigenous, locally produced, small in scale, uses local renewable energy sources, easy to operate and maintain, can be serviced locally through deployment of local skill base, and is affordable.

Through local renewable energy sources and decentralized technologies, along with the conventional grid connection, **REST** proposed an *integrated approach for rural electrification*. It aimed at—identification and adoption of technological solutions, review of current legal and institutional framework, and make changes wherever necessary, promotion, funding, financing and facilitating alternative approaches in rural electrification, and coordination with various linked ministries, apex institutions, and research organizations to facilitate meeting national objectives as enshrined in the overall national policy (Chapter 1). Revisiting and reviving creative programs is an absolute necessity rather than reinventing the wheel time and again.

I rest my case with this quote—'*If you want to go places, start from where you are. If you are poor, start with something cheap. If you are uneducated, start with something relatively simple. If you live in a poor environment, and poverty makes markets small, start with something small. If you are unemployed, start using your labour power; because any productive use of it is better than letting it lie idle. In other words, we must learn to recognize the boundaries of poverty. A project that does not fit, educationally and organizationally, into the environment, will be an economic failure and a cause of disruption*- E.F. Schumacher (Dunn, 1978, p. 1).

Prosumerism holds the key to democratization of energy systems in India (Fig. 5.1, Annexure).

Annexure

See Fig. 5.1.

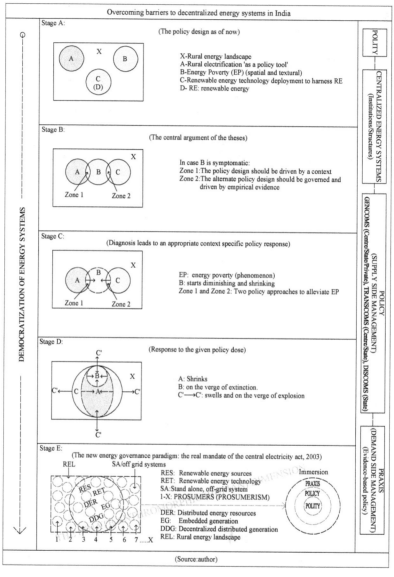

Fig. 5.1 Overcoming 'barriers' to decentralized energy systems in India

References

Aggarwal, V., Fahey, A., Freymiller, S. H., Ramama, M. V., Huang, C. C., Li, S., Moilanen, S., Onda, C., Ratledge, N., Speirs, S., & Wong, J. (2014). *Rural energy alternatives in India: Opportunities in financing and community engagement for renewable energy micro-grid projects, community and economic development/energy and environment* (pp. 1–66). Woodrow Wilson School of Public and International Affairs, Princeton University.

Alghoul, M. A., Amin, N., Lahimer, A. A., Razykov, T. M., Sopian, K., & Yousif, F. (2013). *Research and development aspects on decentralized electrification options for rural household, renewable and sustainable energy reviews* (Vol. 24, pp. 314–324). https://doi.org/10.1016/j.rser.2013.03.057

Annual Report of the Ministry of Power. (2017–2018). *Government of India* (pp. 1–276). http://www.powermin.nic.in

Ashley, C., & Maxwell, S. (2001). *Rethinking rural development, development policy review* (Vol. 19, Issue 4, pp. 395–425).

Bazilian, M., Blyth, W., Hobbs, B. F., Howells, M., & MacGill, I. (2011). Interactions between energy security and climate change: A focus on developing countries. *Energy Policy, 39*(6), 3750–3756.

Bazilian, M., Brew-Hammond, A., Foster, V., Gallachóir, B. Ó., Nussbaumer, P., Pachauri, S., & Rogner, H. H. (2012). Energy access scenarios to 2030 for the power sector in sub-Saharan Africa. *Utilities Policy, 20*(1), 1–16.

Benecke, G. E. (2008). Success factors for the effective implementation of renewable energy options for rural electrification in India–Potentials of the clean development mechanism (CDM). *International Journal of Energy Research, 32*(12), 1066–1079. https://doi.org/10.1002/er.1445

Bhattacharyya, S. C. (2013). Financing energy access and off-grid electrification: A review of status, options and challenges. *Renewable and Sustainable Energy Reviews, 20*, 462–473.

Birol, F (2007). Energy economics: A place for energy poverty in the agenda? *The Energy Journal, 28*(3), 1–6.

Botes, L., & Van, D. R. (2000). Community participation in development: Nine plagues and twelve commandments. *Community Development Journal, 35*(1), 41–58.

Calvert, K. (2016). From 'energy geography' to 'energy geographies', perspectives on a fertile academic borderland. *Progress in Human Geography, 40*(1), 105–125. https://doi.org/10.1177/0309132514566343

Central Electricity Act. (2003). *The gazette of India, part-II* (Registered no. DL-33004/2003) (pp. 1–134). Legislative Department, Ministry of Law and Justice, Government of India, Dated on 26 May.

Central Electricity Authority. (2016a). *Draft national electricity plan (generation)* (Vol. 1, pp. 1.1–6.33), Ministry of Power, Government of India.

Central Electricity Authority. (2016b). *Draft national electricity plan (transmission)* (Vol. 2, pp. 1.11–3.22), Ministry of Power, Government of India.

Central Electricity Authority. (2017). *Growth of electricity sector in India from 1947–2017,* (pp. 1–86), Ministry of Power, Government of India.

Central Electricity Regulatory Commission. (2000). *Availability based tariff (ABT)* (pp. 1–69). Order dated on 4 Janauary.

Chakrabarti, S. (2002). Rural electrification programme with solar energy in remote region—A case study in an island. *Energy Policy, 30*(1), 33–42.

Clarke, S, Cooper, C., Crafton, M., Eidsness, J., Johnson, K., Palit, D., Sovacool, B., & Zoppo, D. (2013). *The trials and tribulations of the village energy security programme (VESP) in India, energy policy* (Vol. 57, pp. 407–417).

Constitution of India. (1950). *Extracts from the constitution of India, as modified on December 1, 2007,* Ministry of Law and Justice, Government of India (pp. 1–443).

Cruickshank, H., & Hirmer, S. (2014). *The user value of rural electrification: An analysis and adoption of existing models and theories, renewable and sustainable energy reviews* (Vol. 34, pp. 145–154).

Department for International Development (DFID). (2002). *Energy for the poor: Underpinning the millennium development goals (MDGs)* (pp. 1–32). produced for DFID by Future energy solutions, DFID. https://www.ecn.nl/fileadmin/ecn/units/bs/JEPP/energyforthepoor.pdf

Draft National Renewable Energy Act. (2015). *Ministry of new and renewable energy (MNRE)* (draft no. 11/3/2014-EFM) (pp. 1–24). https://mnre.gov.in/file-manager/userfiles/dra2015-comments.html

Dunn, P. D. (1978). *Appropriate technology: Technology with a human face.* Macmillan.

Economic Times. (2018). *100% electrification is equal to 100% power politics, politics and nation, news item,* accessed at 9.47 am IST, https://economictimes.indiatimes.com.news.politicsandnation

Electricity Sector Management Assistance Program. (2010). ESMAP. *Modernizing Energy Services for the Poor: A World Bank Investment Review Fiscal 2000–08,* 1–98.

Energy Access Outlook. (2017). *From poverty to prosperity, International Energy Agency (IEA), World Energy Outlook special report, OECD/IEA* (pp. 1–140). www.iea.org

Friebe, C. A., von Flotow, P., & Täube, F. A. (2013). *Exploring the link between products and services in low-income markets—Evidence from solar home systems, energy policy* (Vol. 52, pp. 760–769).

GNESD. (2006). *Poverty reduction—Can renewable energy make a real contribution? Summary for policy makers* (pp. 1–50). http://in.one.un.org

Guidelines for Pradhan Mantri Shaj Bijli Har Ghar Yojana (Saubhagya). (2017). Government of India, Ministry of Power (pp. 1–47). O.M No. (F. No 44/2/2016/-RE). Dated on October 20.

India Energy Outlook. (2015). *International Energy Agency, World Energy Outlook special report, OECD/IEA* (pp. 1–187). www.iea.org

Jain, V. (2006). Political economy of the electricity subsidy: Evidence from Punjab, *Munich Personal RePEc Archive (MPRA)* (paper no. 240) (pp. 1–10). http://mpra.ub.uni-muenchen.de/240/

Kemmler, A. (2007). Factors influencing household access to electricity in India. *Energy for Sustainable Development, 11*(4), 13–20.

Kemmler, A., & Spreng, D. (2007). Energy indicators for tracking sustainability in developing countries. *Energy Policy, 35*(4), 2466–2480.

Kumar, A., & Chatterjee, S. (2012). *Electricity sector in India- policy and regulation*. Oxford University Press.

Lahimer, A. A., Alghoul, M. A., Sopian, K., Amin, N., Asim, N., & Fadhel, MI. (2012). Research and development aspects of pico-hydropower. *Renewable and Sustainable Energy Reviews, 16*, 5861–5878.

Loka, P., Moola, S., Reddy, S., Skumanich, A., Fulton, S., Siah, S. C., & Mints, P. (2013). A case study for micro-grid PV: Rural electrification in India. In *Photovoltaic Specialists Conference (PVSC)* (pp. 3379–3382). 39th IEEE. https://doi.org/10.1109/PVSC.2013.6745174.

Models of rural electrification. (2007). *Report to forum of Indian regulators* (pp. 1–125). https://www.forumofregulators.gov.in

Narula, K., Nagai, Y., & Pachauri, S. (2012). The role of decentralized distributed generation in achieving universal rural electrification in South Asia by 2030. *Energy Policy, 47*, 345–357. https://doi.org/10.1016/j.enpol.2012.04.075

National tariff policy. (2006). *The gazette of India, extraordinary*, Ministry of Power (Resolution number.23/2/2005-R and R) (Vol. 3, pp. 1–21). dated 6 Janauary.

National tariff policy. (2016). *The gazette of India, extraordinary*, Ministry of Power (Resolution number. 23/2/2005-R and R) (Vol. 9, pp. 1–38). dated on 28 Febrauary.

NITI Aayog. (2015). *Report on India's renewable electricity roadmap 2030: Towards accelerated renewable electricity development* (pp. 1–108).

Nussbaumer, P., Bazilian, M., Modi, V., & Yumkella, K. K. (2011). *Measuring energy poverty: Focusing on what matters* (Working paper no. 42) (pp. 1–27). Oxford department of international development, University of Oxford, Oxford poverty and human development initiative (OPHI).

Ostrom, E. (2008). Tragedy of the Commons. In *The new Palgrave dictionary of economics* (Vol. 2).

Ostrom, E. (2010). A long polycentric journey. *Annual Review of Political Science, 13*, 1–23. www.annualreviews.org

Pachauri, S. (2011). Reaching an international consensus on defining modern energy access. *Current Opinion in Environmental Sustainability, 3* (4), 235–240.

Painuly, J. P. (2001). Barriers to renewable energy penetration—A framework for analysis. *Renewable Energy, 24*(1), 73–89.

Palit, D., Clarke, S., Cooper, C., Crafton, M., Eidsness, J., Johnson, K., Sovacool, B., & Zoppo, D. (2013). The trials and tribulations of the village energy security programme (VESP) in India. *Energy Policy, 57*, 407–417.

Planning Commission, Government of India. (2006). Integrated energy policy. *Report of the Expert Committee.* (pp. 1–147).

Planning Commission, Government of India. (2011, May). *Interim report of the expert group on low carbon strategies for inclusive growth.* (pp. 1–114).

Planning Commission. (2014). *Annual report 2013–2014 on the working of state power utilities and electricity departments.*

Putnam, D. R. (1993). *Making democracy work, civic traditions in modern Italy.* Princeton University Press, ISBN 0-691-07889-0.

Press information bureau (PIB) release. (2016). *Pradhan Mantri Ujjwala Yojana: A giant step towards better life for all.* Press information bureau (PIB), Government of India (GoI), http://pib.nic.in/newsite/printrelease.aspx?relid=148971, dated the 17 August, 14:49 IST.

Report of the National Development Council (NDC) committee on power. (1994). *Planning commission* (pp. 1–173).

Report of the conference of the parties on its 21st session (COP21). (2015). *United Nations Framework Convention on Climate Change (UNFCCC)* (pp. 1–36), FCCC/CP/2015/10/Add.1. https://unfccc.int/resource/docs/2015/cop21/10a01.pdf

Samanta, P. K. (2015). A study of Rural Electrification Infrastructure in India. *Journal of Business and Management (IOSR-JBM), 17*(2), 54–59, version IV.

Simpson, R., & Williams, A. A. (2009). Picohydro-reducing technical risks for rural electrification. *Renewable Energy, 34*(8), 1986–1991.

Sovacool, B. K. (2012). The political economy of energy poverty: A review of key challenges. *Energy for Sustainable Development, 16*(3), 271–282.

Srivastava, L., Goswami, A., Diljun, G. M., & Chaudhury, S. (2012). Energy access: Revelations from energy consumption patterns in rural India. *Energy Policy, 47*, 11–20.

Stern. P. C., & Aronson. E. (Eds.). (1984). *Energy use, the human dimension.* W.H. Freeman and company. ISBN 0-7167-1620-8, https://nap.edu/catalog/9259.html

Toffler, A. (1980). *The third wave,* First published by William Morrow and company (p. 544). ISBN0688035973.

Transitions in India Electricity Sector. (2017–2030). *The Energy and Resources Institute (TERI)* (pp. 1–29), 2018. www.teriin.org, visited on April 26, 2018.

Twelth five-year plan document. (2012–2017). *National planning Commission of India* (pp. 130–194), Chapter 14, 2018. (www.planningcommission.gov.in)

IEA/UNDP/UNIDO. (2010). *Energy poverty: How to make modern energy access Universal?* Special early excerpt of the World Energy outlook 2010 for the UN general assembly on the millennium development goals, OECD/IEA, Paris, (pp. 1–52).

Yadoo, A., & Cruickshank, H. (2010). The value of cooperatives in rural electrification. *Energy Policy, 38*(6), 2941–2947. https://doi.org/10.1016/j.enpol.2010.01.031.

Bibliography

Alanne, K., & Arto, S. (2006). Distributed energy generation and sustainable development. *Renewable & Sustainable Energy Reviews, 10,* 539–558.

Anderson, C. W. (1978). The logic of public problems: Evaluation in comparative policy research. In D. E. Ashford (Ed.), *Comparing public policies: New concepts and methods* (Chapter 1, pp. 19–41). Sage.

Anderson, J. E. (1975). *Public policy making.* Thomas Nelson and Sons Limited.

Agterbosch, S., Vermeulen, W. J. V., & Glasbergen, P. (2004). Implementation of wind energy in the Netherlands: The importance of the social-institutional setting. *Energy Policy, 32,* 2049–2066.

Agterbosch, S., Meertens, R. M., & Vermeulen, W. J. V. (2009). The relative importance of social and institutional conditions in the planning of wind power projects. *Renewable and Sustainable Energy Reviews, 13,* 393–405.

Bailey, I. H., & Rand, W. G. (2010). Some things old, some things new: The spatial representations and politics of change of the peak oil re-localization movement. *Geo-Forum, 41*(4), 595–605.

Barbara, C. F., & Houston, H. A. (1996). *Willingness to pay for Electricity from Renewable energy* (NREL/TP-460–21216 • UC Category: 1320 • DE96007944).

Bardouille, P., & Muench, D. (2014). *How a New Breed of Distributed Energy Services Companies can reach 500mn energy—Poor customers within a decade. A commercial solution to the energy access challenge.*

Barnes, F. D. (2005, March). *Draft for Discussion: Meeting the Challenge of Rural Electrification in Developing Nations: The Experience of Successful Programs.* Energy Sector Management Assistance Program (ESMAP).

Barry, M., & Chapman, R. (2009). Distributed small-scale wind in New Zealand: Advantages, barriers and policy support instruments. *Energy Policy, 37*, 3358–3369.

BP P.I.C. (2018, June). *BP statistical Review of World Energy*. London, United Kingdom.

Bradford, J., & Fraser, E. D. G. (2008). Local authorities, climate change and small and medium enterprises: Identifying effective policy instruments to reduce energy use and carbon emissions. *Corporate Social Responsibility and Environmental Management, 15*, 156–172.

Chambers, R. (1993). *Challenging the professions: Frontiers for rural development*. Intermediate Technology Publications.

Charmaz, K. (2006). *Constructing grounded theory: A practical guide through qualitative analysis*. Sage.

Clift, R. (2007). Climate change and energy policy: The importance of sustainability arguments. *Energy, 32*(4), 262–268.

CNPC. (2018). CNPC Economics and Technology Research Institute, Energy Outlook 2050.

Collier, U. (1995). *Privatization and environmental policy: The UK electricity sector in a changing climate*. Robert Schuman Centre, European University Institute.

Collier, U., & Löfstedt, R. E. (1997). Think globally, act locally? Local climate change and energy policies in Sweden and the UK. *Global Environmental Change, 7*, 25–40.

Couture, T., & Gagnon, Y. (2010). An analysis of feed-in tariff remuneration models: Implications for renewable energy investment. *Energy Policy, 38*, 955–965.

Cox, S., Gagnon, P., Stout, S., Zinaman, O., Watson, A., & Hotchkiss, E. (2016). *Distributed Generation to support development-focused climate action*. Emerging climate change and development topics for energy sector transformation: An EC-LEDS white paper series, NREL-USAID initiative.

del Rio, P., & Mercedes, B. (2009). An empirical analysis of the impact of renewable energy deployment on local sustainability. *Renewable and Sustainable Energy Reviews, 13*, 1314–1325.

Devine-Wright, P. (2005). Beyond NIMBYism: Towards an integrated framework for understanding public perceptions of wind energy. *Wind Energy, 8*, 125–140.

Devine-Wright, P. (2011). Enhancing local distinctiveness fosters public acceptance of tidal energy: A UK case study. *Energy Policy, 39*, 83–93.

Dincer, I., & Marc, R. (1999). Energy, environment and sustainable development. *Applied Energy, 64*, 427–440.

Dincer, I. (2000). Renewable energy and sustainable development: A crucial review. *Renewable and Sustainable Energy Reviews, 4*, 157–175.

Dukes, J. S. (2003). Burning buried sunshine: Human consumption of ancient solar energy. *Climatic Change, 61*, 31–44.
Easton, D. (1965). *A framework for political analysis*. Prentice Hall, Inc.
Ebinger, K. C. (2016). *India's energy and climate policy: Can India meet the challenges of industrialization and climate change?* Brookings Energy Security and Climate Initiative.
EIA. (2017, September). *US Energy Information Administration* (International Energy Outlook 2017). Washington, D.C., United States.
Elliot, D. (2000). Renewable energy and sustainable futures. *Futures, 32*, 261–274.
Ellman, D. (2015). *The Reference Electrification Model: A Computer Model for Planning Rural Electricity Access*, thesis submitted at MIT (for the Degree of Masters of Science in Technology and Policy).
Empowering Rural India: Expanding Electricity Access by Mobilizing Local Resources Analysis of Models for Improving Rural Electricity Services in India through Distributed Generation and Supply of Renewable Energy. 2010. South Asia Energy Unit, Sustainable Development Department, The World Bank.
Energy Poverty Handbook. (2016). *The Greens/EFA group of the European Parliament*. ISBN 978-92-0286-5. https://doi.org/10.2861/94270
Energy Saving Trust. (2004). *Wind Energy Case Study: Community-owned wind turbine in the Dulas Valley*. Energy Saving Trust Wales.
Equinor. (2018, May). *Energy Perspectives 2018—Long-term macro and market outlook*.
ExxonMobil. (2018, February). *2018 Outlook for Energy: A View to 2040*.
Farrow, A., Miller, K. A., & Myllyvirta, L. (2020, February). *Toxic Air: The price of fossil fuels* (44p). Greenpeace Southeast Asia.
Fernando, C. Y., & Isaac, D. (2014). *Assessing Sustainable Development of Isolated Communities: The Role of Electricity Supply*. International Conference of the System Dynamics Society. Delft: 13.
Fudge, M. P., & Sinclair, P. (2010). Mobilizing community action towards a low-carbon future: Opportunities and challenges for local government in the UK. *Energy Policy, 38*, 7596–7603.
Gasper, D., & Apthorpe, R. (1996, June). *Chapter for arguing development policy—Frames and discourses* (R. Apthorpe & D. Gasper, Eds.). Frank Cass, 1996, and a special issue of the *European Journal of Development Research*, 1–15.
Gilbert, N. (2001). *Researching social life* (2nd ed.). Sage.
Gilliat, S. (1984). Public policy analysis and conceptual conservatism. *Policy and Politics, 12*(4), 345–367.
Green, A. (1992). *An introduction to health planning in developing countries*. Oxford University Press.

Grindle, M. S., & Thomas, J. W. (1991). *Public choices and policy change: The political economy of reform in developing countries*. The Johns Hopkins University Press.

Gubbins, N. (2007). Community energy in practice. *Local Economy, 22*(1), 80–84.

Gubbins, N. (2008, January 29). *Community ownership models for renewable energy projects*. Conference presentation Practical Solutions to Scotland's Renewable Energy Challenges: Edinburgh.

Hain, J. J., Ault, G. W., Galloway, S. J., Cruden, A., & McDonald, J. R. (2005). Additional renewable energy growth through small-scale community orientated energy policies. *Energy Policy, 33*(9), 1199–1212.

Halfacree, K. H. (1995). Talking about rurality: Social representations of the rural as expressed by residents of six English parishes. *Journal of Rural Studies, 11*(1), 1–20.

Harper, G. D. J. (2009). *The Handbook of Sustainability Literacy: Energy Literacy: Understanding and communicating energy issues* (p. 2010). University of Brighton.

Heinberg, R. (2014). *The Purposely Confusing World of Energy Politics: Society beyond fossil fuels*, originally published as Richard Heinberg's, muse letter.

HM Government. (2005). *Securing the future: The UK Government Sustainable Development Strategy*. HMSO.

Hoffman, S. M., & High-Pippert, A. (2005). Community energy: A social architecture for a renewable energy future. *Bulletin of Science, Technology and Society, 25*, 385–401.

Hoffman, S., & High-Pippert, A. (2008). *It takes money to buy whiskey: Local energy systems and civic participation*. MPSA Annual National Conference. Palmer House Hotel, Hilton, Chicago.

Hoppe, T. M., Bressers, J. T. A., & Lulofs, K. R. (2011). Local government influence on energy conservation ambitions in existing housing sites—Plucking the low-hanging fruit? *Energy Policy, 39*(2), 916–925.

Hyldelund, K. (2010). Decentralized Energy Systems. Directorate General for Internal Policies, Policy Department: Economic and Scientific Policy-(Industry, Research and Energy), European Parliament.

IEA. (2018, November). *New policies Scenario, International Energy Agency* (World Energy Outlook 2018). Paris, France.

IEEJ: Institute of Energy Economics Japan. (2018, October). *Outlook 2019- Energy transition and a thorny path for 3E challenges*. Tokyo, Japan.

IHS. (2018, July). IHS Markit, Rivalry: The HIS Markit view of the energy future (2018–2050).

Integrated Energy Policy. (2006). *Report of the expert committee, planning commission*. Government of India.

International Energy Agency. (2018). *Energy Balances of Non-OECD Countries*. Paris, France.
International Energy Agency. (2018). *Energy Balances of OECD Countries*. Paris, France.
IEA. (2018, November). *Sustainable Development Scenario, International Energy Agency* (World Energy Outlook 2018). Paris, France.
IPCC. (2018, October). *P1 Illustrative Model Pathway, Global Warming of 1.5 degrees Celsius*. Inter-governmental Panel on Climate Change.
IRENA. (2016). *Policies and regulations for private sector renewable energy mini-grids*. ISBN: 978-9295111-45-5.
IRENA. (2017). *REthinking Energy 2017: Accelerating the global energy transformation*. International Renewable Energy Agency.
Jenkins, W. I. (1978). *Policy analysis: A political and organizational perspective*. Martin Robertson.
Jordan, R. (2013). *Incorporating endogenous demand dynamics into long-term capacity expansion power system models for Developing countries* (163 p). Massachusetts Institute of Technology, Engineering Systems Division.
Jorgensen, M., & Phillips, L. (2002). *Discourse analysis: Theory and method*. Sage. ISBN:0761971114.
O'Neill, K. M. (2016, January 21). *Going off grid: Tata researchers tackle rural electrification*. MIT Energy Initiative. http://news.mit.edu/2016/tata-researchers-tackle-rural-electrification-0121
Kemmler, A. (2006). *Regional disparities in electrification of India—Do geographic factors matter?* Centre for Energy Policy and Economics.
Larsen, E. R., & Bunn, W. D. (1999). Deregulation in electricity: Understanding strategic and regulatory risk. *The Journal of the Operational Research Society, 50*(4), 337–344.
Liserre, M., Sauter, T., & Hung, Y. J. (2010). Future Energy Systems, Integrating renewable energy sources into the smart power grid through industrial electronics. *IEEE Industrial Electronics Magazine*. https://doi.org/10.1109/MIE.2010.935861
Levin, T., & Thomas, V. M. (2014). Utility-maximizing financial contracts for distributed rural electrification. *Energy, 69*, 613–621.
Lovins, A. (1977). *Soft energy paths*. Penguin.
Macnaghten, P., & Jacobs, M. (1997). Public identification with sustainable development: Investigating cultural barriers to participation. *Global Environment Change, 7*(1), 5–24.
Madlener, R. (2007). Innovation diffusion, public policy, and local initiative: The case of wood-fuelled district heating systems in Austria. *Energy Policy, 35*(3), 1992–2008.

Manzo, L. C., & Perkins, D. D. (2006). Finding common ground: The importance of place attachment to community participation and planning. *Journal of Planning Literature, 20*(4), 335.

Massey, D. (2004). Geographies of responsibility. *Geografiska Annaler Series B, Human Geography 86 B*(1), 5–18.

Middlemiss, L., & Parrish, B. D. (2010). Building capacity for low-carbon communities: The role of grassroots initiatives. *Energy Policy, 38*(12), 7559–7566.

Miller, D., & Hope, C. (2000). Learning to lend for off-grid solar power: Policy lessons from World Bank Loans to India, Indonesia, and Sri Lanka. *Energy Policy, 29*, 19.

Mini-grid policy toolkit and business frameworks for successful mini-grid rollouts, European Union Energy Initiative (RECP, REN21 and Alliance for Rural Electrification), Eschborn, 2014.

Mitchell, C., Bauknecht, D., & Connor, P. M. (2006). Effectiveness through risk reduction: A comparison of the renewable obligation in England and Wales and the feed-in system in Germany. *Energy Policy, 34*, 297–305.

Mitchell, C. (2010). *The Political Economy of Sustainable Energy, Energy, Climate and the Environment Series*. Palgrave Macmillan. ISBN 978–0–230–00800–7 (hb) 978–0–230–22150–5 (pb), first published in 2008.

Modi, V., McDade, S., Lallement, D., & Saghir, J. (2005). *Energy services for the millennium development goals*. The International Bank for Reconstruction and Development, The World Bank, United Nations Development Programme.

Moe, N. (1991). *Presentation of Sweden's Legislation and Work in Respect of Municipal Energy Plans*. NUTEK.

Moner-Girona, M. (2009). A new tailored scheme for the support of renewable energies in developing countries. *Energy Policy, 37*, 2037–2041.

Moonga, H. C. (2006). Rural electrification policy and institutional linkages. *Energy Policy, 34*, 17.

Mulugetta, Y., Jackson, T., & van der Horst, D. (2010). Carbon reduction at community scale. *Energy Policy, 38*(12), 7541–7545.

Musall, F. D., & Kuik, O. (2011). Local acceptance of renewable energy—A case study from southeast Germany. *Energy Policy, 39*, 3252–3260.

National Energy Map for India: Technology Vision 2030, summary for policy makers, TERI. ISBN 81-7993-064-5.

Navarro, A., Sambodo, M. T., & Todoc, L. J. (2013). *Energy Market Integration and Energy Poverty in ASEAN* (Discussion Paper Series). PIDS.

Negro, O. S., Alkemade, F., & Hekkert, P. M. (2012). Why does renewable energy diffuse so slowly? A review of innovation system problems. *Renewable and Sustainable Energy Reviews, 16*, 3836–3846.

Niez, A. (2010). *Comparative Study on Rural Electrification Policies in Economies: Keys to successful policies* (Information Paper). International Energy Agency.

Nouni, M. R., et al. (2009). Providing electricity access to remote areas in India: Niche areas for decentralized electricity supply. *Renewable Energy, 34*(2), 430–434.

OPEC. (2018, September). *Organization of the Petroleum Exporting Countries* (World Oil Outlook 2040).

Ostrom, E. (1998). *Coping with Tragedies of the Commons*. Workshop in Political Theory and Policy Analysis Center for the Study of Institutions, Population, and Environmental Change, Indiana University.

Ostrom, E. (2000). Collective action and the evolution of social norms. *The Journal of Economic Perspectives, 14*(3), 137–158.

Panelli, R., & Welch, R. (2005). Why community? reading difference and singularity with community. *Environment Planning A, 37*(9), 1589–1611.

Pepermans, G., Driesen, J., Belmans, R., & D'haeseleer, W. (2005). Distributed generation: Definition, benefits and issues. *Energy Policy, 33*, 787–798.

Perry, M., & Rosillo-Calle, F. (2008). Recent trends and future opportunities in UK bioenergy: Maximizing biomass penetration in a centralized energy system. *Biomass & Bioenergy, 32*(8), 688–701.

Peter, D. F. (1986). *Management-tasks, responsibilities practices*. Truman Talley Books/ E.P. Dutton.

Peters, M., Fudge, S., & Sinclair, P. (2010). Mobilizing community action towards a low-carbon future: Opportunities and challenges for local government in the UK. *Energy Policy, 38*(12), 7596–7603.

Petts, J. (2007). Learning about learning: Lessons from public engagement and deliberation on urban river restoration. *Geographical Journal, 173*, 300–311.

Preston, I., White, V., Lloyd-Price, L., & Anderson, W. (2009, May). *Best practice review of community action on climate change* (Final Report). Centre for Sustainable Energy on Behalf of the Energy Saving Trust.

Raco, M., & Flint, J. (2001). Communities, places and institutional relations: Assessing the role of area-based community representation in local governance. *Political Geography, 20*(5), 585–612.

Report on assessment of achievable potential of new and renewable energy resources in different states during 12th Plan period and determination of RPO trajectory and its impact on tariff. (2012). Forum of Regulators, CRISIL risk and infrastructure solutions limited.

Ricci, M., Bellaby, P., & Flynn, R. (2010). Engaging the public on paths to sustainable energy: Who has to trust whom? *Energy Policy, 38*(6), 2633–2640.

Roberts, J., Elliot, D., & Houghton, T. (1991). *Privatizing Electricity: The Politics of power*. Belhaven.

Rogers, J. C., Simmons, E. A., Convery, I., & Weatherall, A. (2008). Public perceptions of opportunities for community-based renewable energy projects. *Energy Policy, 36*(11), 4217–4226.

Rose, R. (1976). *The dynamics of public policy*. Sage.

Roseland, M. (2000). Sustainable community development: Integrating environmental, economic, and social objectives. *Progress in Planning, 54*(2), 73–132.

Schneider, A., & Helen, I. (1997). *Policy design for democracy*. University Press of Kansas.

Shucksmith, M. (2000). Endogenous development, social capital and social inclusion: Perspectives from LEADER in the UK. *Sociologia Ruralis, 40*(2), 208–218.

Smith, A. (2007). Emerging in between: The multi-level governance of renewable energy in the English regions. *Energy Policy, 35*, 6266–6280.

Smith, J., Blake, J., Grove-White, R., Kashefi, E., Madden, S., & Percy, S. (1999). Social learning and sustainable communities: An interim assessment of research into sustainable community projects in the UK. *Local Environment, 4*, 195–207.

Smith, J. L. (2008). A critical appreciation of the "bottom-up" approach to sustainable water management: Embracing complexity rather than desirability. *Local Environment, 13*(4), 353–366.

Sperling, K., Hvelplund, F., & Mathiesen, B. V. (2011). Centralization and decentralization in strategic municipal energy planning in Denmark. *Energy Policy, 39*, 1338–1351.

St. Denis, G., & Parker, P. (2009). Community energy planning in Canada: The role of renewable energy. *Renewable and Sustainable Energy Reviews, 13*, 2088–2095.

Steward, F., Liff, S., Dunkelman, M., Cox, J., & Giorgi, S. (2009). *Mapping the Big Green Challenge: An analysis of 355 Community Proposals for Low Carbon Innovation*. http://www.swslim.org.uk/documents/themes/lt18-resource48.pdf

Strachan, A. P., Cowell, R., Ellis, G., Sherry-Brennan, F., & Toke, D. (2015). Promoting Community Renewable Energy in a Corporate Energy World. *Sustainable Development, Sustainable Development* (23), 96–109. in Wiley Online Library (wileyonlinelibrary.com) https://doi.org/10.1002/sd.1576

Thollander, P., Danestig, M., & Rohdin, P. (2007). Energy policies for increased industrial efficiency: Evaluation of a local energy programme for manufacturing SME's. *Energy Policy, 35*, 5774–5783.

Walker, G. P. (1997). Renewable energy in the UK: The Cinderella sector transformed? *Geography, 82*, 59–74.

Walker, G. P. (2008). What are the barriers and incentives for community-owned means of energy production use? *Energy Policy, 36*, 4401–4405.

Walker, G. P., & Devine-Wright, P. (2008). Community renewable energy: What should it mean? *Energy Policy, 36*, 497–500.

Walker, G. P., Devine-Wright, P., & Evans, B. (2007). *Community energy initiatives: Embedding sustainable technology at a local level* (ESRC End of Award Report).

Walker, G. P., Devine-Wright, P., Hunter, S., High, H., & Evans, B. (2010). Trust and community: Exploring the meaning, contexts and dynamics of community renewable energy. *Energy Policy, 38*, 2655–2663.

Warren, C. R., & McFadyen, M. (2010). Does a community ownership affect public attitudes to wind energy? A case study from south-west Scotland. *Land Use Policy, 27*, 204–213.

Wolsink, M. (2007). Wind power implementation: The nature of public attitudes: Equity and fairness instead of 'backyard motives'. *Renewable and Sustainable Energy Reviews, 11*, 1188–1207.

Thomas, M. (2014). *Innovative Business Models and Financing Mechanisms for PV Deployment in Emerging Regions* (IEA PVPS Task 9, Sub-task 5, Report IEA-PVPS, T9-14: International Energy Agency Photovoltaic Power Systems Programme). ISBN 978-3-906042-27-5.

Trier, C., & Maiboroda, O. (2009). The green village project: A rural community's journey towards sustainability. *Local Environment, 14*(9), 819–831.

UNFCC. (2007). *Climate Change: Impacts, vulnerabilities and adaptation in developing countries*. United Nations Framework Convention on Climate Change.

University of Waterloo. (2016). *Open Access Energy: Power to change the world*. Waterloo Global Science Initiative.

van der Horst, D. (2008). Social enterprise and renewable energy: Emerging initiatives and communities of practice. *Social Enterprise Journal, 4*(3), 171–185.

Vencel, G. B. (2011). *Overcoming the sociotechnical barriers of sustainable renewable energy policies: Path dependency and technological change*. Department of Public Policy, Central European University.

Woodman, B., & Baker, P. (2008). Regulatory frameworks for decentralized energy. *Energy Policy, 36*(12), 4527–4531.

Yildiz, O. (2014). Financing renewable energy infrastructures via financial citizen participation—The case of Germany. *Renewable Energy, 68*, 677–685.

Zerriffi, H. (2007). *Making small work: Business models for electrifying the world*. Stanford University.

Index

A
AADHAR, 29
aboriginals, 67
above poverty line (APL), 31, 257
accelerated electrification of 1 lakh villages and one crore households, 20
accelerated rural electrification program (AREP), 20
acceptability, 13, 377, 378
access, xvii, xix–xxi, xxiv, xxv, 2–4, 6–17, 19, 23, 25, 27, 88, 131, 134, 139, 141, 142, 156, 158, 159, 162, 163, 167–170, 172, 177, 206, 216, 218, 245, 247–249, 253, 258, 260, 261, 263, 270, 272, 274, 335–339, 341, 342, 345, 347, 348, 350, 353, 361–366, 370–373, 375
access rate, 372
action arena, xvii, xxiv, 25, 37, 39, 109, 115, 116, 142, 167, 168, 176, 208, 252, 264, 266, 270, 271, 274, 277, 338, 342, 347, 349, 354, 384
action-theoretical, 15
active engagement, xviii, xxviii, 38, 88, 343, 353
actors, xix, 14, 115, 116, 132, 144, 168, 170, 177, 178, 206, 209, 210, 262, 264, 270, 276, 277, 338, 341, 342, 349, 352, 367, 380, 382, 383
adequate, xix, 4, 177, 242, 270, 379
ad-hocism, 265
administration, 33, 69, 72, 131, 132, 157, 170, 173, 177, 179, 191, 241, 272, 342, 346
administrative, xxii, 28–31, 34, 36, 67, 115, 132, 133, 156, 159, 264, 334–336, 346, 347, 350, 351
administrative astuteness, 346
administrative efficacy, 346
administrative efficiency, 346
adobe photoshop, 37
advanced fuels, 7

affordability, 3–5, 10, 13, 18, 278, 371
agents, 14, 36, 141, 167, 168, 170, 200, 202, 349
alleviation, 5
allocation of business, 350
alternating current (AC), 143, 338, 339
anaerobic digester, 194, 268
anaerobic digestion, 35
analysis, xxii, xxiv, xxviii, 10, 15, 16, 25, 27, 28, 30, 31, 37, 77, 89, 92, 115, 141, 173, 203, 261, 270, 335, 375
analytical approach, 38
Andaman trunk road, 71, 72, 242
animal waste, 17, 33, 34, 193, 196, 205, 241
anthropogenic, 23, 25, 72, 239, 242, 245, 369, 377, 380
anthropomorphic, xviii, xxviii, 144
apolitical institutionalism, 220, 329
appliances, 9, 12, 16, 26, 27, 31, 32, 73, 87–89, 92, 121, 131, 162–165, 167, 173, 241, 243, 246, 249, 254, 256, 259, 337, 339–341
appliances–based usage, 32
appropriateness, 353, 384, 385
arid, 240, 253
articles, 203, 333–335, 347
assemblages, 3
associations, xxii, 37, 110, 117, 135, 142, 263, 265, 367
asymmetric, 14, 199, 274, 379
asymmetric pluralism, 348
authoritarianism, 177, 271, 277
autocad, 37
availability, xviii, xxii, 2, 13, 38, 70, 243, 374, 376, 380, 386
availability based tariff (ABT), 375
average cost of supply, 71, 370

average power purchase cost (APPC), 115, 118, 267

B
backward caste (BC), 162, 167, 190
barriers, xxv, 4, 68, 193, 207, 277, 351, 371, 375
baseline, xvii, 242
base load, 86, 87, 244, 247, 336, 385
basic human needs, 10, 244, 247, 260
behavioural dysfunction, 141, 261
behaviourism, 13
below poverty line (BPL), 31, 209, 257
benign, 144
big push, 348, 376
biodegradable waste, 33, 90
biogas, xvii, 28, 30–35, 38, 73, 90–92, 191, 193–198, 205, 208–210, 212, 215, 218, 219, 236, 241–244, 246, 247, 249–253, 255, 256, 258, 260, 261, 268, 269, 272–275, 342, 361, 380, 382
biogas plant, 191–193, 195, 196, 206, 211, 212, 214, 215, 217, 268, 272
biomass, 7, 9, 205, 210, 218, 275, 361, 363, 364, 380
black cotton soil, 245
boundary problem, 215
bourgeois, 266
business as usual (bau), 72, 120

C
cabinet committee on economic affairs (CCEA), 209
capacity building, 117, 208, 265, 274, 277, 377
CAP algorithm, 372
capitalists, 207, 266, 276

case studies, xx, xxii–xxiv, xxviii, 27, 37–39, 261, 265, 271, 276, 278, 345, 376
cash transfer, 364
caste homogeneity, 139
cattle refuse, 194
causal, 5
central electricity act (2003), 22, 271, 335
central highlands, 240, 250
centre, xxiv, 23, 77, 117, 133–135, 144, 156, 158, 163, 168, 169, 190, 197, 208, 210, 256, 265, 267, 269, 334, 335, 343, 347, 350–352, 354, 363, 366, 368, 373, 375, 384
chief electrical inspector (CEI), 114, 117, 264, 265
choice framework, 142
choice option, 341
civil structure, xvii, 17, 25, 26, 29, 32, 89, 161, 167, 242, 337, 342, 372, 384
clean development mechanism (CDM), 209
closed system, 173, 217
coal, 7, 8, 363, 364, 381
coercive federalism, 351
collection efficiency, 370
collective action, xxii, xxiii, 169, 176, 194, 199, 204–206, 212, 217, 218, 220, 270, 273
collective identities, 368
collectivization, 212, 348
combined heat and power (CHP), 210, 274
commercial enterprise, 120
commodious living, 374
common pool resources, 203
common property resources (CPR), 199, 203, 204, 217
community-centric, xviii, 192, 255

community development block (CD), 30, 131, 177, 242
community resources, 192, 194
compact fluorescent lamp (CFL), 32, 89, 90, 165
comparative, xxviii, 28
complexity, xxi, xxiii, xxv, 1, 2, 14, 16, 18, 157, 163, 169, 204, 247, 273, 343, 345, 368
composite index, 7
compulsory supply hours (CSH), 178
concurrent list, 18, 335, 376, 386
consensual democracy, 190
Constitution of India, 18, 156, 334, 335, 380
constitutive, 10
consumer base, xix, 92, 363, 369
consumerism, 39
consumers, xix, 71, 72, 89, 138, 139, 144, 178, 276, 370, 382, 385
consumption, xvii, xix, xx, xxiii–xxv, 2, 10, 12, 16, 17, 25–27, 30, 32, 39, 67, 68, 73, 77, 89, 91, 92, 119, 120, 131, 140, 141, 158, 160–162, 165, 195, 242, 247, 250–254, 257, 258, 260, 261, 269, 275, 337, 339, 341, 343, 345, 348, 351, 353, 362, 364, 368, 369, 373, 375, 376, 378, 379
contemporary, xxiv, xxv, 14, 17, 18, 37, 158, 169, 170, 177, 258, 261, 264, 277, 340, 342, 367, 379, 382, 384
context, xvii, xx–xxv, 1, 5–7, 12–15, 17–19, 24–28, 34, 36–39, 92, 119, 134, 138, 159, 169, 173, 179, 199, 213, 214, 240–242, 245, 248, 266, 278, 336, 342, 343, 347, 349, 351, 362, 365, 366, 368, 369, 373, 378, 379, 383, 384

contextual, xviii, xxv, xxvi, 10, 12–14, 17, 18, 37, 118, 169, 204, 240, 241, 255, 269, 341, 343, 347, 354, 362, 383–385
contrarian hues, 13
conventional energy sector, xviii, 382
conventional fuel, 208, 269
conventional power (CP), 36, 38, 92, 113, 117, 171, 252, 261, 265, 338, 350, 380, 381
conventional system, 122, 266, 364
conversion efficiency, 32
conversion loss, 33
conversion percentage, 35
cooking fuel, 9, 12, 38, 191, 193–195, 208–210, 212, 218, 241, 244, 246, 247, 249–251, 254, 256, 259, 260, 268, 272, 274, 341, 345, 364, 384
cooking fuel needs, 26
cooperative federalism, 348
co-productive, 2
corporate social responsibility (CSR), 140
cost-benefit ratio, 368
course correction, xviii, xxiv, xxvi, 145, 176, 276, 369
coverage rate, 372
cross sectional, 16
cross-subsidization, 370, 374
cultural practices, 72
cultural singularity, 139
culture/cultural, xvii–xix, xxv, xxvi, xxviii, 2, 6, 12, 13, 18, 19, 24, 25, 28, 29, 36–38, 89, 90, 122, 138–140, 142, 144, 157, 162, 165, 177, 179, 199, 211, 212, 239, 240, 242, 247, 250, 254, 257–261, 263, 266, 267, 269, 339, 341, 345, 349, 350, 354, 363, 366, 368, 369, 376–378, 380, 385, 386

D

daily rated mazdoors (DRMs), 34
decentralization, xxv, xxvi, 15, 92, 157–159, 168, 169, 171, 177, 179, 212, 218, 252, 269, 270, 273, 278, 342, 345, 346, 348, 349, 367, 376, 377, 384, 386
decentralized distributed generators (DDG), 252, 366, 381
decentralized energy system (DES), xxiii, xxv, 379
declared usage, 26, 131
de-concentration, 169
de-congestion, 169
deconstruction, 199, 215
Deen Dayal Upadhyay Gram Jyoti Yojana (DDUGJY), 20, 156, 366
definitional flaw, xxi, 20
delegation, 158, 169, 177, 367
demand, xvii, xix, xx, xxiii, xxv, 2, 14, 15, 26, 27, 39, 69, 70, 73, 78, 86, 91, 92, 132, 134, 144, 163, 165, 197, 241, 243, 244, 246, 247, 249–256, 258–260, 265, 267, 269, 275, 337–339, 341–344, 354, 362–364, 366, 370, 373, 376, 379–381, 384, 385
demand aggregation, xx, 24, 25, 145, 367
demand capture, xxiv, 158, 172, 276
demand profiling, xxv, 30, 31, 88, 162, 341, 374, 384
demand realism, 336, 383
demand side management (DSM), xviii, xxviii, 26, 27, 31, 38, 39, 67, 88, 89, 92, 269, 276, 278, 369, 375, 383, 384, 386
democratic institutions, 204, 207, 212, 215, 344, 348
democratization, 158, 387

demonstration project, 115, 116, 118, 119, 122, 143, 144, 264, 267, 339, 377
deprivation, 4, 7
descriptive, xxii, 37, 88
design–reality gap, xvii, xx, xxvi, 354, 375
desk research, 27
devolution, 157, 158, 169, 177, 367
diagnose, 37
diesel-based, 70, 117, 120, 265
differential, xviii, xxiv, 3, 25, 142, 263, 382
digester efficiency, 35
dimensions, xxii, xxviii, 1, 2, 5, 7, 17, 23, 28, 72, 169, 199, 202, 214, 239, 240, 277, 342, 343, 369, 377, 380
direct current (DC), 92, 121, 167, 173, 337, 339
directionality, 13
discrimination, 4
distributed energy generation, 15
distributed energy sources (DERs), 376, 386
distributed power generation, 92
distribution, xxv, xxvi, 13, 15, 18, 25, 69, 113, 115, 119, 140, 144, 158, 166, 171, 177, 178, 195, 196, 198, 206, 207, 212, 216, 236, 244, 249, 250, 266, 270, 271, 274, 276, 277, 337–339, 343, 344, 346–348, 350, 353, 362, 367, 368, 370, 372, 374, 376, 378, 381–383, 386
distribution chain, 350
distribution lines, 22, 23, 171
distribution losses, 370
distribution transformer (DT), 22, 23, 245
district census handbook (DCHB), 190

District Rural Development Agencies (DRDAs), 208
doctrine of liberal construction, 347
doctrine of plenary power, 347
documentation, 25, 28, 38
domain experts, 142, 263
domestic consumer, 24, 26, 70, 178, 257, 373, 374
Draft Renewable Energy Act (2015), 22
Dual Polity, 334
dynamic pricing, 89
dysfunction, 141, 142, 261, 262, 338
dysfunctional functionality, 159
dystopia, 143, 211, 348

E
EBP approach, xxi, xxiii, xxiv, xxviii, 1, 25, 27, 39, 341, 354, 379, 384
economic, xvii, xviii, 2, 4, 6, 12, 15, 29, 36, 72, 89, 116, 120, 122, 133, 134, 142, 158, 165, 199, 205, 207, 209, 212–220, 242, 245, 251, 255, 258, 267, 273–277, 333, 343, 364, 365, 367, 369, 371, 372, 380, 385
efficacy, 15, 176, 216, 270, 342, 347, 349, 384
efficiencies (fuels), 247
efficiency, xxiii, 4, 7, 16, 73, 254, 268, 274, 349, 370, 384
electrical loads, 88, 89, 142, 164, 242, 243, 246, 249–252, 254–256, 263, 339, 341
electricity, xix, xx, xxiv, xxv, 4–7, 9, 10, 12, 18, 19, 22, 23, 27, 69–71, 77, 88–90, 111, 131, 134, 139, 142, 156–160, 165, 168, 169, 171, 172, 178, 194, 195, 210, 241, 244, 245, 249, 251, 254, 256, 257, 260, 262,

269–271, 274, 334, 336, 338, 340, 341, 343, 345, 346, 352, 361–367, 370–375, 381, 382
electricity consumers, 364, 367
electricity governance, 18, 346
electricity sector, 39, 350, 363, 366
electrified dwelling units(EDUs), 29
electrified village, xxi, 1, 22, 23, 156, 159, 372
eleventh schedule, 334
elites, 132, 158, 168, 169, 350, 353
embedded generation, 139, 250, 368
empirical, xviii, xxv, xxviii, 2, 24–27, 33, 37, 119, 202, 203, 244, 250, 252, 255, 256, 261, 268, 275, 278, 339, 341, 342, 345, 380
empirical data, xxii, 34, 240, 242, 373, 377
empirical database, 28, 145, 241, 242, 340, 342
endemic, xxvi, 2, 13, 240, 252, 255, 269, 276, 340, 377
end-use, xvii, 2
energy, xvii–xx, xxii, xxiii, 2, 4, 5, 9, 10, 12 16, 18, 19, 21, 23, 25–31, 34–39, 70, 73, 77, 86–88, 90, 91, 110–113, 115–118, 120, 121, 138–141, 156, 158–160, 162, 163, 165, 167, 169, 170, 172, 173, 177–179, 196, 210, 211, 239–242, 244, 246, 247, 249, 251–253, 255–258, 260–262, 264, 265, 268–270, 274, 275, 278, 334, 336–338, 340–342, 344, 347, 348, 350–354, 361–364, 366–369, 371–375, 377–380, 382, 383, 385, 386
energy access, xviii–xxi, xxiii–xxvi, 1, 2, 4, 10, 12, 14, 15, 19, 20, 23, 36–39, 69, 88, 156–159, 162, 163, 171, 177–179, 260, 270,
272, 278, 335, 336, 338, 342–344, 354, 361–363, 376, 382, 384–386
energy action, xxv, 14, 167, 176, 276, 340, 343, 344, 384, 386
energy alloy, 93, 269, 374
energy baskets, 13, 17, 26, 240
energy budget, xx, 26, 247, 249, 254, 256
energy centric, 368
energy consumption(s), xvii, xviii, xx, xxi, xxiii, xxv, xxvi, xxviii, 2, 5–7, 9, 12, 13, 15–17, 19, 24, 26–30, 37, 38, 70, 144, 162, 165, 177, 209, 239, 240, 242, 243, 245, 246, 250, 254, 255, 257, 260, 267, 269, 278, 342, 344, 345, 363, 366, 368, 373, 376–378, 380, 384, 385
energy cooperative, 132, 141
energy croppers, 117, 118, 121, 265, 266
energy demand, xvii–xxi, xxiv–xxvi, 2, 18, 19, 23–25, 32, 36, 172, 242, 244, 267, 276, 278, 338, 340, 341, 345, 362–365, 368, 369, 381
energy development index, 1, 6
energy efficiency services limited (EESL), 21, 165
energy exclusion, 6
energy expenditure, 5, 32
energy flow, 2, 242, 385
energy generation, xxv, 2, 25, 28, 120, 178, 247, 269, 271, 277, 343, 351, 352, 367, 368, 374, 382, 384, 385
energy governance, xxi, 15, 18, 176, 270–272, 276–278, 334, 335, 340, 342–344, 348, 350, 351, 366, 367, 376, 378, 383
energy inaction, 14, 143, 369

energy infrastructure, 4
energy ladder, 1, 7, 10, 247, 341
energy literacy, 276, 378
energy management, 88, 92, 269, 276, 368, 383
energy-mix, 364
energy needs, xxiv, xxv, 3, 10, 217, 246, 252, 271, 344, 345
energy poverty (EP), xx, xxi, xxiv–xxvi, xxviii, 1–7, 10, 12–18, 23, 24, 27–29, 36, 37, 39, 240, 241, 244–247, 252, 261, 340, 341, 354, 362, 378, 379, 383, 384
energy poverty survey (EPS), 16
energy production systems, xvii, 27, 38, 120, 139, 173, 218, 250, 275, 338, 341, 350, 351, 364, 377, 381, 382, 385
energy provisioning, 15, 159, 338
energy regulator, 178, 272, 339
energy security, 5
energy service company (ESCO), 38, 168, 169, 171, 177, 339
energy services, xx, xxi, xxiv–xxvi, 2–4, 7, 10, 11, 14, 16, 17, 24, 26, 157, 158, 162, 165, 167, 172, 176–178, 249, 256, 257, 260, 267, 269, 270, 335, 339, 345, 349, 350, 353, 361, 362, 373, 374, 382
energy source, xxiii, 16, 23, 88, 118, 243, 350, 369, 371, 375, 378, 383
energy Swaraj, xxviii, 385
energy system, xviii–xx, xxv, xxvi, xxviii, 10, 19, 25–27, 72, 93, 118, 119, 144, 210, 212, 218, 244, 254, 255, 258, 267–269, 273, 275, 334, 342–344, 346, 349, 353, 364, 368, 369, 373, 374, 376, 378, 379, 385, 387

energy transition, 117, 265, 275, 368
energy use dynamics, 24
environmental impact, 209, 352
episodic, 14, 17, 133, 241, 340, 343
epistemological harmony, 67
equitable institutional mechanisms, 346
equity, 4, 10, 141, 273, 386
estrangement, 173, 214, 262
ethnography, 36
evidence, xvii, xviii, xxi–xxiii, xxvi, xxviii, 13, 14, 17, 37, 77, 92, 93, 144, 169, 240–248, 250, 252, 255, 256, 258–261, 264, 266–269, 272, 275, 276, 336, 338, 339, 341, 342, 344–346, 351, 354, 362, 375, 377, 379, 380, 382, 384
evidence-based policy (EBP), xx, xxiv, xxv, xxviii, 37–39, 276, 341, 346, 354, 379, 384
evidence collection, xxv, 25, 28
exclusion, 172
expectations, 3, 72, 73, 138, 139, 141, 143, 159, 210, 262, 263, 336
experiential learning, 197
explanatory, xxii
exploratory, xxii, 37
external actor, 216

F
farmyard green manure, 194
federalism, 334, 335, 346, 347
feeder, 159, 245
feed in tariff (FIT), 121
fermentation, 34, 196, 268
filament bulb (FB), 9, 32, 89, 165, 259, 260
financial, 4, 20, 118–121, 138, 139, 170, 199, 209, 266, 368, 370, 371, 375, 385

flow diagrams, 278
fluvial, 248
foliage, 72
food chain franchisee, 197
formal access, 26, 169
formal connections, 26, 88, 90, 144
formal state intervention, 336, 337
framework, xvii, xix, xxii–xxvii, 4, 15, 23, 27, 36, 72, 157, 158, 173, 202, 203, 207, 208, 211, 216–218, 239, 270, 271, 274, 277, 334, 335, 338, 339, 342, 343, 348, 351–354, 363, 366–370, 372, 373, 378, 379, 382, 383, 385, 386
free supply, 197, 215
fuel mix, 26, 244, 250–252, 254, 260, 364
fuel poverty, 3, 4, 6
fuel wood, 10, 30, 364
functional domain, 18
functional order, 116, 138

G

gendered, 4
genealogical tree, 191
generation, xviii, 18, 33, 67, 69–71, 73, 77, 88, 90–92, 115, 121, 139, 140, 144, 158, 171, 173, 177, 178, 191, 192, 196, 203, 210, 214, 236, 242–244, 246, 251, 252, 255, 256, 260, 261, 263, 267–272, 274–276, 278, 340, 348, 350, 351, 363, 364, 368–371, 374–376, 380, 381, 383, 386
generators, 91, 178, 194, 244, 367, 370, 375
geo-climatic zones, xvii, xxii, 26–29, 35, 37, 67, 239, 240, 243, 246, 248, 250, 253, 255, 259, 275, 337, 342, 368, 378

geographical spaces, 163, 242
geographies/geographical, 2, 3, 10, 13, 15, 17, 24, 29, 69, 133, 190, 239, 248, 250, 268, 336, 368
geo-spatial, 13, 14, 17, 157, 240, 342, 362, 367, 378, 379, 384
gestation period, 38, 119
government, 6, 18, 19, 68, 72, 112, 115, 122, 136, 137, 156, 157, 167, 208, 216, 248, 251, 253, 256, 334, 335, 337, 338, 346, 347, 351, 352, 366
granular, xvii, 2, 15
great plains, 240, 248, 253
green energy bonus, 113, 120, 121
grids, xxvi, 4, 27, 29, 31, 37, 39, 69, 91, 108, 111, 114, 117, 121, 131, 132, 135, 136, 145, 167, 171, 244, 247, 249, 259, 261, 265, 269, 337–339, 349, 364–366, 369, 370, 373, 386
groundwater conservation bonus, 113, 118, 121
groundwater management, 108
Gujarat energy development agency (GEDA), 113, 114, 264, 337, 338
Gujarat energy research and management institute(GERMI), 113, 264
Gujarat Urja Vikas Nigam Limited (GUVNL), 108, 112

H

heterogeneity, xix, xx, xxii, xxiv, 18, 343, 363, 379
heterogeneous, 19, 24, 25, 379, 386
high sulphur diesel (HSD), 70, 77, 91–93, 244, 267, 269
Himalayan zone, 255
horizontal spread, 375

household (hh), xx, 3, 5–7, 9, 10, 15, 16, 20, 23, 24, 26, 30, 31, 34, 36, 68, 90, 109, 143, 156, 165, 170, 172, 190, 192–199, 203–205, 209, 212, 213, 217, 243, 244, 246, 249, 250, 254, 256, 268, 336, 361, 362, 366, 370–373
human, xix, xxv, 2, 5, 25, 27, 28, 35, 39, 90, 144, 202, 212, 218, 239, 242, 245, 249, 268, 269, 275, 277, 278, 342–344, 361, 369, 374, 384, 385
human behaviour, 204, 207
human capital, 192, 345, 367
human control, 206
human data, 28
human development index (HDI), 5, 374
human dimension, xxv, 18, 19, 25, 26, 241, 242, 343, 376, 384
human interaction, 206
human intervention, 196
humanistic, xviii
human waste, 33, 34, 241
humid sub-tropical, 240, 248, 250, 259
hydraulic retention temperature (HRT), 268
hydro, 363, 364, 380, 381
hypotheses, 7, 10, 247, 341

I
immersive, xx, 36
impolitic polity, xxiv, 335
inadequate, 4, 177, 379
incandescence, 167
income poverty, 5, 16
Indian renewable energy development agency (IREDA), 210
indicators, xxvii, 3, 6, 247, 362

indigenous, 38, 195, 205, 211, 255, 385, 386
Indira Awas yojana (IAY), 337
inductive, 36
inequality, 10, 207, 333
informal connections, 32, 338
information asymmetry, 38, 86, 141, 142, 206, 220, 262, 263, 277, 340
informed policy formulation, 25
infrastructure, xxiii, 3, 4, 22, 23, 139, 215, 258, 259, 350, 370–372
institutional distancing, 177, 342
institutional heterogeneity, 348
institutions/institutional, xx, xxii, xxiii, xxvi, xxvii, 2, 4, 14, 15, 18, 27, 108, 115, 121, 132, 137, 140, 141, 156–159, 170, 171, 173, 176–179, 190, 199, 202–207, 209–220, 239, 264, 267, 270–277, 333, 335–340, 343–351, 364, 366, 367, 377, 378, 382, 383, 386
institutions of self government, 334
instrumentalities, xxi, 23, 208, 347, 366
instrumental rationality, 119
instrumentation, 33, 236, 239
integration, 19, 179, 202, 272, 350, 351, 364, 371
intensity, 5–7, 12, 33, 90, 91, 157, 167, 210, 256, 269, 367, 368, 379, 384
interdisciplinary approach, 27, 39, 379
interest groups, 218, 274, 342, 345
internal rate of return, 368
International energy agency (IEA), 6, 29, 361, 362, 364
International solar alliance (ISA), 21
interpersonal communication, 207
irrigation system, 264

island, 67–71, 91, 240, 243, 267, 268
island ecosystem, 245

J
Janta model, 198
Jawahar Lal Nehru National Solar Mission, 21

K
katiya connections, 162, 169, 338
Khadi and Village Industry Commission (KVIC), 208
kitchen waste, 33, 241
Kutir jyoti scheme, 20

L
lease deed, 136–138, 140
least count, 33
legislative, 156, 334, 335, 347, 351
lessee, 136–138
lessor, 132, 136–138, 142, 263
Leviathan, 216
lifeline consumption, 156, 336
lifestyle, 2, 12, 19, 72, 73, 144, 239, 240, 244, 247, 253, 255, 258, 377, 384
light emitting diode (LED), 9, 32, 89, 90, 164, 173, 251, 337, 339
lighting, 9, 13, 17, 19, 23, 26, 30, 73, 89, 90, 92, 163, 164, 167, 171, 172, 241–244, 246, 247, 251, 252, 254, 361
lighting load, 27, 32, 89, 165, 241, 243, 244, 246, 249, 251, 252, 254, 256, 259, 260
lighting needs, 26, 31, 241, 245, 252, 260
lignite, 363
linkages, 2, 7, 171, 275

liquefied petroleum gas (LPG), 7, 9, 10, 30, 205, 208, 209, 213, 244, 246, 247, 249–251, 254, 256, 260, 272, 361, 364
livestock data, 28
load demand, xx, 26, 33, 88, 89, 131, 145, 162, 163, 165, 243, 244, 246, 247, 254, 256, 258–261, 267, 336–338, 341, 345, 353
load demand profile, 26, 32
load estimation, 32
local, xvii–xxvii, 2, 13–15, 17, 24, 26, 28, 29, 33, 36–39, 73, 88, 90–92, 112–114, 117, 132–135, 138, 142, 143, 145, 156–159, 163, 165, 167–171, 176–179, 190, 196, 203–206, 211, 212, 218–220, 239–241, 243, 244, 246, 247, 250, 251, 253–258, 260, 261, 264, 265, 267, 270, 272, 274–278, 334, 336, 338–346, 350, 353, 362–364, 366–381, 383–386
localism, 176, 343, 344
local power structure, 38, 157, 163, 339
local resources base, 25, 92, 220, 276, 342, 344, 347, 348, 369, 384
lock-in, 28, 172
Lohia awas Yojana (LAY), 251, 252, 337, 338
low-carbon sources, 364
LPG re-filling cycle, 30

M
macro, xix, 12, 30, 140, 179, 209–211, 272, 277, 335, 336, 348, 351, 363, 368
magnitude, 3, 13, 240
mangrove forests, 68, 69
market imperfection, 350
mean sea level (MSL), 68, 255, 256

measurement, 5, 6, 15, 77
median income criteria, 244, 247, 249, 255, 260
meso, 176, 210, 270, 272, 335, 340, 371
metis, 211, 347
metrics, 3, 12, 240, 247, 261, 384
micro, 12, 14, 36, 168, 176, 179, 254, 260, 269, 270, 272, 362, 371
micro-analysis, 39, 245
micro-culture, 6, 278, 342
micro-realities, 15
milch cattle management, 195
mini-grid operator (MGO), 178
minimalist state, 143, 263
minimum needs program (MNP), 20
Ministry of New and Renewable Energy (MNRE), 20, 21, 208–210
ministry of power (MOP), 19, 22, 23, 366
mixed method, xxi, xxiv, xxvii, 1, 2, 239, 341
mix methods research, 27
modern, 3, 4, 6, 7, 10, 13, 16, 17, 88, 167, 241, 247, 256, 258, 261, 333, 353, 361, 364, 365, 384
modern needs, 12
modern state, 211, 348
monolithic, 132, 169, 210, 217, 275, 350
monopoly, 38, 178
montane, 240, 255, 259
multi-dimensional, 14, 36, 362
multidimensional energy poverty index (MEPI), 7
multipurpose gadgets, 13, 17, 241
myopic view, 210

N
naqli bijli, 263
National Biogas and Manure Management Programme (NBMMP), 21, 208, 209, 275
National Electricity Policy (2005), 22, 156, 336
national rural electrification policy (2006), 272, 336
national rural employment guarantee scheme (NREGS), 110
National tariff policy (2006), 22, 375
National tariff policy (2016), 22, 271, 375
natural gas, 7, 361, 363, 364
natural resource preservation, 267
nazari naqshas, 28
negotiated solution, 144
net discounted value, 368
non-comparative, 369
non-conventional fuel, 269
non-conventional power (NCP), 121, 142, 262, 348, 381
non-electrical dwelling units(NEDUs), 29, 338
non-energy croppers, 266
non-government organization (NGO), 138, 167, 170, 171
Nonia community, 38, 131, 262
non-revenue power, 143, 250, 338, 350
non-state actor(s), xxiii, 14, 15, 159, 167, 171, 177, 178, 270, 272, 338, 339, 341, 378, 385
normative, 2, 10
norms, 2, 36, 114, 139, 143, 177, 207, 215, 378
norms of reciprocity, 207, 344, 367
North Bihar power distribution company limited (NBPDCL), 131, 132, 134, 145
not for profit (NFP), 201

nuclear, 363, 371

O
objective function, 369
off-grid, 29–31, 108, 117, 119, 121, 140, 142, 252, 262, 265, 266, 278, 337, 338, 341, 345, 367, 381
oil, xviii, 10, 12, 16, 30, 243, 244, 246, 363, 364, 380
ombudsman, 344
open access, 118, 206, 277, 372
operationalization/operationalize, 3, 12, 13, 240
operation and maintenance costs, 172, 195
opportunism, 132, 141
options, xviii, 13, 17, 25, 144, 205, 216, 217, 240, 276, 341, 370, 373
organised consent, 215
overdraft, 118, 266
overhead service reservoir (OHSR), 120

P
panchayati raj institution (PRI), 190, 215
panchayat sachivs, 34
paradigm, xvii, xxi, xxv, 1, 27, 37, 38, 169, 179, 214, 239, 250, 267, 341, 346, 354, 374, 379, 384
paradoxical, 14, 18, 241
parameters, 2, 35, 140, 142, 193, 262, 263, 268
pareto-optimal, xxiii, 204, 218, 274
Paris accord, 381
Parliament, 156, 334, 335
passive communication, 207

passive consumer, xxv, 13, 14, 18, 19, 27, 88, 92, 145, 267, 340, 341, 343, 348, 354, 366, 378
passive consumerism, xvii, xxiv, 14, 31, 158, 339–341, 362, 372, 373, 380
paternalistic design, 212
patriarchal, 262
penetration rate, 373
per-capita, 5, 6, 244, 247, 249, 251, 252, 256, 259, 363
per capita consumption of power, 70, 243, 244, 246, 251, 254, 259
per capita demand for lighting, 243, 254
phenomenon, xxi, xxvi, xxviii, 1, 3, 5, 13–15, 17, 27, 36, 169, 201, 239–241, 266, 341, 379, 383
philanthropists, 142, 263
photography, 36
photomosaics, 248
physical terrain, 13, 37, 92, 240, 245
physiographic divisions, xvii, xxii, 26–30, 35, 37, 67, 239, 240, 248, 255, 259, 267, 275, 337, 342, 368, 378
planimetric base map, 29
plant load factor (PLF), 368, 371
policy, xvii–xxi, xxiii–xxviii, 1, 4, 5, 7, 12, 15, 19, 21–25, 27, 37–39, 92, 108, 112, 115–120, 122, 132, 157–159, 169, 177, 178, 199, 203, 207–210, 214, 218, 250, 252, 255, 257, 258, 264, 265, 268, 271, 274–278, 333, 335, 336, 338–341, 344–354, 363–369, 371–373, 375–385, 387
policy apparatus, 266
policy communique, 132, 376
policy communities, 38

INDEX 417

policy conception, xxiv, xxv, xxviii, 18, 274–276, 343, 349, 373
policy conduit, 376
policy constructs, 23, 211, 382
policy design, xvii, xxiv, 12, 24, 39, 115, 116, 119, 158, 208, 210, 211, 252, 264–267, 269, 274, 275, 333, 336, 340, 342, 347, 353, 368, 371, 378, 379, 383, 385
policy documents, 27
policy estate, xxiv, 158, 210, 261, 262, 264, 275, 342, 349, 382, 383
policy infusion, xxiv, 158
policy making, xxiv, 12, 18, 342, 351, 363, 380, 383
policy parallelism, 209, 272
policy pluralism, xxvii, 209, 218, 378
policy prescription, xxvi, 19, 144, 145, 179, 205, 216, 244, 347, 354, 377, 379
policy problem, 347
policy recipients, xx, 2, 14, 38, 116, 117, 141, 159, 264, 265, 354, 378, 382
policy sweeteners, 118, 266
political affiliations, 88
political allegiance, 349
political economy, xxii, 177, 215, 271
political impact, 209
political structure, 165, 350
political trust, 207
politics/political, xvii, xxvii, xxviii, 12, 15, 18, 24, 25, 36, 116, 117, 132, 133, 139, 142, 157, 163, 199, 205, 207, 216, 251, 263, 265, 273, 276, 277, 333, 335, 340, 345, 346, 349, 350, 352, 354, 362, 368, 376, 377, 383
polluting technologies, 10
polycentric nodes, 367

polycentrism, 177, 270
polychromatic, 13
polysemy, 12, 340
positivism, 344
potential resource, 92
poverty, 7, 15, 108, 365, 387
power distribution network (PDN), 178
power for all (PFA), 23, 159, 385
power purchase agreement (PPA), 70, 112, 113, 118, 119, 264, 266
power rating, 32, 132, 173
power relations, 25, 142, 160, 167, 345
power system, xix, 88, 340, 364, 370, 380
practices, 2, 3, 10, 19, 112, 119, 120, 159, 173, 177, 179, 192, 200, 254, 266, 274, 336, 365, 368, 376, 378, 385
Pradhan mantri awas yojana (grameen) (PMAY)G, 337
Pradhan mantri gramodaya yojana (PMGY), 20
Pradhan Mantri Gram Sadak Yojana (PMGSY), 245, 259
Pradhan Mantri Sahaj Bijli Har Ghar Yojana (SAUBHAGYA), 21, 366
Pradhan Mantri Ujjwala Yojana (PMUY), 21, 209
praxis, 15, 19, 38, 385
PRAYAS, 135, 139, 140, 143, 144, 262
preferences, xxv, 12, 13, 17–19, 24, 25, 92, 157, 158, 240, 254, 267, 276, 340, 343, 350, 354, 384
prenatal history, 191
pre-stressed cement concrete (PSCC), 249
primary census, 28
primary energy, xvii, xxi, 2, 5, 16, 31, 269, 348, 365

primitive, 13, 14, 17, 241
prisoner's dilemma, 204
private energy entrepreneurs, 344
private energy service companies, 336, 339
privatization, 216
probability sampling (PS), 30
problem-oriented approach, 38
procedural rationality, 119
process, xvii, xviii, xx, xxiii, xxv–xxvii, 6, 19, 29, 37, 113, 120, 141, 142, 157, 158, 173, 179, 196, 197, 199–202, 206, 211, 217, 220, 258, 262, 268, 271, 273, 277, 340–342, 344, 346–350, 352, 354, 369, 372, 373, 377, 380, 384, 385
procreative, 2
productive uses, 10, 260, 373
proletariats, 266
prosumerism, 387
public good, 176, 205, 206, 217, 270, 348
public works department (PWD), 250, 253
pump-set energization, 18
Punjab agricultural university (PAU), 196, 198
purposive sampling, 31
pyranometer, 33

Q

quality, xxiv, 2, 7, 10, 15, 18, 25, 32, 33, 87, 88, 91, 142, 156, 159, 171, 177, 178, 212, 241, 242, 244, 245, 256, 258, 336, 340, 349, 366, 367, 370, 372, 373, 385
quantitative, xxi, 16, 26, 27, 32, 34, 73, 77, 89, 92, 241, 342, 369, 384

quantitative analysis, 25, 31, 32, 37, 90, 91
quantity, 2, 15, 16, 25, 26, 32, 33, 77, 114, 121, 167, 241, 242, 256, 262, 373, 375

R

radiometer, 33
Rajiv Gandhi Grameen Vidyutikaran Yojana (RGGVY), 20, 156
random sampling, 29
rational choices, 277
reciprocity, 139
recognition, xix, xxv, xxvi, 13, 17, 19, 240, 363, 368, 379
redistribution, 277, 346, 386
reference electrification model (REM), 38, 139, 140, 261–263
refugees, 68
regulators, 15, 70, 114, 118, 139, 143, 156, 157, 178, 195, 263, 270, 271, 336, 339, 370
relational, 368
relational dynamics, 115, 132, 157, 169
relationship, 2, 5, 14, 139, 159, 169, 349, 362
relative, xviii, 3, 13, 14, 17, 86, 142, 173, 241, 263, 377, 379
relativist, 379
reliability of supply, 13, 17, 32, 140, 178, 241, 340
reliable, 3, 4, 13, 17, 135, 140, 156, 178, 240, 244, 246, 258, 260, 336, 361
remote village electrification (RVE), 21
renewable energy resource potential (RESP), xxi, 2, 24, 90, 270, 368
renewable energy sources (RES), xviii, xxvi, 178, 210, 271, 275, 351, 372, 378, 382, 384, 386

renewable energy technologies (RETs), 27, 353, 376, 377, 379, 380, 382, 386
renewable purchase obligation (RPO), 115
rent-seeking, 132, 349
research design, xxi, 2, 19
reserve, 92
resilient energy system, 353
resolution, 22, 36, 140, 173, 177, 192, 218, 270, 274
resource allocation, 38, 165, 168, 170, 273, 277, 346, 350, 362
retail supply, 89
retrospective, 37
rolling topography, 255
rural, xvii–xxi, xxiii–xxvi, xxviii, 1, 2, 4, 7, 10, 13–20, 23–28, 36, 39, 90, 93, 108, 117, 121, 134, 140, 143–145, 159, 162–164, 170, 172, 173, 176, 208, 209, 240–242, 245, 251–254, 257, 258, 265, 268, 269, 271, 275, 276, 335–342, 345, 348, 352–354, 362–368, 370, 373, 374, 376–379, 382–385
rural dimension, 14, 39, 362
rural economy, 261, 353
rural ecosystem, 13, 14, 18, 19, 267–269, 346, 362, 366
rural electricity sector, 278, 354, 364, 383
rural electricity supply technology mission (REST), 20, 22, 386
rural electrification (RE), xx, xxiii, xxv, xxvi, 18, 19, 22, 23, 27, 156, 158, 179, 250, 252, 253, 272, 334–336, 339, 349, 351, 365–369, 371–373, 381, 382, 384, 386
rural energy ecosystem, 18, 25, 73, 144, 343

rural integration, 372
rural load demand, 336
rural market, 372
rural/renewable energy service company (RESCO), 15, 38, 159, 162, 167, 170, 271

S
sale, 114, 119–121, 257
sale of power, 111
sampling frame, xxi, 29, 31
sampling method, 29, 31
sampling procedure, 29
sampling unit, xxi, 29, 31, 241
sampling universe, xxi, 28, 29, 31, 34, 239, 241
scale, xvii, xix, xxiii, xxv, xxvii, 2, 3, 14, 38, 88, 157, 173, 176, 210, 213, 214, 260, 269, 270, 277, 278, 342, 343, 362, 369, 374, 375, 378, 383, 384, 386
schedule eleventh, 334
schedule seventh, 18, 334
secondary residue, 196
sectoral centralization, 211
self-determination, 205
self-expression, 142
self-governance, 168, 170, 217
semi-arid, 240, 246
service provider, 142, 173, 176, 177, 262, 343
services, xvii, xix, xx, 2, 3, 6, 13–17, 24, 26, 36, 73, 92, 114, 131, 135, 138–142, 156, 157, 161, 165, 168, 171–173, 177, 178, 197, 198, 202, 205, 239, 240, 243, 246, 252, 255, 256, 258, 260–263, 267, 270, 271, 273, 278, 334, 336–340, 342, 344, 349, 350, 362, 363, 366, 370, 372–374, 376, 380, 386

settlement, 31, 68, 72, 131, 190, 204, 206, 215, 217, 242, 245, 248, 250, 253, 368
settlers, 67, 68, 72, 243
shamilat, 253
shared responsibility, 349
signals, 14, 17, 88, 250, 341, 362
simulation tools, 369
single-phase connections, 26, 29, 249
single stage prototype, 35
size, 2, 31, 109, 132, 133, 193, 196, 213, 214, 243, 248, 253, 338, 364, 382
social acceptance, 172
social capital, 192, 199, 207, 217, 218, 343, 345
social contractors, 263
social dilemmas, 277
social economy, 199, 215
social enterprise (SE), 199, 202, 214, 215, 220, 272, 274
social entrepreneurship, 38, 199, 200, 202, 215
social fabric, 193, 215, 346
social impact, 199, 214, 215, 217, 352
social inclusion, 172, 202, 361
social innovation, 207, 210, 215, 219, 274, 344
social learning, 382
social structure, 37, 142, 169, 170, 205, 207, 262
social theory, 19, 179
social value, 197, 200, 202, 214, 215, 217, 218, 272–274
society, xxvi, 2, 25, 37, 108, 111, 113, 117, 118, 135, 140, 157, 158, 206, 207, 212, 213, 239, 265, 273, 277, 345, 348, 353, 361, 362, 373, 374, 377, 380, 386

socio-cultural, 3, 12–14, 24, 25, 36, 131, 138, 142, 144, 163, 170, 242, 245, 251, 255, 256, 260, 264, 266, 268, 273, 276, 343, 345, 346, 350, 362, 379, 384
socio-cultural polarity, 346
socio-cultural space, xxv, 2, 14, 15, 17, 24, 26, 30, 241, 345, 362, 378, 384
socio-economic, 12–14, 18, 21, 24, 67, 71, 73, 115–117, 163, 168–170, 190, 218, 242, 248, 257, 258, 265, 266, 268, 273, 336, 337, 344, 345, 349, 362, 376, 384
socio-economic caste census (SECC), 209
socio-technical, xviii, xxiii, xxiv, xxvi, xxviii, 27, 142, 143, 169, 345, 348, 349, 368, 374
socio-technical transformation, xxviii
software planning tool, 262
solar, xvii, xix, xxiii, 28, 31–34, 38, 70, 73, 83, 90–92, 108, 110–113, 115–121, 131, 135–137, 141, 172, 210, 240, 242–244, 246, 247, 250–253, 255, 256, 258, 262–266, 268, 269, 274, 339, 351, 363, 364, 368, 371, 375, 380–382
solar curve, 34
solar cycle, 34, 90
solar home lighting system (SHLS), 168, 251
solar insolation, 33, 90, 91, 241, 243, 246, 249, 255, 256, 260, 268
solar irrigation pumps (SIPs), 108, 115, 266
solar micro-grid, 134, 135, 138, 142, 143, 261–263
solar photovoltaic (SPV), 108, 138, 140

INDEX 421

solar power packs (SPP), 337–339
solar power policy, 112, 115
solar pumping, 121
solar pump irrigators' cooperative enterprise (SPICE), xxii, 38, 108, 109, 117–119, 264–266
spaces, xvii, xviii, xx, xxiii, xxv, xxvi, xxviii, 2, 12, 14, 17, 19, 24, 28, 29, 37, 38, 118, 119, 139, 142, 144, 173, 239, 242, 245, 267, 342, 366–368, 374, 378, 384, 385
spatial, xxi, 13, 131, 214, 248, 268, 368, 371
spatial identities, 10
spending measure, 5
stack diagram, 89, 90
stand-alone systems, 39, 367
standardization vacuum, xxiv, 159
standard of performance (SoP), 178
standards, 13, 18, 34, 35, 140, 178, 197, 258, 259, 346, 354, 381
state actors, xxiii, 15, 338, 377, 385
state driven development (SDD), 348
state highway (SH), 245, 253
state-led development, 157
state legislature, 156, 334
state list, 382
state nodal agency (SNA), 15, 22, 113, 114, 178, 272, 337, 338
state(s), xxii, xxiii, 18, 28–30, 32, 36, 38, 109, 112, 114, 116, 118, 132, 135, 156, 157, 168–171, 176–179, 191, 197, 199, 203, 207–211, 214, 216, 220, 240, 241, 248, 251, 252, 256, 257, 264, 270, 271, 274, 333–335, 337, 346–348, 351, 352, 366, 370, 374–376, 383, 385, 386
state utility, 110, 112–115, 165, 264, 339, 370, 371
statutory, 22, 178

strategic, 368
structured survey, 27
subsidy, 90, 115, 118, 120, 244, 257, 350, 371, 374
sub-station, 159, 340
substrate, 35
supply side, 4, 92, 247
supply side management (SSM), xxv, 19, 267, 340
surplus power, 111, 114, 115, 120
sustainable, xxviii, 16, 108, 120, 134, 135, 344, 365, 374, 378
sustainable development goals (SDGs), 361–363
symbolic, 14, 369
symptomatic, xxvi, 13, 14, 17, 241, 349, 354, 384
symptomatic problem, 25, 144, 379
symptoms, xxi, xxvi, 3, 13, 14, 17, 28, 240, 241, 252, 341, 362, 369, 384
systematic, 4
systematic random, 29, 30
systemic, 15, 20, 211, 270, 368
systemic policy design, 362
system(s), xxv, xxviii, 2, 15, 24, 25, 28, 29, 38, 69, 77, 88, 91–93, 112–114, 116–118, 120, 121, 139, 141, 142, 144, 157, 170–173, 178, 179, 195, 196, 198, 203, 210–216, 218, 219, 236, 243–247, 250, 252, 261, 263–270, 274, 277, 333, 337, 338, 340, 341, 343, 348, 350, 353, 365, 368–370, 373–375, 377, 378, 380–383, 386

T
tariffs, 71, 89, 142, 257, 263, 370, 372, 375, 382
taste, 13, 17, 92, 163, 240, 254, 267, 384

Tata power Delhi Distribution limited (TPDDL), 134–136, 140, 262
taxonomy, 15, 207, 277
TBP approach, xxi, 1
technical, xxiii, xxvii, 4, 36, 39, 86, 113, 114, 118, 122, 167, 168, 171, 192, 196, 262, 264, 338, 345, 349, 352, 353, 368, 370, 372, 377, 380
techno-economic, xxvi, xxviii, 115, 172, 269, 346, 368, 370, 374, 375
techno-economic model, 344
technological acculturation, xix, 348
technological dysfunction, 141, 262
technological imperialism, 266
technological implant, 264
technological lock-in, 118, 131, 265
technology, xix, xx, xxvi–xxviii, 3, 10, 35, 36, 38, 92, 110, 112, 115–119, 121, 122, 134, 138, 139, 142, 167, 171, 172, 177, 191, 196, 197, 254, 255, 262–268, 271, 277, 340, 343, 350, 353, 361, 364, 369, 373–381, 385, 386
technology adoption, 386
technology diffusion, 267
technology partner, 117, 264, 265
temporal, 13, 214, 341
terminological, 3
text, xvii, xviii, xx–xxii, xxiv–xxviii, 1, 13, 17, 18, 25–28, 39, 116, 117, 159, 239, 264, 347, 384, 385
third party, 113, 114, 117, 137, 265
three tier institution, 168, 346
time of day (ToD), 73, 86, 92
topography, 29, 242, 250, 253, 259, 268
total installed capacity, 69
traditional fuels, 7, 10

tragedy of the commons, 203, 204, 216
transaction costs, 141
transmission, xxv, 69, 144, 269, 277, 343, 348, 368
triangulation, 379
tropical wet, 240, 243
trust deficit, 170, 206, 213, 215, 217, 262, 273, 276, 344
tube light (TL), 32, 89, 165, 251, 259, 260, 337, 338

U
un-electrified, 159
union list, 382, 383
union territory, 28, 31, 32, 192, 240, 242
unitary, 334, 348
universal, 3, 7, 13, 134, 156, 158, 249, 252, 260, 278, 336, 345, 363, 366, 377, 385
universal service obligation (USO), 156
Unnat Jyoti by Affordable LEDs for All (UJALA), 21, 164
urbanization, 363
usefulness, 24
user-value, 372
utilitarian philosophy, 168
utility maximizer, 168, 172
utopian, 134, 136, 142, 263
Uttar Pradesh Electricity Regulatory Commission (UPERC), 178, 271
Uttar Pradesh New And Renewable Energy Development Agency (UPNEDA), 179, 272, 337, 338

V
value-behavior gap, 378
value system, 2
vector design, 142

vertical integration, 375
village electrification, 18, 365
village energy security programme (VESP), 21
village headman, 161, 162, 168, 171
village level workers, 34
virtual power, 263
visible infrastructure, 262, 340, 350, 369
visual ethnography, 36, 37, 239
voltage fluctuation, 32, 87, 88
voluntary governance, 38, 177, 271
vulnerabilities, 1, 3, 12, 17, 240, 340, 344, 353

W

waste quantification, 33, 34, 241
well-being, 2–5, 16
west coast plains, 240, 246
wet, mesophilic digesters, 35
wind, 91, 118, 210, 262, 274, 351, 363, 364, 371, 375, 380, 381
win-win situation, 194, 206, 273

CPSIA information can be obtained
at www.ICGtesting.com
Printed in the USA
LVHW022037120222
710984LV00004B/620